The
Academic's
Handbook

The Academic's Handbook

FOURTH EDITION

Revised & Expanded

Lori A. Flores and
Jocelyn H. Olcott,
EDITORS

DUKE UNIVERSITY PRESS
Durham and London   2020

© 2020 DUKE UNIVERSITY PRESS
Printed in the United States of America on acid-free paper ∞
Cover designed by Matthew Tauch
Text designed by Courtney Leigh Richardson
Typeset in Whitman and Constantia by Westchester Publishing
Services.

Library of Congress Cataloging-in-Publication Data
Names: Flores, Lori A., editor. | Olcott, Jocelyn, [date].
Title: The academic's handbook / edited by Lori Flores and
Jocelyn Olcott.
Description: Fourth edition, revised and expanded. | Durham :
Duke University Press, 2020. | Includes index.
Identifiers: LCCN 2020003436 (print) | LCCN 2020003437
(ebook) | ISBN 9781478010067 (hardcover) |
ISBN 9781478011118 (paperback) | ISBN 9781478012641
(ebook)
Subjects: LCSH: College teachers—United States. |
Universities and colleges—United States.
Classification: LCC LB1778.2 .A24 2020 (print) |
LCC LB1778.2 (ebook) | DDC 378.973—dc23
LC record available at https://lccn.loc.gov/2020003436
LC ebook record available at https://lccn.loc.gov/2020003437

Contents

Acknowledgments

Many thanks to all the wonderful authors in this volume who generously contributed thoughtful, creative, often provocative ideas about how to approach various aspects of academic life and life beyond the academy. Duke University Press put together its characteristically expert team to bring this volume into the world, starting with soliciting reports from two very helpful anonymous readers. Editorial associate Alejandra Mejía shepherded this volume through its complicated journey. Project editor Ellen Goldlust carefully directed the production process, polishing prose and eradicating typos along the way with Suze Schmitt. Chad Royal, Christopher Robinson, and Matthew Tauch and Courtney Leigh Richardson also assisted with getting this book into print. Above all, Gisela Fosado brought the two of us together and inspired us with her vision for a new edition of *The Academic's Handbook* that would reflect the many ways the academy has changed as well as the many ways it has yet to change. It has been an honor to endeavor to live up to that vision.

Introduction

LORI FLORES AND JOCELYN OLCOTT

What might I be able to negotiate for when accepting a new job? What service requests are okay to say "no" to? What goes into writing a renewal, promotion, or tenure letter (my own or somebody else's)? How do I successfully balance my work and personal responsibilities? How do I get funding for my research and publish my research? What strategies will make my teaching more manageable and pleasurable? This handbook helps demystify academia and answer common questions we encounter over the course of our careers.

The amount of time and physical and emotional energy required to make it through graduate school, and then pursue and keep a career in academia, is significant. Most of us embarked upon our academic journeys because we love the combination of research, writing, and teaching; helping others learn and being lifelong learners ourselves; saying something valuable to our discipline or the wider public; and being able to live—to varying degrees—a "life of the mind." It can be hard, however, to remember that passion when you encounter the realities of sustaining an academic career. There is Impostor Syndrome ("Everyone will discover that I don't really belong here"), isolation ("Is anyone else here? Am I the only one feeling this way?"), the uncertainty of the job market, burdensome teaching loads, financial strain, the need to navigate delicate political relationships, and the challenge of building a supportive network that promotes your intellectual vitality and personal wellness. Academia itself has changed so dramatically in recent years that trusted mentors may be struggling themselves to navigate this new terrain.

This Fourth and Revised/Updated Edition of *The Academic's Handbook* aims to provide helpful advice to academics at every career stage, from entering the job market, through one's first job and (for those on this track) the process of getting tenure, and then onto negotiating the challenges of accepting leadership and administrative roles at their institutions. The last edition of the handbook was published in 2007, and we are excited to offer an updated edition that reflects important changes and trends in academia over the last decade. We not only prioritized the gathering of contributors who more accurately reflect the diversity of scholars in the academy but also have included essays that acknowledge the reality that there is no longer a "conventional" or "typical" academic or academic position. This edition tackles topics such as the increasing "adjunctification" of the academy; the debates around technology, social media, and free speech in classrooms and wider campus communities; successful publishing and grant-writing strategies in a changing landscape of resources; and the rising number of mental illness diagnoses among students, staff, and faculty.

Between the last edition and this one, there have emerged many useful academic advice essays, blogs, websites, books, and coaching services. So, what is the added value of a handbook like this one, in an age when you can type in a question or phrase into a search engine and find multiple sources of wisdom? This handbook serves as a complement to these other resources, offering a curated collection of advice from a diverse array of academics and a starting point to formulate questions for an online search or a professional coach. We envisioned, and believe in, this handbook as a tangible thing you can hold in your hands, keep on and pull off your bookshelf, and read and mark up in those times when you want to unplug from the digital realm. Presented together in one volume, these essays will hopefully encourage you to step back and look at your present situation in terms of the longer arc of your career and the wider community of academics. We want this handbook to be not only a gift to the new academic as they embark on their first position but also a resource and comfort to those who have labored in academia for longer—perhaps approaching challenges and opportunities for the first time or perhaps seeking new ways to navigate them. If you're feeling stuck or alone, or wondering about how to take a next step, or want to be inspired by the words and suggestions of your peers, this handbook can be useful in all of those moods and moments.

The amount of daily interaction among colleagues is dwindling, not because we want it to, but because of the increasing demands upon our time and attention. Our present culture of "busyness" and overcommitment, as well as the corporatization of higher education, has resulted in us feeling as if we cannot give ourselves the permission to slow down for something that won't appear on our annual reports, to have longer conversations with our peers and reflect upon how our life is going inside and outside of the workplace. We all have to come to realize that academic work is never done, and will take up as much time and space as we allow it. While we often consider scheduling flexibility as a perk, it can easily foster the feeling that one *should* be working all the time on a big idea, a pile of grading, or an inbox full of email. Think of this handbook as part of your support network as you balance your life's particular set of responsibilities. It holds within it the voices of multiple colleagues who, in wise and accessible language, affirm for you what is exciting and fulfilling about academic work while reminding you that maintaining boundaries around your labor is not only okay but necessary.

Our contributors—who represent a wide range of personal experiences, disciplines, job titles, and career stages—have generously shared their thoughts because they care about professionalization, demystification, and reckoning with the changed realities of the academic landscape. First, the students we are encountering and teaching have changed. Since 2000, the number of low-income students enrolled in college has increased 15 percent; the number of students who identify as female, Asian/Pacific Islander, or Native American/Alaskan Native have each increased 29 percent; the number of Black students has risen by 73 percent; and the number of Latinx students has increased by 126 percent. In 2015, 41 percent of college students were 25 or older.[1] Our students are diverse not just along these lines of race, sex, class, and age, but able-bodiedness and learning ability, sexual orientation and gender identity, religious and political ideology, immigration and citizenship status, and can range in educational background from "legacy" to "first-gen." In their essay "Teaching the Students We Have, Not the Students We Wish We Had," Sara Goldrick-Rab and Jesse Stommel point out that "Today's college students are the most overburdened and undersupported in American history. More than one in four have a child, almost three in four are employed, and more than half receive Pell Grants but are left far short of the funds required to pay for college."[2] These challenges are only compounded by other personal concerns such as being a transfer or international student, a student in need of learning accommodations, someone who has experienced trauma, or someone who lives with the constant fear that they or their family members will be deported. Faculty members must give attention, care, and compassion to this wide range of students.

Academia has not kept up, however, with recruiting and retaining faculty members who meet and reflect this level of student diversity. According to the National Center for Education Statistics, in the fall of 2013, Asian/Pacific Islander faculty made up only 10 percent of full-time faculty at postsecondary degree-granting institutions, Black faculty only 6 percent, Latinx faculty only 4 percent, and Native faculty less than 1 percent (these numbers exclude faculty who identified as multiracial). In 2015, the number of faculty members of color (including adjunct and visiting faculty) stayed fairly consistent at 23 percent. When we count only tenured faculty, the number falls to 17 percent.[3] Women, though they are getting hired almost on parity with men for academic positions, suffer a tremendous pay gap upon hiring that follows them throughout their career if unchecked. Their numbers also drop upon tenure (only 38 percent of tenured faculty were women in 2015). If one is a younger woman or woman of color, statements that directly or indirectly communicate "you don't look like a professor" have sparked Twitter hashtags and movements such as #ThisIsWhat-AProfessorLooksLike to demand the same respect and recognition readily conferred upon many white male faculty members.

This failure to retain and promote underrepresented academics is multifaceted. Real sexism and racism are at play, along with the burnout of faculty of color and women through too many service and mentoring demands. For many of us, these requests appeal to the aspirations that first drew us to academia, but they also can leave us feeling overburdened and exhausted. In addition, a lack of robust mentoring structures and transparency about expectations may result in many feeling as though they aren't properly "clued in" to the game of academia and how to reach its continuously moving goalposts.

A second sea change that has taken place since the last edition of the handbook has been the increasing casualization and precarity of academic labor. The recession of 2008 had tremendous ripple effects that have been compounded by the 2020 pandemic. Graduate school applications increased, while a backlog of people already looking for academic jobs piled up as presidents and deans instituted hiring freezes. Today, the academic job market is fiercely competitive, as immensely qualified scholars contend for a shrinking number of jobs and an even smaller number of tenure-track jobs. Some of the essays here discuss academic life off the tenure track and its different destinations, which range from leaving academia altogether to embracing and thriving in a non-faculty position in an educational setting. Those in privileged tenured positions must become better attuned to how to advocate for their colleagues and students in more vulnerable positions, even as they endure their own pressures and frustrations. Very few academics today can enjoy comfortable travel and research funding, or take for granted the autonomy and stability of their departments and programs.

Although academic life has changed radically since the previous edition of this handbook, we still have the capacity to shape the terms of our employment (as ever, in conditions not of our own choosing) through the choices we make about where to dedicate our time and energy. To that end, the three parts of the handbook offer aerial-view and close-up advice that will help you feel better prepared for changing times. Part I, "Your Career Arc from Grad School to Retirement," opens with an essay that guides you from the job market to signing a job contract. The essays that follow address how to negotiate contracts, navigate departmental politics, and consider a variety of careers. For those who pursue a career on the tenure track, two chapters explain how to make strategic choices along the way to tenure, and words of wisdom about how to keep working in a healthy and sustainable way after this milestone is reached.

Part II, "The Trinity of Academic Life: Research, Teaching, and Service," delves into these three components of faculty life. The section opens with practical pieces of advice about how to find and apply for sources of funding for your work, make the most of the modern research library, and develop ethical research practices. It continues with seasoned advice on how to prepare your scholarship for journal and book publication, particularly in the changing world of e-publishing.

Amid debates on the usefulness of the lecture and "flipping" the classroom, several contributors offer their take on what works for them when they teach. Two contributions take up the thorny question of how to handle the presence of digital devices in their classrooms, with one describing the benefits of banning them and another stressing their value for promoting inclusivity and neurodiversity. A pair of chapters provide concrete strategies for teaching in large lecture halls and smaller seminars, one of the creators of the #FergusonSyllabus attests to the power of crowdsourcing, and we experimented with crowdsourcing to gather suggestions for creative assignments. Along that vein, we have included a compilation of assignment and assessment ideas that we crowdsourced from professors over social media. Several contributions in this section offer advice about how to make classrooms welcoming to all students, including those historically underrepresented in college classrooms. The final four pieces in the section on teaching explore ways to take teaching into the broader world, whether in your home communities, local prisons, or on another continent.

The section about service discusses mindful mentorship and advising; the significance of peer evaluations; questions to ask yourself before deciding to take on a service commitment; and how to design a course that engages with and serves the wider community.

Part III, "Issues in Today's Academy," discusses the big questions we might have about fashioning our identities and lives as academics. Two public intellectuals discuss their relationship with social media, while another essayist discusses academic freedom and free speech. The following piece considers another aspect of the digital revolution's impact on academia, pointing to the need to redesign student evaluations in the age of internet bullying. A co-written piece on balancing work and family, penned by two professors who adopted children in the United States and in Scotland, provide a transnational perspective of academic parenthood. Essays on the corporatization of the university, sexual harassment, and building up intellectual community and town-gown relations round out this final section.

The experience of meeting each other and working together on *The Academic's Handbook* has taught us so much about the need for dialogue and collaboration, on multiple levels. We come from different personal backgrounds and teach at different kinds of schools, but we share important observations about what's exciting and what's problematic about academia that made us eager to update this volume. We want our readers (and ourselves) to be able to pick up this handbook when it's been a hard day, when we need some inspiration in our classroom or department meeting, or when we need to remind ourselves that it's okay to say a "yes" or a "no" to something. This handbook is a part of your community of support, and we look forward to continuing to update this work as it is needed. While there is so much more to discuss beyond what is covered here, the essays here continue much-needed conversations and hopefully extend the promise that academia can be a profession you can navigate, shape, and enjoy.

NOTES

1. Manya Whitaker, "The 21st-Century Academic," *Chronicle of Higher Education*, 2 January 2018 (https://www.chronicle.com/article/The-21st-Century-Academic/242136/).

2. Sara Goldrick-Rab and Jesse Stommel, "Teaching the Students We Have, Not the Students We Wish We Had," *Chronicle of Higher Education*, 10 December 2018 (https://www.chronicle.com/article/Teaching-the-Students-We-Have/245290).

3. Whitaker, "The 21st-Century Academic."

PART I

Your Career Arc from
Grad School to Retirement

When the first edition of *The Academic's Handbook* was published in 1995, there was more of an agreed-upon sense of what a "normal" or "traditional" academic career looked like, though changes were already afoot. Now, there are many pathways to follow after graduate school, including the more conventional (if increasingly rare) tenure-track career as well as other possibilities both within and outside the academy. There are nearly infinite possibilities for putting your research and teaching skills and specialized knowledge to use outside the academy, but, given this volume's scope, the chapters here focus mostly on pathways running through or near academic institutions. Karen Kelsky ("The Professor Is In"), who left a tenured position to launch a career as a professional academic mentor, offers advice on how and when to approach the academic job market and how to negotiate your first contract. Yuridia Ramírez describes her experience cultivating an academic identity without stifling her own ebullient personality. We offer some advice for negotiating a higher salary (and other benefits) at various career stages. Bryan Pitts and Cynthia Greenlee discuss their decisions to pursue non-faculty careers—Pitts directing an area-studies program at a university, and Greenlee outside of the academy but still occasionally dipping a toe in when she desires. Sylvanna Falcón explains how to cross the difficult terrain from signing a contract to securing tenure by cultivating appropriate support systems at your institution and beyond. We offer some basic guidelines for talks and presentations, including everything from job talks and conference presentations to invited lectures. Sarah Portnoy discusses how to navigate academic life off the tenure track, making use of institutional resources while recognizing the different expectations and protections for non-tenure-track faculty. Finally, Sarah Deutsch offers counsel about how to manage the inundation of service, mentoring, and evaluating requests that follow a successful tenure review. While the privilege of tenure does come with expectations that you will mentor and support those climbing the ladder behind you, it does not mean you have to turn your life over to service or that you will no longer need mentoring yourself.

While there are now, for better and for worse, many ways to be an academic—and even more ways to be an intellectual—they still all require smart and practical strategies for balancing research, teaching, service, and life.

1. The Tenure-Track Job Search, Start to Finish

KAREN KELSKY

Every department has its own culture with regard to hiring, so it is impossible in an essay to encompass the full range of practices. Places wherein departments differ include the point at which the whole department is or is not involved in decision-making, and the relative power of the department, search committee, department head, or dean to make the final decision about the person offered the job. I will share with you the process that prevailed in all of the departments with which I was associated, as it is a very common one. It will at least get you into the ballpark of how the typical American tenure-track job search is conducted and provide a comparison point for any deviations you encounter moving forward. As with all things job-search related, general advice can only go so far. Do weigh this chapter against practices you've observed in your own department and what mentors in your field tell you about your own field. The single most important thing any job seeker can do is to participate in searches in your own department—minimally by attending job talks and participating in department-wide conversations, even better by serving as graduate student representative on an actual search committee.

Step 1

For a tenure-track job opening to exist, there needs to be a line. A line is permission that a department receives from the dean to hire in a certain area. While the acquisition of a line is not something the candidate plays a part in, it is useful to start the summary of the job search here, because it sets the stage for what follows. The effort to get a line starts the year prior to the job search itself.

In most cases, departments are asked to present their ranked list of hiring requests to the dean during the spring term. These lists must include a rationale for each line request, in terms of programmatic need, teaching demand, leveraging current strengths to fill as many gaps as possible with one person in a strategic way, and promises of enrollment and funding that this hire will bring in. This rationale and the ranked list itself has to be fought out in the department; by the time the line is requested, feelings are oftentimes already running rather high about the urgency of the hire.

The dean gathers all the requests from all of the departments under his or her purview and evaluates them against the budget available for new hires. In any case, eventually the decision is communicated to the department: you have been approved to search for a line in xxx. In almost no cases do departments get approved for all of the lines they request. Large, wealthy departments in STEM and Business tend to get more lines approved; small humanities departments may get no lines approved at all. In the current impoverished state of higher ed, departments may go years without a single new tenure-track hire, and indeed may be seeing their department shrink precipitously with years of retirements or departures going unreplaced.

I share this background because it is my view that the single most important mental exercise for all job seekers hoping for success on the tenure-track job market is learning to see the hiring process from the search committee's perspective rather than their own. Job seekers who look at the search from their own perspective will be prone to make several very common errors of approach:

— Drone on tediously about their own research interests and the minutiae of the dissertation
— Express interest in teaching only tiny, obscure courses that revolve around the identical preoccupations as the dissertation
— Treat interviews as monologues
— Focus entirely on their own research and teaching "wants" rather than departmental needs.

By grasping the year-long departmental effort that precedes the listing of the job ad, you have a better sense of the stakes of the hire for the department. They had to confer, debate, rank, request, and wait while the request was considered. The job ad is the outcome of that long process, and the successful candidate is going to be the one who both meets the priorities listed in the ad *and* acts as an engaged colleague who understands that all hires are an intense and significant (and increasingly rare) department-wide process.

Step 2

Moving on, once the line is approved, the department establishes a search committee, which finalizes the details of the job ad and places it, usually in about August. The ad will include specific area or topical priorities (which may be more targeted than the general line request that was previously sent to the dean), specific items required for full consideration, and a deadline that is often around October 15, November 1, or December 1. The search committee will likely include approximately five people—both senior and junior members of the department, and, if a PhD-granting program, one grad student representative.

This is where you, the candidate, encounter the ad. Here is what you must know: the deadline is sacrosanct. Because of H R and affirmative action rules, files that are not complete at the time of the deadline cannot be considered; they will be thrown out. In former decades, candidates might have received a note to alert them that they were missing a letter or document, but those days are gone. Now any incomplete file is simply disqualified. This means if one of your letter-writers fails to get their promised letter in on time, your file is probably disqualified. Know this, and make sure you have backup letters on file with a dossier service to send in a pinch (if that isn't already your main mode of submitting letters).

Send all the material they ask for, and don't send any material they did not ask for. Every committee has its own established criteria, and to stay on the right side of affirmative action rules, they must evaluate all candidates equally, i.e., on the basis of the requested documents only.

At this point, the committee has the unenviable task of whittling down what may well be a huge number of complete applications (ranging from 200 in smaller fields and smaller campuses to 1000 for high-profile jobs in large fields like American literature) down to a manageable long short-list. This list will likely contain somewhere between 10 and 25 files. As you can see, a frenzy of rejection is required to get from, say, 500 applications to 25. In this scenario, 475 applications must be rejected quickly, by faculty members who are just as stressed out, distracted, and overworked as you are.

Here again, remember the search committee! It's not a magical black box, and it's not a form of faculty relaxation. It's work. Work that is entirely uncompensated, and that occurs on top of all the other poorly compensated, poorly supported, time-stressed work that faculty members are burdened with in the neoliberal academy. Spare a moment to imagine your hypothetical search committee member: she was up at 6:00 a.m. to get her kids up and dressed and fed, in order to get out the door in time for school. She rushes in to work for her first meeting of the day, this one with her TAs, and then to teach her first class. The next hour is filled with tedious course recertification paperwork, before a lunch meeting about the latest 10 percent cut to the department budget and demand for more work on the budget committee. Her afternoon class comes next, followed by office hours and a line of disgruntled undergraduates challenging her grades on the midterm. She barely makes it to yet another (mostly pointless) faculty meeting at 4, from which she must slip out early at 4:50, to the judgmental glares of her colleagues, to make it to school to get her kids in time to get them to piano and soccer. She only gets home in time to throw some dinner on the table and spend an exhausted hour or two of family time before getting the kids bathed and into bed, folding some laundry, and then hastily writing her lecture notes for the next day's class. She hasn't yet gotten to the unfinished grading, but . . . oh, the damned search! And that meeting is . . . tomorrow! So she opens the file and starts racing through the applications. "How fast can I reject these files," she asks herself, "so I can just get to bed?" The whirlwind of rejection that follows is not personal; it is structural. It finds the lowest hanging fruit of applicant errors, and pounces on them.

The things that lead to instant rejection: an incomplete file; applications from people clearly unqualified or unfit; applications filled with typos and grammatical errors; applications that show no connection to the advertised priorities; applications that are endlessly long, self-involved, and verbose, and bury the actionable evidence in a forest of impenetrable verbiage; weak applications that show insufficient publication or teaching record; strong applications but from applicants whose theoretical or methodological orientation is too far removed from the department's; confusing applications that reference a scattered assortment of interests but no clear central disciplinary focus; and so on. Nobody at this stage is likely to get a second look. There is simply no time.

Step 3

All of the search committee members construct their long short-list, and then come together in the meeting to hash it out and agree on a final, official version. Obviously, those candidates who are on everyone's lists will be automatically added. Those who are on, say, four out of five lists are probably also automatically added. But those on only two or three lists will be argued over. Pros and cons, rationales, supporting evidence drawn from other department colleagues or emergent programmatic emphases or gossip heard outside the dean's office, etc., will be marshaled. Of course, the fit with the job ad will play a major role. However, it's not always a completely decisive role. This is because the priorities for the search were to a large degree set an entire year earlier, and in that time, personnel change, priorities change, departmental and campus budgets change. Faculty go on leave or take other jobs. New departmental or campus initiatives might suddenly arise. So, while the ad matters a great deal, there can be some mission creep at the point when the search committee members actually begin to rank the candidates for short-listing.

In the end, the search committee will agree on a final long short-list (although some disagreements at this and other parts of the search can arise and carry over to the bitter end). The individuals on this list are then asked for additional materials such as writing samples, and depending on the discipline's practices, are probably invited to a preliminary interview at a conference or by video. In most departments, the long short-list does not require approval by the whole department.

Step 4

The long short-list candidate interviews are typically about thirty minutes in length, and happen live at conferences held in late November and beyond, or by video. These are prescreening interviews, meant to provide the search committees with an encounter with the live human behind the packet of application materials. The goal of these interviews is to get a sense of the candidate's personality; academic persona; ability to articulate research topics, methods, conclusions, and publication plans effectively; fit with both the advertised job and the departmental priorities; and ability to speak with energy and skill about teaching. While the encounters are short, thoughts of potential collegiality will arise at this stage. The key to these short interviews for the candidate is to provide all essential data points being sought by the search committee. These include: Is your dissertation finished/almost finished? Do you have clear publication plans? Can you teach our most essential courses effectively? Do you grasp the kind of department and campus we are—i.e., slac, r1, regional teaching—and what that means for the job? Do you communicate through dialogue not monologue? And so on.

Step 5

With the results of these preliminary interviews and/or extra materials such as writing samples or letters of recommendation in hand, the search committee meets again to hash out a short short-list of candidates invited for campus visit. A common number for this list is three invitations with two alternates, although departments with larger or smaller budgets, or particular hiring agendas (read: inside candidates) may deviate. The decision will be made based on the criteria described in Step 4. Some departments will require the search committee to get this final short short-list approved by all faculty members, and some will not. In any case, once this list receives final approval, the main individuals are invited to campus, sometimes by the search committee chair, sometimes by the department head.

Step 6

In the system that prevailed for the past thirty years or so, the campus-visit invitations went out around December or January for visits in February or March. However, recently the market has accelerated, and more and more invitations go out in October or November, for visits in late November or December. In general, the purpose of this acceleration is to grab excellent candidates before they have a chance to fully explore all possible jobs. The buyers' market of the academic job market makes this possible.

In any case, whether in late fall or winter, the campus visits take place. These too permit of a great deal of variation, but I will again describe the conventional practices that prevailed at my R1 institutions: a two-night visit packed with scheduled meetings and events. In that typical structure, the candidate flies in late afternoon, and is picked up at the airport and taken to the hotel and then to dinner. The next morning begins with breakfast and continues through meetings and meals, with the all-important job talk taking place at 4 p.m. A reception and dinner follow that. The next morning begins with another early breakfast, additional tours and meetings, and then the candidate is driven to the airport for departure.

Common elements of a typical campus visit, in no particular order, include the following (those that are core elements are marked with an asterisk):

* Individual meetings with interested department faculty in their offices (30 minutes each)
* Official search committee meeting (1–2 hours)
* Meeting with department head (1 hour)
* Meeting or lunch with graduate students (if a grad program; 1–2 hours)
* Breakfast (2x), lunch (2x), dinner (2x) with different configurations of faculty and graduate students
* Meeting with dean or provost (if a small campus; 30 minutes)
  Tour of campus (1 hour)
  Tour of town in a faculty member's car (1 hour)

* Job talk and Q and A (2 hours)
  Teaching demo (1–1.5 hours)
  Post-job-talk reception (1 hour)
  Reception at faculty home (varies)
  Examination of (potential) lab space/equipment (1 hour)
  Visits to relevant interdisciplinary centers on campus (1 hour)
  Visits to special library collections (1 hour)

The purpose of the campus visit is for the candidate to show that they can comport themselves like a faculty peer; behave like a good-natured colleague; flexibly engage with a range of colleagues; present, explain, and defend their research verbally in the high-stakes environment of the job talk as well as in more casual interactions over lunch or dinner; directly or indirectly display good teaching skills; and demonstrate the fit of their work to the needs of the department.

The campus visit is grueling. The candidate is being surveilled. It's critical that candidates do what they can to ensure sufficient sleep (so bring sleep aids if you use them) and sufficient sustenance (bring protein bars to fill up on as needed, as meal times may be consumed with conversation rather than eating). A good campus visit will include a few rest slots, and a sensitive department will provide the candidate with an office space to use during the visit, but these are not guaranteed.

Step 7

After the campus visits are all completed, the search committee meets to evaluate the candidates, first deliberating on whether any are to be considered unacceptable and removed from consideration (this regularly happens), and then ranking the rest. The grad student member, if there is one, will have also polled the graduate student population, and will come to the meeting prepared to represent their opinions and concerns. At this point, in most cases, the search committee will share this ranking with the entire faculty, and at least one departmental meeting will be devoted to discussing the candidates, the ranking, the acceptable/unacceptable decision, and the need to invite any alternates. If no one candidate emerges from these deliberations to be offered the position, then alternate candidates will be invited. Assuming, however, that at least one of the original candidates is acceptable, that person's file is forwarded to the dean with a request to make an offer.

In most cases, deans simply rubber stamp a department's final decision, but not always. There are times when a dean will overrule a department's choice and insist on another candidate. This is a very bad thing for everyone, as the department feels terribly disrespected, and the person hired comes in without the goodwill or support of their colleagues. Thankfully, that is rare. In most cases, deans recognize that they are not qualified to opine on hires, and will approve the department's choice and provide guidance to the department head on the terms of a permitted offer, encompassing salary, startup range, and so on.

Step 8

The department head or search committee chair contacts the successful candidate and offers the job. The candidate then generally has a week or two to consider the offer and to negotiate some of the terms. The elements of an offer that are negotiable differ widely based on discipline, area of study, status of the department, leverage possessed by the candidate (i.e., competing offers), and the rank and type of the institution. R1 offers can be negotiated the most, while tiny regional teaching college offers can be negotiated the least. Similarly, STEM and Business/Finance offers can be negotiated more, while deep humanities offers (like Classics, Philosophy, Comparative Literature, etc.) can be negotiated less. Negotiating is generally expected but can be fraught with various risks, so candidates should certainly get help from an experienced mentor. In any case, once elements of the offer such as salary, startup funding, annual research support, teaching load and teaching releases, moving support, summer salary, lab space and equipment, and grad student/lab assistant funding have been negotiated, then the contract is mailed, the candidate signs it, and the search is officially finished.

In my decade of running The Professor Is In, I have continually been amazed by the way that brilliant PhDs with highly developed minds and research skills suddenly transform into helpless, passive victims vis-à-vis the job market. Time and time again, scholars who can ferret out obscure nuggets of insight from the most complex sets of data will throw up their hands in hopeless despair at the job search, saying things like, "It's impossible to understand," "It's a crapshoot," "It's all who you know," and so forth.

Let me hasten to confirm: the academic job market is catastrophically bad. It is in a state of near-total collapse. Only between 5 and 35 percent of PhDs will ever get even a single tenure-track job offer. Almost 75 percent of university instructors across every rank and type of institution are hired on a contingent basis.[1] Among adjuncts, 25 percent are paid so poorly that they qualify for public assistance.[2] It is the academic career that is the exception and the alt-career now the norm. The normative career track for PhDs is outside the tenure track and likely outside the academy entirely.

However, these truths about the academic job market do not mean that the market is utterly devoid of its own logic. It has a logic—one that is entirely drenched in (continually disavowed) neoliberal markers of productivity. And it has a set of values that mostly track onto a (continually disavowed) prestige hierarchy. Job seekers do not have to consider themselves helpless in the face of it. All PhD job seekers can learn the logic and values that govern the academic job search and from the beginning of their time in graduate school can avail themselves of the excellent advising on the nonacademic job search available across the internet.

PhD training renders its subjects more and more enmeshed in systems of external validation. Effective career strategizing—whether in the academy or outside—hinges on rebuilding the capacity for internal validation, recovering your own values and motivations, and charting an independent course separate from the outdated expectations of departments and advisers.

NOTES

1. Colleen Flaherty, "A Non-Tenure-Track Profession?," *Inside Higher Ed*, October 12, 2018, https://www.insidehighered.com/news/2018/10/12/about-three-quarters-all-faculty -positions-are-tenure-track-according-new-aaup.
2. Ken Jacobs, Ian Perry, and Jenifer MacGillvary, "The High Public Cost of Low Wages: Poverty-Level Wages Cost U.S. Taxpayers $152.8 Billion Each Year in Public Support for Working Families," UC Berkeley Center for Labor Research and Education, April 2015, http://laborcenter.berkeley.edu/pdf/2015/the-high-public-cost-of-low-wages.pdf.

2. Developing an Academic Identity: Lead with "You"

YURIDIA RAMÍREZ

Whether confronting the challenges of entering graduate school or beginning a new position, it is imperative that we fashion our own unique identities as academics as we navigate the people around us and the spaces we inhabit, despite a prevailing culture that generally promotes conformity. Authenticity is possible, though, and in this essay, I will share some personal anecdotes of how I navigated the journey to stay true to my authentic self, as well as offer some suggestions and advice as to how others might be able to do the same.

It remains the case that underrepresented scholars—including differently abled and LGBTQ+ scholars, veterans, religious minorities, women in the sciences, and scholars of color—are often encouraged or pushed to develop an academic persona that seems properly "intellectual." We should be easily confident and articulate; our dress should be sleek and sophisticated but neutral; and our temperament competitive though muted. We should be comfortable and knowledgeable about marketing our work and ourselves. Most importantly, we should refrain from ever being vulnerable or revealing too many details about our personal lives. I remember mentors telling me as an undergraduate to straighten my hair when I attended academic conferences, because women with straight hair were seen as demure and composed and thus would be received more positively than those with curly hair, which might connote a bigger presence. As a graduate student, I was told to avoid wearing my hoop earrings while I presented my work, lest I distract people in the audience. It never occurred to me then, as it does now, that instead of muting my personality to conform to an academic realm not originally designed to include Latina intellectuals, I should challenge this culture and create space for others like me by committing the radical act of being myself.

I struggled with accepting my authentic self long before graduate school. A first-generation college graduate and the daughter of working-class Mexican immigrants, I grew up in a small town in rural Wisconsin where my "foreignness" and "brownness" were magnified by my name, skin tone, and language. School personnel Anglicized my name to "Judy," while friends and classmates criticized and ridiculed me for being "loud," a characterization of me that has since persisted. As I navigated these spaces of institutional and structural whiteness, I greatly desired to be one of many, rather than the only. It was not until high school that I embraced and reclaimed my name, writing "Yuri Ramírez" on my assignments, and it was not until my graduation ceremony that a school administrator announced me using my full name. In college, I felt deeply committed to developing my personality and character without sacrificing my happiness. In many ways, this phase felt like a rebirth. I cultivated relationships with people who accepted me just as I was and pursued experiences in the community that only augmented and strengthened my light. I volunteered at after-school programs devoted to supporting Latinx migrant youth and worked with refugee and immigrant high school students—many of whom were young parents—as they worked on history research projects that reflected their experiences. Their stories reminded me so much of my own family's journey to this country. These realizations led me to discover that my identity was grounded in teaching and working with—and being in—community. I came to see these students as representations of myself and my family, and I felt an intense responsibility to continue my academic journey because I wanted to become someone of whom they could be proud.

Graduate school, though, has a way of making even the most confident person self-conscious, and I felt it within days of beginning my coursework. Some of the students in my cohort whispered about how they could not believe a state school graduate like myself had been accepted to Duke, deducing that I most certainly was a diversity recruit. On multiple occasions, these white graduate students and one white male professor commented on how I very seldom offered anything of significance in class discussions, going so far as to ridicule the words I had chosen to express myself. One time, after one of our senior white professors—who identified as both a woman and an ally—led a seminar discussion about the additional burdens placed on women of color in the academy, my cohort colleagues loudly claimed within earshot that that was a lie, invalidating not only me, but also the lived experiences of our professor. Their words tormented me because they verbalized what I most feared—that I did not belong. Other times, my vibrant and gregarious personality led colleagues and professors to question my academic credentials and intellectual prowess. Because they perceived me as not being serious and formal, they assumed I also could not be intellectually rigorous. For the first year of graduate school, I was broken, a shadow of myself, and had no idea what to do or who to be.

So, I sought out faculty of color, especially women, in my department and across the university. I emailed them, introduced myself, and invited them to coffee or lunch. I also reached out to one of my mentors from college, and she emailed professors in her network who lived in North Carolina, who in turn reached out with a desire to mentor me. Over these coffee dates with women of color faculty, I told them my story—often crying—and sought their advice. Their wisdom and words affirmed my experiences and made me feel as though I did belong and was part of a community. I also befriended other students of color in my program through a graduate student group focused on students of color and found refuge among them as well. Because I had mentioned to the student group's main organizer, an African American woman in my program, that two of my cohort members had said I was a diversity recruit, she made it a point to ask a graduate school dean if any of the students gathered in that room were diversity recruits. When the dean responded with an unequivocal and resounding "no," that colleague looked over and smiled reassuringly as tears streamed down my face. I later reached out to the dean to introduce myself and tell her how much it had meant to me to hear her say those words when I needed them most. She followed up by inviting me to lunch, and talked with me for hours about what I had experienced in graduate school thus far. Becoming a mentor, the dean was determined to prepare me professionally, as well as academically, for academia. She invited me to participate in graduate school programming, panels, and even search committees, so that I could meet more graduate students of color across the university, as well as grow more comfortable over time in academic and professional settings. Throughout it all, she constantly reminded me, "you, as you are, belong."

If the majority of students in graduate school feel some sense of Impostor Syndrome, I offer my memories of these microaggressions along my personal journey to show how obstacles of various kinds can derail not only individuals' academic trajectories, but also their very personal identities that existed before pursuing academia as a career. So how can we stay true to the people we want to become, or continue to be, in the face of others who might doubt our capacity to be an equal among them? My advice is to recognize early on that these institutions of higher learning, like many spaces throughout this country, were never intended to include or promote certain communities. Thus, simply taking the step of enrolling in academic programs and studying to be among the new cadre of professors is a fundamental challenge to the system. Change is happening but not fast enough to make everyone feel welcome and comfortable. The pressure to "fit in," no matter how benignly someone thinks they are placing that pressure upon you, seeks to maintain the status quo.

Aim for the authenticity of being radically you. Use your personal statement for graduate school or cover letter for jobs to say something about who you are and your values. I always wanted people on search committees to remember me and my story, so I made it a point to emphasize that I was a first-generation graduate and intimately tied to community work and public history. Especially when I was on the job market, I realized that if I was going to be happy anywhere, I needed my future department to know exactly who I was and the type of work and organizing in which I was intimately invested. Be forthcoming with who you are and what you value, because—in the long run—not only will you save yourself the trouble of maintaining a facade, but you'll also be in a place that values you for all of your complexities. We all deserve to work in an environment that makes us feel the most human and the most like ourselves, even if it takes time to find it.

To feel the most like ourselves, we also have to feel comfortable and confident in our skin. When I go to conferences or symposiums, or when I teach, I always wear clothes that make me feel powerful and that allow me to exude confidence and security, which usually means embracing colors, patterns, and my natural curls. Because I understand myself as deeply rooted in community, I write and speak in ways that are clear and concise. I also am visibly racialized as "other," so especially when I am with my students, I am open about being a first-generation graduate and the daughter of Mexican immigrants. My work and values also transmit my political views, so I encourage my students to be open about their opinions and ideas, all the while respecting each other and me in the process. There is so much about who we are that is innately invisible to others, so I encourage you to lean in to those particularities and find strength and power in them.

Find those who will brighten your light without feeling threatened that you are dimming theirs. Other scholars of color, especially women, at my graduate institution were integral in reiterating to me that I was not a diversity recruit, and there was nothing wrong about who I was or how I carried myself. I networked at national conferences and developed relationships with scholars of color who supported me throughout my career, validating both my work and my experiences. I quickly realized that the type of scholar I wanted to be did not replicate the systems of learning I had confronted in graduate school—the posturing, the competitiveness, the performance—but rather were fundamentally premised on the notion that all people, including myself, had a critical and integral role in the production and dissemination of knowledge.

Of course, the academy and our disciplines continue to have particular conventions to which we must adhere, so there is a strategic way in which we can remain true to our multiple identities even while existing within these structures. Reach out to colleagues at other institutions and develop a panel to participate in conferences, as panels tend to be accepted at higher rates than individual submissions. Attend the presentations of more senior scholars at conferences and introduce yourself to them after their panel. If there is a scholar whom you are particularly excited to see at the conference, reach out via email before and ask for a coffee meeting. I cannot emphasize enough how crucial it is to develop relationships with senior scholars in your field, since they can serve as models for how you should present and engage with intellectual inquiry, introduce you to other scholars in your field, and continue to support and advise you throughout your career.

The relationships you build and experiences you pursue will only support your professional and academic growth. The more I organized in my community, participated in academic conferences, and engaged on campus through professional development opportunities, the stronger my academic voice became. I learned to graciously accept critique and think through ideas with others, while remaining steadfast to my intended arguments and interventions. If you have decided to research and narrate stories of people who share a particular background of yours, do not shrink in the face of those who would call you "too close" to your research. We must not forget that white scholars have been researching white communities for years. We must continue to push through the externally and internally imposed doubt to change how academia views certain types of research and the scholars who choose to pursue them.

Perhaps the most significant advice I can offer is to be respectful of your colleagues and mentors without being self-abasing or obsequious. Too often in graduate school, I made the mistake of positioning myself as a novice, as someone not on the same level as my fellow students, because I believed it. I desperately wanted to be "allowed in" to this academic world but felt myself not smart enough. So often, in front of others, I attributed my triumphs to good fortune and luck, downplaying the merits of my work. There is a way to assert that academic success takes a village without eliminating your own hard work and unique talents from that equation. Years later, I still have to be mindful of recognizing and asserting my accomplishments, scholarly production, and collegiality. Once you have identified your strong suits in your department or discipline, play to them and assert them—not boastfully, but with a steady confidence and trust that your work is valuable, relevant, and meaningful. Academia has its own milestones and markers that center on external validation; remember, however, that the internal validation you give yourself is important not only to your perseverance in this career, but also for the people whom you might not realize are observing you, including your own students or community members. By being yourself, you empower others around you to do the same. Take up equal space, and notice when others need your help in claiming theirs. Instead of "fitting in" to the academy as it is, we have the opportunity to completely transform the academy by opening the doors to countless students who see themselves and their experiences reflected in those of us who are rising now in the ranks. The best academic identity you can develop is one that stands poised in your intellectual capacity without sacrificing all of the other complex identities that make you the person you are.

3. How to Negotiate for a Higher Salary

LORI FLORES AND JOCELYN OLCOTT

Most of us enter academia because we are passionate about teaching and inter-ested in a life of ideas and critical inquiry. But, let's face it, we also have to eat and pay the rent. What's more, it's demoralizing to realize that the colleague down the hall from you takes home ten or fifteen percent more than you do, or that the hotshot your department just hired right out of graduate school signed for a salary close to what you're making after a decade on the job.

Asking for salary increases is awkward, particularly since even well-resourced institutions tend to cry poor when faced with such requests. There are, however, some considerations to keep in mind that can help you in the process. As with most things in academia, it's worth spending time to do some research. Here are the questions you'll want to ask:

1. How much information do I have about peers' salaries?

In most public institutions, salaries are part of the public record. Finding out what your colleagues earn may be as easy as finding the appropriate website or as arduous as performing a records request, but you should be able to learn it one way or another. In private universities, salaries are usually undisclosed. The only way to learn what colleagues are earning is often to ask them directly, which—depending on institutional culture—may only be appropriate with those who are also close friends and confidants. You'll also want to know how the institution arrived at those salaries. Many departments have some version of merit-increase pools, but there are widely varying criteria for determining who is meritorious. Some departments have union contracts that determine when raises occur and how they will be distributed. Whatever the system is, you'll want to have a handle on its mechanisms in order to make sense of salaries.

2. Who are my peers, anyway?

Particularly if you are in a public institution (or thinking about joining one), you'll be able to compare your salary to a broad range of colleagues. Before you embark on negotiations, make sure you are making an apples-to-apples comparison. The most obvious pool is colleagues at your same rank in your home department (i.e., the department where you have or anticipate getting tenure) who have a roughly similar record of teaching, research, and service. Such comparisons may not be possible in small departments or in departments where there are widely disparate modes of performing different aspects of your job (e.g., in a music department that may include composers, performers, theorists, musicologists, etc., each of whom may have quite different duties in teaching, research, and service). In these instances, it may make more sense to compare your salary to someone whose work bears some material similarities to your own. It might make more sense for the associate professor of musicology to compare their salary to a similarly ranked cultural anthropologist than to a similarly ranked performing musician. For someone negotiating their first contract in a small English department that hasn't hired in a while, it might make more sense to look at salaries for recent hires in other humanities departments.

3. How much leverage do I have?

There are only a few moments when you really have leverage at academic institutions; you should use them wisely. The first and most obvious moment is when you first get hired at an institution. Since benefits and subsequent raises are based on a percentage of this first number, it's worth negotiating for as much as you can. If you don't have another offer, your best guideline is the salaries of other recent hires at your rank and in your department or similarly situated departments (i.e., departments in the same division, similarly ranked, and with comparable expectations). You might ask for five percent above that number, but you should be aware if there is a clear cap—sometimes set by a union or a legislature, and sometimes de facto based on the lowest-paid colleague at the next rank up.

The other obvious moment when you have leverage is when you have an outside offer. There are many opinions within academia about the advisability and ethics of seeking outside offers if you're not serious about accepting them. But the fact is that neoliberal institutions increasingly leave it to the market to determine employees' value. The most effective way to command a higher salary from your current institution is to show that another institution would pay a salary that, after factoring in cost-of-living differences, would amount to a raise. That said, it is inadvisable to apply for a job that you have no intention of accepting if it were offered—even putting ethics aside, you would gain a professional reputation that would not serve you well in the long run. Prospective employers can usually tell when you're not serious about a job, and your current institution might decide they don't have the interest or resources to retain you.

A third moment when you might exert some leverage is when you've just received some sort of recognition or distinction such as a book award or a teaching prize. Particularly if the prize comes from outside the institution—from a professional organization or similar entity—it signals to your chair and your dean that other institutions might try to court you. That's a good time for the institution to remind you how valuable you are.

Last, but definitely not least, you have some leverage in instances of salary compression, particularly if it also follows a pattern of discrimination against an underrepresented group. Once again, such information is easier to obtain in public institutions, where you can see how your salary stacks up against your colleagues' and whether there is a pattern of underpaying particular demographic groups. If you are underpaid compared to colleagues in your rank or if you think that there may be an issue of salary discrimination, you should seek remediation.

4. What are my institution's policies for remediation?

The two circumstances described above are, of course, a bit different. Salary discrimination is illegal and should lead to immediate remediation (and possibly back pay) if there is a clear pattern. Salary compression is not illegal and not even unusual, although it sometimes also follows demographic lines. For example, parents of young children or of children with special needs often have found it more difficult to publish at the same rate as their colleagues. If you have not received a raise in a while (but your colleagues have), it may make sense to ask your chair whether you are eligible for a compression raise, which would bring your salary in line with colleagues at your rank.

5. What can I negotiate for besides salary?

When you have the opportunity to negotiate, you might consider what else you might negotiate for besides salary. Because salaries come with fringe benefits and payroll taxes, employers are often more willing to grant nonsalary requests. You might ask for additional start-up funds, a larger moving allowance, or a larger research account. You might request course relief during your first year or several releases that might be distributed over several years. Some private institutions offer a tuition benefit for your dependents, but you'll want to check to see if there is a vesting period and if there's a limit to how many dependents may take the benefit. Institutions in areas with a higher cost of living may offer some possibilities for making housing more affordable—renting out subsidized housing, offering low- or no-interest mortgages, granting a one-time housing subvention, etc. As with salary, it makes sense to find out as much as you can about what packages your institution has given to similarly situated colleagues.

6. With whom should I negotiate?
Different institutions have different practices regarding negotiations. In some places, you will negotiate with your chair, and in others with a divisional dean or dean of the faculty. If you are already employed by the institution, it likely makes the most sense to start with your chair. If you are short-listed for another position, you should notify your chair promptly. Some institutions will make preemptive retention offers, and it's always better that your chair hears this news from you rather than from someone else.

7. What if I push too hard?
It is exceedingly rare—although not unheard of—for an institution to retract an offer of employment because the candidate asked for too much during negotiations. It makes sense to ask for everything you want, including the high end of the salary range, and to explain why these demands make sense (e.g., to match another offer, to allow you to set up a lab, etc.). That said, demanding salary and benefits that are considerably out of line with what your colleagues make can definitely ruffle feathers and may get things off on the wrong foot with your new department chair. In some cases, particularly in public institutions, there may be strict limits on what your institution can offer; in others, there is a salary pool such that offering a generous salary to one colleague will come out of future raises for others. The more information you have about how salaries are structured in your department, the more effective you'll be in negotiations. If you make what your chair or dean sees as an excessively high demand during retention negotiations, they may decide not to counteroffer. Many institutions specify in their retention offers that they will not tender another retention offer for a set period of time (generally five years).

4. Scholarship and Life off the Tenure Track

BRYAN PITTS

In 2006, my first year of doctoral work, my fellow history PhD students and I would spend parties discussing the sort of university where we might like to end up. What were our dream jobs? What places would be acceptable as a stopgap measure? What sort of schools would we never settle for? We treated the job market like the college application process, with dream universities and safety schools. From the vantage point of today's job market, it appears silly: a mixture of youthful pride and naive optimism. Of course, in 2006, it wasn't so silly at all, because it seemed everyone was getting jobs. I attended more than one dissertation defense for my adviser's previous students, who had had to scramble to finish their dissertations after two or three years at a school that had hired them with a single chapter written. It never crossed my mind that someday I would not be a college professor.

How much can change in a decade. In the wake of the 2008 financial crisis, cuts to public education, and the changing composition of state legislatures and Congress after 2010, tenure-track jobs are nearly impossible to come by. In my own subfield, Latin American history, a 2017 analysis by the American Historical Association revealed that there was an average of 136 applicants vying for perhaps 15–20 tenure-track jobs per year. Between 2010 and 2017, I applied for 141 tenure-track jobs, adjunct positions, and postdocs. I managed 25 first-round interviews, 9 on-campus visits, and 0 offers. I watched as one by one, my friends made jubilant announcements on Facebook: they were accepting a tenure-track position. Everyone assured me that my turn would come. In the meantime, my department at Duke generously offered me a two-year visiting position. I left a semester early for a Fulbright postdoc in Brazil, then returned for what would turn into a three-year postdoc at the University of Georgia. Surely the teaching experience, the Fulbright, and the UGA postdoc—not to mention articles in the top journals in my field in both the US and the country I studied—would be my ticket to the tenure track, I thought. I was wrong.

Those of us who didn't land tenure-track jobs undoubtedly all endured a similar process of soul-searching. Why did we fail where others succeeded? Our colleagues all sought to reassure us that we shouldn't see it as a failure, as a measure of our self-worth. It's just a bad market. The logic of committees is inscrutable. Maybe if only we'd been a man, or maybe a woman. Maybe our skin was too dark, or wait, maybe too light. Maybe we were too heteronormative, maybe not queer enough. Maybe we look like amateurs because we didn't teach or publish or present enough. Maybe we did too much of one of those, or all of them, intimidating insecure committee members with our brilliance. Maybe our outgoing personality comes across as aggressive; maybe our caution seems shy. But no matter how we explain it to ourselves, it all comes back to the same conclusion, doesn't it? We didn't pull it off.

By 2016, I reluctantly began to accept the inevitable. I had been done with my dissertation for three years. My book was nowhere near finished. A year had just passed with four tenure-track jobs in my subfield, Brazilian history. I had interviewed for all four and had campus visits for two, all to no avail. I was stale on the market, and if I hadn't landed a job in a year with four ads that seemed written for me, I never would. A close friend from undergrad began encouraging me to transition into his field, management consulting. After all, teaching had given me the ability to speak fearlessly in front of others and explain complex topics in terms that laypeople could understand; surely I could help factory workers understand easier ways to organize their workflows. I began to accept that whatever the reason, I would never make it in academia. All the same, I kept applying to academic jobs. It only takes one, right? Hope springs eternal.

I did have one card left to play: I had earned an MA in Latin American Studies, and I was finishing a postdoc in a Latin American Studies program, where I'd spent a little bit of time helping with grant writing, data collection, and budget management. Perhaps this was a way to stay close to academia without being on the tenure track. So, in 2017, when a position posted for Associate Director of the Center for Latin American and Caribbean Studies at Indiana University, I decided to throw my hat in.

It's funny how everything looks different depending on your perspective. My perspective was that of someone who'd spent seven fruitless years on the market, who was in a near-panic about where his salary and health insurance would come from after the school year ended. As I heard later, the greatest concern among the search committee at IU was whether I was serious about staying at the job. In the end, luckily for me, IU decided to offer me the job, with a start date barely a month later.

As I write this from Bloomington, Indiana, I count myself among the lucky ones. Although research is not a component of my position, our affiliate faculty have nonetheless treated me like a colleague and scholar. The Latin Americanist faculty in the Department of History—some of the most renowned scholars in my field—have welcomed me with open arms, inviting me to talks in their department and receptions with their grad students. A graduate student asked me to serve on her dissertation committee. I teach a seminar every fall for MA students in Latin American Studies and PhD minor and certificate students. In many ways, this is the best of both worlds: I get to teach and write, without being overwhelmed by either, or by the rat race of a looming tenure review. In fact, I'm convinced that it's the lower teaching load that's enabled me to finish four journal articles in the last year and a half; instead of spending my evenings grading and prepping, I spend them writing. And if you asked me whether I'd prefer to be at this job, or to be an assistant professor at a school in a town of ten thousand people, with a 4/4 teaching load, for a similar salary, I'd take my job at IU every time. There's also something to be said for the fact that rather than living isolated in a department, I have a position that offers an interdisciplinary perspective and the opportunity to build a top area studies program. My friends who are on the tenure track have told me that they wish they had the opportunity to do something more than teach classes and debate degree requirements for their major and minor. As associate director of an interdisciplinary program, this is what I do every day, and it's an integral part of my job, not a nebulous "service" component that takes a distant back seat to research and teaching.

At the same time, there are drawbacks. For one, I am paid about 25 percent less than an assistant professor at IU. I am also classified as an "academic specialist," which is a strange hybrid between faculty and staff. What this means in practice is that when it would be advantageous to me to call myself faculty, the university considers me staff, and when I would benefit from a staff designation, they tell me that I'm faculty. For example, when I attempted to join the employees' union, I was told that I was ineligible because I was faculty, but when the faculty senate voted to allow representation for non-tenure-track faculty, academic specialists were excluded because we were considered staff. Most disappointing has been the fact that my ability to continue doing research and being treated like a scholar depends entirely on the goodwill of whoever my center's director happens to be at the time. While I have been lucky to have two directors who encourage me to keep researching and writing, the precarity of my status as a "scholar" is constantly driven home.

What would I tell a recent PhD going through the same process as I did? First, I'd tell them that it's really not their fault; the market really is terrible, and unless we improbably manage to undo the neoliberalization of the academy and the corresponding devalorization of skill sets that aren't applicable to STEM or professional fields, this won't change any time soon, if ever. And no one should base their self-worth on whether they manage to convince a committee of four (probably) socially awkward people, safe in that ivory tower of tenure, that they're worthy of a job offer. Second, I'd tell them not to be afraid to look completely outside academia; in many cases, they can work fewer hours (imagine leaving your work completely behind when the clock strikes 5:00 p.m.!) and earn more than they would on the tenure track (not the case with my position, but certainly the case with consulting jobs). Third, I would encourage them to do everything they can to hone their skills in administration, grant writing, and staff supervision. For me, it turned out that these skills were far more useful for landing a job than any of my research or teaching. Fourth, I'd tell them that there are ways to be fulfilled in academia without a tenure-track job. My work as associate director may be tedious at times, but is it any more tedious than grading three hundred world history final exams? And fifth, I'd tell them that it's still possible to write articles and a book without a tenure-track job; in some ways, it's easier, because there is no pressure to earn tenure, and no one can get upset if you focus exclusively on your scholarly writing when you leave the office. Just be adamant that when your forty hours are up, your own writing takes priority. In the end, as the tenure-track job market narrows ever further, the definition of the jobs in which one can produce scholarship is expanding. And I know that after seven agonizing years, I'm pretty happy with how things turned out.

5. The Dangers of Doing Other Things: Why I'm a Scholar but Not an Academic

CYNTHIA R. GREENLEE

During my first-ever meeting with my department's director of graduate students, the avuncular white male professor asked me all manner of questions: What are my goals? What did I want to do in the program? Noting my then-hyphenated name, he asked what my spouse did professionally and inquired about whether we had children—questions that would be off-limits or at least unseemly in a job interview. But more than the probing getting-to-know-you chitchat, he dominated the conversation with heartfelt, booming monologues about the beauties of the intellectual life, the eventual payoffs of graduate-student drudgery, and how this department would retrain me to write the academic way. I listened, understanding that though I had been a journalist and high-level communications professional for global international health organizations, I must learn the conventions of scholarly writing. I carefully wiped my face of any expression—what some in the hard-of-hearing world call "dead face"—when he repeatedly affirmed how much he and the department wanted to support me because, no offense, I was an at-risk student.

I paused, wondering if I had earned this designation simply by being a Black woman student at Duke University. He quickly and tactlessly clarified: I was older, had had a successful career, had a family. And he said, in an exaggerated stage whisper, should I not fare well in my doctoral studies, I could easily decide "to do other things." My hoary age of 33, as well as my professional and life experience, were potential liabilities. It was an epically inauspicious beginning (though the director also turned out to be helpful in many ways).

As it turned out, PhD in hand, I did decide to do "other things." I've worked to maintain a foot in the scholarly world while not being a professor. I am a scholar but not an academic. I am specifically an independent historian who studies African American women and girls in the post–Civil War South, and the intersections where race, reproduction, and the law collide. I have a book proposal circulating, a literary agent, an almost-done manuscript, a coedited anthology coming out in the near future, and various publications of which my traditional academic colleagues would approve.

It must be said, I am an *intentionally* independent historian who had that coveted R1 tenure-track offer with a 2/2 teaching load; multiple dissertation and postdoctoral fellowships and graduate-student writing prizes; and the support of academic mentors at the top of their fields. I said no to that job before the ink on the offer was dry.

But I embarked on a different path than many of my fellow students, working as a scholar outside the academy, as the senior editor at a social-justice journalism publication, and as a freelance author who writes history-informed pieces for a reading public unlikely to pick up a monograph. My public-facing writing has appeared in dozens of publications and won a coveted mention in the 2018 *Best American Essays* volume. And, after co-founding a reproductive-health nonprofit while in graduate school and working consciously to merge my intellectual and activist interests, I'm a well-respected thought leader on reproductive health, rights, and justice in both past and present.

My optimistic side believes that education is the ultimate possibility generator. But my cynical side consciously front-loaded this essay with a partial list of credentials. Why? Because so many assume that I was one of the newly minted PhD masses who could not land a position or was consigned to scrape the bottom of the job-market barrel in multiple-year job searches. Or that I was unqualified. Academics whose departments depend on low-paid labor and who barely know me sometimes ask if I'm able to support myself by writing, editing, and my other pursuits. I don't have the heart to tell them that I almost certainly make more money than they do.

That may sound insulting, but it's no less so than the routine insults and thoughtless structural barriers put in the way of "alt-ac" scholars or workers. The realist in me rarely explains my decision not to pursue a tenure-track job; I know that the hardest thing about being an independent scholar is how university-based academics and associated institutions treat you. My colleagues in the teaching life inundate me with unpaid requests to help their students every semester, and some invite me to speak on their campuses at lower compensation rates than tenure-track professionals, if they offer honoraria at all.

I'm automatically ineligible for many research fellowships, which administrators or nonprofits tie to affiliation. Academic research that I began as a graduate student and was hailed for its rigor then suddenly has become "advocacy" since I left the academy. And while I might be sensitive to these snubs, I am not mistaken in understanding the patronizing, pitying, and inaccurate assumptions that tend to undergird the curious "What are you doing now?" or "How are you doing?" questions that greet me whenever I attend academic gatherings.

Even those academic colleagues who are miserable (and perhaps especially those who are miserable) tend to interpret my choice as an incomprehensible rejection of what they hold dear and, interestingly, as a repudiation of their own aspirations. Some just can't fathom opting for a nine-to-five life (the horror!) or other labor arrangements such as freelancing or consulting.

Being a scholar but not an academic was my choice. To date, that choice has worked for me.

So why the decision to hit the eject button before I had settled into a relatively cushy tenure-track gig? It was a combination of factors specific to me, the institution where I would have launched my "formal" academic career as a junior faculty member, reservations about the academic life, and—probably most importantly—the knowledge that I had marketable research and writing skills that I had possessed before graduate school and that my doctoral education had enhanced, but not created.

In the final analysis, I entered a doctoral program not because I believed that the attainment of a degree and a teaching position were the end goals; neither did I believe those were the only goals. I never intended to be only a professor, but instead planned to continue writing for the public and doing advocacy around issues of reproductive autonomy, especially for Black, brown, and marginalized communities. As I figured it, my identity and research would not be totally or forever contained within the structure of a college or university. My PhD was to be another gadget in the toolbox, one that could open doors and opportunities, rather than narrow them. And I left the door open to return to academia, if I wanted to and should an attractive opportunity arise.

At the root of my decision to be a scholar, not an academic, were two key epiphanies. First, I recognized that I did not need to be a classroom instructor to teach in the world. I also knew the difficulty of teaching about race, Blackness, and sexuality, particularly as a young Black woman who was likely to teach in a predominantly white institution. In a related revelation, I considered whether I needed to be faculty to create the work I desired to do. I realized—as I talked to peers, mentors, creatives, people outside my discipline and outside higher education—that I did not need to be a professor to publish. Such a simple fact, but seemingly hard to grasp because academic publishing is so geared to the exigencies of the tenure track. And while academic publishing is inherently stacked against those who don't have research funds or leave, subventions, or built-in feedback networks, I can submit my work to peer-reviewed journals as much as the next person. Furthermore, I have the added boost of experience pitching editors at nonacademic publications and winning them over with compelling reportage that people actually want to read. What could academia do for me in terms of publishing that I couldn't do myself, with my own writing skills, journalism contacts, inside knowledge of how editors work, and hustle?

Indeed, my writing for nonacademic audiences built my reputation, but the reality is that the academic world and the world "outside" overlap. I'm known as an expert in the reproductive history of Black women, especially abortion, because I wrote about it for online publications. Then that work traveled on social media and fed my reputation as a scholar and, more specifically, a scholar-writer who comfortably straddles the popular and the esoteric.

But let me also speak of more concrete and practical concerns—because these are the factors that few people talk about if and when they talk about choosing to enter or leave academia. As a Black woman with a Black male partner, I didn't subscribe to the default "go anywhere you find a job" philosophy. Black life and safety in the United States are always precarious. It is one thing to consider departments where I would be "the only one" (that's simply a burdensome reality of many departments), but living in an area with little diversity and few cultural escapes was not an option. Neither was it an option to work across the country from my extended family, including an ill parent. As that director of graduate studies made clear in my first meeting, family connections and existing social networks should be strategically deprioritized if one wanted to succeed. Though this view was not necessarily representative across my department, the louder voices—in public or in private advising like that session—prevailed.

Beyond those very critical concerns, I objected to two pillars of graduate education as I saw them: the constant delaying of gratification, and the notion that the tenure track was the sole or best destination for people who spend five to seven years earning a humanities doctorate. Perhaps my well-intentioned DGS was right: I had been lucky enough to have a career and professional success, which taught me how to negotiate even in the lopsided power dynamic that is graduate school and convinced me that I could thrive if a tenure-track job didn't materialize. I could use my research skills but have a more immediate impact in my work as a journalist and advocate instead of waiting or preparing for the next milestone: graduate school acceptance, passing my first exams, making it through my comps, defending my dissertation, going on campus visits, learning how to teach my first classes as a professor, publishing my first journal article, making it to that third-year review, and getting to tenure. Some academic aspirants may be comforted that the rocky and tedious road to achievement and job security comes with many guideposts, but these markers are not as satisfyingly clear as they appear in the distance.

And though academia offers some flexibility in focus and scheduling as long as one produces, I wanted more freedom to experiment. When I entered graduate school in the fall of 2007, I entered a program and a field that was supportive but nevertheless deeply invested in the tenure-track position as the pinnacle of success.

Those attitudes are changing and must, if only because we know the market for academic posts is finite and creates a perpetual surplus of emerging scholars. If they have been taught to think big when it comes to their dissertations but small when it comes to their prospects, that's a lamentable and preventable failure of both imagination and education, which should widen possibilities and close access gaps.

Educators need an education to better assist their students. For many professors who advise graduate students, the tenure track is the burnished brass ring. But it's not the only prize, by far.

Still, faculty may find themselves at a loss to help students renegotiate having a PhD and finding a job where, to be fair, potential employers may deem them overqualified or out of touch. Here's where universities could benefit from the examples of industries that have "training of trainers" (TOT) to teach students about their career options. This is not a far-fetched idea, especially since many programs tackle pedagogy in this way, using master teachers and resources to build better instructors.

Those educators need to know that the options are many. Among the obvious choices of career for people armed with impeccable writing and research skills (and some don't require extra training): policy analyst, translator, academic editor, consultant, higher-education administrator, public historian or curator, archivist, instructor at high schools or community colleges, curriculum designer, positions that require data analysis or synthesis of large amounts of information, and many more that are less obviously connected to the scholarly life.

This diversity of opportunity would be clear if departments rustled through their alumni files regularly and tracked down their own former students. Those one-time students are the best resources, especially since they have navigated the job search far more recently than their advisers and are likely reckoning with the worst of the gig economy inside and outside academia. Faculty and administrators have, within their reach, a corps of people who are already working in other venues—with varying degrees of success and happiness, just like the people dedicated to conquering the tenure ladder.

Their experiences—and those of other nonalumni whose work lives outside higher education—cannot only be the subject of the occasional departmental brown bag. And opportunities to try out different forms of writing, knowledge production and dissemination can be integrated into the curriculum—like teaching students to write op-eds to newspapers and popular media. Similarly, advising can counsel students on best practices of success, but also ask them if they are considering a nonacademic path and then help them plan ways to explore as much as they can and as early as they can.

I am lucky. I arrived at graduate school ready to embrace the study of humanities and also aware that I did not leave other interests at the door. And I became increasingly aware that my research and my life's passions did not have to reside in different places or be dependent on the counsel of tenured scholars who disapprove of my nonacademic leanings, stigmatize "outside work" as a less desirable outcome, or might not have the tools to adequately offer suggestions or direction. After receiving readers' reports on this piece, an editor suggested I think more deeply about what to say to mentors who may need reassurances that it wouldn't be negligent to counsel students and junior colleagues to think outside the tenure-track box. I suggest a reframe of that concern. Is it not rather more negligent to single-mindedly direct students to one path—where the coveted prize is so elusive—and foreclose discussion about all the places they *could* go?

6. From Contract to Tenure

SYLVANNA M. FALCÓN

First, congratulations on *earning* a contract. I use the term *earn* intentionally because you have worked hard to arrive at this post-PhD stage of your academic career. You likely went up against hundreds of applicants for your position, and probably experienced some heartache too in the process. The academic job market is very hard to endure financially, emotionally, and physically, and it is a mysterious process to nonacademics. Even casually referring to it as the "market" normalizes the neoliberal competition one tolerates to secure a contract, including going into debt to apply to jobs and for interviews.

On the Inside Higher Education website's *Conditionally Accepted* blog, I wrote about negotiating a job contract in which you are well positioned to thrive. The negotiation stage is the most important step in the process from contract to tenure.[1] In too many cases, the mere exhaustion of the job market itself results in signing a sub-par contract. You've earned the job offer, and it is important to step back and try to negotiate into place the elements needed to succeed as a junior scholar. This process requires consulting far and wide about what other colleagues have negotiated in their contracts at similar institutions, and what they regret or have learned from their own mistakes. You need to believe that you deserve the structural benefits (i.e., course releases, research funds, software programs, lab space, and so forth) as you embark on a tenure-track position.

Much of what I offer here as food for thought is based on my experience at a public university, but I believe it will be useful for those entering jobs at private institutions as well. Though not a steadfast rule, a shroud of secrecy can exist in private institutions, particularly around the tenure process. Yet in both public and private settings, you must learn to navigate the political waters, advocate for yourself and others, and manage the various demands on your time.

As an assistant professor, you will now be interacting regularly with a wider array of people than just your fellow cohort members, department faculty, and dissertation committee. The primary base is your department, followed by your division and entire university institution, and then professional associations. The first place to start cultivating relationships is within your department. I recommend spending most of your first year getting to know these colleagues, including the department staff, through informal office conversations, occasional lunch or coffee meetings, and seeking advice as you transition to and familiarize yourself with the bureaucracy of your new institution. Forming a relationship with the department staff is vital because an academic position is not just about research and teaching—it is about forming professional work relationships and understanding where to go to get information about anything from benefits and retirement to copy codes and a library card. It is important to build rapport with staff who understand the institution's bureaucracy in a different capacity than faculty colleagues.

The next step is setting up your various mentor networks with both senior and peer-level colleagues. If your new department does not have a mentor system set up for junior faculty, then propose one. The assigned department mentor should never be the chair to avoid any conflicts of interest. As the department's administrator, it may be too much to expect the chair to always have your best interests in mind at the expense of the department. Depending on the size of your department, this mentor can be someone from the core faculty or someone affiliated with your department. Then, inquire if your Academic Senate has a faculty welfare committee with a mentor program. If so, sign up for a faculty mentor from any department on campus in your division—it can be very helpful to have a connection to someone who is not in your department. Next, consult with your professional association networks to see if they have mentor programs. For instance, Sociologists for Women in Society has an established mentor program, and the National Women's Studies Association offers mentor sessions at their annual meetings. In other words, developing your mentor networks means going beyond your department to form a combination of trusted advisers and a peer cohort to minimize the isolation of academia. Cultivating these mentor relationships takes time; embrace the process of forming your mentorship team here.

Your campus should be offering a personnel review and tenure workshop through its Academic Personnel Office (APO). Do not ever miss these sessions. I attended every single one through submitting my file for tenure review and learned something new every time. You retain different types of information as you get closer to the tenure review process, depending on your stage. It is in your interest to understand the bureaucracy of the personnel review process and to understand that staff at the APO can offer you an additional perspective on the process that is internal to your campus. You should ask if these conversations with APO staff are confidential, in case you have any department concerns to convey to them.

Academia can be about navigating a web of alliances and rivalries that you just cannot fully comprehend because they formed long before you started graduate school. If we consider the longevity of the department for a moment, you may be entering a space in which people have been colleagues for over fifteen years, if not more. I can assure you that kind of longevity can mean it has not always been smooth sailing. Bitter feelings can linger for decades, and it is in the interest of your well-being to not decipher what happened. People are complicated in general and academics are no exception. I have seen and heard fights over hires, over an imbalance (often gendered) of service expectations, over incompetent leadership, and about people's personal and family lives (i.e., seeming that faculty with kids may not be saddled with as much service or evening classes). Apply your observation skills to familiarize yourself with your department and campus culture; take notice of who speaks the most often in department meetings and how your new colleagues interact with each other. In addition, assess when a campus issue merits speaking up or not. I do not believe that assistant professors should be completely silent until after tenure because having integrity in academia means voicing concerns when necessary, even at the risk of upsetting colleagues. Nurture a healthy balance between asserting yourself when it's important and accepting that every single battle does not need you to be on the front lines.

A junior faculty member must learn how to prioritize. A common mistake I see in junior faculty colleagues is that they say "yes" to every ask because they want to make a good impression, they really believe in the task or service, or because they feel they should step in for less involved colleagues. I often counsel junior faculty mentees that their priorities will change over time. If you envision a thirty-year academic career trajectory, it is important to clarify what is a priority now, and what can be a priority later. In my second year of a new tenure-track job, a group of women of color graduate students asked me to be their faculty adviser. I initially thought this would be great—I would get to meet and mentor women of color who needed the same guidance I probably did in graduate school. But then I had to be really honest with myself: at the same time of that ask, I was experiencing enormous challenges in getting my first book published that I was only sharing with my most trusted circle of sister-friends. Was I inclined to say yes to take my mind away from the mental fatigue I was experiencing navigating the book-publishing process? Was I inclined to say yes to instill some purpose in being a woman of color academic? I had to reflect and wonder why an already tenured or senior woman of color was not being asked instead of me. I then came to accept that the only way I could eventually be a tenured woman of color academic myself was by saying "no" now, but knowing I would say "yes" to this kind of request later. Though I tried to explain to these fierce women of color that the timing just did not work, this did not stop the talk of my being a "sell out" and not a "true feminist." I could have predicted that would have been the reaction but I paid it no mind, knowing that one day they might understand my position. Sure enough, when one of them entered a tenure-track job about two or three years later, she said "I get you; I totally get why you had to say no." And now that I have earned tenure, I have said yes to mentoring many people at the graduate and faculty levels because I can now prioritize this important service work.

Obtaining clarity on what is expected in a tenure file early can help you map out your next several years. You need to approach the tenure process with some thoughtful advance planning, not with blinders. Depending on what your institution requires for tenure files, you can better evaluate the service demands that get asked of you along the way. For example, if you are at a Research-1 institution where you know research and publications are the primary aspect of your file, then any service request should be assessed as follows: is this ask worth taking time away from my research, writing, or relaxation time? If you can answer yes, then it is a service request to consider. If it is a clear no, then consult with your mentor team on how to say no in a way that does not close doors in the future. The service requests will continue to come your entire career; knowing when to say yes and when to say no is key to maintaining longevity in the profession. I have yet to hear of a case in which someone earned tenure because they said yes to every service request made of them. These requests can be time-consuming and can introduce unanticipated political issues that can be exhausting. You may become resentful of the people who asked you to do this service in the first place if it turns out to be far more labor-intensive than you were led to believe.

Women of color academics (and many others) not only have to confront Impostor Syndrome, but its sibling or cousin, Presumed Incompetent.[2] Impostor

Syndrome has more of a personal and internal aspect to it (i.e., "I don't think I belong here") while Presumed Incompetent has an external element (i.e., someone treating you as inept). Being perceived as incompetent by another person—whether a peer or someone more senior—is based on assumptions about your social and cultural capital and can lead to feeling undermined. Not every negative interaction is about presumed incompetence; thus, it is important to disentangle being challenged (even if in a gruff or rude manner) and being undermined. Challenging presumed incompetence is about learning how to advocate for yourself, determining who to go to in your mentor community to discuss the matter, and in particularly egregious cases, documenting problematic incidents. Someone isn't going to be fired or denied tenure for being a jerk, but they could be approached about their behavior by a department chair or another colleague.

The tenure process can also involve an external reviewer element that perhaps feels the most unsettling because it can be impossible to know who you upset or annoyed at a professional conference, or if you're dealing with a fragile senior ego that does not want their work to feel passé. When you attend professional conferences, be intentional about your networking and try to acquire information about various people in your field—who has a reputation for being toxic or holding a grudge? Who are the scholars you should ask to coffee? Who might be a good tenure letter writer in the future? Conferencing is exhausting, yet it's necessary for you to attend and be visible to other scholars who may be asked to review your file. Since I was the parent of a young child while I was on the tenure track, I limited myself to two professional conferences every year. For me, family time was just as important as my job, so I was very selective about which conferences to attend and mindful of what networking I wanted to do at these meetings.

Public talk invitations are a nice way to meet colleagues at other institutions and, in general, can be a far more generative way to form relationships that could be part of the external review process. If you are invited to give a public talk at an institution in which there is a cohort of scholars who engage in the kind of work you do, then it is a good idea to give that invitation serious consideration. If that is not the case, wait until your first book is published or you have launched your next major research project to accept these invitations. Save your energy and use it wisely.

To thrive in this profession, it is important to constantly do internal check-ins. Ask yourself: How am I doing? What is challenging my teaching or writing process? Am I eating in a balanced way? Am I getting the exercise I need? Am I sleeping well? Am I developing bad habits that need to be addressed (e.g., skipping meals, working through lunch, not taking breaks)? Am I feeling isolated? Should I talk to a therapist about some of my struggles? Am I spending enough time with family and nonacademic friends? These can be difficult questions to ask yourself, but they must be asked constantly. Being an assistant professor is a very demanding job that merits proper attention to our bodies and mental health.

As I stated above, it is important to have a loose plan to prepare a file for tenure. Tenure itself is a political process so you should not be under any illusions that people's personal biases or grudges against you won't come back at the time of tenure. If a university wants to deny you tenure, they will find a way to do so. Submitting a solid file can serve as a shield from people's pettiness and jealousy and position you to take legal action if necessary. Pay attention to the faculty who have earned tenure prior to your case—what was in their file? How were they evaluated? In other words, do some homework.

The department in which you start the tenure track may not be where you earn tenure. If you realize you are in a department in which you feel unhappy and unsupported, create an exit plan. As one friend told me, you write your way to another job. Getting your work out there and published should be part of your exit plan. Having good colleagues, being happy about where you live, and doing the research and teaching you want to be doing makes all the difference in how you walk through this profession. Rather than feeling embattled and consumed by negativity, you can seek contentment and acceptance about what the university structure can and *cannot* offer you.

In closing, I share my list of "top ten best practices" for striving to be a happy academic.

1. **Have a life outside of work** because no one should work 24/7. Have nonacademic friends as part of your life and community circle.
2. **Know when to say "yes" and when to say "no."** You will be asked to participate in events, give talks, organize workshops, review articles or books, etc., for the rest of your career. It is OK to say "no" if it's not a good time for you. Sometimes these opportunities are cyclical so one year may be "yes" and the following year may be "no."
3. **Establish a reputation as a person with integrity** and who is trustworthy.
4. Accept everyone will make mistakes and **learn from yours or ones made by others**. Avoid repeating those same mistakes and do not hold grudges.

5. When you encounter hostility and negativity, realize that it is about them and not you. **It is important for your sanity to steer clear of toxic people** in academia or, if avoidance isn't an option, to minimize those interactions as much as possible.

6. **Avoid working in isolation.** Too often academics work and think alone; try to establish a scholarly community where you break that culture of isolation.

7. If something happens that leaves you upset, **then communicate your frustrations to someone in a manner that is respectful, engaging, and fair**. It is not necessary to yell at peers, faculty, staff, and students to make your point.

8. **Protect chunks of your weekends as much as possible** for downtime.

9. **Maintaining balance is intentional**; it will not organically emerge. Balance your academic life with having a life!

10. **Remember that your intellectual and research life really matters,** so seek support when needed and, if sole-authored work is paramount to your tenure file, then treat writing as a craft that needs constant love, nurturing, and attention.

NOTES

1. Sylvanna Falcón, "You Deserve Better," *Conditionally Accepted* (blog), Inside Higher Education, September 16, 2016, https://www.insidehighered.com/advice/2016/09/16/faculty-color-should-not-just-accept-initial-job-offer-essay.

2. See *Presumed Incompetent: The Intersections of Race and Class for Women in Academia*, edited by Gabriella Gutiérrez y Muhs, Yolanda Flores Niemann, Carmen G. González, and Angela P. Harris (Boulder: University Press of Colorado, 2012).

7. A Few Rules of Thumb about Conference Presentations and Invited Talks

LORI FLORES AND JOCELYN OLCOTT

1. The first rule of public presentations: every talk is a job talk. That is to say, every time you present your research, you have an opportunity to convey not only your interesting findings and the sophistication of your analysis but also your collegiality and ability to convey material effectively. You never know who might be in the audience who might one day be evaluating your tenure file or grant proposal or considering hiring you as a colleague. You should approach every speaking engagement with the professionalism and respect that you would a job interview.

2. Know what the standard protocols are within your field as well as the expectations for this particular event. How long will presenters speak? Will most people have visual aids? Do people tend to read from a prepared text (perhaps circulated in advance to a commenter or the audience) or from a looser set of notes? It takes about a minute to read one hundred words at a pace that people can listen to. If you plan to include visuals, make sure you leave time to navigate and discuss those. Do not try to cram in more material than you have time for! If you speak too quickly, whether in person or during an online talk, you'll lose your audience, and if you go over time, you'll annoy everyone in the room.

3. Find out about the audience you'll be addressing. Will you be speaking mostly to specialists or to a more general audience that might include undergraduates or members of the public? Will the audience be mostly native speakers of the language in which you are presenting? Will there be

simultaneous translation or ASL support? Make sure that your language and presentation are appropriate to the audience. This can be difficult if your hosts aren't sure who the audience will be or if you expect a mixed audience. Ultimately, though, giving a talk is just another form of teaching—you'll want to make sure that your audience is with you about the basic concepts before you delve into more challenging material.

4. Dress appropriately. The more junior you are, the more you should probably err on the side of sartorial formality, but you also want to make sure you're comfortable. Conferences and invited talks often involve spending long hours sitting in one place, alternating with seemingly interminable walks through a rabbit warren of a convention center. If it's winter, you may need a coat and hat for outside, but the conference rooms could be overheated and airless. Make sure you can take off layers without feeling overexposed.

5. Be on time. If you are on a panel with a commentary, make sure to ask when you need to submit your paper and *meet that deadline.* Commenters are often performing an act of professional generosity squeezed in among countless other professional commitments; do not abuse their goodwill. Whether giving a lecture or participating in a panel, make sure you arrive in plenty of time to set up technology, introduce yourself to fellow panelists, and avoid leaving any guessing about whether you'll show up.

6. Have a backup plan. Many of us rely on laptops and digital projectors for supporting materials. If you are giving a presentation that simply will not work without this support, make sure you test your technology in advance in the space where you will present. If such testing is not possible, make sure you have a plan for how to present the material without this support.

7. Be gracious. If you are invited to give a talk on campus, be mindful that the administrative staff arranging your visit also have many other responsibilities. If an audience member asks a question that seems completely bananas, try to turn it into something that lets you share a new aspect of your work that didn't fit into the talk. If things go sideways with logistics and equipment, roll with it as best you can.

8. Finding My Way in Academia: My Non-Tenure-Track Path to Success in Food Studies

My non-tenure-track position has not been without its challenges, but it also has brought many unexpected rewards. I have been in my current job at the University of Southern California in Los Angeles for the past twelve years. My current position is associate professor (teaching) in the Department of Latin American and Iberian Cultures.

Much like the rest of the 73 percent of academics off the tenure track, I expected that my career would be in a tenure-track job. I have a PhD from a top program at a renowned university and worked with some of the most well-known scholars in my field of training. Life, however, does not always go as planned. When I went on the job market, I learned that my sexy-sounding, interdisciplinary, transatlantic research and fieldwork did not translate easily into fitting into a canonical box. Additionally, I had a non-portable fiancé who was starting his own local business in the San Francisco Bay area. Despite these and other challenges that came my way, I carved out my own path in a non-tenure-track position that allowed me the flexibility to raise young children without the stress of those early high-pressure years non-tenured young professors face. Over time, I let go of the chip on my shoulder and took advantage of my academic freedom to build a successful and gratifying career.

Currently, I teach a variety of food studies courses at USC in the Departments of Latin American and Iberian Cultures, American Studies and Ethnicity and, most recently, Anthropology. These are all courses that I have created over the past eight years and are taught in both English and Spanish. I also lead a study-abroad program on food culture and food sovereignty to Oaxaca, Mexico every May. In December 2016, I published a book, *Food, Health, and Culture in Latino Los Angeles* (Rowman and Littlefield), based on my teaching and research. I assign chapters from this book in my classes. Most recently, I received a $20,000 grant from the university to co-teach a new class, Documenting Latinx Food Culture, that I created with a colleague related to my other seminars but with a more theoretical and ethnographic focus.

The experience of creating and teaching food studies courses at USC has been an exciting and unexpected journey, one that I relish now, but that has not been without its frustrations and challenges. I completed a PhD at the University of California, Berkeley in Romance languages and literature in 2005, with the intention of eventually being offered a tenure-track job. My dissertation was on Hispanic ballads (narrative poems) that have their roots in medieval Spain and that still exist in oral tradition in certain parts of the Spanish-speaking world. I did fieldwork in Spain, Cuba, and Mexico for my dissertation on one particular ballad, and wrote about women's voices in the Spanish ballad tradition. My dissertation enabled me to do fieldwork in interesting places and learn about gender and agency in traditional cultures, but it did not put me squarely in one box for applying for a job. I did not write a dissertation exclusively about medieval Spanish literature, nor had I written one only about contemporary Latino cultural studies. The study of folklore crosses both time and place, something that proved to be both a blessing and a curse for me when applying for jobs. "Your research sounds so interesting," interviewers would exclaim, only to offer the job to someone whose research fit squarely in the boundaries of the field they were filling.

Despite my non-conventional profile, a non-tenure-track position would never have been on my radar as a graduate student. I had worked with well-known professors in my field and never questioned my anticipated career path. While we were prepped for the academic job market, conversations about non-tenure-track jobs and jobs outside academia were nonexistent. My grad school peers ahead of me received tenure-track jobs and I assumed I would, too.

Until my personal life got in the way. As I was writing my dissertation in early 2004, I met my husband, a budding entrepreneur opening pharmacies for the Latino market in the Bay Area. In other words, he was *not* portable. I was thirty years old when we got engaged and starting to feel ready to have a family. He told me not to sacrifice my dreams for him, but that he could not relocate either.

In 2005, I finished graduate school and accepted a job as a visiting assistant professor at Oberlin College. My fiancé stayed in San Francisco while I spent the year at this small liberal arts college in Ohio. My job at Oberlin was challenging and fulfilling. The students were intellectually curious, demanding, and bright. I had the opportunity to devise a seminar based on my dissertation and to figure out how to teach specialized courses. However, my fiancé was back in San Francisco and this job ended with the close of the academic year. I was not going to apply for positions far from him. Therefore, I was geographically limited and had been trained in a fairly narrow field. My outlook for a successful academic career path was not optimistic.

Returning to San Francisco in 2006, I had no idea what I would do next. There are not many universities in the Bay Area and I didn't see academic jobs that matched my profile. "Maybe it's time to explore work outside of academia?" I thought to myself. I assumed I had skills in research and writing, even if I lacked actual work experience beyond the ivory tower. I applied to dozens of jobs at museums, foundations, and nonprofits. Most didn't bother to interview me. Those that did said I had a "very interesting profile" but "lacked work experience." "Sorry, you are overly educated and underqualified," I was told repeatedly. No job offers. After a few months, I grew increasingly frustrated and decided to apply to jobs at local universities. I received an adjunct position at San Francisco State University in early 2007, teaching Spanish language and conversation, far from the lofty tenure-track job I had envisioned and not nearly as interesting as my Oberlin position had been, but it was something.

Soon after, my husband and his busy partner decided to expand their chain of Hispanic pharmacies to the closest big growth market, Los Angeles, and it was agreed he would be the one to relocate to Southern California. Fortunately, a friend learned about our plans and forwarded me a job announcement for the University of Southern California. It was a non-tenure-track job teaching upper-division courses in the Department of Spanish and Portuguese. It seemed like it could be an interesting prospect.

At thirty-six weeks pregnant, I flew to Los Angeles to interview at USC. I was excited about this possibility. They wanted me to teach a poetry seminar and Spanish composition classes. I would be able to teach material I found interesting and meaningful at an elite private university that could provide at least short-term job security. A weight was removed from my shoulders.

The salary offer was very low for the cost of living in Los Angeles. The university offered to match the salary I had been given at Oberlin College. Since I had no other job offer, I had no leverage to bargain with them. It would have been very hard to live in Los Angeles on this salary as a single person. Fortunately, my salary was only supplementing what my husband earned, and I could afford to take the job and continue my career path. If I had been a single person, life on this salary would have been far more challenging.

In August 2007, I began my non-tenure-track position at the University of Southern California, a job I am still in twelve years later. My career path is one that I could never have taken had I been in a tenure-track job. A tenure-track job would not have given me the opportunity to explore so far beyond my field of training and to research and publish on whatever I choose. While these advantages come with disadvantages—there is no financial support for my research, and I teach far more than my tenured colleagues—I still cherish the academic freedom I enjoy. I didn't *have* to publish a tenure book. I wrote my book because I *wanted* to do so, because it was enjoyable, and because it was a vehicle to tell the stories of so many of the amazing people and organizations I have worked with over the years.

While I had no time off to write the book—no sabbatical or course release—I carved out the time with a singular focus during the eighteen months it took me to complete.

My appreciation for my career path did not come overnight, however. For the first few years, I was still frustrated and somewhat embarrassed by my position. My grad school friends were all in tenure-track jobs. Were they *better* than me? I knew I had opted for this route and was happy not to be under the pressure they were while raising two young children. I could enjoy the time with my children without the pressure to churn out publications for tenure. Yet, I knew I wanted something more—but what would it look like?

Then, one day, the *what* started to take shape. In the fall of 2009, at a department faculty meeting, one of the tenured professors was throwing out ideas for courses that would attract new majors and minors to the department. He suggested a course about Spanish food. "Spanish food," I remember thinking to myself. "We are in Los Angeles. Why would you teach a course on Spanish food at a university that is surrounded by *taquerías* and *pupuserías*? That doesn't make sense." USC is in the middle of South Los Angeles, an area whose population is over 60 percent Latino. Many Central American immigrants moved there in the 1990s and as a result it is ripe with *panaderías*, Salvadoran pupuserías, *carnicerías*, and endless taquerías. Despite the Latino neighborhoods surrounding USC, my students taking classes in the Department of Latin American and Iberian Cultures had very few opportunities to interact with the surrounding community and use Spanish in real-life situations. They were "locked" on campus with few incentives to explore beyond.

As a folklorist, food seemed like an interesting lens through which to explore and learn about culture, one that I had always enjoyed as a traveler to new and different places and one that would be both accessible and exciting for students. Studying folklore and doing extensive fieldwork in different countries gave me the tools to know how to conduct food ethnographies; interview people to learn their food stories; and understand that cuisine, just like the ballads I had once studied, travels and adapts to new environments while still preserving its "authenticity" (a loaded term in my field, since what is authentic is slippery and dynamic: what is authentic to one person in one place can vary significantly). The authentic mole in Oaxaca is different from the one in Puebla. These ideas resonated with me and I began to research this exciting field I knew nothing about, food studies, in order to put together a new community-based class in which students would use technology (blog posts) to post their findings.

During the spring of 2010, I applied to USC's Center for Excellence in Teaching to create a new course that would use technology as a tool to enable students to write about and share their experiences and theoretical knowledge with each other via a blog site. I received a grant for five thousand dollars to apply toward the creation of my new course and set about to meet leaders and activists in the Latinx food industry who could help me create this experience.

In 2011, I began teaching the Culture of Food in Latino Los Angeles in the Spanish Department, a course that turned out to be life-changing in many ways. While creating opportunities for my students, I met many people outside academia: chefs, restaurateurs, museum professionals, community organizers, and journalists, as well as other academics who work in related fields in food studies. I had found a field that was exciting and that allowed me to move back and forth between academia and the "real world." I enjoyed forming these new professional relationships and have benefited from them immensely over the years.

I also got to know other parts of this vast city as I shared them with my students. My students visited markets, street vendors, taco-truck owners, and many other gastronomic delights in East Los Angeles and Boyle Heights, areas that are 95 percent Latino and are rich in Latino culinary culture. Yet, I started to realize that these same areas that abound in taquerías and panaderías come up short when it comes to full-service grocery stores, playgrounds, and parks. Instead, they are saturated with corner stores, liquor stores, and vacant lots.

This growing awareness led me to create a second course in 2015, Food Justice in Latino Los Angeles. This course has allowed me to teach students about the lack of access to healthy, affordable, culturally appropriate food, and its consequences. It has enabled students to interact with members of the community and, once again, use their Spanish in real-life situations. This time, however, it is with the goal of having them be aware of the inequities that exist between USC and the surrounding low-income community. My goal is not only to have students interact with community members but to work side by side with them, doing volunteer work through various nonprofit organizations. As a result, I have developed close ties with local organizations, been involved in projects that have benefited the community, and opened my students' eyes to social justice issues through hands-on community-based work. This community-based engagement has been very rewarding for the students—as well as for me.

My book, *Food, Health, and Culture in Latino Los Angeles*, is part of a food studies book series and came out of the experiences teaching my courses and the relationships I formed with various nonprofit organizations. It allowed me to profile the amazing grassroots work of local community and school gardens and to tell the stories of leaders in the food justice community. I used the book to tell local stories that are important on a larger scale.

Writing the book was a challenging experience because I had no support from my institution or outside grants; at the same time, it was very gratifying. Since I was not writing the book as a requirement for tenure, I had complete freedom to tell my own story in the way I chose. I did not have to use an academic press. This allowed me to choose a press that had published other related monographs and that gave me a contract on the basis of an abstract, instead of one or two complete chapters.

Instead of bemoaning the fact that I had to teach three classes while writing my book and raising two young children, I just woke up earlier and made extra time in my day to write. I was lucky to have a supportive husband and the flexibility in my work schedule to dedicate blocks of time to writing. I completed the book in about fifteen months and spent the final months on details such as photographs, the index, etc.

The book opened doors that I could never have imagined. I gave a well-attended book talk soon after publication at the university that gave me greater recognition both on campus and in the wider community. The university magazine wrote about the book, as did other publications. As a result, the *Los Angeles Weekly* contacted me to see if I would be interested in writing articles with a food justice focus. (I was thrilled!) A few months later, the local PBS television station asked if I would write an essay for their website. Soon after, I published my first article for the *Los Angeles Times*, and have written two more since.

My non-tenure-track position gives me the freedom to write for a non-academic audience without the pressure of having to dedicate all my time to academic publications. Writing for the mainstream press is rewarding and enjoyable. It allows me to provide exposure for the entrepreneurs and organizations I have gotten to know, and to support social justice causes I find important. I am very grateful for this opportunity to give back to the people who have taken time to talk to my students year after year.

The book's publication also opened doors on my campus. The chair of another department asked if I would be interested in teaching a seminar based on my book. This was an opportunity I had been asking department chairs for during previous years with no success. Now I was able to move outside the confines of my home department and create a course for a different student demographic. To say that I was very pleased would be an understatement.

I have taught this course once a year for the past two years and found it to be a very meaningful experience for the students and for me. Instead of teaching in Spanish, where the students' goals include using the language in written and verbal contexts, the class is taught in English in an American studies and ethnicity department. This allows for greater critical thinking and attracts a different student population.

In 2019, I applied to co-teach an interdisciplinary course with a colleague in anthropology. We were awarded $20,000 to use on the course during the 2019–2020 academic year. I plan to bring in amazing speakers and take the students to visit places that are normally not in my budget. While funding opportunities for new courses are fewer in non-tenure-track jobs and even less likely at a public university, they do exist in non-tenure-track positions—if one seeks them out and takes advantage of them.

Would I have been allowed to create these kinds of courses as a tenure-track professor? It is highly unlikely. I would have been tied to the field in which I was hired to teach. My priority would have been to teach those courses that students needed to complete a major before I created something else, and I would have been under pressure to publish a peer-reviewed book with a top academic publisher. Instead, I charted my own course and wrote the book that I wanted to write to use in my classes, and that highlighted and honored the stories of the people I had met and worked with over the years.

How can one make a non-tenure-track position fulfilling? Of course, this question is subjective and the answer will vary depending on your field, but here are a few general suggestions:

— Don't settle for just doing what is expected of you.
— Think outside the box. Use your skill set to come up with course offerings that are exciting and marketable to students.
— Find a niche that is innovative and interactive! Students are always writing that my course was their "favorite course they took at USC and they wish they had taken it sooner. . . ." I am not the world's greatest teacher and certainly not the most organized, but I offer an experience they don't have otherwise.

— Promote yourself! It took me years to feel comfortable with this, but I have had articles published about my classes on the university website, Spanish-language press including Telemundo, and other places. This allows the university and my own department to know what I am doing and (hopefully) value it. Otherwise, there is little to no awareness of the contributions I have made. This awareness has opened doors to teaching in departments beyond my home department and hopefully, in the future, to receiving financial support for my scholarship.

— Create experiences that you find personally gratifying. For years, I worked to help legalize Los Angeles's street vendors. I was part of a citywide working group, attended numerous meetings and hearings, and wrote a feature article on their struggles. When they were finally legalized after an epic battle, I was proud of the small part I had played and the many community members I had gotten to know along the way.

— Serve on a departmental or university-wide committee that is doing something meaningful. Service is a part of my job contract, but the service obligations are not as clearly outlined in my position as in the tenure-track ones at my university. I was asked to be on a committee to address food insecurity and homelessness among students. While this contributes toward service, it is also something I am passionate about.

— Make a difference in your larger community! Be an activist for something you believe in. I serve on the board of Garden School Foundation, a nonprofit that teaches garden-based education, where many of my students volunteer as part of my classes, and I am on the advisory council of a local museum the students have been visiting with my class for years. The flexibility of my job has allowed me to form these relationships and serve the larger community.

— Join a larger community of scholars doing related work and attend their conferences if the financial support from your institution makes it possible. I have been going to food studies conferences for the past six years, where I interact with scholars who are not concerned with my job status. We exchange ideas for our classes through workshops and learn about each other's scholarship. I have been asked to co-write articles and speak on conference panels with other leading academics in my field over the years. They respect my work and I have formed relationships with my colleagues. This places me within a larger community of scholars so that I do not become isolated at my institution.

Despite the early years of struggle, I eventually found my way to a satisfying career. It has not been a perfect situation by any means. I write this as I plan for an upcoming book project in which I hope to spend a year with my husband and children, conducting research while based in Mexico City. We are planning this academic year away for both personal and professional reasons. We would like to provide our children with a true immersion experience beyond the visits with family in Mexico City or speaking Spanish at home. I am interested in researching the recent interest in indigenous cuisine and how indigenous ingredients such as corn, agave, and cacao are becoming trendy, yet inaccessible to the lower-income consumer. I would like to spend time on the ground in rural communities of Oaxaca with growers. I would also like to deepen my knowledge of Mexican gastronomy by learning about the history and traditions of its rich and varied foodways. Yet unlike tenure-track colleagues, I have no guaranteed financial support for this project from my university. I plan to apply for a research grant that would cover one semester and I will apply for outside grants as well. These grants, however, are few and are not guaranteed. I understand that these are the limitations of my job, but I am hopeful that I will receive support for my next research project.

Leading my classes on street-food tours of Los Angeles, taking students to meet sidewalk vendors and learn about their struggles, organizing excursions to a school garden in a low-income Latino neighborhood, exploring farmers markets that have programs to increase access to healthy, fresh, culturally appropriate food—these are just a few of the highlights of the community-based learning experiences I have developed over the years. While your field may be very different, how can you create experiences that are more engaging for your students, that challenge them to think differently, and that push the boundaries of your non-tenure-track position? How can you find a way to do research that is meaningful to you, even with limited support for it? How can you contribute to the university by serving on committees that demonstrate your commitment to a cause? How can you turn this job into something that you are proud to be doing, rather than a last resort you are stuck with?

I don't have the answers to these questions, but hopefully I have provided some food for thought.

9. Surviving the Dream

SARAH DEUTSCH

This Is So Cool!—Being in Demand

After tenure, I began getting all kinds of invitations. People invited me to speak at far flung places! People wanted me to review books and manuscripts! People wanted me to sit on important university committees! People wanted me to organize conferences! People wanted me to assume leadership positions in the community and the profession! People cared what I thought! It was fabulous! Until it wasn't.

Even before I got tenure, I found service obligations and speaking invitations mounting. After tenure, they multiplied alarmingly. It had never occurred to me that I would have more invitations to do things I thought were interesting than I could possibly manage. I was traveling three out of four weekends a month. Whenever I wasn't teaching, I was in committee meetings. I was doing course preparation between 11:00 p.m. and 5:00 a.m. One semester, I taught three regular undergraduate courses at my own campus, two graduate student biweekly seminars, and one course at another university as a favor to my mentor. At the same time, I had committed to revising and resubmitting two articles and one book. I sat on two nonprofit boards in the community, directed a program at the university, and supervised a number of graduate students. Then I got an infection I could not shake, and it was a wake-up call (not that I had time to sleep).

This crunch is particularly acute for faculty underrepresented at their institution. When I first got to MIT as an assistant professor in the 1980s, there were so few women faculty members that I was in meetings whenever I was not in class, leaving only the late night and early morning hours for class preparation and the fantasy of scholarship. Since every committee needed to have a woman on it, I was on what felt like every committee. What is more, women students (and even men students) eager for a sympathetic ear headed to the offices of women faculty members, often breaking down in tears. An external review team for our Women's Studies Program told us in no uncertain terms to stop performing these functions for our students. We could tell they were from Mars.

Such demands are even more weighty for faculty of color at most institutions. Rising diversity in the student body has not been matched by rising diversity in the faculty. Ever-increasing demands for faculty who understand the dynamics of being the anomaly, for faculty to "represent" their color or sex on committees, and for these faculty members to provide liaisons between the college or university and the community imperil faculty of color not only regarding their scholarly success, but regarding their physical and mental health. I have only worked at one university that recognized this extra burden by providing a course release. Most colleges and universities and colleagues, if they recognize it at all, see the burden as purely elective.

Not all faculty of color want to engage in this work, and some few succeed in keeping it at bay. But many such faculty, often first-generation doctorate and even bachelor's degree holders, feel an obligation or desire to pay it forward. They see a fundamental part of their role as mentoring and as working to change the institution to make the path easier for those who follow. It is crucial that they, collectively if possible (and so necessarily, usually, across departments), make chairs, deans, provosts, and presidents aware of this dynamic. It will help if they can mobilize the support of sympathetic faculty members who have influence with the administration, whatever their demographic. To do so effectively, it is crucial to provide the studies (some cited here but there are others) to support the claims.[1] Even so, the most effective argument may be that such work demands can lead not just to attrition but to departure for other institutions. Deans and provosts and presidents tend to be highly competitive people. The idea that they are behind or are losing out to other institutions is often a powerful motivator, even if other aspects of their listening skills seem to be wanting.

Some people feel that everyone who makes it to tenure should have suffered as they have suffered, that it made them stronger and proved their merit. Others feel no one should have to suffer in those ways. We have choices when we get tenure, not just about our own careers but about our bystander behavior. To me, this is an issue of creating the community in which you want to live. It is always better, however, to speak with someone rather than for someone. If you think something inequitable is occurring, whether it's structural or individual, engage the colleagues targeted. Ask them what they think, and what would be helpful. If they are junior colleagues, they may not know what is possible, and they may feel too vulnerable to want it raised as an issue. If they are overwhelmed with service, take the issue to an administrative meeting of chairs or deans as a larger structural issue—assistant professors at research-one universities, for example, should not be tasked with launching a new program while trying to finish their book and establish their teaching. Similarly, take the lead in collecting colleagues across departments to articulate the extra burdens that fall on faculty of color and how to address them. Be noisy in your department around the composition of search committees and the nature of short lists. It's always better not to be noisy alone. Bring your colleagues on board. We only have to look at the demographics of the academy in the last three decades to know that diversity is not inevitable.

Given these pressures, it is particularly important to remember that tenure offers a chance to set your own priorities and rebalance your life, but that means more than thinking about what kind of work most engages you. It means thinking about what kind of life you want to lead. How often do you like being on the road? How many manuscripts are too many manuscripts? How many tenure and promotion committees and reviews (which are incredibly time-consuming) can you handle without sacrificing everything else? How many students can you responsibly mentor without losing sleep? What role do you want to play in your community? Remember, your community is the department, the university, the academy, and your town. Even one committee for each of those communities would be four committees at any given moment. Sit down and have a conversation with yourself. What's important to you? How many trips a month are really too many? Is reading article or book manuscripts more important? Or doing book reviews? What kind of service matters? How much time do you reserve for yourself and your family?

Service is a way we can have some control over our environment. You don't want to shun service entirely. By the time we get tenure, many of us have a lot of pent-up institutional energy. There are things we want to see happen both in terms of restructuring or reforming and in terms of initiatives at a variety of levels in the department, at the university, and in the wider community. It's satisfying to be able to take steps toward our vision. So you want to take part. Even minor service sometimes builds relationships across departments, outside of work, and up the food chain that make it easier to create change later.

Create criteria for how you choose where to put your energy. Regarding committees, at the university or in the community, do you want to lead or just be in the room? For some committees, if you cannot have some significant say in the direction of the committee, the service may be more frustrating than gratifying; for other committees, the relationships that emerge may be the main benefit, and just being in the room may fit best with the other demands on your time. In the same vein, what would make a manuscript worth reviewing? The topic? The publication? The author? What makes a talk worth giving? Some people decide by having a minimum honorarium level. Others base their decisions on the impact, including whether the audience is an underserved community—a prison or a high school in a low-income area. Some people use a combination of factors. Try to be clear in your own mind what you want from any particular service opportunity.

Try to take an active hand rather than just responding to requests. That can be the best way to make sure your service lines up with how and where you want your voice to be heard. It may be that parking is, in fact, the most meaningful committee at your university with the greatest impact on your colleagues' daily lives. Or not. If there's a committee on which you would rather serve, you can step forward and request assignment. Those responsible for creating committees tend to go back repeatedly to the same trusted names, but they're not averse to welcoming volunteers—indeed, since finding faculty to staff the myriad university committees can be overwhelming, they're often grateful.

Here's the catch—you can pour your energies into work that suits your own priorities, but if your priorities do not align or are even at odds with the priorities of your institution, it is unreasonable to expect the institution to reward you for it. If you can garner a clear sense of the college's or university's priorities (often articulated in mission statements and strategic plans), sometimes, with a little work, you can frame yours to align—a conference or curricular initiative or even outreach of certain kinds can bring in grant money, for example, or open a new field of inquiry, or help an institution fulfill its mandate.

Other times it would be a greater stretch. When I chose to write a book and then edit documents collections aimed at junior and senior high schools, I knew it would not only delay my second academic monograph and so my promotion, it would also be irrelevant in the eyes of the administration. That choice would not bring greater glory or visibility to the institution, bring outside grant money, or raise our standing in national rankings. I was okay with that. In this case, my desire to get a different kind of history into the hands of teenagers outweighed my desire for other kinds of rewards, and I was simply tremendously grateful that tenure allowed me to make that choice.

You can, if it is important to you, decide to spend time and energy trying to shift institutional priorities, an exacting and often exasperating all-consuming endeavor, but not entirely impossible. But choose your battles—there may be other areas in which shifting the institutional ground matters more to you.

In any case, it is easier to make these choices if you can get a sense of the structure of decision-making at your university or college. You can ask for an organization chart, though not all universities have them ready to hand out, and even a chart may not reflect how things really work. But it's hard to be effective at creating change or building a program without knowing the lines of power. Seek the advice of long-serving faculty and staff members you trust who may have both a broader perspective and insider knowledge of not only structures but personalities.

Even if you don't have something particular in mind you'd like to see happen at your institution, everyone should expect that at some point they'll have to step up. Leadership skills can be learned—from how to run an effective meeting to how to build consensus—and once you have them, leadership positions seem less daunting. Take the opportunity to learn leadership skills where you can—it turns out they are far more transferable than you might think. Go to a few good workshops at your university or your professional meeting or elsewhere.

The nonprofits I was serving sent me to a day-long workshop on nonprofit board leadership that I was unenthusiastic about attending. I went to two sessions. I have completely forgotten one of them, but the other I have drawn on almost every year since then. In my two nonprofits—the state affiliate of the National Endowment for the Humanities (NEH) and a regional rape crisis center (RCC)—one set of board meetings was always well attended, the members deeply engaged; the other, RCC, had sparse attendance. Both nonprofits' directors were effective at their jobs, leading well-run organizations. The difference mystified me.

At the workshop I learned the secret: successful meetings have clear agendas distributed to attendees, with adherence to the time allotted on the agenda for each item, meaningful but not overwhelming work for each member, and substantive discussion and meaningful outcomes for each meeting—outcomes that the transparent decision-making process made clear were affected by what was said and who was in the room. That was how the NEH affiliate meetings ran, and we felt respected and essential. By contrast, the RCC, in an effort to spare the board members, required no work and little to no input from us, only that we be willing to be arrested for not turning over counseling records in rape trials. It turned out we were perfectly willing to go to jail for the rape survivors who sought RCC's services, but less willing to attend seemingly pointless board meetings.

I am pretty sure I am not the only person who has suffered through interminable meetings in which little, if anything, of import transpires. This lesson about running meetings turns out to apply equally well to department meetings, committee meetings, and probably even family meetings. Your institution may not have the resources to provide such workshops where these and other leadership lessons are taught, but some corner of your community probably does.

Being Intentional

Without planning and making priorities, you can grab each enticing opportunity and widely disperse your energy while building neither your community nor your career. Make an aspirational five-year plan and be ready to revise and revisit it from time to time. Where do you want to be in five years? How can your department help you get there? Share the plan with your chair.

When you make your plan, try to balance taking chances on new things that might send your mind in new directions with steadily building community in your major field through giving talks, consistent attendance at conferences, and putting together panels and even whole conferences. Make sure the conferences you create, the ones you put time and energy into, serve your own intellectual and community-building goals as well as offer opportunities to your students and colleagues.

Think about your teaching in the same way. Create at least one course that maps, even if only in the broadest sense, onto your current research question. If you can make at least one of your courses lie within the largest questions of your research, you can have an entire class of students help you brainstorm about your current obsession. Even in an undergraduate class, their research can become pieces of your research. Indeed, you can try out your chapters on the class. This has several benefits—it lets students know that we, too, revise; it puts audience eyes on our prose; and it shows students we respect them and value their intellectual input. They rise to the occasion, and it has definitely benefited my own work. It's a bit of a shocker, what they pick up in my work that I miss. And the students love being part of a larger enterprise with a tangible outcome.

The Whiteboard

Keep track of the categories of opportunities coming your way. These might include requests for independent studies, requests to serve as an adviser or on committees at your own or other universities, conference participation, reviews, etc. Make quotas for each. Be loyal to them and get your lines straight. I did six separate independent studies in one semester—that was crazy. Now I put all my categories on a whiteboard, and when I agree to do something, I write it under the appropriate category. When the third person asks me to do an independent study, I glance at the whiteboard and let them know how sorry I am that I am already doing two, and cannot accommodate them this semester. Sometimes you can clump independent studies and do them jointly, sometimes you can put them off, but don't go beyond your limit.

Getting to "No"

It can be really hard to say no. When people ask you to do something, it is more than flattering. They make you feel as though only you can possibly do this task. At first, I put a Post-it note on my phone that said "no!" But I was shocked when I saw it that it was totally ineffective. So I put one below it that said, "I'll get back to you." I explained to people that I made it a rule never to say yes to anything without thinking about it for at least twenty-four hours. I found people universally respected that rule. Twenty-four hours gave me time to check my other commitments and to consult my partner. It also gave me time to think about whether I knew someone for whom this would be a real opportunity rather than an impossible added task. When I passed on a request to someone else, it made me a good colleague or mentor, helping to develop someone else's career. That felt great!

Letting People Know What You're Up To

You may be worked to the bone and appalled when someone at your university asks you to do yet another thing, but you have to realize no one but you knows the sum total of things you're doing. If the person asking is a powerful person at the university, you can tell them, "I would love to do that! Here are the twelve other things I'm doing for the university—which one should I drop so that I can do this one?" Let people know what you're doing in the wider academic and nonacademic universe. Don't think of it as tooting your own horn. Think of it as letting people plan in a realistic way and letting them get a realistic sense of your position, not only in the department but outside it.

At the same time, it's important not to forget entirely about your scholarly trajectory. There are only so many hours in a day. Try to spend at least fifteen minutes a day on your own project, your best fifteen minutes, even if it is only checking a footnote. That way when you have two hours, you are not starting over. At the same time, if you are going to pour yourself into the institution, make sure the institution will respond by giving you release time while you're doing it, or with release time after you've done it so that you can get back to your scholarship. In an ideal world, you can work with the institution to make the innovations line up with your projects, even if loosely. That benefits both you and the institution. Remember, having granted you tenure, the place wants you there for the long haul. Courting burnout can lead to resentment and make you want to go some other mythical place where no one will ask you to do anything. It is in the best interest of the university as well as yourself to find a sustainable balance.

Where to Go from Here—Moving Up and Moving Out

Now that you have tenure, you are set for your career and never have to move again. But you might want to change things up. You might want to check out administration at your home university, or jobs elsewhere. There are benefits and pitfalls to doing so.

The great thing about going on the job market post-tenure is that you already have a job. The stakes are dramatically lowered—for you. Having witnessed the job search from the vantage point of graduate student, tenured faculty member, chair, and dean, I know the stakes for the institution and your colleagues remain high. Searches are enormously time-consuming, and the institutional commitment is one-way—once you have tenure, they have to keep you, but you don't have to stay. There are good reasons to explore your options, but be aware that every year the academic world is illuminated by bridges inadvertently set afire by someone carelessly dropping a lit match as they gazed at the prospect before them. No one likes to be played. Word gets out when people perpetually go on the job market simply to leverage up their home salary. In such situations, retention negotiations, too, can go south unexpectedly swiftly. You can wind up someplace you never intended to accept. Be careful. Be thoughtful. Don't be a toad.

The reasons to go on the job market can resemble the reasons to move into administration. You may be bored with teaching, with your colleagues, or with your community. In an era of restricted hiring, when not many new voices come into your department, you may feel you can predict every word that's uttered. You may have come up against a brick wall in your institution, or you may be stuck. You may want or need more resources academically or personally, including a spousal appointment.

An administrative position—whether it's director of undergraduate studies, director of a program or center, or a deanship—can offer new challenges, new conversations and perspectives, and an opportunity to implement your own ideas. The timing is tricky. I know people who have been incredibly productive in their scholarship while serving as dean or chair. I am not one of them. Taking up such a position between projects can give you breathing space to conceptualize the next project in the context of a new set of dynamics that can shift your thinking. And, at the other end of the project, if it is well along with sufficient momentum, you could bring it to closure. But for many of us, taking up a new set of tasks and demands—usually more time-consuming than teaching and taking more social energy—in the early or middle stages of a new project makes it hard to make steady forward progress. This is particularly true if we also have small children at home. On the other hand, sometimes it can offer a nice excuse when we weren't ready to move forward on that project in any case. The poet Stevie Smith, writing about Coleridge's claim that he never finished his Kublai Khan poem because of the sudden, distracting arrival of a person from Porlock, intoned, "I long for the Person from Porlock."[2] It's generally a good idea to be honest with yourself about what's really delaying you.

Try to be as clear as possible about what the new position entails. I took on one position and was told by its previous tenant that "you'll figure it out from the emails you get." Not helpful. Find out the variety of tasks and the amount of support available in terms of financial resources, mentoring, and staff—and whether there are any staff battles. Managing staff, for which few of us have any training, can be the most challenging part of an administrative position. Find out how much responsibility the position entails, and the amount of control you'll have over decision-making (often at odds). Think about what this particular position will allow you to do in terms of your institutional priorities. It can be really satisfying to have a shaping hand in a program or department, to change the culture, to nurture people through tenure, or to watch a new program come to fruition. There is, of course, stupid stuff that comes with every position, so you want to make sure the satisfactions are likely to outweigh the annoyances.

You also want to be careful to limit your hours. If you do take on an administrative position, choose only one or two initiatives within that position on which to focus, no matter how many other attractive ideas crop up. Management studies show that longer hours do not make for better decision-making, and I certainly found that to be true. Emails are like rabbits—they multiply alarmingly. I let people know I dealt with email once a day, midday, and so responded only once a day. If it's an ongoing conversation, sometimes a phone call is a better use of your time. If it's truly an emergency, there are other ways people can find you.

Protect some time for your own work, your family, and yourself. Don't say you're available at those times—treat them as sacrosanct, as if you were teaching a class. I know of no one who said on their deathbed, "I wish I had spent more time at the office." See one of your tasks as to model a sane work life. As a dean, I let the people appointing me know I would not work more than one weekend a month or more than one evening a week, and I would leave an hour early twice a week to pick up my child. I did once offer to meet someone higher up the food chain on the playground, but he found another time.

For those who are restless, sometimes a fellowship away or a visiting gig can offer a way to recharge without leaving your institution permanently. Like a new job, it can put you in dialogue with different scholars who have different paradigms or pet theories, new ideas and perspectives. Sometimes, it can also make you appreciate your home institution and community more than you had.

Should you decide to reenter the job market, the best time is usually when you have just published something or successfully created a program or completed a grant—in other words, a time when people can see you as an active colleague who will contribute to their institution. That is also when you are most likely to field letters of interest from other institutions.

There is an etiquette to the post-tenure job market. Your institution is happier to find out you're sought after (a retention risk) than that you're seeking. Let your chair know if you are getting nibbles from institutions with higher standing or more resources. If, on the other hand, you are actively seeking, don't depend on the discretion of others. Make sure your institution knows why you are looking—that is, as long as it's not personal. It's best to tell your home institution how much you value it, how great it's been, and if only there were X (spousal appointment, more money, more resources, more people in your field, more or any graduate students, the opportunity to run a center or build a program, etc.), you would never even think of leaving. It's also best not to bad-mouth your home institution when on the search—it always gets back. If your university sees you as disaffected and determined to leave, it may disinvest as well.

When responding to solicitations for applications, it's okay to be uncertain whether you'd really go. It's up to the seeking institution to convince you it would be a good fit. And once you have an offer in hand that you like, if there is any way you would stay at your home institution, let them know and let them counter. No one wants to get in a bidding war, however, and few institutions will do much back and forth, so you need to be clear in your own mind what is important to you.

As with the other advice here, try to know yourself. I have heard that you lose a year every time you move. I have not found it so. I have found moves enlivening. There have always been losses as well as gains, both in terms of communities and amenities, and certainly I have bouts of nostalgia, but I always had what I saw as good reasons for the move. Think about what your "good reasons" would be. If you possibly can, give the place a trial run. Visit for a semester or a year before giving up tenure at your home institution. Never give up the tenure you have without first securing tenure anew. I have known more than one case in which a prominent scholar accepted a position, and then failed the tenure process at the new institution and had to scramble to retrieve his old position. Weird things can happen in the tenure process, and that's a nightmare no one wants or has to have.

Finally, remember every day—even if you have to post it above your computer—that you love this job you worked so hard to get. We lead a life rich in ideas and exchanges, and its anomalous security gives us a long horizon filled with possibilities.

NOTES

1. Stephen R. Porter, "A Closer Look at Faculty Service: What Affects Participation on Committees?," *Journal of Higher Education* 78.5 (2007): 523–541; Laura E. Hirshfield and Tiffany D. Joseph, "'We Need a Woman, We Need a Black Woman': Gender, Race, and Identity Taxation in the Academy," *Gender and Education* 24.2 (2012): 213–227; Caroline Sotello Viernes Turner, Juan Carlos González, and J. Luke Wood, "Faculty of Color in Academe: What 20 Years of Literature Tells Us," *Journal of Diversity in Higher Education* 1.3 (2008): 139.

2. Stevie Smith, "Thoughts about the Person from Porlock," Poetry Foundation, accessed April 2, 2020, https://www.poetryfoundation.org/poems/46848/thoughts-about-the-person-from-porlock.

PART II

The Trinity of Academic Life: Research, Teaching, and Service

Depending on the kind of institution where you find yourself working, the three responsibilities of research, teaching, and service will fall in a particular order of priority and significance for your continued time there. If you are at a larger research-oriented school, your department chair or promotions and tenure committee might tell you (formally or informally) that your research and publications should form the centerpiece of your reappointment or promotion file. If you work at a community college or small liberal arts college, they might tell you that your teaching and student evaluations are the most important considerations. At certain schools, evidence of dynamic teaching *and* research are expected, a double whammy that strikes fear into those who can't see how they'll muster the energy to accomplish both those things. And amidst all of this, service to one's department or program, university, and professional field must also be performed and can even feel like the most compelling parts of our jobs. Despite refrains of "service doesn't matter" or "service matters much less," we cannot ignore that certain scholars—particularly younger scholars, women, and people of color—are saddled with service obligations that can either drain their internal resources or not benefit them professionally as much as they hope they will. The passionate (and compassionate) essays in this part of the handbook offer advice on how to navigate the demands and mysteries of research, teaching, and service.

Beginning with how to acquire funding for your research, a coauthored piece by three academics—Miroslava Chávez-García, Luis Alvarez, and Ernesto

Chávez—who have all served on prestigious funding committees in the humanities gives practical and comprehensive tips for how to craft a successful grant application. Next, Deborah Jakubs and David Hansen remind us of what resources to ask for and take advantage of in our institution's libraries, which increasingly function as sites of both research and publishing. A pair of essays by James Sutton and Nanibaa' Garrison discuss IRB requirements and ethical questions to consider and answer while designing your research plan and data collection. Neuroscientist and memory researcher Rosanna Olsen offers helpful advice for publishing your scholarship in journal article form, whether it is a single-authored or coauthored piece, and Cathy Davidson and Ken Wissoker update their essay from the handbook's previous edition to discuss the process of book publication from the perspective of a university press.

Our subsection on teaching is filled with exciting pieces by scholars who impart thoughtful strategies and assignments in their very different-looking classrooms. Literature professor Magda Mączyńska reflects upon teaching intimate seminars at a small college in New York City and offers a useful bibliography for further reading on teaching philosophies and strategies. Chicana/o studies scholar Genevieve Carpio and biochemist Neil Garg discuss their techniques for teaching large lecture classes at UCLA. Historian Marcia Chatelain, who became famous inside and outside of academia with the creation of the #FergusonSyllabus following the 2014 police brutality protests in Ferguson, Missouri, gives us a deeper look into the process of creating a crowdsourced syllabus that very explicitly speaks to contemporary social issues and tensions. In the spirit of experimenting with format and reaping the benefits of social media, we include a crowdsourced piece from ten academics, sharing their favorite or most successful assignments that will hopefully provide inspiration for your own classrooms and syllabi. Counseling and higher education professor Laura M. Harrison addresses the debate of how much technology to allow in the classroom by explaining the benefits she believes her students derive from her laptop ban. On the other hand, in their discussion of promoting neurodiversity in the classroom, John Elder Robison and Karin Wulf explain the ways that digital devices can make classrooms more accessible to a greater range of students. Two contributions offer suggestions about how to support underrepresented students: Eladio Bobadilla speaks to the experiences of veterans and of undocumented students, while Antar Tichavakunda explains the phenomenon of microaggressions and how to diminish their impact. Finally, four contributions discuss strategies for taking teaching outside the classroom. Lynn Stephen discusses how she and her co-teacher engage students in a collaborative project of knowledge production by and for the local Latinx population. Kathryn Fox and Keri Watson offer reflections from their respective experiences starting and running prison education programs. Finally, anthropologist Charles Piot discusses the meaning and benefits of service-learning opportunities, and how to successfully take one's teaching skills abroad.

Service in academia takes many forms, and we cannot deny that one's identity can influence how much one is asked to perform. Younger scholars, women, and people of color are often expected to mentor more passionately and frequently, and to be more available and visible in their departmental and university communities. The essays in this section offer advice about how to create realistic and healthy boundaries around your time and energy. How do you determine when a service request deserves an unequivocal yes, or when it deserves a graceful but firm no? How do you even *craft* a graceful but firm no? What should you keep in mind when deciding if serving on a certain committee will ultimately serve *you*? Outside of your immediate campus environment, you will be asked to evaluate your peers as a form of service. Joy Gaston Gayles and Bridget Turner Kelly draw from their experience mentoring across a diverse array of backgrounds. Sharon Holland dispenses much-needed reminders about your visibility and impact as a reviewer, and what to be aware of when writing article or manuscript reviews, letters of recommendation, or tenure and promotion letters for others in your field. The editors offer a final list of questions to ask yourself when considering whether to accept an invitation to professional service.

10. Applying Successfully for Grants and Fellowships

MIROSLAVA CHÁVEZ-GARCÍA, LUIS ALVAREZ, AND ERNESTO CHÁVEZ

In 2009, the three of us came together to provide some words of advice on how to apply successfully for grants and fellowships. We did so as a result of a recent stint reviewing applications for a national fellowship competition and realizing that many applicants struggled with the process. Whether it was composing a personal statement, identifying the significance of the major themes, or highlighting the contributions or intervention of their work in a larger body of scholarship, we knew many lacked the knowledge—often gained through mentorship—to pull together a winning proposal.

We then decided to draw upon our experiences, as applicants and reviewers, to compile a few words of wisdom in the *Organization of American Historians Newsletter*.[1] In response, we received warm praise for sharing our insights with junior colleagues. Those insights, however, have become outdated, as we know that the application and review process is not static, especially with the veritable explosion of online resources facilitating—and perhaps overwhelming us with—opportunities to strike it big in our area of study. Here we provide an expanded update to our advice on why, where, and how to apply to grants and fellowships. Specifically, we address how to write personal, research, and proposed project statements as well as how to compose bibliographies. We also suggest what to consider before hitting "submit" and the larger end goal and point of this process.

Why Apply

Applying for grants and fellowship is a necessary skill as well as an expectation in academia. The processes and purposes are somewhat different, however. Grants support specific research activities needed to carry out a larger project. For instance, if you need to travel to a research site to investigate a specific question related to your work, you would apply for a travel or research grant. Those grant applications almost always ask for a detailed budget. In most cases, you will need to contact your institution's office of research (or equivalent) to have your budget and proposal approved. While doing so may seem like a bureaucratic delay, those offices review your proposed submission with an eye toward strengthening the proposal. They often will streamline your budget and prepare it along the lines of what is expected from a particular sponsoring agent. Fellowships, in contrast, allocate funding that allows you to work on your project without having to teach or labor in another way to support yourself. Normally, fellowships are semester- or year-long packages and rarely, if ever, need to include a budget, though you will have to discuss how you will spend your time to achieve your stated goals. Arguably, managing your time wisely is one of the most challenging aspects of fellowships. We say more about this below.

Applying for fellowships and grants gives you the opportunity not only to acquire financial support for your work but also to better recognize and articulate the purpose and significance of your research. Your application can inform your peers that your work is serious and significant to the field and academia more broadly (as reviewers are not always in your area of research but can be so compelled by your proposal that they believe your work merits support). Practically, fellowships and grants allow you the privilege of amassing data or an archive, enabling you to advance the analysis and writing of your findings. Grants and fellowships also bring added recognition in most academic fields and among colleagues and, if on the tenure track, work toward promotion at all levels. A record of successful grants and fellowships contributes to your image as a fully engaged and active scholar, which, in turn, will motivate other funding agencies to support you down the road. Many researchers, especially those in the social sciences and STEM fields, apply for large grants (those totaling $40,000 or more) to work collaboratively with other scholars and to support graduate and undergraduate students as well as staff. Grants can enable the mentorship of young investigators; the compensation of underpaid administrative assistants, budget analysts, and grant writers; and exciting interdisciplinary, inter-institutional projects.

Where to Apply

Fortunately, today we have databases that allow you to search among hundreds, if not thousands, of funding possibilities. Among the most comprehensive is Pivot, a search engine of ProQuest that enables you to look for grants and fellowships as well as scholarships and awards across the globe, and to collaborate with other researchers who have subscribed to the database. Many, if not most, research-based institutions subscribe to Pivot, and users can set up profiles delineating specific areas of interest and research, applicant level, funding type, funding sources, career goals, and other parameters. Many similar but more specialized databases exist, such as Graduate and Postdoctoral Educational Support (GRAPES); H-Net Humanities and Social Sciences; the Chronicle of Higher Education; Pathways to Science; Simons Foundation: Funding Opportunities in Math, Life Sciences, Physical Sciences, and Autism; and the *National Science Foundation Newsletter* subscription for STEM and non-STEM sources. You can also search specific foundations whose mandates include excellence through diversity and diversifying the professoriate. They include the Ford Foundation, American Association of University Women, Woodrow Wilson Foundation, American Council for Learned Societies, Spencer Foundation, and Annie E. Casey Foundation, among others. To find opportunities in your area of research, join professional associations in your field, both nationally and internationally. Remember, many of these have graduate student and assistant professor level memberships, providing specialized funding opportunities. Most importantly, check with your campus's office of research for more opportunities, as they are invested in your success. When you win, they win.

Before You Begin

Before you begin, try to obtain a previous year's successful application or two. That application does not have to be for the specific funding agency to which you plan to apply, but it should be in a similar field or source of support. The sample or samples will help you understand what a winning proposal looks like; zoom in on its language, organization, and structure. While successful applicants make the process look easy, the reality is that strong proposals take time to cultivate and often evolve as the projects develop, contract, and grow in different ways. Give yourself at least a month, if not more, to pull together your submission, assuming that you already have a working proposal or prospectus in hand. If this is a completely new study, give yourself several months to outline and refine the themes, central questions, sources and methodology, preliminary findings, and significance to the field. An underdeveloped proposal will signal to the reviewers that the project is in its infancy and likely not viable in the time frame or approach suggested. As you flesh out your ideas, make the appropriate changes to the proposal, refining the innovative nature of your work, the main themes and arguments, research findings and approaches, theoretical frameworks, and timeline for completion. Pay attention to deadlines and requirements as well, as no two grant and fellowship applications are alike. A well-thought-out and thorough proposal is a winning proposal.

Getting Started

Once you have identified the grants and fellowships in your area of research and for which you are eligible to apply, read over the application requirements carefully. Use a calendar and work backward in setting deadlines for yourself. Ideally, you will want to have a draft of the application ready at least two to three weeks or more in advance to provide it to those who are writing your letters of recommendation.

Rest assured that each component of the application serves a purpose—the applications were not designed to annoy. Rather, each part has been thought out and likely is meant for you to link your project with the interests of the funding organization, and to facilitate the evaluation of your project. Your job is not to challenge or refute the requirements—doing so will likely lead to a rejected proposal. In the process, you need to take advantage of every component of the application to demonstrate the strengths of your project, particularly the innovative nature of the study and ways in which it advances knowledge in a particular field or area of scholarship. Avoid repetition as well. Spend time addressing each part of the application separately and treat them independently. Think of the application as a puzzle with each piece offering an opportunity to convey the most significant aspects of your work. The sum of the parts should come together to form a bigger picture of who you are, what your project is about, and why it deserves support.

The Personal Statement or Perspective

Grant and fellowship organizations often ask you to provide a personal statement or perspective as part of your application. This is more than a brief autobiography. It is an opportunity for you to tell the funding agency more about yourself and how prepared you are to successfully complete your proposed project. Your task is to show how past experiences have equipped you to carry out the proposed project and contribute to the funding agency or organization.

Take this charge seriously! Be sure to address your personal background, professional history, and accomplishments beyond the academy. All can enhance your file and help make the case that you will be able to execute and complete your study in ways that will intersect with the goals of the funding program. This means connecting the dots between your experience and what you are proposing to do. Be as clear as possible about how your upbringing, previous education, and achievements position you to see your project through and propel the vision of the funding organization. In the world of competitive grants, it is not always enough to be experienced and have a generative proposal. Your chances of being successfully funded are better when you can show how the two are linked.

When writing your personal statement, be true to who you are and your unique perspective. Have confidence that the trajectory of your career has positioned you to make valuable contributions in research and writing, in your fields specifically and academia generally. The personal statement is your chance to show that you are the right person to do your project. While being confident in your ability and project is good and necessary, try to refrain from outright boasting about your accomplishments and ability to pull yourself out of difficult circumstances. Likewise, avoid portraying yourself as a victim, the "only" one studying a given subject, or someone whose project will "save the world." Instead, take the time to discuss who or what organizations, programs, philosophies, or individuals supported you along your academic and professional journey. Share with reviewers who or what inspired you to ask the research questions that frame your work. Consider how challenges or obstacles have sharpened and strengthened your approach to your work. Describe how you have come to see the importance of your work. Demonstrate your commitment to diversifying the academy by sharing specific examples—whether positive or not—from your own journey to this point in your career, and what you learned or gained. Explain how you plan to continue to engage others and promote the kinds of programs that enabled you to accomplish all that you have. Be mindful and respectful of those who supported you, and be a responsible citizen who is cognizant of and grateful for what you have and what you plan to give back. Remember, those reviewing your application may not know anything else about you. Your personal statement is your chance to introduce yourself and help them understand why you should be among those offered a grant or fellowship.

Research Statement

Just like your personal statement, your statement of previous research can showcase how prepared you are to tackle and successfully complete your proposed project or plan of study. Use this section of your application to discuss the most significant projects you have completed. If you are unsure, ask a trusted mentor, adviser, or peer. Avoid generating long lists of titles, sources you have consulted, or research trips you have taken. What is most important is your research process, your findings, and the skillset acquired. This is the place to convince reviewers that you have the experience, ability, and wherewithal to see your project through to the end. Use your past projects to make your case! Discuss the form of your previous projects, including unpublished writings, conference papers, journal articles, and books. Highlight your key arguments and the methods, theoretical frameworks, and narrative approaches that informed your finished product. Equally important, consider your past projects as parts of a greater whole that paints a portrait of your approach to scholarship and larger body of work. While many of us conduct projects that do not always directly feed into a larger project, your previous research can underscore skills you have refined and thinking you have done that may provide links, however small, with your newly proposed project.

Just like your proposal itself, your statement of previous research can show reviewers you have what it takes to complete an innovative project. It summarizes your existing body of work, but also demonstrates that you know how to produce a finished product and can develop and follow a plan to get there. Depending on the nature of your past work, you might highlight several key ingredients that have made you successful. Emphasize your primary research questions, indicating the central thematic, theoretical, or historical problems you addressed. Convey your main findings by accentuating your most important arguments and answers to the questions you asked. Underline your interventions in existing literatures, taking care to chart how your original contributions moved the field rather than summarize what other scholars have said. Identify the methods and sources you used to complete your projects and, if relevant, include significant archival or ethnographic experience that may shape your new project. If appropriate, do not hesitate to explain how inventive organization or narrative presentation were instrumental to past projects. Statements of previous research tend to lose themselves in detail or be too general. To avoid this, do what you would with any other essay. Be sure your main point is clear and evident throughout. Make an argument about how your previous research has positioned you to produce more innovative scholarship. This is a chance to demonstrate your maturity, your investment in your field, and, more importantly, that you will continue to be a productive scholar.

Bibliographies

Some grant and fellowship committees ask you to compile concise bibliographies of the most relevant sources for your project. The reasoning behind this component is that the bibliography will display your awareness of both the literature related to your project and the relevant sources that will allow you to complete your study. Thus, the bibliography should be composed of secondary and primary sources, or the data you will use. If you have been asked to present an annotated bibliography, be sure to summarize the individual entries by pinpointing not only the main argument, but also how it informs your project and moves, challenges, or reaffirms key debates in a particular field. For the primary sources, the annotation should discuss how it will be utilized in your project and thus make clear that there are indeed sources that are accessible, that you are aware of them, and that they will allow you to complete your project.

Proposed Project

In *On the Art of Writing Proposals*, a dated but nevertheless indispensable guide, the Social Science Research Council reminds us that the first sentences are the most important component of an application because they have the ability to capture or lose the reader's interest.[2] We can attest that after many hours of reading proposals, many of which are unclear and uninspiring, we are left bleary-eyed, bored, and starved for some excitement. Your goal is to develop a first sentence or paragraph that captures the reader in a compelling way. This can be done by opening with a story that encapsulates what your project is about, or a "bait" statement that shows where your study fits into the literature in the field and how it will advance our knowledge of a given subject. Whether you choose a creative way or a more traditional manner to seize the evaluators' attention, make sure that your approach is clear, concise, and precise. Also ensure that your proposal is written in essay form and includes an introduction that conveys the project's importance. Provide a thesis statement (preferably at the end of the first paragraph) that charts out the study's major contours, your main argument or findings, and, perhaps, suggests your methodological approach and other innovations in your work. Many times, after reading an application, we had no idea what the project was about. Letters of recommendation often do a better job of explaining the project, especially those of emerging or early career scholars. However, leaving it up to your letter writers to do your job sends a message to the reviewers that you are not quite sure about what you want to do. More importantly, it conveys that you are not equipped (at the present moment) to carry out the study.

Beyond the first paragraph, the project proposal should provide a significant discussion of the main argument and your study's contribution to the field(s). You should also point out the main themes and questions being asked, the theoretical framework and methodology, sources you will utilize, the project's scholarly contribution, and how the project will be manifested (via chapters or sections). If required, a timeline to completion should also be prepared. When crafting this calendar, you want to be realistic and provide a month-to-month projection of the work you will do during the fellowship or grant tenure. If you do not think you will finish in the time required, do not say you will be able to do so because the reader will know—based on the quality of the proposal—whether the project is feasible in the time projected. Address questions such as: What is the significance of the project? What is your contribution to the field and general knowledge? What will we learn that we do not already know? In other words, why is the work important? Do not assume that the reviewers—or anyone else for that matter—know that your project is important. You need to convince them of that fact. One of the more difficult aspects of grant and fellowship applications is that they essentially ask you to convey clearly formed arguments and descriptions about work that you have yet to complete. This is a challenging task, but one that is made immensely easier if you are aware of the constitutive elements that need to be addressed in your proposal. Moreover, it forces you to take a stand on your work.

Before Pressing "Submit"

Before you submit the application, budget the time to send out the completed application to mentors, peers, and other colleagues for feedback. When seeking readers, choose those you trust and know will be honest and offer constructive criticism. If you are unclear about the instructions of the application or any aspects, do not hesitate to call or email the fellowship or grant office and speak to relevant staff. Reach out to scholars you know who have received funding from the source you are applying to and ask, as noted earlier, if you could perhaps view their application packet. Successful proposals are most often those that have been read by several people ahead of time to provide comments, suggestions, and clarity in overall presentation. Lastly, proofread using a hard copy that you can write on. Sometimes it helps to read the document backward so that your mind does not recognize the words in context and can spot misspellings. Reading it aloud also helps tremendously and allows you to look for inconsistencies in sentences and meaning. Typos and contradictions instantly turn off the reviewers.

Final Bit of Advice

The most important thing to remember is that although applications for funding are time-consuming, they are part of the academic experience and more than pay for themselves if and when you get a grant or fellowship. Also, once you write one fellowship or grant proposal, it is easier to write another. It only takes one grant or fellowship for you to have the opportunity to continue your research and writing without having to hustle multiple jobs or responsibilities to make ends meet. Receiving support from a competitive source also looks good on your resume, and evaluators will take notice. In short, one grant or fellowship begets more grants or fellowships. Given all the benefits that will come with receiving a grant or fellowship, submitting an application is time well spent. Lastly, when it comes to seeking grants or fellowships, we encourage you to start early and apply often. Good luck!

Resources

These resources were generously provided by UCSB Graduate Student Resource Center with the help of Noreen Balos, Funding Peer. These are only samples of the resources available. You may contact Miroslava Chávez-García (mchavezgarcia@history.ucsb.edu), Ernesto Chávez (echavez@utep.edu), or Luis Alvarez (luisalvarez@ucsd.edu) for more advice.

FUNDING DATABASES

Cornell Fellowship Database: https://gradschool.cornell.edu/fellowships
Duke Research Funding Database: https://researchfunding.duke.edu
NSF Funding for Graduate Students: https://www.nsf.gov/funding/index
.jsp
Oak Ridge Institute for Science and Education (ORISE) (internships, fellowships, and research experiences): https://orise.orau.gov/stem
/internships-fellowships-research-opportunities/index.html
Pivot: https://about.proquest.com/products-services/Pivot.html
The Scholarship Connection, UC Berkeley: http://scholarships.berkeley
.edu

UCLA GRAPES (Graduate and Postdoctoral Extramural Support): https://grad.ucla.edu/funding/

University of Chicago Fellowship Database: http://grad.uchicago.edu/fellowships/fellowship-database

University of Illinois Urbana-Champaign Fellowship Database: https://www.grad.illinois.edu/fellowship/

LISTSERVS FOR FUNDING OR BY FIELD

American Association of University Women: http://www.aauw.org

American Council for Learned Societies, Advancing the Humanities: http://www.acls.org/

Annie E. Casey Foundation: http://www.aecf.org/

Ford Foundation Fellowship Program: http://sites.nationalacademies.org/pga/fordfellowships/index.htm

GRAPES "Grad Fellowships-L List Subscription": https://grad.ucla.edu/funding/financial-aid/gradfellowships- l-list-subscription/

H-Net Humanities and Social Sciences online: https://networks.h-net.org

Interdisciplinary Humanities Center Funding Opportunities: http://www.ihc.ucsb.edu/about-research-development/

NSF Newsletter Subscription (STEM and non-STEM): https://service.govdelivery.com/accounts/USNSF/subscriber/new?qsp=823

Pathways to Science Funding and Research Opportunities: http://www.pathwaystoscience.org/index.aspx

Simons Foundation: Funding Opportunities in Math, Life Sciences, Physical Sciences, and Autism: https://www.simonsfoundation.org/funding/funding-opportunities/

Spencer Foundation: https://www.spencer.org/

Woodrow Wilson National Fellowship Foundation: https://woodrow.org/

SUMMER OPPORTUNITIES

Brooklyn College Summer Research Opportunities Database: http://www.brooklyn.cuny.edu/web/academics/centers/magner/students/research.php

National Institute of Health (NIH) Summer Research Opportunities: https://www.training.nih.gov/programs/sip

Pathways to Science Summer Research Database Search (STEM and non-STEM) (also includes non-STEM opportunities, searchable by theme: social sciences, business, arts & media, or all general programs): http://www.pathwaystoscience.org/programs.aspx ?descriptorhub=SummerResearch_Summer%20Research%%20 20Opportunity

Rand Corporation Graduate Student Summer Associate Program: http:// www.rand.org/about/edu_op/fellowships/gsap.html

Stanford Fellowships, Internships, and Service Programs Database: https://haas.stanford.edu/students/cardinal-careers/fisp

University of Illinois Fellowship Finder: https://www.grad.illinois.edu /fellowship/

NOTES

1. Miroslava Chávez-García, Luis Alvarez, and Ernesto Chávez, "Preparing a Successful Grant or Fellowship Application," *Organization of American Historians Newsletter* 37.3 (2009): 7, 14.

2. Adam Przeworski and Frank Salomon, *On the Art of Writing Proposals: Some Candid Suggestions for Applicants to Social Science Research Council Competitions* (1988; New York: Social Science Research Council, 1995), https://www.ssrc.org/publications/view/7A9CB4 F4-815F-DE11-BD80-001CC477EC70/.

11. The Modern Research Library

DAVID HANSEN AND DEBORAH JAKUBS

It is undeniable that research libraries are undergoing dramatic change. The impact of new and constantly evolving technologies on library collections and services, while not unanticipated, has brought about a transformation in both the kind of resources offered and the relationship of the library to its users. The availability of new formats has also transformed teaching and research. It is common to read about "the changing nature of research libraries in the information age," and yet the library's traditional role has endured, albeit within an environment that is very much in flux.

The modern library still fulfills its established role by providing materials for research, teaching, and study, but it does so in very different ways and has assumed important new functions as well. This is especially true across five important areas of the changing scholarly information landscape: (1) library collections (both general and special); (2) scholarly communications and publishing; (3) digital infrastructure; (4) digital scholarship; and (5) teaching. This chapter aims to help new faculty learn how, across these areas of support, they and their libraries can (and already do, at many institutions) form close partnerships to significantly advance research and teaching.

The modern library is a dynamic organization at the heart of the learning process within the university, and librarians are increasingly active partners with faculty in the academic enterprise. Research libraries today spend a significant—and growing—proportion of their collection funds on the intangible: access to electronic databases, online journals, and e-books. In effect, libraries are "renting" these resources. New service models target user needs, and librarians have come out from behind that once-forbidding reference desk to be increasingly active partners with faculty. Technology has made research and teaching easier in some ways, but more difficult in others. With so much information available, it is more important than ever that students and faculty learn to discriminate, to pick and choose, to analyze, and to select carefully. Technology has decentralized many library functions, making it unnecessary to set foot in a library building, but the array of resources can be overwhelming, and users of these resources need guidance. Librarians are essential not only to provide a general introduction to collections and services, an orientation to the literature of a particular field, or a specialized session on a certain research topic, but also to help students learn how to be careful and discerning in their work with websites, databases, blogs, and other online sources.

These new roles for research libraries do not come without a price. Striking the balance between conducting traditional collection development, for example, and moving decisively into the digital era, presents a challenge to libraries. Supporting the needs of all disciplines—those that rely on print materials, or rare books, or film and video, or foreign-language resources, as well as those whose literature is mostly or completely online—all within a finite budget, is one of the most significant tightrope acts that research libraries must perform. The array of databases and other digital resources available is dazzling, and these costs, and their often inexplicably and outrageously large annual increases, must be factored into the larger equation of library budgets. At the same time, library budgets have, on average across the United States, shrunk as a percentage of total university spending. Faculty can be effective allies in advocating for increased library funding.

What do these changes and challenges mean to you as a new faculty member? As a graduate student, you developed a special relationship to the library where you conducted your own research, in the institution where you wrote your dissertation, worked as a teaching assistant, designed your courses. That was most likely an intense relationship, based on your broad and deep knowledge of the library's book and journal collection in your specific field of research, perhaps the primary sources available to you in the special collections department, as well as your discovery of digital resources relevant to your own work. The odds are that you gave very little thought to how those materials got to the library, or how the librarians made decisions about resource allocation. As a faculty member, you may have the same relationship to the collections that you had previously, but you also have responsibilities with regard to the library. You will have the opportunity to learn more about the internal workings of the library, to advocate for the library on campus and beyond, to understand the budget process and the tensions when trade-offs are necessary, and perhaps to advise on decisions about resources. Library administrators will welcome your active participation in determining how the library can best meet your needs and those of your students, and how to set priorities amid a climate of practically constant change.

Collections: The Foundation of Libraries

For the 120-plus libraries of the Association of Research Libraries (ARL), deep and broad historical collections, including rare books and primary resources, are central. These collections were developed over the years through various means: the efforts of librarians and faculty; as gifts and exchanges; and through subscriptions and standing orders for books by certain publishers or on particular topics. Subject specialist librarians, basing their decisions on explicit or implicit collection policies, purchased those materials they considered to be of importance to the research and teaching of the university, in the process building especially strong collections in certain areas. Faculty returning from research trips abroad often donated their books to their university library, or made contacts with organizations that contributed materials. Many of the resulting collections are the richest and deepest in the world, and reflect the intellectual interests of the faculty of a given institution at a particular time. Gifts of books and journals have also contributed to the creation of strong library collections, as have materials received on exchange from research institutes or universities around the world.

That was the print environment. With the shift to electronic formats and the integration of multimedia into teaching, the definition of "collection" has changed dramatically. Internet resources, along with the proliferation of databases, online journals, and e-books, have transformed the collection development function in libraries. Beyond call numbers for print books, the library's online catalog connects the user to thousands of links to e-books and other digital resources that are licensed, not owned.

"I never use the library anymore," quips one faculty member in the physical sciences. What they mean is that they never go into the library to check out books. But as they read e-journal articles at their desk, or check facts in a database from their lab, they are, in fact, using "the library," since those resources are acquired—or rather access to them is contracted—by the library. For professors in Classics, the bound journal collection is their bread and butter and their carrel in the stacks is their lab. For geologists, the digital map collection is critical to research, the library's GIS experts are their partners, and they tailor their assignments so that students will develop a familiarity with those resources. Historians of South Asia depend on the British Parliamentary Papers for their work. Slave diaries in the special collections department form the focus of a colonial US history class. A database containing the publications of nongovernmental organizations (NGOs) offers information on the public health aspects of AIDS in Africa. A website that gathers and preserves the web pages of Latin American political candidates, hosted by a university with a strong Latin American studies program, serves as an important resource for students in a political science class. A collection of Chinese videos supports both a language class and a course on popular culture. The list goes on and on; the array of formats has changed dramatically, and the sheer volume of information to which the library serves as a gateway has grown exponentially. Research and teaching are increasingly interdisciplinary. The library has multiple user communities, each with distinctive needs.

Nowhere is this effect more apparent than in the area of online journals. As new areas of inquiry develop, they spawn other journals. In a phenomenon known as "twigging," new journals take on more and more specific emphases as subfields emerge and scholars specialize further. As if the rise in the number and diversity of journals were not enough of a new variable for libraries, the costs of online journals have increased from exorbitant to outrageous, particularly in the STEM fields. What is often not apparent to library users is the fact that the individual subscription rate is considerably lower than the institutional rate. Libraries are, on average, charged a subscription fee that is ten times higher than what individual subscribers pay. It is not unusual for a subscription to a single scholarly STEM journal to cost libraries in the range of $10,000 to $20,000 per year.

Distinctive Collections: The Value and Versatility of Primary Materials
Special collections—the rare books and primary documents that are truly distinctive and often unique—are what most differentiate research libraries from one another. Once restricted to on-site use, requiring travel to the holding institution, these collections have been gaining visibility and use through libraries' digitization programs, which have greatly expanded access, not only for scholars around the world but also for the general public and even K–12 students and their teachers, who may discover online a useful resource connected to their curriculum. Thus, ambitious digitization efforts have greatly extended the reach of libraries and enabled scholarship much more broadly than was previously

possible. Depending on your discipline and field of interest, the rare book and manuscript collections at your home institution, in combination with digitized special collections that are housed elsewhere, may be important research materials for you.

That said, as technology has become more pervasive, and communication and learning platforms encourage increasingly virtual and intangible engagement, students—particularly undergraduates—are more and more drawn to primary documents in their original format. Accustomed to conducting their work through electronic means, students find rare materials to be novel and often particularly moving as concrete manifestations of historical events, works of literature, and even data. Libraries' special collections are seeing an upsurge in interest in primary research among undergraduates. Librarians and archivists work closely with faculty to identify collections of primary materials that can illustrate or embellish on the lessons of a course. In some cases, a particularly rich archive may serve as the basis for an entire course, offering opportunities for students to take a "deep dive" into the documents for research papers, presentations, or curated exhibits. These collections are not limited to humanists; they can offer remarkably rich curricular components in a wide variety of fields.

The Transformation of Scholarly Communications

New faculty face an incredible number of options for publishing their research. The internet has fostered the ability to quickly and easily transmit scholarship to colleagues, collaborate with partners at other institutions around the world, and engage with new audiences to expand the reach and impact of research. But the scholarly publishing system also faces significant challenges.

One of the more significant challenges is money. Scholarly publishing is big business. It's not uncommon for a large research library to pay out multi-million-dollar annual subscription contracts, much of which goes to five large publishers. Those five publishers have grown as the result of industry consolidation, which accelerated rapidly over the last few decades, particularly in the STEM fields. A recent study by Larivière et al. (2015) examines this phenomenon, showing that consolidation has left certain fields with a particular lack of alternatives. Clinical medicine, for example, went from fewer than 20 percent of all articles in that field published by the big five publishers in the early 1970s to over 60 percent of all articles in that field published by the big five publishers in 2013. Other fields show similar consolidation, including chemistry (around 70 percent of all chemistry articles in 2013 were published by the big five publishers), earth and space (around 50 percent), and mathematics (around 50 percent). This means that universities and the libraries that serve them have few choices but to purchase access from publishers with dominant market positions.

Unsurprisingly, as the industry has consolidated, we have witnessed dramatic publisher profits. For example, Elsevier, one of the largest publishers, recently reported annual operating profits nearing $1 billion, on margins of nearly 40 percent. The other big publishers report similar figures. Taken together, those figures represent several billions of dollars leaving college and university budgets each year. While commercial publishers understandably seek a return on their investment, the sheer amount of money flowing out of the research system and into corporate profits does not align well with academic priorities. It means fewer resources for faculty positions, postdocs, labs, librarians, and a whole host of other needs that are at the core of the research enterprise.

A closely related challenge is in how published scholarship is made available to readers. Although the internet enables global, low-cost access to research, most scholarship is accessible only behind a paywall at prices beyond what most readers can afford. The big five publishers have embraced and promoted this system, though there are some significant changes afoot. Nonprofit publishers such as Public Library of Science (PLoS) have pioneered an open-access model that covers publishing costs with article processing charges (APCs) that are billed to authors, enabling the journal to distribute articles online for free (termed "gold" open access). The open-access APC model has proven viable enough that commercial publishers have begun to adopt it for some of their journals. Although other open-access business models exist, the APC model has become one of the more significant. But it is not a panacea; APCs raise their own risks. When APCs are high (which they are for most commercial publishers who have engaged in open-access publishing), researchers may be trading an "access to research" problem with an "access to funds to publish" problem. Depending on the publisher and journal, APCs can vary significantly, from a small fee of $50 to over $5,000 per article. Average costs for major publishers are around $1,500, which for many researchers can still represent a significant barrier.

The proliferation of publishing options, especially for articles, has also raised the challenge of how to evaluate scholarship. Promotion and tenure committees, now faced with candidates whose scholarship is published across a diverse range of journals, have looked to metrics to help understand the impact and importance of that scholarship. Unfortunately, the most commonly used tool, the Impact Factor, is also among the crudest and least well-suited for the task.

Originally developed in the 1960s to determine which journals to include in the Science Citation Index, the Impact Factor has emerged as an important (though incomplete) metric for evaluation across a broad range of scholarship. Impact Factor is essentially the measurement of the average number of citations per article in a given journal over a given period of time. While still helpful to understand long-term trends in citation patterns across journals, the impact factor can say almost nothing about an individual article. Much more precise and revealing metrics are available today.

The availability of these tools is reflected in recent calls for changes in how funding agencies and academic institutions go about evaluation. In December 2012, a prominent group of editors and publishers of scholarly journals released the San Francisco Declaration on Research Assessment (DORA), which makes several recommendations, the core being that scholarship should not be evaluated using journal-based metrics, but rather should consider a "broad range of impact measures including qualitative indicators of research impact, such as influence on policy and practice." As of January 2020, DORA had been endorsed by eighteen hundred organizations, including several major universities, as well as more than fifteen thousand individual researchers.

The field of metrics and tools used to provide article-level impact assessment is fast developing. Among those currently in use are standard citation indexes such as Web of Science and Scopus, though new entrants are now emerging in the field, including Digital Science's "Dimensions," and even Google Scholar. In addition, tools to expand the universe of potential impact assessment are now in common use. Altmetric, a tool also owned by Digital Science, tracks references to scholarly outputs across the web, including in public spaces such as on Wikipedia and social media, as well as across more serious citations in government and NGO reports.

Finally, infrastructure control is perhaps the most significant challenge for the future of scholarly publishing. While the act of publishing itself involves a relatively discrete and distributed set of technologies, the process of knowledge discovery, production, dissemination, and evaluation involves a large and disparate set of tools. Just as publishers have horizontally consolidated by acquiring journals, they have also begun to vertically consolidate by acquiring a variety of systems that manage data and content, including everything from grant administration to article submission, publication, and evaluation. For example, researchers from the University of Toronto–based project the Knowledge Gap, Posada and Chen (2017), have documented how just one publisher, Elsevier, has created or acquired over the last decade or so major pieces of the knowledge production infrastructure. This includes everything from basic research discovery platforms such as Scopus and ScienceDirect, to funding, methods, and data collection tools such as SciVal and Hivebench, through to distribution via platforms such as bepress and ssrn, and into research evaluation through tools such as Pure, SciVal, and Scopus.

While we are only just beginning to experience the effects of this vertical integration, it has already raised some difficult questions. Conflict of interest is a major one: can one organization be trusted to both produce content and evaluate its significance and impact? Vendor lock-in and data portability is another real concern. Once a researcher has begun with a given set of tools, how feasible is it to move that research out and onto another publisher's technology ecosystem? Ultimately, these questions devolve into some basic concerns about academic freedom. While journal publishing has firmly established norms and codes of ethics to support academic freedom, it remains unclear how other parts of a corporate-owned knowledge production system will respect those values.

So how do libraries fit into all this? Aside from the self-interest in controlling journal subscription rates, for the most part librarians have found corporate publishers' massive profits and accompanying business models antithetical to libraries, and their universities' core mission of promoting access to knowledge. In response, libraries have actively supported faculty in their efforts to push back, both on campus and off. Since 2012, more than seventeen thousand scholars have publicly signed on to a boycott under the banner of a website titled "The Cost of Knowledge," agreeing not to author, referee, or do editorial work for Elsevier-published journals to protest their business practices, including their high prices. Libraries have loudly amplified those objections to congressional representatives, campus administrators, and research funders. As a result, many federal agencies have now implemented open-access requirements for funded research, requiring that published research be made available for free online twelve months or less after initial publication. Funders such as the Wellcome Trust and the Bill and Melinda Gates Foundation have gone a step further by investing in alternative publishing arrangements that would cut out or minimize commercial publisher involvement.

On campus, libraries have been active partners with faculty in developing campus open-access policies to ensure that faculty research is widely accessible. In the United States these policies have commonly followed the "Harvard Model," preserving a preexisting license in all faculty-authored journal articles so that no matter the bargaining power between the author and the journal, the right to post a copy of the article online for free is always preserved.

Working with individual faculty, many libraries now also employ in-house scholarly communication experts who can consult with authors on publishing contracts, options for online distribution, and tools to maximize and track the reach and impact of scholarship. Libraries have also taken on management of open-access funds, which have primarily been directed at supporting individual faculty who need assistance to pay for APCs in open-access journals. Some have recently expanded to also support open-access monographs published by university presses.

For new faculty, the key takeaway is that the scholarly communication system is complex and evolving, and that it is driven in part by business concerns that have nothing to do with the integrity of the scholarly record, research ethics, or the dissemination of ideas. Faculty are at the core of the system, however, and have considerable power to make changes. Faculty have, in libraries, willing partners to help amplify that message and achieve changes that more closely align the publishing system with academic and research priorities.

Digital Infrastructure

Since the early 1990s, the digitization of scholarly resources has been a driving force in the transformation of library services and of the scholarly enterprise itself. Virtually every research library in North America has undertaken digitization projects over the past decade, although the scale, complexity, and long-term viability of these projects vary significantly. Some of the largest projects, such as the Google Book and HathiTrust projects,[1] which involved the University of Michigan, Stanford, the University of California, and others, have been transformational in opening up online access to millions of volumes of works. Libraries are challenged not only to build and maintain large-scale digitization services, but to take actions necessary to sustain their digital assets over the long term and migrate them to formats and systems of continued relevance for modern researchers.

There is a diverse set of technology pressure points for supporting knowledge discovery, production, and dissemination. In contrast to the commercially owned digital infrastructure, libraries have been active in software development and implementation in an effort to offer open, alternative platforms on which researchers can create and share knowledge.

Early digital archive efforts focused on making available via the Web electronic versions of theses and dissertations or preprint articles in a few scientific fields. Those efforts have flourished, resulting in a large number of software options for both institution-specific repositories of scholarship and subject-based repositories, such as ArXiv (physics, math, computer science, and other fields) and HumArXiv (humanities), along with broader alternatives such as those hosted by the Open Science Foundation. Driven in part by campus open-access policies as well as by library and faculty pressure on publishers to open up their standard publishing contracts, those repositories now host millions of scholarly works for free distribution online. The Directory of Open Access Repositories (Open DOAR) now lists nearly 4,000 such platforms, many of which feed scholarship directly into discovery tools such as Google Scholar, which has contributed to broad dissemination and readership.[2]

A second and emerging area of library support is in hosting not just the final research products, but also the data underlying the research. To ensure research integrity and fuel reproducibility, many funders and journals now require researchers to share the data underlying their work. Libraries have collaborated closely with repositories such as DataDryad, which integrates directly with publishers. Many libraries have built their own infrastructure to support local faculty needs, which in many cases involves the hosting and preservation of large and complex data sets. Beyond the technical support, some libraries offer consulting services for faculty to help them navigate funder data management plan requirements, data formatting and structuring, and deposit.

Supporting New Forms of Scholarship

Closely related to the digital infrastructure support, libraries have become active partners with faculty who seek to conduct and disseminate their research in new forms of scholarship, particularly in the area of the digital humanities. There are new opportunities to use computational analysis, software integration, and online research portals to help make scholarship more interactive, deep, and understandable to broader audiences. These opportunities have increasingly driven faculty to take on such projects, and libraries to develop suites of services, to support both technology needs and the project management, organization, and planning needed to produce digital scholarship.

When digital scholarship projects first emerged in the 1990s,[3] the technical and practical barriers were high. Devoting resources to these projects was viewed as risky; presses didn't publish them, and there were no real avenues for peer review. The technology was so rapidly changing that neither libraries nor anyone else knew how to preserve them for the long term. Today, digital humanities projects are still somewhat experimental and risky, but support for them has become more robust. Many libraries support web-publishing tools such as Omeka and Scalar, data-mining and text-analysis tools that facilitate text encoding and comparison, and offer trainings and consultation for both faculty and their graduate students to evaluate, plan out, and run a digital project.

University presses are now beginning to experiment with publishing these projects—Stanford University Press recently published *Enchanting the Desert*, a first-of-its-kind digital project with author Nicholas Bauch—and libraries are increasingly looking to collaborate with them. Not every library everywhere is equipped to address all the challenges posed by digital scholarship, but many are in a position to help faculty get started on these types of projects.

Partners in Teaching

As a new faculty member, you will find librarians to be creative and willing partners in the process of educating your students. Beyond the more informal and spontaneous interactions between students and librarians at the service desk, or through online "chat" reference, there are opportunities to engage library subject specialists for in-class sessions to focus on research methods and the specific resources on a topic. Some libraries offer more formal instruction programs that address information literacy, plagiarism, and critical thinking, among other topics. These sessions may or may not be required, and will orient students to the library, its collections, and its services. They will teach students how to evaluate websites for accuracy and to identify bias and "fake news," how to determine the comparative advantages of print and electronic sources, how to cite references, and how to incorporate, when appropriate, primary materials into their papers and presentations. Librarians and archivists can contribute in multiple ways to the learning process and are valuable partners with faculty.

In addition to generalist instruction librarians, most college and university libraries have expert staff with deep subject or international/area studies or language expertise. Other specialists in data analysis and management, visualization, digital humanities, instructional technology, and other areas may also be available to you as partners in designing your courses, assisting students with assignments, and ensuring that you have the collections resources you need.

Conclusion

Expanded partnerships between faculty and the library in a variety of arenas bring not just new intellectual challenges, but broad benefits to scholarship and to research institutions. For example, as more faculty become familiar with and concerned about the alarming rise in the costs of STEM journals and the resulting crisis in scholarly communication, they enter the fray as strong, articulate advocates for new publishing models and adequate funding for library collections. As librarians engage more actively in teaching—whether it is through formal library instruction programs or team-teaching with faculty—students and faculty alike acquire new skills in information retrieval and research methods. Technology in support of teaching and learning depends on new collaborative relationships. For a new faculty member, this is a time of change, challenge, and experimentation in research libraries. You will undoubtedly be part of the transformation that is underway, and you will find willing partners in librarians.

NOTES

1. Google is estimated to have digitized some 30 million volumes. Most of those scans were made from the collections of research libraries, which in turn together created their own digital library, HathiTrust, which is tailored to academic researchers' needs. See https://www.hathitrust.org/. While the majority of those scanned books are not available to users in full-text due to copyright restrictions, both digitization initiatives have greatly improved research use of collections by enabling text searchability, access for blind and print-disabled users, and preservation access for books whose physical copies are deteriorating.

2. Some good examples from US institutions are Duke University Libraries, *Duke-Space*; Harvard Library, Office for Scholarly Communication, *DASH*; and University of California, *eScholarship*.

3. A good example is Ayers, *Valley of the Shadow*. Some exemplars of more modern projects include papyri.info (papyrological focused), ProjectVox (https://projectvox .org/ [accessed April 2, 2020]; online community highlighting the work of early modern women philosophers), Hypercities (www.hypercities.com [accessed April 2, 2020]; thick mapping in the digital humanities), Southern Spaces (https://southernspaces.org [accessed April 2, 2020]; online journal focused on real and imagined places in the US South).

WORKS CITED

Association of Research Libraries. http://www.arl.org.

Ayers, Edward L. *The Valley of the Shadow: Two Communities in the American Civil War.* 1993–2007. http://valley.lib.virginia.edu/.

Bauch, Nicholas. *Enchanting the Desert*. Stanford, CA: Stanford University Press, 2016. http://www.enchantingthedesert.com/home/.

Buranyi, Stephen. "Is the Staggeringly Profitable Business of Scientific Publishing Bad for Science?" *The Guardian*, June 27, 2017.

Duke University Libraries. *DukeSpace: Scholarship by Duke Authors.* Accessed April 2, 2020. https://dukespace.lib.duke.edu/dspace/.

Freeman, Geoffrey T. "The Library as Place: Changes in Learning Patterns, Collections, Technology, and Use." In *Library as Place: Rethinking Roles, Rethinking Space*. Washington, D.C.: Council on Library and Information Resources, 2005. http://www.clir.org/pubs/abstract/pub129abst.html.

Harvard Library, Office for Scholarly Communication. *DASH: Digital Access to Scholarship at Harvard*. Accessed April 2, 2020. https://dash.harvard.edu/.

Larivière, Vincent, Stefanie Haustein, and Philippe Mongeon. "The Oligopoly of Academic Publishers in the Digital Era." *PLoS ONE* 10(6): e0127502 (2015). https://doi.org/10.1371/journal.pone.0127502.

Maxwell, John W., Alessandra Bordini, and Katie Shamash. "Reassembling Scholarly Communications: An Evaluation of the Andrew W. Mellon Foundation's Monograph Initiative (Final Report, May 2016)." *Journal of Electronic Publishing* 20.1 (2017). https://doi.org/http://dx.doi.org/10.3998/3336451.0020.101.

Posada, Alejandro, and George Chen. "Preliminary Findings: Rent Seeking by Elsevier." *The Knowledge Gap: Geopolitics of Academic Production*. 2017. http://knowledgegap.org/index.php/sub-projects/rent-seeking-and-financialization-of-the-academic-publishing-industry/preliminary-findings/.

"San Francisco Declaration on Research Assessment." Accessed January 27, 2020. https://sfdora.org/read/.

University of California. *eScholarship: Open Access Publications from the University of California*. Accessed April 2, 2020. https://escholarship.org/.

12. Suggestions for Alleviating IRB Angst

JAMES E. SUTTON

The Office for Human Research Protections (OHRP) within the US federal government mandates that academic institutions have an Institutional Review Board (IRB). These IRBs are charged with protecting the rights and welfare of human subjects who participate in research, and they ensure that research involving human subjects complies with ethical principles and relevant local, state, and federal laws. Before research involving human subjects can be carried out, it must first undergo an IRB review and receive approval.

Submitting a proposal to the IRB evokes universal angst amongst researchers within academic settings. I have experienced IRB-induced anxiety when embarking on my own research, so I am empathetic toward other researchers. At the same time, however, I have also gained a better appreciation for the IRB process from being an IRB member and serving as my institution's current IRB chair. In the following paragraphs, I share some practical insights with the goal of increasing the odds that others will have favorable encounters with the IRB when doing research with human subjects. Rather than generating an exhaustive list of technical tips, I instead offer some general suggestions and commentary on a handful of themes that are often taken for granted or simply overlooked.

Regulations, Procedures, and Ethical Principles

When planning a new study, my first suggestion is to become well versed in the formal regulations and procedures that are associated with IRBs. Aside from the IRB webpages that most academic institutions have put together for their constituents, there are a number of helpful governmental resources that are easily accessible online. In particular, I would begin by reading the *Belmont Report*, which was prepared in 1978 by the National Commission for the Protection of Human Subjects of Biomedical and Behavioral Research (US Department of Health and Human Services, Office of Human Research Protections 1979).

The *Belmont Report* outlines the basic ethical principles for conducting research with human subjects, and it guided the development of our federal policy for human subjects protection, typically referred to as the Common Rule, in 1991. The Common Rule was recently revised to better protect human subjects while simultaneously reducing common inconveniences faced by researchers when going through the IRB process. This revised policy was published in the *Federal Register* in 2017 (Federal Policy for the Protection of Human Subjects 2017) and has implications for research commencing on or after January 21, 2019. More information on the *Belmont Report*, the Common Rule and its recent revisions, and IRBs in general can be found within the OHRP section of the US Department of Health and Human Services webpage.

The three basic ethical principles outlined in the *Belmont Report* are respect for persons, beneficence, and justice. More thorough elaborations on each of these ideals can easily be found elsewhere, including on the OHRP webpage noted above. Generally, the Belmont Report calls for researchers to avoid the exploitation of vulnerable populations, minimize and make human subjects aware of potential risks and harm from participating in research, and provide human subjects with the opportunity to make an informed and voluntary decision to participate in research.

While the *Belmont Report*'s objectives seem straightforward enough, in practice they often manifest themselves in unforeseen, complex, and discipline-specific ways. In the following two sections, I provide some selected examples pertaining to prison research and research with indigenous populations. The point I hope to make is that researchers need to think critically about how to best reconcile the spirit of our ethical principles with the situational contexts and other unique considerations that affect their research.

Ethical Principles in Situational Context: Research in Prisons

I have previously written about some unique and challenging human subjects concerns that may arise when doing research in prisons (see Sutton 2011; Sutton 2017). Two examples from my prior work that I elaborate on here pertain to informed consent and providing compensation in exchange for research participation. I intentionally selected these two examples for their mundanity in order to underscore the need to think critically about the specific contexts in which human subjects research occurs.

It is conventional practice to give participants a copy of a consent form when carrying out research with human subjects. When conducting research in prison, however, having prisoners keep a consent form could potentially put them at risk. Should staff or other prisoners find a research participant's consent form, they may incorrectly assume that the participant was providing sensitive information about them or certain incidents, and deem the participant a snitch. Snitching is a cardinal sin in most correctional settings, and repercussions can range anywhere from disdain, stigma, and harassment to violence in more extreme cases.

It is also common to provide participants with some form of compensation when doing research with human subjects. However, perceptions of preferential treatment and feelings of exclusion and injustice may emerge if those who participate in a study receive a benefit that is not made available to everyone else in prison. Even a form of compensation as seemingly minor as a candy bar can potentially cause serious problems within restrictive prison environments, with reactions again ranging anywhere from disdain, stigma, and harassment to violence in more extreme cases.

As these examples show, best practices for adhering to the *Belmont Report's* principles are ultimately situationally determined. Accordingly, every step of the research process should be thought through thoroughly and should not be taken for granted. Simple practices such as providing a consent form or a token of compensation are consistent with the intent of the *Belmont Report* in most settings, but they can be at odds with it in others. For instance, blindly following these precepts when doing prison research could inadvertently violate the principle of not harming human subjects. Upon recognizing that potential harms from research participation can be physical, psychological, economic, legal, and reputational, it is the responsibility of researchers to then anticipate the unique human subjects implications and challenges that are more specific to their respective substantive areas.

Ethical Principles in Situational Context:
Research with Indigenous Populations

In addition to giving each step of the research process careful deliberation, it is incumbent upon researchers to think more broadly about the research itself. For instance, researchers should critically reflect upon the ethics of what they are doing and how and why they are doing it. Some examples from research with indigenous populations in the United States are instructive.

Anderson (2015) and Deloria (1991) recount myriad ways in which many of those who have studied American Indians have engaged in exploitation. For instance, researchers have often produced works of poor quality and put forth inaccurate observations. A problem that has resulted from this is that negative and oppressive ideas about American Indians have been spread.

Even if incorrect ideas are eventually corrected, "the book remains in the library where naïve and uninformed people will read it for a decade to come" (Deloria 1991, 459). As Anderson (2015, 163) points out, "efforts to control present research cannot often remedy the residual of past research. There are many theories and presumed 'facts' inscribed in existing publications now taken as fact and permeating other publications." In light of these dynamics, Deloria (1991) argues that quality and accuracy are fundamental ethical issues given the harms experienced by American Indians when these expectations have been violated.

Whether they are pursuing "repetitive" research objectives dictated by external funders that have no connection to actual community needs (Deloria 1991) or simply advancing their careers through the "commercialization" of indigenous people (Anderson 2015), a problem that has exasperated ethical challenges is that self-serving researchers have not felt any obligation to treat indigenous populations ethically. For this reason, Deloria (1991) calls for researchers to assist and otherwise give back to the indigenous communities they study. Collaboration and reciprocity have in turn become objectives pursued by many scholars, though Anderson (2015) has identified a number of contradictions in these approaches in practice. Most fundamentally, he observes that "While reciprocity, equality, and authenticity can be achieved inside the collaborative situation, the core irony remains that larger conditions are always present, actively imposing structural inequalities and contradictions that no agency of the researcher . . . can dissolve or resolve" (150–151).

I have drawn from insights offered by scholars who have studied indigenous populations in the United States to show how the ethics in play have real consequences for living human subjects and, potentially, whole communities. The lessons presented here about exploitation and the harms caused by poorly executed research should be taken to heart by others who will then ideally contemplate implications that are specific to their own substantive areas. As should now be clear from the illustrative examples offered from prison research and research on indigenous populations, adhering to ethical principles entails more than simply applying a standardized set of procedures.

Pedagogical Research and IRB Considerations

It is important to remember that IRB considerations also apply to scholarship on teaching and learning. I have reviewed several proposals for pedagogical research projects over the years and could write about myriad IRB-related themes pertaining to this kind of work. In light of space limitations, I will briefly highlight two issues here that I have found to be especially common.

The first is that instructors need to recognize that they are in a structural position of power over their students. For this reason, special care must be taken to ensure that students do not feel as though they will suffer repercussions for not participating in a research project. Adopting an anonymous design can often address this concern, though it may be difficult to ensure anonymity in smaller courses where instructors know their students well enough to connect them with their data.

Informed consent is a second issue that has frequently come up in pedagogical research proposals that I have reviewed. Consistent with other forms of research, those who study students must provide them with the opportunity to make an informed decision to participate. Accordingly, researchers cannot use information from students' work as data without their consent, nor can they go back and draw from prior students' work for research purposes unless those students previously provided their consent to do so. It may be possible in some cases to gain informed consent retroactively, but in practice it is onerous and logistically challenging to track down former students.

Practical Tips for Increasing Positive Engagement with the IRB

Academic researchers commonly perceive IRBs as persnickety with an overarching reach. I suspect these perceptions stem in part from the fact that many proposals need to be revised in accordance with IRB feedback and then resubmitted for additional review. One way to minimize these kinds of hindrances is to be thorough and clear when providing the details solicited within an IRB proposal form.

It is important to recognize that IRBs were originally designed to ensure the protection of human subjects in biomedical and social psychological research. The details solicited within an IRB proposal form therefore typically align well with these lines of inquiry. In recent years, however, a number of scholars in fields such as sociology (Blee and Currier 2011; Cameron 2016), political science (Yanow and Schwartz-Shea 2016), and anthropology (Dobrin and Lederman 2012; Lederman 2004; Lederman 2006) have written about the ways in which traditional IRB protocols poorly fit other forms of inquiry.

Ethnographic field research is a prime example of an approach that may be unduly restricted by conventional IRB procedures that reify the traditional scientific method. It is often the case that IRB proposal forms require researchers to address certain ethical considerations that do not readily apply to ethnography, while simultaneously neglecting other ethical considerations that do. For those who conduct this kind of work, I recommend reviewing Lederman's (2007) suggestions and sample template for "educating your IRB" members about research approaches that they may not fully understand.

Keep in mind that IRBs are composed of members with a range of backgrounds and roles both on and off campus. It is therefore likely that just a few at best will have discipline-specific knowledge on any particular proposal. If IRB members are confronted with information that is either unclear or too limited for them to adequately assess risks, they will likely revert to apprehension. While this may result in project delays and require researchers to do additional work on their proposals, it is ultimately the IRB's job to err on the side of caution when contemplating matters that could potentially pose harm to those who are gracious enough to participate in human subjects research.

In the event that a proposal does come back with questions, discouraging feedback, or a disappointing decision, it is crucial to maintain a positive attitude when addressing the IRB's concerns. I recall one instance when we received a proposal for a project that we all found exciting. However, we were unable to approve it in its first iteration because we were not provided with sufficient information. Had the proposers simply responded to our feedback, they could have made some relatively easy fixes to secure IRB approval.

Instead, the proposers were defensive, failed to address our concerns, and then ultimately abandoned what should have been a neat project. The lesson to learn from this case is that attitude can be everything. While I cannot speak for all institutions, the IRB on my campus strives to enable, rather than derail, research while fulfilling our obligations to protect human subjects. Indeed, one of the main reasons we voluntarily do this work is that we genuinely enjoy learning about the research that our faculty, staff, and student colleagues are doing. Unfortunately, the proposers in the example that I just shared failed to understand this.

Concluding Thoughts

I have emphasized some general steps that those who do research with human subjects can take to alleviate angst and minimize delays when going through the IRB process. While my focus has been on federally mandated IRBs in academic settings, I want to note that in some cases, researchers may also need to secure additional authorization from other entities prior to conducting their research. For instance, my prison research had to undergo a separate human subjects review by the prison system's review board, and Anderson (2015) secured approval from a commission of elders and educators when studying the Northern Arapaho Nation.

Becoming familiar with policies and procedures, understanding and appreciating the IRB's role, and maintaining a positive attitude are all basic suggestions that any researcher can benefit from. Moreover, it behooves researchers to take deliberate efforts to anticipate how our more abstract ethical principles unfold differentially in practice, depending on one's specific research objectives and context. All of this is crucial, as our ethical principles ultimately have real consequences for living human subjects and, in some cases, broader communities. On a final note, it is important to recognize that each IRB has its own culture. When in doubt, you should therefore ask the IRB at your institution to share their suggested best practices for dealing with any issues that you may be struggling to resolve.

WORKS CITED

Anderson, Jeffrey D. 2015. "Ironies of Collaborative Research in the Northern Arapaho Nation." *Collaborative Anthropologies* 7.2: 142–179.

Blee, Kathleen M., and Ashley Currier. 2011. "Ethics beyond the IRB: An Introductory Essay." *Qualitative Sociology* 34.3: 401.

Cameron, Abigail E. 2016. "The Unhappy Marriage of IRBs and Ethnography." *Contexts* (blog), March 19. https://contexts.org/blog/the-unhappy-marriage-of-irbs-and -ethnography/.

Deloria, Vine. "Research, Redskins, and Reality." 1991. *American Indian Quarterly* 15.4: 457–468.

Dobrin, Lise M., and Rena Lederman. 2012. "Imagine Ethics without IRBs." *Anthropology News* 53: 20.

Federal Policy for the Protection of Human Subjects. 2017. *Federal Register* 82.12 (January 19): https://www.govinfo.gov/content/pkg/FR-2017-01-19/pdf/2017-01058.pdf.

Lederman, Rena. 2004. "Bureaucratic Oversight of Human Research and Disciplinary Diversity IRB Review of Oral History and Anthropology." *Anthropology News* 45.5: 8.

Lederman, Rena. 2006. "The Perils of Working at Home: IRB 'Mission Creep' as Context and Content for an Ethnography of Disciplinary Knowledges." *American Ethnologist* 33.4: 482–491.

Lederman, Rena. 2007. "Educate Your IRB: An Experiment in Cross-Disciplinary Communication." *Anthropology News* 48.6: 33–34.

Sutton, James. 2011. "An Ethnographic Account of Doing Survey Research in Prison: Descriptions, Reflections, and Suggestions from the Field." *Qualitative Sociology Review* 7.2.

Sutton, James. 2017. "Doing Reflectively Engaged, Face-to-Face Research in Prisons: Con-
    texts and Sensitivities." *Handbook of Research Methods in Health Social Sciences*: 1–16.

US Department of Health and Human Services, Office of Human Research Protections.
    n.d. Accessed January 20, 2020. https://www.hhs.gov/ohrp/.

US Department of Health and Human Services, Office of Human Research Protections.
    1979. *The Belmont Report: Ethical Principles and Guidelines for the Protection of Human
    Subjects of Research*. https://www.hhs.gov/ohrp/regulations-and-policy/belmont-report
    /index.html.

Yanow, Dvora, and Peregrine Schwartz-Shea. 2016. "Encountering Your IRB 2.0: What
    Political Scientists Need to Know." *PS: Political Science and Politics* 49: 277–286.

13. Informed Consent and the Ethics of IRB Research: A Case Study of the Havasupai Tribe's Lawsuit against Genetic Researchers

NANIBAA' A. GARRISON

In 2003, Carletta Tilousi, a member of the Havasupai Tribe of northern Arizona, learned that DNA samples she had donated for a genetic research project on type 2 diabetes in 1989 were in fact being used in non-diabetes-related genetic studies by researchers at Arizona State University (ASU). In Tilousi's view, she had not provided consent for any studies beyond the original diabetes-related research. On further investigation, Tilousi realized that the DNA samples that she and other members of the Havasupai tribe had donated had been used for studies on schizophrenia, ethnic migration, and population inbreeding, all of which are highly charged topics that are taboo in the Havasupai culture. The Havasupai Tribe filed a lawsuit against the Arizona Board of Regents in 2004 over the misuse of their genetic samples and lack of complete "informed consent" involved in the samples' collection. The case was an important challenge to the definition and use of informed consent, particularly with vulnerable populations. This essay, after explaining the outcome of this case, examines how Institutional Review Board (IRB) officials understand its significance and its implications for how they conceptualize and enact human subject protections. The case raised awareness about the importance of ensuring that participants are informed of the research and that transparent communication about the research is absolutely necessary to maintain the trust of participants. This essay illustrates a cautionary tale of research gone wrong, and a reminder to strive for justice and transparency when working with communities in research.

Between 1990 and 1994, DNA samples were solicited from approximately four hundred Havasupai Tribe members in conjunction with the Diabetes Project led by researchers at ASU. The stated intent of the project was to understand why more than half of Havasupai adults were afflicted by type 2 diabetes. The Havasupai, a small tribe living in a remote part of the Grand Canyon, had limited access to fresh food and health care. The Diabetes Project included education about diabetes, the collection and testing of blood samples, and genetic association testing. To obtain informed consent, ASU researchers made oral statements recruiting the tribal members to the research study. When they agreed, participants were asked to sign informed consent documents written in English. Although the consent form said that the samples would be used for research on "behavioral/medical problems," tribe members were told that their samples would be used specifically for genetic studies on diabetes.

However, initial studies failed to find a genetic link to type 2 diabetes. The samples were stored and, as was common practice at the time, subsequently used in other unrelated, ongoing genetic studies, and distributed to researchers within ASU and their collaborators at other institutions. The researchers obtained IRB approval from ASU for studies on diabetes and schizophrenia; however, Havasupai participants alleged that researchers had failed to make clear that the samples may be used for studies on schizophrenia and that no expanded informed consent was sought. Since mental illness is highly stigmatized in the Havasupai culture, tribe members asserted that they would not have consented to such research had they been properly informed. The tribe also alleged that researchers gained illegal access to Havasupai medical records by entering the local medical clinic and removing secured files without permission from tribal officials or clinic administrators.

In April 2010, the *Havasupai Tribe v. Arizona Board of Regents* case reached a settlement in the tribe's favor: tribe members received $700,000 in direct compensation, funds for a tribal clinic and school, and, most significantly from the standpoint of several tribe members, the return of the tribe's DNA samples. The settlement signified closure for tribe members, and they took the DNA samples home to properly dispose of them in a culturally appropriate ceremony. Many Native Americans view DNA as a valuable part of one's personhood, not as a material object. However, in the contemporary US research context, DNA samples are generally considered the property of the research institution once they are obtained, and researchers almost never return biological material to participants. The return of the Havasupai samples meant the end of all future studies with those samples.

The return of DNA samples is of great significance because it challenges notions of biomaterial ownership in research, and what constitutes value and for whom. DNA is essential to genetic research: samples are typically banked or kept in laboratory freezers, sometimes for decades, and used for multiple studies across many years. Researchers value the ability to use these samples to study disease association, population substructure, evolutionary history, and other biomedical studies. Fewer restrictions on sample usage allows researchers to stretch their research dollars by using samples for multiple studies. Researchers study DNA to make important discoveries, publish the findings, and advance their careers, all of which bring financial gain and recognition. Because researchers and institutions assume ownership of DNA samples, many researchers have used them without much thought about how the donors of the samples might react. However, the case brought by the Havasupai Tribe challenged these notions of ownership, introducing a power struggle over appropriate use and stewardship of the samples.

In May 2003, the Havasupai Tribe issued a "Banishment Order," barring all ASU researchers and employees from the Havasupai Nation and halting all research. The Inter Tribal Council of Arizona and the National Congress of American Indians each passed resolutions supporting the Havasupai Tribe. Coincidentally, the year before the Havasupai Tribe learned of the sample misuse, the Navajo Nation passed a moratorium in 2002 on genetic research within their boundaries. The lawsuit brought by the Havasupai Tribe raised several new questions for the Navajo Nation and other tribes. The lawsuit revealed not only distrust in outside medical researchers, but also several claims of injustice: harm and lack of human subject protection, the unequal distribution of "benefits" from participating in research, and questions of community exploitation by researchers. In doing so, the lawsuit has made tribes reluctant to alter research policies, and the moratorium remains in effect in 2020. As a consequence of the lawsuit and prior instances of genetic research injustices, many tribes continue to refuse participation in genetic research despite researchers' ongoing efforts to recruit them.

The effect on the scientific research communities, however, is largely unknown. Because the case was never tried in court, the settlement left no formal legal precedent for changes in informed consent procedures, recommendations on secondary uses of samples, or considerations for vulnerable populations in research. Researchers and oversight boards, such as IRBs, were given no clear guidance on what changes should be made to existing procedures. But the lawsuit brought by the Havasupai Tribe challenges notions of informed consent, particularly with vulnerable populations, by signaling that broad consent forms and incomplete disclosure did not bring about the full understanding of research participation necessary for truly informed consent. When the case settled, it was covered in numerous scientific publications, including *Nature* magazine and the *New England Journal of Medicine*, in addition to appearing on the front page of the *New York Times* and in *Phoenix Magazine*.

The case raised issues of just and respectful research practices involving Indigenous people. In particular, it highlighted the effects of research harms on the community, challenged the appropriateness of certain types of research, and questioned the adequacy of informed consent. Yet several questions remain: what is just research, by whom and from whose perspective is justice determined, and how might research be conducted in a more just manner? The specific implications of this case on the conduct of genetic researchers and IRBS in the United States has not been thoroughly explored. As such, the broader impact of the lawsuit on biomedical research remains largely unknown.

In a journal article published in *Science, Technology & Human Values* in 2012, I examined the way researchers and IRB experts think about and implement informed consent practices in research studies, particularly in light of the settlement of the case brought by the Havasupai Tribe. I interviewed IRB chairpersons and biomedical faculty researchers engaged in human genetic research at six top National Institutes of Health–funded medical schools across the United States. In particular, I focused on the silence around justice and equity in genetic research involving Indigenous populations. By only addressing consent and not cultural concerns, I argued, researchers will fail to achieve justice for those communities participating in research. IRBs follow human subjects regulations to ensure that requirements are met regarding minimal risk, informed consent, and participant confidentiality. However, there appears to be a constant "slippage between norms and practices" when IRBs generally fail to take a step further to ensure just and equitable research inclusion across all populations.

Most of the researchers and IRB chairs that I interviewed either reported hearing about the case through the *New York Times* article or could not remember the exact news source from which they learned of it. Some also alluded to institutional discussions and mentions of the case at national meetings. Knowledge of the case ranged from limited (i.e., not being able to remember the tribe name, the correct researcher institution, or that the case resulted in a settlement) to extensive (i.e., knowing the case complaints, the issues that were raised, and the settlement terms). Some respondents defended the investigators at ASU, arguing the informed consent form may have been adequate, and one researcher thought the consent forms may have been "sufficiently broad" (Researcher Int11) to allow them to carry out additional studies unrelated to diabetes. This researcher continued:

I'm not necessarily stating that there should have been sanctions. I think it does serve as a wake-up call, probably to both investigators and IRBs that they be a little more careful and more specific as to what they say they're going to do and what they do do, and certainly can put blame on both parties. Not criminal blame, again I don't think anybody did anything illegal but bordering on unethical.

The IRB chairs showed more concern than did researchers about ensuring that informed consent forms were worded in a way that protected the participant, the researcher, and the institution. However, just and equitable research inclusion cannot be achieved if we do not address the main cultural concerns of smaller populations that deter them from participation in research. In short, a "one size" informed consent form does not fit all persons for all time.

Furthermore, science is constantly changing, so informed consent must change with it. However, it is difficult to predict the studies that one can do with old samples that exist today, as another researcher (Researcher Int17) described by asking, "How do you deal with the dynamic nature of science? . . . We can't really foresee what we can do with the sample now versus what we can do with it 10 years from now." This burdensome and confusing issue in dealing with old samples puts some researchers and IRB chairs in a complicated situation: Do they hold onto the samples and apply the standards of informed consent today, or do they apply the standards from the time the samples were collected? And would secondary uses of old samples undermine the expectation that research participants had for what studies would be performed with their samples? Researchers have shared their samples (gathered with broad consent terms) with others in their labs and their collaborators, or passed them on as "legacy collections" to young investigators who are starting their research careers.

Some researchers choose not to worry about research ethics, forcing the IRB to take a more active role in ensuring that research ethics guidelines are followed and enforced. As whole genome sequencing technologies have advanced, IRB chairs have been creating informed consent templates to ensure that research participants fully understand the study, and to address issues of privacy and implications for family members. However, broad consent forms might prove to be too vague for many potential research participants to understand, as was demonstrated in the lawsuit brought by the Havasupai Tribe, and may not allow for fair and equitable research opportunities for Indigenous participants. Rather, these broad consent forms can act as a "cover" for researchers to do a wide range of research and be legally protected, rather than addressing specific concerns of unique communities of participants.

As IRB protocols stand now, the only choice given to study participants is whether to participate or not; if one chooses to participate, one must opt in to all potential uses. The only alternative posed here is to not participate, leaving little room for negotiation between researchers and research participants. And simply de-identifying samples in order to use them for studies beyond the informed consent is not a solution; the research may have implications for the community that identifies with that population, particularly in cases in which population-based information may reveal potentially stigmatizing information for other individuals of the same population or ethnic group.

As scientists build on published knowledge and advance their careers and discipline, communities seldom receive any tangible benefits from research participation. It is important to note that the lawsuit brought by the Havasupai Tribe was dismissed because of procedural error, resulting in no legal precedent, but it did prompt valuable discussions to happen in scientific fields. Other cases involving issues with informed consent and secondary uses of samples have come to light over the last twenty years: concerns were raised about the syphilis studies on African American males in Tuskegee, uses of newborn screening samples in research without informed consent from parents, and cancer cells removed from Henrietta Lacks that were then cultured and used in research without her knowledge. In response, policy makers, bioethicists, and IRBs have been suggesting more stringent review processes, more detailed consent forms, and additional human subjects protections, including increased communication and disclosure to research participants. Failing to take the initiative to engage a community in discussions about the research that involves them, and to modify informed consent templates to address their specific concerns, will further marginalize these groups and make them less likely to participate in future research.

This case study reveals the necessity of thinking deeply about the role of regulation and justice issues in genomics research or any IRB-approved research in general. We must remain mindful of the diverse views of research participants, and work harder to ensure that just and equitable research practices encourage communication and inclusion of minorities in research in order to break down the barriers of distrust. Open communication and transparency go a long way toward building trust with researchers and are vital to successful research endeavors.

NOTE

For full references, see the original published version of this piece: Nanibaa' A. Garrison, "Genomic Justice for Native Americans: Impact of the Havasupai Case on Genetic Research." *Science, Technology & Human Values* 38.2 (2013): 201–223.

14. Publishing Your Research

ROSANNA KATHLEEN OLSEN

You have completed your final data analysis and are ready to start writing a journal article. You open your laptop, start your word-processing program, and stare at the blank screen. You watch the cursor blink about twenty times as you debate about where to begin. You watch the cursor blink twenty more times before you decide it is time to take a coffee break (surely you will be able to write that first sentence after a cappuccino or strong cup of tea!).

This essay will help you avoid the above scenario and provide advice about how to write more efficiently, avoid common "traps" that plague many academics (whether early or advanced), and offer guidance for navigating the current world of academic publishing.

We all know that the first step in publishing your research is preparing your manuscript. However, "preparing your manuscript" is typically an extended process which can take weeks, even months, to complete. It can be overwhelming to decide where to start and which parts of the manuscript to tackle first. You may even delay the start of the writing process because you do not feel ready to write—because you want to perform further statistical analyses on the data, or perform a more thorough literature review. Try, however, not to put too much pressure on yourself and believe that the first draft has to be absolutely perfect. There will be plenty of time during the revision process to tinker with the data and refine your writing.

Breaking up the manuscript into manageable parts is an important first step so that the task does not feel so daunting. Instead of thinking about the manuscript as one thirty-page document, think of it as four (or more) smaller portions, and this will make the task of writing your paper feel much more manageable.

Note that while this essay was written from the perspective of a scientific researcher, much of this advice will be of value for scholars who work in other disciplines.

1. PREPARING YOUR MANUSCRIPT

My students, who primarily have backgrounds in psychology, biology, and neuroscience, often assume that a manuscript should be written in the order that it is typically read (i.e., Introduction first). However, if you are writing up a scientific experiment, or set of experiments, I recommend preparing your manuscript in the following order: (1) Methods section; (2) Figures and Results; (3) Introduction; (4) Discussion. These recommendations will help you complete each section of your paper.

The methods section of your manuscript should be the first one that you prepare. Ideally, this section should be written during the planning or data-collection phase of your study. Writing down the pertinent details about your experiment (e.g., number of trials, duration of study phase, etc.) can save tremendous amounts of time, frustration, and backtracking if completed concurrently with data collection. It can be easy to overlook this when you are hyperfocused on data collection, but your future self will be extremely grateful to have at least most of this section written prior to the completion of the study. Of course, this does require updating any details that get tweaked along the way during the piloting of your study. Even if the details of your experiment change, many aspects of your study will not (e.g., computer screen resolution used in the experiment) and can be easily described. Furthermore, the methods section will typically be written in the same way (or in a similar way) no matter where you submit your paper, so this section can usually be written without knowing where the paper will be published.

In addition to saving time and heartache later in the writing process, writing the methods section helps obviate the anxiety that comes with staring at a blank screen and blinking cursor. Even just setting up a title page (with a tentative title), thinking of keywords, inserting page numbers, and formatting your document according to the journal-specific format can help ease the anxiety. In addition, starting with the methods section does not require the same type of pontification that is required by the discussion section, which can bog down the academic. You will likely need to write and rewrite the first sentence of your introduction to get it "just right," but the methods section is straightforward, and doesn't require the brainpower needed for other portions of the paper.

Now that you've written the methods section, it's time to mock up some figures and start writing up the main results of the paper. These are the meat and potatoes of the paper, and it is important to work on this section while the data and analyses are still fresh in your mind. Think about which figures will be necessary for the depiction of your study, and create some draft figures that will serve as anchors as you write the results section. I typically spend a significant amount of time perfecting my figures; however, this beautification step can wait until you know which figures will make the final cut prior to submission. To start, make sure your figures are in decent-enough shape to send to your coauthors, and then you can return later to the figures to finalize the font sizes and other elements. If possible, try to automatize as many steps of your figure creation as possible, so that you can make any necessary adjustments as efficiently as possible. Document any computer code that you use to make your figures, and make sure you have a system in place that allows you to track which piece of computer code was used to make each figure. Remember that your figure numbers may change during the revision process, so you might not want to name each file by the figure number alone. When preparing the figures and figure legends, you can keep a note for yourself and your coauthors within the manuscript document with a link to the analysis code or filename you used for each figure.

I find that writing the results section is also more straightforward than writing the introduction and discussion sections, as you are simply reporting the analyses you conducted and the patterns in the data. However, you may want to begin thinking about the journal to which you plan to submit your paper at this stage. Some journals may have their own idiosyncratic reporting style, or they will direct you to a particular style guide (e.g., *Publication Manual of the American Psychological Association*). Moreover, some journals will require you to report effect sizes along with other more traditional statistical values such as t-scores and p-values. Paying attention to any field or journal-specific nomenclature or formatting requirements at the outset will save time down the line, so that you do not need to repeat your data analyses or spend time editing the style. This information can typically be found on the journal website, under a section usually titled "Instructions for Authors." Remember, as you finalize your results section, you will likely need to update the methods section with additional details of the statistical analyses performed on your data.

After finishing a draft of the methods, figures, and results, it is time to write the introduction. The introduction section should contain 1) a summary of the existing background literature on the topic of the current study; 2) a description of the unanswered questions in the literature your study will address; and 3) a brief description of the current study. Some authors opt to include a brief description of the study results in the introduction as well. As with the results section, you will need to keep any journal or field-specific style requirements in mind when writing the introduction. If you know that the journal you plan to submit to has a word limit on the length of the introduction, you will want to keep this in mind while writing. However, I typically find it is easier to write the first draft of my introduction "long," and then trim and rewrite this section to fit the word limit during the editing process. Be very careful to perform a thorough literature search and reference any similar papers appropriately. Remember, reviewers will be very upset to read, "this is the first paper to do X . . ." when five other papers have examined a similar research question!

Finally comes the discussion section. Some authors love writing this portion, while others loathe it. The discussion section should summarize the results of your study and explain how your findings relate to current theory and the existing literature. This is also the part of the paper in which you will explain any surprising or unexpected findings and mention any limitations which need to be taken into consideration when interpreting the data. You will also want to include a section which describes any next steps or future directions that would be interesting to pursue, given your current data and results.

2. SELECTING A JOURNAL

Selecting a journal for your paper is an issue that many graduate students, early career academics, and even experienced researchers struggle with. Some scholars—especially those who might be on the job market or trying to strengthen their resume—might want to try to publish their work in the most prestigious journal possible. However, journal prestige is not the only factor to consider when selecting a home for your paper. It is important to choose a journal that has the right audience for your work. Even in this digital age, when most academics read work digitally through online journal subscriptions provided by their university, selecting a journal that has the correct readership for your work can still play a role in whether your paper is read or cited.

In general, I make this decision by first thinking about which journals publish work that I typically read, and especially work that is similar in theme to the work I am attempting to publish. Pay attention to the "Instructions for Authors" page on the journal website, so that you do not waste time submitting your paper to a journal that has a policy to not publish manuscripts of a given type (e.g., some neuroscience journals will publish descriptions of single clinical cases and some will not). If you are not sure where to send your paper, ask colleagues in your subject area which journals they typically read. Similarly, you can ask your more senior colleagues whether a certain journal has a good or bad reputation in terms of the quality of the research that they publish.

When you select a journal, it can also be helpful to look at the members of the journal's editorial board. This is important because in some cases, you can request that a particular editor be assigned to your paper. You can then ask your mentor or a colleague whether they have had a good experience at a certain journal or with a certain editor. Journal editors vary in terms of their responsiveness to authors' questions and concerns, and this variability will play a role in your publishing experience.

Other issues that can influence your journal decision is whether the journal has an "open-access" policy, or whether the journal typically has a fast or slow turnaround on either their desk rejections (i.e., when the editor decides not to send a paper out for review), or the review process. Regarding the former, some newer online journals are open access by default, whereas other journals that are edited by more established publishing houses will sometimes offer an "open-access option" for authors who want to make their papers available without a journal subscription. Keep in mind that both open-access journals and journals that offer an open-access option will typically charge a significant publication fee (which is generally paid by the author, using grant or departmental funding), ostensibly to cover the lost revenue that comes along with fewer journal subscriptions or paid-access articles.

Many students ask how long it will take to hear back from a journal once they have submitted their paper and it gets sent out for review. This varies widely from journal to journal, and can range from about one month to six months (or more). Remember that journal editors are usually researchers or professors too, with a number of other obligations associated with their "regular job," not to mention their family and personal lives (I know that many editors often attend to their journal duties late at night or on the weekend). Always keep this in mind when you are sending correspondence to an editor (or complaining on social media about a slower response from a journal).

Be aware that there are a number of predatory journals that will often solicit research using a "pay-to-play" model. Some of these journals even falsely claim to provide the same type of peer-review process as a traditional journal. However, it has been revealed that many of these predatory journals do not provide the same level of peer review as more traditional journals. There have been shocking examples of completely fabricated hoax papers that seem to not have even been proofread prior to publication (see "Testing Inter-Hemispheric Social Priming Theory in a Sample of Professional Politicians—A Brief Report," by Gerry Jay Louis [pseudonym], at the fictional Institute of Interdisciplinary Political and Fecal Science, for one amusing example).

If you have not heard back from a journal after three or four months, I recommend contacting the editor to politely ask about the delay. Typically, they will be able to give you an update soon thereafter about the status of your paper. In some extreme cases, an editor might have a difficult time finding appropriate reviewers for your paper, or a reviewer might not be able to complete the review on time, which will extend the review process. Sometimes, a paper can "fall off the editor's radar" and just needs to be called back to their attention. If you have not heard back from the editor in six months or longer, or you find out that the paper has not been sent out for review in that same amount of time, I would consider pulling it from the first journal and submitting to another journal.

3. RESPONDING TO REVIEWERS

After your paper has been peer-reviewed, the handling editor will recommend whether your paper should be accepted as written (this is very rare); whether minor or major revisions are needed (more common); or whether the paper should be rejected or is not suitable for the journal to which it was submitted. If the editor decides, based on the reviewers' comments, that you can revise and resubmit, you should give yourself a pat on the back. This does not necessarily mean that your paper will be accepted, but it does mean that if you can adequately address the reviewers' questions and concerns, your paper will have a good chance of acceptance at that journal.

Responding to reviewers can be time-consuming and frustrating, but your manuscript can be considerably improved by the editor's and reviewers' suggestions. The review process can reveal which sections of your paper are not clear, or if you accidentally forgot to provide certain details that are important for understanding the data or paradigm. Thank the reviewers for their helpful suggestions and time, as this will signal that you have taken their suggestions seriously. Reviewers will sometimes have different theoretical interpretations for the data, and these conflicts will have to be addressed. Always be respectful and polite when responding to your reviewers (even if they have misunderstood a part of your paper) and remember that you will be on the "other side" of the review process soon enough.

Keep in mind that you should try to comply with as many of the reviewers' requests as possible, within reason. If a reviewer suggests that you use a completely novel tool or start your data analysis from scratch without sufficient justification, you as author can use your discretion regarding whether this request is reasonable. When in doubt, ask the journal editor for guidance, and they can offer their opinion regarding the reviewer's suggestions.

4. AUTHORSHIP AND COAUTHORSHIP

Authorship issues are another area that can be difficult to navigate. I recommend having a conversation with potential coauthors as early as possible, so that you are aware of your colleagues' expectations regarding inclusion or exclusion from the author line. Similarly, it is important to have an open dialogue with your coauthors about the order in which you will be listed on the author line. In some fields, the person who writes the article is the first author (often a graduate student or other trainee), and the person who funds the study is the last author (often the research supervisor). However, these traditions are field-specific and will vary across disciplines. The number of authors included will also vary quite widely across research areas, depending on the collaborative or multidisciplinary nature of the work. In some fields, it is common to give authorship to undergraduate research assistants who assist with data collection; in other fields it is not. In either case, it is important to have an open conversation with your mentor, colleagues, and trainees about what is expected from them in order to "earn" authorship for a given project. Similarly, if you borrow data or collaborate with another researcher during a limited time period of the project, you should discuss with them as early as possible whether their contribution was substantial enough to warrant authorship. In cases that a collaborator assists with the project but is not listed as an official coauthor, it is good practice to thank them for their contribution in the acknowledgments section of the paper.

5. MAKING DATA "OPEN"

There is now a good deal of momentum behind the debate about making data and code used in your research "open" or available to the public after your manuscript has been published. There are clearly many scientific and economic advantages of data sharing and open-access data. For example, trainees and more junior researchers who do not have the same financial resources as more established researchers can ask follow-up questions or perform novel analyses on published data without having to pay for an entirely new dataset. In addition, data on similar topics can be combined across research sites to increase statistical power. Some federal funding bodies now encourage providing access to data to improve transparency. Similarly, some journals now require data sharing, although adherence to these data-sharing requirements seems to be quite mixed. It does seem that in the future, more and more journals will require access to data and code, so this should be kept in mind even during the data collection and analysis stages of your study. If you plan to share your data and code, you will want to make sure that your data is organized and well documented. Keep detailed notes so that a person unfamiliar with your study will understand how the data are coded, and that the critical information for the replication of your data analyses is available.

Prior to sharing your data, additional logistical issues need to be considered. For example, when participants signed their consent forms, did they consent to having their data shared? How will you protect privacy and other personal information from being inadvertently transmitted if you share your data? These are issues that your Research Ethics Review Board can help you navigate. Many research institutions are now working to put procedures in place to facilitate data sharing and protect participant privacy. The standardization of data-sharing procedures will help researchers comply with data-sharing requests by funding bodies and collaborators.

To conclude, here are my Dos and Don'ts of Research Manuscript Writing:

Do write your methods section as soon as you collect your data, or even as you design your study.

Don't wait until your data is analyzed to start writing your research methods section. It will be much easier to remember or check these methodological details during the design/collection phase than months (or even years) later!

Do set deadlines for yourself and break up your manuscript into manageable parts.

Don't get stuck in the "just one more analysis before I start writing" trap.

Do stay open to change—the final paper might look very different from the one you originally planned to write.

Don't remain inflexible with regard to the "story" you want to tell. The data are the data.

Do use a reference manager (e.g., EndNote, Mendeley, Paperpile) to take care of your reference list and format your references for the specific journal to which you are applying.

Don't wait until you finish writing your article to add the references. Try to add them in as you write.

Do have someone else read over your paper one last time before submitting to catch any typos or spelling mistakes that you (or your computer program) missed.

Do use language that is accessible to readers not in your immediate discipline.

Don't use too many subfield-specific acronyms that will confuse your reviewers and/or journal editors.

Do provide the names of a number of potential reviewers—journal editors appreciate this! However, avoid suggesting potential reviewers you know personally, or who will appear to have a conflict of interest.

15. Academic Book Publishing

CATHY N. DAVIDSON AND KEN WISSOKER

Academics share ideas and information in many forms. Over much of the previous century, that would have included face-to-face lectures or conversations by letter or phone, in addition to publication in books and journals. Now, at the time of this writing, if you ask an academic where they saw the smartest thing they read that week, the answer might be on a blog; in a born-digital project; on Twitter, Facebook, or another social media location; or in an email exchange, as well as in any of those earlier forms. These new modes of scholarly communication have changed book publishing several times over. They also offer new considerations for scholars deciding how best to publish their work.

Despite these massive changes in the scholarly ecology, books still have a central place. Around the turn of the millennium, many prognosticators predicted the book would not survive the first decade of the new century. Instead, books are alive and well, though now widely available in digital as well as paper form. That is in part because a book allows the presentation of a long-form argument where a scholar can present both their research and its implications, allowing space for depth and development not always available in shorter forms. Even the short book composed around a long essay will have more room for ideas and narrative than the longest *New Yorker* article. A journal article in a field can present a good reading of a novel or a focused ethnographic or historical study. A book needs to have a greater reach and ambition, so is a different kind of challenge for authors and publishers. While a book is now one of a greater number of alternative ways to convey one's research and ideas, it is still a central form to master.

In most humanities fields and many in the social sciences, the publication of a book with a reputable academic press is the key to jobs, advancement, merit raises, and professional status. As with anything with such life-altering power, the academic publishing process is often shrouded in mystery and fraught with anxiety. We hope to demystify that process by providing clear guidelines for selecting a press, submitting a manuscript for publication, seeing your manuscript through to its publication as a book, and then shepherding that book once it is out in the world.

What Is Academic Book Publishing?

Academic publishing is that slice of the large and varied publishing world dedicated to books geared to higher education. There are many kinds of academic publications: textbooks, short introductions, handbooks, reference guides, collections of essays, readers or anthologies of previously published materials, monographs, and broad synthetic works. Some of these publications are meant primarily for students, some for colleagues in a field or subfield, some for academics working across fields on a topic or area. Some works are aimed primarily at academics, others primarily at the general public; some assume the reader knows most of what the author knows, others assume the reader will be brought into the terrain for the first time.

Different kinds of books are associated with particular kinds of publishers. There are textbook publishers as well as publishers that specialize in scholarly editions for teaching. Some publishers aim to reach the broadest public and others specialize in a specific discipline. While most publishers stretch across at least some of these categories, they are also mostly organized to focus on the areas most central to their enterprise.

A textbook publisher hires college representatives, salespeople who will go door to door from school to school, urging professors to adopt their company's books rather than another publisher's. Such a textbook can be immensely successful without ever appearing on a bookstore's shelves outside the area set aside for course sales. By contrast, a trade publisher hires sales representatives who visit bookstores, presenting the new books that are about to be published in the next few months. These books may or may not be adopted in a course, but, in most cases, course adoptions will not be crucial to their success. Their primary audience is the book-buying public.

This essay will concentrate on scholarly book publishing. Writing textbooks or reference works are their own subjects, and the reader will need to consult other guides.

The bulk of this essay will focus on university press publishing but, before we turn our attention to that topic, we will look briefly at the other forms of scholarly book publishing. For scholarly writing, there are three main classes of publishers: trade publishers such as Random House or Norton; academic commercial publishers such as Palgrave or Wiley; and university presses. The first question you must ask is which type of press is best suited to your work and your goals. This is a complex question and there is no simple answer. However, once you have signed a contract with a press, your book will be published according to the implicit and explicit rules of that particular type of publishing. Before you make a decision about which kind of press to choose, you need to be realistic about how your book will be treated, what its sales might be, and how long it will be kept in print, for these matters all vary with the type of publisher.

Trade Presses

Trade houses, now largely parts of bigger international conglomerates, are looking to make money from the books they publish. They are also looking for certain kinds of prestige, but on a very large scale. A book must have strong potential to reach a general audience—the so-called literate general public. That means that trade potential will vary with subject. World War II historians will have more possibilities for a trade publication than will their counterparts studying the working class in Buenos Aires.

For trade publications, writing style is at a premium. These are books written for those who are not obligated to read them. They are not assignments; they are not part of the scholarly requirements of others in a specific field. Trade books need to be accessible to readers with no background on the subject, while not condescending to their readers. For trade books, the academic is assumed to be the expert on the subject. The publisher will not be obtaining peer reviews or checking to see if the theory is up to date or the right experts in the field cited. The publisher may, however, have the book rigorously evaluated by the house lawyer to make sure there is nothing that can be seen as potentially libelous about any living subjects mentioned in the book. (The dead have to fend for themselves.)

With few exceptions, the way into a trade publisher is through an agent. Agents are the gatekeepers. They sort out what even gets presented to trade editors. But that makes it often difficult to obtain an agent. Agents make money by taking a percentage (generally 20 percent) of the proceeds of a book, so they have no reason to take on projects that they are not confident they will be able to sell at a high price. There are many places that list agents, but referrals from colleagues that have them may be the most successful way of getting a hearing. Agents also have specialties, so locating one who handles your type of project is essential.

In the world of trade publishing, nonfiction books are usually sold by a prospectus. An interested agent will spend a good deal of time with you to help craft a proposal the agent feels is saleable. Such proposals form their own genre, and, in the course of shaping a prospectus, you may find that your project has taken on forms you hadn't considered or predicted. This is, once again, because an agent's charge is to find the most saleable angle, not the angle that will make the biggest impact in the author's discipline. Methodological issues may need to disappear, while a gripping but minor part of the narrative is brought to the fore. If you don't like shaping your subject in this way—and having an editor shape your project for you, according to a trade concept of "market"—you should think twice about trade publishing.

Once an agent deems the proposal to be satisfactory, they will then pitch the book to all the editors they think will like it. The pitch may start with a lunch conversation or with emailing the proposal to likely editors. Hopefully, there will be a few editors interested. Perhaps they will want to meet the author and, ideally, they will make a bid on the book. If not, the agent will go to a next set of possibilities. If a satisfactory bid on the book is made, the agent will negotiate the contract. It is not infrequent now for an author to be asked to hire a "book doctor" (also known as a "developmental editor") who will work on the text for a fee paid by the author herself. Some editors still line-edit their books, sometimes agents will offer editorial advice, but being asked to hire a professional book doctor—often a former editor or agent who has gone into business for herself—has become very common. None of this is hard or fixed.

In the time that *The Academic's Handbook* has gone through its four editions, the publishing world has undergone drastic changes. Besides the consolidation of independent houses into larger international publishing conglomerates such as Hachette or Bertelsmann, there has been a decrease in the amount of space for academic work at this level of trade publishing. Some of the largest publishers who used to publish scholarly books no longer do so, and the number of trade publishers specializing in these high-end areas has decreased. Again, this varies a good deal by discipline and topic, but most would agree that the bottom line has become more and more important over this period, leaving less room for the serious book coming out of the academy.

At the same time, the growth of social media and academics on social media has given some academic authors an audience and a space for their ideas that is new and, in many cases, truly inspiring. Scholars are able to reach audiences beyond their field and the academy. Those with a following may have readers seeking out their books—and agents or editors who are eager to work with them. This might be similar to a kind of public intellectual success an academic might have had in an earlier era through writing for magazines or newspapers. The current moment is more democratic and also rewards a different set of writing and networking skills.

The advantages of trade publishing have also changed over this period. Bookstores and review media are now only part of a wider landscape of sales and publicity. Over the last few decades, the number of independent bookstores has sharply decreased from what it was, though some such stores have bounded back in this "shop local" moment. Chain bookstores that once drove independents out of business are not in good shape themselves. Chain stores have carried serious and even academic books at times, but they are very bottom-line oriented and mostly feature the titles that sell the best. To have a book included in a display in these stores often requires paying a fee, something trade publishers are in a better position to do than are scholarly presses. Over the last ten or fifteen years, book review sections in newspapers and magazines have shrunk or been cut almost entirely, making it even less likely that your book will be reviewed there. In these and other ways, there are more and more books trying to get attention in fewer and fewer of the older conventional spaces.

Again, there is a counterstory here. At the same time that other venues have shrunk, participatory media—online book clubs, Amazon reviews, Goodreads, and blogs with book recommendations—have increased in popularity and in reach. In some ways, the shrinking of the physical independent or chain bookstore has been replaced by the expansion of online reading recommendations. For any author with a new book, a social media platform is a way of getting out their ideas. These platforms include relevant and often topic-specific book groups, blogs, participatory forums, and a variety of mainstream and specialized journalistic outlets. Other features of the new social media publishing landscape include Twitter threads with hashtags, author websites, and author profiles on the sites of publishers, booksellers, distributors, and beyond. This wide array of social media sites helps to publicize work both in specialized fields and in related other fields, and have become a substitute for or complement to the remaining actual, physical neighborhood bookstores. Even as there are signs of some of those bookstores reappearing again, especially in academic communities, the online interaction amplifies while, conversely, also competing. It's more than anecdotal that people wander through the local bookstore taking photos of books that they will then order at a discount on Amazon or for their Kindle.

A publisher with clout and resources can be a huge advantage, at least if you are trying to reach a general audience. That large publishers have tools at their disposal doesn't mean they use them on every book. Not by a long shot. Someone estimated that at the big houses, 95 percent of the resources go to 5 percent of the books, which are expected to bring in 95 percent of the revenue. It is not uncommon to hear academics, perhaps used to a more hands-on university press experience, or having big crossover dreams, complain that their trade press didn't take out ads or support their book in the ways they thought they could expect. Academics are often unrealistic about sales figures. Serious scholarly books published by commercial presses, even with the best advertising, may well sell less than ten thousand copies. The academic's fantasy of getting rich through trade publication is, in 90 percent of the cases, just that: a fantasy.

Still, there is no question that having the trade name on the spine, having a sales force dedicated to selling the publisher's books, and having coordinated and connected publicity can be an advantage for certain kinds of books. A particular book may do better as a big fish in a smaller pond at an academic publisher, but such examples—and they are plentiful—are notable because they buck the trend. Typically, if a trade publisher pays a large advance for a book, the company will work as hard as is necessary to recoup that cost. Once the book is no longer new, there is often a significant diminishing of attention to the book or its author. The familiar adage of trade authors is that a book has ninety days to make its mark; after that, the publicists and editors at trade houses turn their attention to new books or to their list's top sellers. In the end, once a book is no longer selling, it is likely to be shredded or remaindered. Trade publishers are not known for their sentimental attachment to keeping books in print after they've stopped paying their way. They are not known for giving up rights either, so the book may stay in print, but only be available as an e-book or in a print-on-demand form.

University Presses

University presses are justly known for their attention to scholarly content and for keeping books in print. But, of course, publishing with a university press comes with its own positives and negatives. University presses themselves vary greatly, from small presses that publish a handful of books a year to large ones that have multiple divisions and publish hundreds—or in the cases of Oxford and Cambridge, thousands—of books each year. Some may focus more on regional concerns, others are more heavily academic. Most publish some books aimed at nonacademic audiences, and most have at least part of their list devoted to scholarship. Within the scholarly part of the list even the largest presses have areas in which they specialize, and whole other fields that are barely represented.

With few exceptions, book manuscripts submitted to university presses will be peer-reviewed. Though procedures vary greatly (as will be explained later in this essay), scholars in the field read a manuscript and it also goes before a press board composed of faculty of the hosting university, who must give their imprimatur on behalf of the university before the book can be published.

While in some countries a university press will publish work primarily or solely from its own university, in the United States, university presses almost always operate independently in choosing which titles to publish. It's rare for more than a small percentage of titles to originate at the press's home institution and these will generally be the result of a particular coincidence of interests, rather than some preplanned program or obligation.

University presses can be expected to speak the language of scholarship. Acquisition editors at most presses have one or more areas of academic responsibility, depending on the size and structure of a particular press. While they do not necessarily have formal academic training in these areas, they attend scholarly meetings, track intellectual trends, and are responsible for guiding presses' presence in these disciplines. They solicit manuscripts and choose which books their press should publish, and then help explain and situate the scholarship for other people at the press. Marketing departments at a university press will be familiar with many of the meetings, journals, and priorities in the fields in which the press publishes. However much they are also concerned about sales, the press as a whole will take pride in the recognition and awards that a book receives from its scholarly audience.

Approximately one hundred university presses publish the work of all the scholars from all the universities in the United States. Not every university has a press and almost all university presses lose money publishing academic books. They publish scholarly books because that is their mission. University presses exist to publish scholarship that would not be viable in an open market. Some presses make up their losses from scholarly publishing through subsidies from their own institutions. A few are fortunate to have endowments or publish certain kinds of books (varying from regional guides and histories for state presses to ESL—English as a Second Language—texts and Bibles for Oxford or Cambridge) that are perennially strong sellers.

Sometimes one part of the press cross-subsidizes another part. For example, a large journal-publishing operation might cross-subsidize the books division of the press. Still other presses run warehousing operations that make enough money to pay for scholarship. More and more, individual authors in the humanities and social sciences are being asked to help seek subventions from foundations or their own institutions (in a manner analogous to the way scientists pay a per-page fee for articles published in refereed science journals).

At this point in time, scholarly publishing will only succeed with one form of subsidy or another. Every scholar must be concerned about the economics of scholarly publishing because, in a way different from and yet also analogous to trade publishers, trying to stay as close as possible to a "break even" point makes a difference in which scholarly books university presses publish. A press can be proud when a book wins the prize for best in its field—but if that book then only sells five hundred copies, the press will have to publish another book, somewhere, that will make up the amount of money that book lost.

Most university presses have sales representatives who sell their books to bookstores, but only the very few largest presses have representatives who work for the press itself and only sell the books of one particular press. Most presses sell their books through consortiums or the use of independent sales groups that work on commission. This means your scholarly book is most likely to be in a bookstore in a college town or in an urban area. Nearly all the books will be available through the main book wholesalers (it's a very concentrated industry) and from online booksellers, which now represent the largest portion of the market. But there is no denying that over the last decade, the amount of bookstore space devoted to university press books has declined as a result of commercial pressures.

University presses will pitch their trade books—the books deemed to be of the most general interest—to reviewers. Although they compete over shrinking space, university press books are still reviewed in major newspapers and magazines. Since university presses operate in the academic sphere, they generally give greater marketing emphasis to reaching the audiences for their books by advertising in academic journals and sending those journals review copies; by direct mail and email to all or part of a disciplinary organization or to those teaching a particular subject; and through displays at academic meetings. Most have active Twitter, Facebook, and Instagram presences as well. The combination of online presence and the easy availability of online purchase has put university presses on a more equal footing than has been the case for many decades.

Commercial Academic Publishers

Within the world of scholarly publishing, there is a good deal of variety. Commercial academic publishers combine aspects of the academic and trade publishers with additional characteristics of their own. They are commercial, often multinational, and frequently part of larger corporate entities that expect a substantial rate of return on their investment. Routledge and Wiley are two examples. Commercial academic publishers may be more academically focused than a given university press, or may have a balance of general-interest titles and specialized ones. Some are oriented toward bookstores; others put most of their marketing energy into reaching scholars directly.

Peer review may or may not be a requirement. Since commercial academic publishers deal with scholars all the time, they are comfortable with peer reviews, but these may be more optional or less binding than at a university press. As with university presses, many scholarly presses specialize in a discipline or group of disciplines; the largest will cover at least as wide a range as the largest university presses.

If university presses can barely break even publishing scholarship, how can commercial academic publishers make a profit doing it? There are a number of answers to this question. Some commercial presses may see less need to publish monographs in a given area, putting more emphasis on general introductions or other works meant for teaching. Some publishers are able to use benefits of scale, in multinational reach or in cutting costs in production. Some mainly publish scholarship in prohibitively expensive library editions. Many publishers are also journal publishers, or reference or textbook publishers, and other parts of the same larger corporation may be involved in distribution or other aspects of the publishing business. Commercial academic publishers may also devote less attention to the details of publishing your work than university presses (which can be artisan-like in attention to details or quality in editing, design, and production).

A Caution about Predatory Publishers

In addition to these three kinds of academic publishers, there are some kinds of publishers at the fringes that one would be wise to be careful about. An older form would be a vanity press, one that requires a fee to publish the book. Such presses will do little to promote the book, or to help a scholar's career. Even the most metrics-oriented administrator pressing their faculty to publish will generally recognize and discount such publications. Similarly, recent years have seen the rise of what are referred to as "predatory publishers" who might aggressively market their services to scholars but do little for the book. In some cases, their model is arranged around collecting open-access fees or publishing with little editorial or design work at inflated prices.

Choosing a Type of Publisher

There are some books that one could imagine having a successful life at all three types of reputable publishers. There are many more books that could be published at either a university press or a commercial academic one. How does one choose which press is right for a given book? This requires a good deal of honesty with oneself about the book itself, a realistic understanding of who is going to read it, and one's reasons for publishing it. What will the reader be expected to know ahead of time? What questions will seem relevant and expected, what citations familiar, what will make the argument convincing? Is the book directed at a particular subdiscipline, or an interdisciplinary space, at those working through a particular question? Is the hope that the book will get the author tenure or promotion? Or to influence national policy? To get on television? To make as much money as possible?

It is difficult to sort through these hopes, plans, and motivations. Often the needs of different readerships guide the text from section to section or paragraph to paragraph, with parts meant to reassure colleagues sitting uneasily next to sentences addressed to an imagined wider audience. Academics will sometimes judge their own work as available to a general audience based on its topic, or because there are large sections that are written with narrative verve. When the work is published, reviewers in general-interest periodicals focus not on these sections but on academic arguments or language, citations, and references to other academic work. Since they expect the whole book to read like trade nonfiction, reviewers point out the parts least accessible and often use them to dismiss the work as "too academic."

You need to be honest about what you are writing and for whom. Beyond that, the best advice is to look at your own bookshelves. What has been published recently in your area, with the slant that you find appealing, and who published it? You will find certain kinds of books clustering at certain presses. If you see yourself in that company, then you should begin the process of trying to place your manuscript by writing to the editors at those presses.

Among university presses, there will usually be a number of plausible options for a given field or subfield. In some fields, senior people will think of those as firmly ranked, in others they will be seen as equally good options. You will want to balance the stature of the publisher, your own rapport with the editor, the place of a given list in the overall direction of the field, and the degree of interdisciplinary orientation in your work and in the press's approach, along with more material considerations such as pricing, the availability of paperback and digital editions, and book design.

Approaching a Scholarly Publisher

If you've decided your book is best suited to a commercial academic press or a university press, what do you do next? At this juncture, the advice is the same for both kinds of academic publishing: Check out the websites. Most presses will have directions for submitting proposals and a list of editors and their areas. The best, most basic advice is to follow those instructions carefully.

After selecting presses that seem best suited to your work, you can contact the press to see if they are interested in you. You might start with a list of five or ten possibilities—this will vary with your field—and then choose to write to your top choice first, or to write to five or six viable ones at the same time, depending on how sure you are of where you would like the book to end up.

There are several common pieces of advice to bear in mind. In general, it is better to write to someone in particular rather than to "Dear Editor" or "Dear Social Science Editor." It shows that you have done some homework. (Using a first and last name is perfectly acceptable for someone you do not know; a first name is fine if you are comfortable using a first name, and an honorific or title is okay if you wish to use one. It turns out this is a question that stymies many authors preparing to send an email. Basically, be polite and go with the form of address with which you feel comfortable and professional.)

Few if any editors will want to see a whole manuscript at this initial query stage unless they have previously requested it. Editors usually will be willing to see a short proposal sent by email attachment, but it's best to check the press's website to be certain. An initial email inquiry about the editor's interest in seeing a prospectus or the suitability of the project for a press is generally welcome, though not at all necessary.

A standard proposal consists of a cover letter explaining the project, a chapter by chapter breakdown, a cv, and a sample chapter or two of the text. The cover letter should emphasize the most important information first: the field of the author, the argument or contribution of the proposed book, and how it will fit into the list of the particular press. It's useful to say something about the intended audience—"graduate students and faculty in political philosophy"—but not useful to extend that audience unrealistically to "everyone interested in issues of race and justice." Remember that the editor will know much more about the market for books in the areas in which the press publishes than you do, so elaborate lists of courses or areas of interest will rarely show you in a good light. Similarly, a shorter cv is fine; the press will not need to know every course you have taught or every guest lecture you gave.

The letter should also explain how much of the manuscript is now ready for review, and your timetable for completion of the full manuscript. If the manuscript is a revision of a dissertation, say so. Explain where you are in the process of revising and the scope of your revisions. If it is a new work, explain what parts are finished. If the editor is interested, they will want to see more. The proposal should be timed so that they can; if an editor writes back excited about the project and soliciting more material, you will want to be able to provide some, not say it will be ready in six or ten months.

From Dissertation to Book

If you are sending an editor a manuscript based on a dissertation, you should not only acknowledge its origins but you should also indicate the ways that the new book departs from the dissertation that spawned it. Almost no scholarly publishers in the United States will publish a dissertation as is, but many first books start their lives as dissertations. The reason that no one will publish them is not pride (or prejudice). It is because in very concrete ways, a dissertation is a radically different genre of writing than the book that arises from that dissertation.

Much has been written about the topic of revising a dissertation into a book. William Germano's *From Dissertation to Book* (2nd ed., University of Chicago Press, 2013) is the best and most comprehensive guide to how to transform a dissertation into a book. And "transform" is the operative word in most cases. The crucial difference between a dissertation and a book is that your committee members are paid to read your dissertation. You wrote it knowing who your readers would be. By the end of the dissertation, you may have made an argument but the purpose of the dissertation is to show you have mastered the field and added something of substance to it. Its purpose is not to argue a position and marshal evidence in a way that supports that argument. Because no one has to read a book, it becomes the author's job to move the reader from the first sentence, paragraph, page, or chapter to the second. Rather than assuming the reader will be willing to slog through all the genuflections and summaries of other scholarly work before getting to the writer's own contribution, in writing a book, you have to present your argument from the start. It becomes the arc and measure of everything else you include in the book. Unlike a dissertation, which may include parts adapted from seminar papers or written so you can make a case that you deserve a job in a particular field (e.g., the chapter on Phillis Wheatley might qualify you for an early Americanist position), every part of a book needs to develop the argument and push it further along.

In short, revising a dissertation is not about salvaging as much of the original as possible. One or even several chapters may turn out to be journal articles and not be part of the final book at all. This may seem frivolous, but it isn't. Finding the best way to make the book's argument is more efficient in the long run than trying to salvage that dissertation—and leads, in the end, to a book manuscript more likely to be accepted for publication.

Submitting Your Manuscript

Presses receive many more proposals than they can possibly publish. Presses often must turn down manuscripts that they could publish with pride, simply because there are more good possibilities than time, staff, or financial considerations allow. Generally, the number of books a press publishes is roughly or even exactly budgeted well in advance. The books it chooses to publish have distinguished themselves in some way from many equally good possibilities.

For that reason, among others, it is worth trying to meet an editor before or at the same time as submitting a proposal. If one is choosing among presses, this is a good way of sorting out who understands the project. The editor can provide much helpful advice not only about how to submit the manuscript but on how to finish it, how long it should be, how it might be organized, and so forth. The editor often has a better grasp of the latest work coming out in a field than many scholars within the field simply by virtue of the stream of new manuscripts constantly coming across her desk.

If you are at or close to the stage of shopping your proposal, you can email prospective editors to see if they will be attending an upcoming academic conference. In general, editors are more likely to attend national disciplinary conferences than local or regional ones, but that will vary with the press, editor, and field. An editor will only have a finite number of slots available to meet with people, and the schedule will include authors and potential authors at all stages of the process, so they may or may not have time to meet at a particular event. Some editors make a practice of being in their press's booth at the conference book exhibit and may encourage you to stop by. Others may offer to make an appointment to talk about your work. They may express interest in seeing a proposal but be too busy at the conference to meet you in person. They may let you know that the project is unlikely to be suitable for their press's list at that time. All of these are productive outcomes.

It is generally not a good idea, at least in most disciplines, to simply plan on walking through the book exhibit hoping to meet editors and talk about your proposal. Editors may or may not be in the booth. If they are there, it's a fine place to introduce yourself, but a poor place to do a standing full pitch for your book, unless asked. It's also not a good idea to pass out copies of your proposal, or to leave copies unsolicited for the editors at the press. Such proposals may or may not make it back to the press itself and rarely would be considered an actual submission requiring a response. You can use your time at the book exhibit at a professional conference to see what various publishers have on display in your area, to talk to the press's representatives in the booth to see what they are most excited about, and, of course, to select the books you most want to buy and read when they are, literally, "hot off the presses."

Once you have made contact with the editor, once you believe your manuscript is ready to be evaluated, you should ask the editor about the next steps. They may want to see a prospectus and a sample chapter, or the entire manuscript. The sample requested may vary if this is a revised dissertation or a second or third book.

If you send a prospectus by mail, the response time will vary from editor to editor and press to press. You may hear back right away or it may take as long as several months. Different editors and presses will have different systems in place—and of course editors' efficiency and habits vary as much as anyone else's. Timing may or may not reflect the level or clarity of interest. Sometimes a quick response will mean an obvious yes or no for the editor; a slow response may mean the editor is traveling or simply backed up. It is fine to check in occasionally after the press has had the proposal for a month or two. One might check with the editorial assistant or contact the editor directly. If a press is your first choice, but other presses are expressing interest, it's usually a good idea to let the editor know.

The Review Process

Typically, an editor reads the material you send and decides whether it suits the needs of the press and has good publishing prospects. The editor may read the whole proposal or just enough to make a decision. That verdict may reflect a judgment about the work itself, its academic interest and importance, or it may be based on the press's priorities—list-building or financial—at the moment. Even if a press has published a lot in an area, they may not be looking for more such books at a particular time. A decision that is based on the work might reflect the topic or the execution, or a combination of both. It's rare to get as much frank feedback about the particulars as you would like, though on occasion a good relationship with an editor can help elicit some guidance.

Once an editor decides to pursue a project, scholarly peer review is the next step in the process. Here, procedures begin to vary from press to press as well as with the stature of the author and the type of book involved. Most academic presses like to have two external reviewers. There are presses that might regularly use more and some that use one reader internal to the press and one external reviewer. Generally, review will be a single-blind process—the readers will know your name, but you will not know theirs, though some presses allow reviewers the option of revealing their identity to the author. In most cases, presses will exclude people at your own institution or, if this is a book developed from your dissertation, members of your dissertation committee or home university. Some editors will be open to suggestions for people who might be appropriate reviewers, or will ask if there is anyone who should be avoided. It's fine to offer to provide such a list. It is not appropriate to try to insist on who the particular readers should be. Some presses will look for a combination of junior and senior readers; or ones presumed to be friendly and less friendly to a particular approach; or someone who knows the theory or method and someone who specializes in the particular subfield; or, in the case of interdisciplinary work, one person from each of the intersecting fields.

With a commissioned book, or a proposal from a very senior person with a long track record in a field, a small amount of material may be all that is required for a review. A reader is presumed to have a lot of extratextual knowledge about the author's ability. In general, the less a reader might know, the more of the manuscript the press might want to send to that reader. Since the readers give helpful advice, the more they see, the more useful their advice can be to first-time authors or to those new at the particular kind of project. Some presses would prefer to send out a whole dissertation with a cover letter about the revision, for example, rather than a revised chapter or two. Writing a single chapter can be like writing a journal article, and may say little about the way the whole argument works.

Reviewers read manuscripts as a service to the profession and are doing this in addition to their other academic obligations. Thus, the time the review process takes is always more unpredictable than presses or authors would like. Some readers read remarkably quickly while others drag on for far too long. You should ask up front how long the press expects the process to take, but also expect considerable variability.

Unlike submission of journal articles, there is no automatic proscription against submitting book manuscripts simultaneously to more than one press. Some presses will only look at some projects if they can look at them exclusively; other presses are willing to compete for a manuscript. If a press asks you if they can consider your manuscript exclusively, it's your choice. If you agree, you are bound by it. The press, of course, is not obligated at all, so if you have initial interest from several presses at an early stage, it would be wise to consult them before agreeing to give one exclusive rights of review.

It is important to know that exclusivity never applies to initial inquiries, only to the review of the manuscript. While exclusivity appears to express enthusiasm, it may also reflect that the press might feel it's not worth their time and effort to send out your book to reviewers if they can't be sure they will be able to sign the book up in the end. If you decide to submit your book simultaneously to more than one press, it is both ethical and useful to let each of the presses know. They will want to know which presses they are competing against, which makes sense. If they want to publish your book, they will need to highlight their strengths against those of the other specific presses.

It is rarely advisable to have more than two or three presses reviewing a manuscript at the same time. The burden of work for the presses and the reviewers in your field grows with each additional press. If your manuscript has made it this far, chances are that if one press wants to go forward to contract, the others will as well. Eventually, you will need to make a decision, which becomes harder as relationships deepen during the process. This is not a situation in which you need a "safety school."

Interestingly, senior scholars, who one might think could have more to gain in a competitive situation, submit simultaneously much less often than junior scholars. If you are a junior scholar with an editor you like who is enthusiastic about your project, you probably will have no need for additional suitors.

After reviews are in, the possible paths begin to vary even more. If the reviews are negative, or discouraging in some way to the press, that may be the end of the process at that press. At some presses, this endpoint may come at the moment of financial reckoning. They might send a manuscript out to see if it seems like a potential prize-winner, but if it is judged to be merely very good, the press may decide that it's not a project they can afford. In most cases, though, if the reviews are generally supportive—even if they make pages of suggestions—the author will be asked to write a response.

Responding to Reviewers

The author response is an unusual genre of writing, and quite different from the response you might offer to a critique of your work in any other forum. In fact, the art of reading and responding to reviews is one of the most important parts of a publishing career.

And it isn't easy. Feedback is seldom easy to accept, especially when it comes on a project on which you've been spending many of your waking hours for three or five years. Learning to accept what you can from readers' reports and to read them with the awareness that someone spent a lot of time reading your manuscript (and for a token fee) is truly an art. Instead of trying to defend your manuscript or arguing that your questioner is off base, when you write your response, you need to assume the responsibility of taking in whatever critique is useful toward the final goal of making your manuscript as good as it can be. Authors often will point to their excellent intentions and good motives. Those are not the issue. The point is how well you are communicating your ideas and your argument.

The review process is the first official test of whether you are succeeding or failing. It can be compared to a Hollywood test screening. If the director expects the audience to be weeping at a certain scene and instead they are giggling, it's not helpful to curse the audience. The director has to go back and recut. The same is true of your manuscript. You control the text; you have to make it work. The response to reviews is an opportunity to say how you will do that.

Sometimes readers will offer contradictory solutions to the same problem. In other words, two readers will focus on the same part of the text but will provide different diagnoses and different prescriptions. Authors often, understandably, feel confused or angered by such contradictions. But what you should try to see is that something important is happening in this aspect of your book, but it isn't quite working. Your readers are trying to find a solution, but you are the author. What they are really saying is that, in one way or another, this is an argument that needs more work, more attention, more development. They may not have the right solution, but they are urging you to pay close attention to this part of your manuscript and to work to develop it successfully.

Editors know that responding to readers' reports is difficult. Your editor will help you write your response and may provide you with some guidelines for the appropriate kind of response necessary to move to the next stage in the publishing process: a contract for your book.

Obtaining a Contract

Once you have responded adequately to your reviewers, procedures will be initiated within the press that will lead to a contract. These procedures vary and your editor will need to explain how the process will work in your case. Often presses have boards, which may be of two types. First, at commercial academic presses and most university presses, there are internal boards involving some combination of editors, sales or marketing people, and the press director; sometimes managing editors, a press financial officer, and managers of design and production also participate. At some presses, the board might be all editors, at others it might include representatives of a number of departments at the press; at some presses, the director may have sole say, at others a wide consensus may be required.

The second kind of board is typically an advisory board composed of university faculty. Some state university presses include faculty and other representatives from the different campuses. These faculty boards "guard the imprint" and represent the academic oversight for the press's list.

Procedures at this stage may vary as well. At some presses, an internal board approves a project which then goes to a faculty board, whose approval is necessary for a contract. At others, an internal board makes the decision on a contract and the faculty board gives its approval later on, when the revised version of the manuscript is deemed ready for production. Most faculty boards consider each manuscript separately; others approve wholesale the press's activity over a longer period.

There are advantages and disadvantages to each of the systems. As an author, you should query your editor about the particular process at the press. Don't assume it will be exactly the same process that colleagues have gone through at a different press.

Once you are offered a contract, read it carefully. Some contracts issued in advance are also final contracts. Others will be replaced by final contracts. Some advance contracts don't commit the press to anything more than reviewing a later manuscript; some are binding unless something unusual happens. Again, the best advice is to ask your editor about the press's own conditions and procedures. If you have questions about the contract, start by asking your editor. If there is some point about which you remain unsure, you might consult colleagues who have published at similar presses.

Most contracts are conventional. Consulting friends or relatives who are agents and accustomed to the substantially different conventions of trade publishing, or lawyers used to poking holes in contracts, rarely turns out to be productive.

Royalties and Advances

Earlier in this essay, we noted that most scholarly publishing loses money. This is important to remember as you read your contract and get to the bottom line. Every contract has a royalty agreement but, for the vast majority of academic books, the actual amount of money earned from the book itself will be trivial, especially relative to the other indirect forms of remuneration (promotions, merit raises, competitive job offers) that result from academic publishing.

Most university and commercial academic presses will pay royalties on sales of the book. Usually these will be on "net receipts"—the amount of money the press receives from sales of the book. Trade publishers generally pay royalties on list price, regardless of the discount at which the book was actually sold. It would be a rare author who could move a press from its normal way of accounting, but if you are comparing arrangements with others, you should understand this difference.

It is fairly common, when books are published simultaneously in library cloth and paperback editions, for authors to forgo royalties on the library cloth edition (which now rarely sells more than one hundred copies). Other than that, an author could expect to have some royalties on most sales, though there are some presses which offer no royalties on the first hardcover monograph sales. This is not the usual practice, however. When presses vary royalties from contract to contract, it usually reflects some combination of the perceived status of the author and the sales prospects for the particular book, together with any competitive considerations.

An advance is the payment of some of the expected earnings from royalties, paid in advance of the publication and actual sale of the book. It is not a signing bonus, in the sense of additional money, but rather represents the faith of the press in the book's eventual sales. It is customary for advances to be paid in parts, such as half on signing and the remainder on final acceptance or publication. In cases that advances are offered—and this also varies from press to press and book to book—the amount can vary from a few hundred dollars to a few thousand. There are cases in which university presses have paid advances in five figures rather than three or four, but they are comparatively rare.

If you have more than one press offering a contract, you should compare the royalties and advance between them, but you should also inquire about how the press plans to publish and position the book. Some things will be negotiable and some not. Presses will often match an offer from another press in some way to get a book. For instance, a press might slightly up an advance or royalties, or a press that would otherwise plan to publish clothbound editions only might agree to a simultaneous paperback. In the end, you will need to decide where you want the book, since ultimately the offers are unlikely to differ by much. A $500 difference in the advance from one press, for example, may not counterbalance another press's reputation in your field, or differences in book design or marketing approach, or an offer to publish the book simultaneously in hardcover and in paper.

Open Access

The publishers discussed here generally depend on book sales to break even, in the case of university presses, or to contribute to the profitability of the company, in the case of commercial academic ones. While open access fulfills one important goal of scholarly publishing—the widest possible distribution of a scholar's work—it has taken some creativity to figure out how to achieve that in a sustainable way. Much of the early interest in open-access publishing came from the high price of commercial scientific journal publishing, which was taking up a vastly disproportionate amount of academic library budgets, much to the concern of the scientists involved and of national agencies that were frequently funding the research. Some commercial publishers responded by allowing authors to pay to have their research published in an open-access fashion, collecting money up front rather than waiting to see if the particular article caught on. Scientists were then often able to build such fees into their grants. This model runs into obvious trouble when applied to the humanities and narrative social science, which are book fields, and where scholars usually do not have extensive grant funding. There have been a few voluntary or foundation-supported open-access presses in the humanities, but for the most part, the open-access efforts are scattered and still in development.

One notable recent effort has been TOME (Toward an Open Monograph Ecosystem), which was jointly created by the Association of American Universities (AAU), Association of Research Libraries (ARL), and Association of University Presses (AUPresses). Participating universities give a significant subsidy for publication of a book by one of their faculty to that professor's press, in return for the press publishing the book in an open-access form. The subsidy is not enough to replace all the revenue that a press would make from selling a reasonably successful monograph, but it can put a book in small-selling field on a more level playing ground with larger-selling ones. There is an ongoing program called Knowledge Unlatched that has a similar effort based on library contributions, and some presses have developed their own programs. If this is important to you or in your field, be sure to ask your editor about it early on.

Most presses will prefer a hybrid approach, wherein they are selling the book through online and conventional bookstores, in digital editions, and at academic meetings, while also having it available as open access for those who cannot afford it or for whom the open version better suits their needs. Sometimes the printed versions are only printed on demand, but in many cases, they are printed as usual.

Subsidies

As noted above, it has become conventional for university presses to inquire whether an author's institution has funds to help support publication of their book. The sources of such funds will vary from institution to institution. At some places, a scholar's dean or department chair will be able to offer such support.

Other institutions may have a centralized fund with set times for applying, or have a competitive process. Any press will appreciate such support, so it is worth asking one's dean or department chair how that works ahead of time. Often such funds can be built into start-up packages or competitive offers. The scholar's press will be able to supply the book's budget or other materials to establish why the funds are needed. Finally, it is worth noting the difference between the general support that helps underwrite the cost of publishing the book, and money required to do something specific, such as including color illustrations. Presses will be hoping for the former, though sometimes the two can be usefully combined into a single ask.

Deadlines and Delivery Dates

A contract signed in advance of the final manuscript will usually contain a date for turning in the revised and completed version. If you are asked to proffer such a date, be kind to yourself. Choose a date that gives you enough time for the many changes in location, institution, partner or family status—not to mention the complications of research and writing itself—that can intervene. Unless the publishing program changes radically while you revise, publishers are likely to understand if you need more time than expected (as long as you aren't churning out books for other publishers in the meantime). Stay in touch with your editor and apprise them of your progress, and if you need more time, ask.

This might be a good time to mention that the full process from contract to publication takes much longer than scholars imagine when they emerge from graduate school, mostly because the process of producing a manuscript and seeing it through all the different stages of peer review and revision is a larger task than anticipated.

When you turn in the revised manuscript, procedures once again will vary by press. If the faculty board voted at the time of contract, they may or may not need to approve the completed manuscript. At some presses, it will be between author and editor to determine if the manuscript is ready for production. At others, the manuscript will go back out to reviewers for their judgment. Again, each of the systems has advantages and disadvantages; you will want to understand the procedures at your press.

Gathering Art and Permissions

Your book manuscript is not complete and is not ready to go into production until you have secured all of the art and the proper copyright permissions for both quotations and images. In most cases, obtaining the art and permissions for a book is the author's responsibility. This should be spelled out in the book contract, but it is worth talking to your editor about early on. The author is generally responsible for paying any costs involved in obtaining acceptable copies of images, and in securing the rights to reproduce them in the book.

The earlier you start gathering and preparing the art and permissions, the better. The requirements will vary from press to press, so it's best to find out what your press will require early on. The press may demand higher-quality images than you expect. The scan that looks perfectly fine posted online or in a PowerPoint presentation may not be of sufficient resolution to work for print.

As books became searchable online, permission requirements have generally tightened. The monograph that once might have had only a small circle of readers, few of whom would have cared about the rights for materials included, is now readily and fully searchable by anyone. Presses are consequently more careful to make sure permissions are secured and that they match the needs of the book. A book that will be distributed around the world will require that the author obtain world rights for the material included. If the book will come out in a digital edition, the permission should specify that.

Many university presses are supporters of fair use. Fair use is an important part of the copyright law that allows reasonable use of material under copyright for the purpose of criticism. It is worthwhile learning about both fair use and public domain—Wikipedia is particularly good here, but there are many sources—and then checking with your editor on how your press sees the issues. Fair use is always a matter of interpretation, and each press will have a different sense about what will count.

From Manuscript to Book

Once the manuscript is finally complete (including with all permissions obtained and approved), it is ready to go into production. Schedules for production are no longer flexible.

Typically, the process of turning a completed university press manuscript into a book takes nine to twelve months. This will usually involve the press's professional copyediting, you reviewing the edits, manuscript clean-up back at the press, design of the interior, typesetting, proofreading, indexing, cover design, and finally printing and binding.

As you have no doubt guessed by this point in the essay, the particulars will vary from press to press and the timing from book to book, depending on length or workloads, even at a single press. At many presses, a managing editor will oversee the copyediting, which is done by freelancers. Elsewhere, it is done in house by press staff. Many presses use freelance design, while others are proud of their in-house designers. Some presses have stock interiors; others design them afresh each time. You may be solely responsible for proofreading or there may be a professional proofreader as well. Indexing is often, but not always, the responsibility of the author. You may be tempted to hire a grad student or a professional and should bear in mind the needs of the audience that will be reading your book, and what they will expect to find in the index. A professional indexer might be perfect for a narrative history, but lost in a theoretical work featuring a variety of unfamiliar terms.

Commercial academic presses tend to be faster, sometimes by skipping, combining, or reducing stages. In all cases, though, there will be absolute deadlines, with tight turnaround times, at several stages in the production. You will be expected to meet these deadlines, even if it means changing your vacation dates or proofreading days after your child's birth.

Your book will be in a catalog, with an announced date, and the production process is geared to ensuring that what is promised in that catalog is available when the press says it will be. That date, by the way, is conventionally a publication date—for publicity—and is usually a few weeks after the physical books are available. This comes from the trade necessity of having books already in the bookstore when reviews appear.

You, your editor, and the press's marketing department will all want the book out in time for important academic meetings. It becomes crucial to treat the schedule for returning copyedited manuscripts or page proofs like a train schedule. You have to show up on time. Once the book is out, you will be certainly glad you did.

Becoming an Author

As with a basketball shot or a golf swing, the follow-through is critical to success after your book is published. Your follow-through is key to the success of the whole effort. The press will work hard, but there are many things that happen for a book primarily because of the attention, presence, and networks of the author.

The moment of publication is not a time to disappear in postpartum abjection. You should make a special effort to show up at conferences or to arrange to give talks about the topic of your book. It's a crucial part of promoting the book and ensuring that it gets into the hands of colleagues and students in your field, and it is also a significant part of your responsibilities as an author.

After your book is published, it's excellent to take advantage of your own social media presence to make sure your book circulates as widely as possible.

You may be given a discount code by the press which you can share, or be able to link to reviews or events. It's a great time to call in favors from your graduate school cohort or the peers you have hosted. If travel isn't practical, even offering to video chat with a class can make a difference.

This is also an exciting part of book publishing and key to being both a scholar and a writer. You might find yourself in dialogue about the book with a scholar you admire but never met, or with grad students eagerly devouring your work. After all the time spent alone writing a book, it is gratifying to see the impact the book is having on others. Fostering that goal is as good for you as it is for those fortunate to read the book on which you have labored for years.

Again, university press books lose money for the universities that own them. Doing your part to ensure that your book sells enough to pay for itself should be seen as a professional commitment—and it is a commitment that will be as good for your career as it is for scholarly publishing more generally.

The best reason to stay engaged with your book even after it has appeared in print is because you've earned it. The whole process of writing a book and seeing it through publication is a long one. It is often frustrating and almost always solitary. Seeing your book actually read and appreciated by others, being part of an ongoing discussion of its ideas, and being able to watch its impact on the thinking of others is one of the joys of publishing. Otherwise, why not simply think one's thoughts? Why bother about a book if it isn't to communicate?

Reaping the personal satisfactions of authorship, of communicating your ideas with the world you may not have known before you began writing, is an extremely positive part of the publishing process. But it is not the end of the process. Not at all. In fact, it may well be simply the beginning of your next book project.

16. Holding the Space: Reflections on Small-Class Teaching and Learning

MAGDALENA MĄCZYŃSKA

A classroom can be many different spaces. Depending on your institution, it can be more or less inviting, more or less conducive to the labor of learning. Its walls may be painted uninspiring beige. Its heating system may not function properly, and you may find yourself alternately opening the window—propping it up with abandoned books and erasers—and slamming it shut. Your classroom may have no windows at all. It may be furnished with a collection of uncomfortable chairs with rickety plastic tops on which students are expected to balance their books, notebooks, writing implements, handouts, and water bottles; or with rows of front-facing, bolted-down tables that cannot be arranged into more egalitarian configurations. If you are very lucky, your classroom is beautifully designed and contains everything you need, including state-of-the-art technology and comfortable seats for all. Alternatively, it may not be a "classroom" at all but a lab, a studio, or a digital platform. Whatever space, physical or virtual, you and your students enter on the first day of class can potentially become a locus of transformation. You are the custodian of this vital space; you are charged with activating and sustaining its transformative powers.

Why dwell on these details of interior design? Because, as Virginia Woolf taught us in "A Room of One's Own," material conditions are fundamental to intellectual and creative endeavors; because, as Ira Shor taught us in his academic ethnography *When Students Have Power* (1996), "classroom furniture helps discipline students into a status quo of inequality"; because, as bell hooks taught us in *Teaching to Transgress* (1994), American university classrooms routinely reproduce racist, patriarchal, and class hierarchies, promote conformity, and refuse to make space for the transgressive energies of pleasure and excitement. Many of our students will arrive numbed to these institutional realities and their material manifestations.

In the last fifty years, radical educators have encouraged us to counter the hierarchical, passive model of learning-as-information-transfer from the professor's full mind to the students' empty ones—what Paulo Freire famously called the banking system of education. Freire's dialogical method, Ira Shor's power-sharing, bell hooks's teaching as practice of freedom, and Ngũgĩ wa Thiong'o's decolonizing curriculum offer powerful examples of critical pedagogies. A growing body of scientific research on human learning confirms what pedagogical visionaries knew all along: the best learning happens when students ask questions and solve problems relevant to their lives and communities; learning is profoundly social and inextricably linked to emotions; learning is deepened by metacognitive reflection. Overcoming academic alienation not only produces a more just education, but a more effective one. Even the fortunate students who already feel at home in academic settings can benefit from a more active, socially embedded, holistic, and reflexive education. And all students can benefit from an education that promotes the kinds of creative, collaborative, and intersectional thinking necessary for navigating today's shifting digital landscapes and multidimensional political and environmental crises.

In a small-class setting, professors are perfectly positioned to foster inquiry-based, community-grounded, self-aware learning. We can begin by inviting students to reflect on where they (and we) are situated within the educational system, and how the educational system in turn is situated within an interconnected network of larger forces, synchronic and diachronic, that have shaped the particular academic classroom where we find ourselves today. Regardless of our disciplines, we have the opportunity not only to teach the *what* of our course (the content or skills we were hired to "cover"), but also the *why*: to demystify the process of knowledge production and dissemination, of which students too often see themselves as passive recipients. This project of de-alienation starts with acknowledging the positionality of each student and each professor, with considering the intersecting dimensions (material, historical, socioeconomic, environmental, political, cultural) of the chairs on which we sit.

The academic classroom has never been a neutral space; our students' histories, no less than our own, shape our shared experience. We may face a group of students reluctant to acknowledge our authority; or, conversely, we may settle too easily into an overconfidence born of unacknowledged privilege. By making visible the lines of power running through our classrooms, and by allowing our students to teach us, and one another, we can build a better academic community. The small class, where everybody knows everybody's name, is the perfect laboratory for such collaborative experimentation. No single pedagogical strategy or piece of instructional technology will automatically guarantee active learning, let alone the development of intellectual, social, or political agency. Nevertheless, some modes of teaching are more conducive to achieving these goals than others. What follows is an overview of evidence-based best practices in academic teaching, informed by my own experience as an immigrant, white ethnic, straight, cis female, neurotypical, able-bodied, middle-class, full-time professor of literature at a small urban liberal arts college. My focus here is small-classroom teaching (even though some of the most exciting learning today admittedly happens outside academic walls: see Charles Piot's and Laura M. Harrison's chapters on virtual and community-based education), but much of what I discuss can be adapted to other settings. Whether you are a novice or a seasoned instructor, whatever your job description and academic discipline, I hope my essay gives you useful ideas for activating your students, renewing your teaching practice, or simply rediscovering purpose and joy in the classroom.

Break the Lecture

The most traditional (and criticized) academic teaching method is the lecture: typically, a single professor talking to a group of silent students in a large hall, or on a screen if in the form of a massive open online course (MOOC). To migrate this format to a small classroom would be a wasted pedagogical opportunity. On the other hand, although many successful teachers forgo it altogether, lecturing can be useful as long as it comes in short segments embedded within a well-designed active learning experience. Human attention generally wanes after about fifteen minutes, so we must intersperse lecture segments with activities that allow students to apply, analyze, synthesize, and evaluate (to borrow Bloom's taxonomy) their newly acquired knowledge.

As with any other text we might assign, we can help students get the most out of our mini-lectures by offering opening, check-in, and closing activities. These can be as simple as asking questions before, in the middle, and after our talk ("How would you define racism to a seven-year-old?"; "What are the three definitions of racism I've discussed so far?"; "If I were to give a one-question quiz on the subject of racism next week, what should be the question?"). A more advanced version might involve posing an opening problem ("Why should Controversial Figure be allowed/disallowed to speak at our campus?"); or asking students to consider the contents of the lecture from divergent points of view

("Summarize the two main points of my lecture in a headline for CNN and for Fox News"); or negotiating the content of future lecture segments with the class ("Which of the legal cases I mentioned today would you want to hear more about next week?"). The idea is to spark student interest; to connect new content to existing knowledge and experience; to guide the listening process and encourage information retrieval; to involve students in decision-making about their own learning; and to allow space for engagement with the material beyond the rote query "Are there any questions?" (which students take as a signal to begin packing their bags). These activities also allow professors to gauge student (mis)understanding of course material, promote student-to-student learning, and learn something new by considering their area of expertise from unexpected points of view.

The model described above clearly abridges the role of content delivery (once perceived as the main business of an academic session), reducing it to a segment within a diverse educational experience. A more radical version of this abridgement, the "flipped" classroom, moves the introduction of new content out of the classroom entirely, asking students to read or watch course materials at home, while reserving class time for more active forms of learning involving higher-order cognitive operations. While the flipped classroom is a recent development (popularized by peer-instruction champion Eric Mazur), a traditional humanities seminar follows a similar format, with students reading a novel or set of archival documents before class, and then analyzing and discussing the texts during class. This way of teaching requires advance scaffolding, but the rewards are many: more efficient use of class time; deeper engagement with the material; and more vibrant, creative, multidirectional exchanges.

Write It Out

One of the most powerful tools for academic thinking is writing. In a traditional classroom, students use writing to take lecture notes and exams. In an active classroom, writing can be used at any point, and for almost any purpose: to warm up, focus, and brainstorm; to summarize, paraphrase, and synthesize; to question, subvert, and dissent; to connect, transform, and create. Writing can be private (freewriting, journaling) or collaborative (peer-to-peer annotations, collective note-taking on digital platforms, small-group assignments). The good news is that our twenty-first-century students already have extensive experience with writing (they do it all day long on their devices), and are adept at adjusting messages to the needs of particular audiences. All we need to do is tap into this expertise. Since listing the many uses of low-stakes in-class writing would require several volumes (see the annotated bibliography at the end of this chapter for excellent examples), I will limit myself to two personal favorites: translation and freewriting.

I use the word "translation" not in the traditional sense of traveling from language to language, but from register to register, genre to genre, medium to medium. Translation exercises give students the opportunity to manipulate and communicate course material by rearticulating it in new ways for new audiences—and for themselves. Rather than asking for a traditional summary of an assigned reading, I ask for a public service announcement, Wikipedia entry, listicle, or poem. Rather than asking students to enumerate the similarities and differences between two theories, I ask them to write a short dramatic dialogue, or to draw a comic strip illustrating an imaginary exchange between the two authors. If time is tight, ultrashort social-media-inspired genres can be very useful: composing a tweet or hashtag is a great way to extract and communicate the main point of a reading, as well as convey attitude. These creative exercises work well for pairs and groups, allowing students to have fun together. Where a more traditional prompt would yield stale, mechanical responses, my students repeatedly rise to the challenge with surprisingly sophisticated and nuanced translations. Finally, I like to ask students to generate quiz questions, exam prompts, and paper assignments for the class. Working in these more traditional academic genres allows students to review course material, select what matters most (which may not be what I, the professor, would have wanted), and have a say in their own education.

While translation exercises demand active, on-the-spot intellectual engagement, freewriting offers a reprieve from the pressures of structured thinking and standard grammar. Peter Elbow, the great champion of the practice, argues that regular freewriting helps increase fluency, facility, and creativity, especially for writers struggling with anxiety or procrastination. In a typical freewriting exercise, students are given a prompt and asked to write continually for several minutes without pausing to think or evaluate their work. A promising idea generated during this first session might become the prompt for a second round of writing; this spiral process (called "looping") can help students deepen and focus their thinking about a topic. While freewriting prompts, generated by the professor or the students, are useful for exploring ideas, a purer form of the technique allows students to write with no prompts and no expectation to share. I am especially fond of this minimalist practice: opening the class with five minutes of freewriting clears the mind, creates a sense of community, and acknowledges emotions that might otherwise interfere with the learning process. On a more practical level, it can reduce tardiness, as students are reluctant to break the shared silence with their shuffling entrances. Any hesitation I might have felt about "wasting" five minutes of class on a "nonacademic" activity was dispelled by my students' palpable relaxation, and their improved focus during the rest of the period.

If my love for in-class writing reveals my disciplinary bias as a professor of literature, many of the ideas discussed above can be translated into oral or non-verbal modes. For example, if everyone's mobility permits, you might ask your students to try freewalking, a kinetic equivalent of freewriting in which students generate ideas while taking a walk, alone or in conversation with a partner. Visual forms of translation could involve diagramming and data visualization ("create a visual representation of the sub-prime mortgage crisis"); poster making ("sketch a poster explaining the benefits of flu shots to college-age students"); planning monuments or theme parks ("design a Black Lives Matter memorial," "draw a Shakespeare ride"); composing visual essays ("assemble a YouTube slideshow on climate change"); or choreographing ("compose a short dance illustrating the challenges of living with PTSD"). The possibilities are endless. Many professors worry that we are not doing our jobs in the classroom if we are not transmitting knowledge or expertise, or at least moderating class discussion. But as we stand there doing "nothing," each of our students is engaged in learning. Using low-stakes assignments is a great way to train ourselves to accept that not everything produced in our classrooms needs to be vetted or graded; that not all learning needs to go through the clearinghouse of the professor. Those of us uncomfortable with the role of onlooker can grab a pencil (marker, computer, instrument) and join in. When we work alongside our students, we model commitment to ongoing practice and show respect for the shared learning space. We can use this time to test the viability of our prompts (a humbling and illuminating experience) or advance our own scholarly projects (I have developed several conference papers during in-class freewriting sessions). In the process, we might just learn something new.

Work Together
Trained by years of schooling, college students often address their comments to the professor exclusively, even if giving feedback to a classmate. To wean students from an overdependence on authority figures, we can strategically de-center ourselves and validate peer-to-peer interactions. One familiar strategy is small-group work. Groups give reluctant public speakers the opportunity to be heard, and encourage multilateral exchanges between students—who tend to be very effective at teaching one another. When organizing group activities,

it is useful to identify a concrete final product (a list of three questions, two competing points of view, a tweet), unless the purpose is informal discussion. To ensure everyone is involved, group members can take on roles (note-taker, moderator, presenter, time-keeper) and establish ground rules for participation. Some professors prefer to create long-term peer groups to reap the benefits of cohort support, while others create new groups for every class to increase the diversity of student interactions. Some prefer larger groups for a greater variety, or smaller groups for increased focus. I am partial to pair work, which requires direct accountability and promotes focused listening. Experimenting with formats in dialogue with students is the best way to find a formula that works for a particular project and population.

On the other end of the spectrum, the class as a whole can function as a large peer group. Class discussion has the potential to activate democratic learning— as long as the professor refrains from overwhelming the conversation with expert comments. Asking students to set rules, prepare questions, and moderate discussions can help redistribute control and promote lateral engagement. More radical forms of professorial decentering include immersive role-playing activities like debates or reenactments. These require extensive preparation, but can yield some of the most exciting learning experiences. One well-established immersive pedagogy is Reacting to the Past (RTTP), developed by historian Mark C. Carnes at Barnard College. In an RTTP course, each student assumes a historical role, fictional or actual, and participates (in character) in debates surrounding a key historical event (Indian Independence, the 1913 Paterson Strike, the French Revolution, etc.). The outcome of the game is not predetermined, and students have the freedom to diverge from the historical record as they learn, from the inside, the complexities of negotiating political conflicts. More than a dozen game scenarios are available in print, and professors can try out the method themselves at the Reacting Consortium's annual conference. RTTP is one example of a pedagogy in which the professor provides initial materials and acts as behind-the-scenes monitor, while students develop the content and direct the trajectory of the class. Not every course lends itself to such radical reimagining, and not every professor has the appetite for being gamemaster, but any class can be enlivened by immersive, participatory, student-directed play.

Preach the Process

In the intimate setting of the small classroom, the professor has the opportunity to model a passion for learning and discuss the challenges and frustrations that are inevitably part of intellectual life. Debunking the myth of academic genius can help students understand the laborious process of knowledge production, overcome feelings of inadequacy, and build resilience. Sharing our own process (including notes, drafts, failed experiments, or revise-and-resubmit letters) can provide a powerful antidote to the awed alienation many students, especially first-generation degree seekers, experience within academia. In addition to offering personal testimony, we can foster a growth mindset throughout the course through process-friendly assignment design (portfolios with built-in revision opportunities, scaffolding complex assignments to help students practice individual component skills); grading systems (contract or specifications grading in which students elect what grade to pursue and revise their work to meet required standards); and feedback style (praising effort over talent, prioritizing process comments over comments that simply justify final grades). Formative feedback is an especially powerful teaching tool: making space for conversations about student work-in-progress is worth the investment of labor, and ultimately saves time. Over many years of teaching writing-intensive courses, I have honed two successful formats for mid-process commentary: feedback workshops and one-on-one conferences. While the examples described below are drawn from coaching student writing, their principles can be adapted to high-stakes academic projects across disciplines.

Many classes use small groups or pairs to elicit peer feedback, but I am a fan of the whole-class feedback workshop, where everyone reads and comments on everyone else's drafts. This is a time-consuming but highly rewarding activity that helps students articulate goals, normalize struggles, identify patterns, and get inspiration from their peers while giving public feedback. In my classes, I ask each author to distribute copies of their draft, and then read it aloud while others listen and underline passages that strike them as particularly strong or weak. After the reading, each person offers one point of praise and one suggestion for improvement, while the author listens and takes notes. The professor follows the same format. The feedback workshop is one of my favorite sessions of the semester: my students continue to impress me with the thoughtfulness, generosity, and intelligence of their comments. This is not surprising, considering that they are all grappling with the challenges of the same assignment—and it provides powerful evidence for the claim that the professor is not always the best teacher in the room.

While the feedback workshop allows students to work collectively with one another, many instructors like to use one-on-one conferences to give individualized attention to each project. This kind of out-of-class contact can be an invaluable experience for students, especially those not comfortable with academic customs such as seeking out faculty in their offices. There are many viable conference formats, but my favorite formula is to read student work in real time rather than collecting and pre-annotating it prior to the meeting. While I read the draft, the author writes a reflection, so we both have notes for the conversation to follow—I want the conference to be a dialogue, rather than a space for telling the student what to do. Reading the draft on the spot forces me to prioritize and resist nitpicking. For the student, witnessing a person engage with their work can be illuminating: the confusion or delight visibly produced by their words is much more clear than professorial marginalia (often illegible to students, figuratively and literally). The conference also gives the student writer a chance to articulate and clarify their developing ideas, a process that often leads to epiphanies and breakthroughs. This kind of in-depth conferencing is ultimately a time saver: annotating the same drafts at home would have taken more time, with lesser rewards. In our era of contingent academic labor, many professors cannot afford to meet students individually, but it might be worthwhile to experiment with in-class conferences, or cancel regular classes to make room for one-on-one or small-group feedback meetings. Even a minimal in-progress check-in during class will communicate investment in the student's work and support for their learning process.

Respecting the process means respecting the fact that our students' learning is affected by a myriad of factors (emotional, socioeconomic, physical, cognitive, political) over which we have no control. As professors, we are not qualified to address many of our students' challenges, but we can take the time to familiarize ourselves with the support systems our institutions offer (tutoring, access and wellness services, food pantries, childcare, etc.) and help students use them to their advantage. We can redesign our courses for maximum access, so students with special needs are not saddled with the burden of adjustments (switching to take-home exams, sharing lecture slides, integrating multimodal materials). We can resist the culture of student-shaming in informal faculty gatherings. We can speak loudly against discriminatory behaviors in and out of the classroom. We can choose to show compassion, patience, and respect. In *Let's Pretend: A Special Report on Solving the Education Crisis in America*, Lenora Fulani and Fred Newman invoke Lev Vygotsky's study of young children who learn to speak when adults *pretend* that their babbling is speech until it *becomes* speech.[1] Through such aspirational performance (treating learners as if they have already become what they are in the process of becoming), we can help students move toward competencies and identities yet beyond their reach.

Go Meta

Students get more from their education when they become self-aware learners. Metacognition helps them gain control and overcome common educational identity myths ("I'm bad at math," "I'm a terrible writer," "I'm a C student"). We can promote metacognition by explaining the rationale behind our teaching strategies, and inviting students to consider what works and does not work for them. A culture of reflection can be established on the first day of class with show-of-hands surveys and conversations about learning habits. Throughout the course, we can build in opportunities for informal reflection in multiple media by asking students to write, discuss, and otherwise illustrate their learning process. One fun way to encourage reflection on in-progress assignments is verbal or visual metaphor-making. Metaphors can help students pinpoint where they are and where they need or want to go: "If your draft were a house, what would it look like at this point in the process? Too many rooms? Foundations but no walls? Asymmetrical structure? Draw your house at the current stage of the project," and so on. To encourage higher-order cognitive work, we can invite students to "talk through" their thinking or creative process, articulating underlying principles behind their work (what Lang calls "self-explaining").[2] In addition to the many informal reflections scattered throughout the course, we can ask for formal capstone reflections. The letter form is especially conducive to this kind of work: students can write cover letters for portfolios, missives to incoming cohorts, or inspirational messages to past or future versions of themselves.

The practice of academic reflection goes beyond individual student learning. As our students reflect on their labors, we should reflect on ours. Students can teach us how to teach them through short surveys and regular meta-conversations about experiences with our course and institution. (Some colleges and universities provide a service wherein a third party checks in with students and gathers anonymous feedback mid-semester; this can also be arranged informally among colleagues.) We can reflect aloud on our own work and involve students in our professorial decisions—by pulling back the academic veil, we denaturalize the academic culture that many students have simply taken for granted. We can encourage the habit of meta-thinking by discussing the institutional history of our disciplines, of the modern university, and of institutionalized education in general. We can invite students to reflect on their own educational histories. We can help them see the walls, chairs, and bodies in our classroom as parts of a more vast and complex picture. Infusing our courses with reflection at every level of the academic experience is the single most powerful low-investment change we can make to support more effective, more integrated, and more politically empowered learning.

Keep Learning

Perhaps the most exciting aspect of academic teaching is the opportunity to learn from, and unlearn with, our students. Each person in the classroom comes with a set of experiences, knowledges, and epistemologies—sometimes not immediately legible to us. Acknowledging and honoring this wealth of knowledge will make our courses more interesting, equitable, alive, and, indeed, more academically successful. It might be easier, especially for the novice professor, to hide behind the wall of expertise that separates the expert from the student; but allowing ourselves to be open, even vulnerable, can lead to more learning, more resilience, and more transformative discovery for everyone.

Ongoing learning for the professor also means turning to the community of fellow educators, many of whom face similar challenges. Like our students, we learn best together. At the end of this section, I include a brief annotated bibliography of pedagogical resources helpful in cultivating professional (and personal) growth for professors at any level. After more than twenty years in the classroom, I often still feel like a novice, but I have come to understand that this is a feeling to be embraced. When we see ourselves as learners, we can help students become better learners themselves. My bibliography does not pretend to be representative or exhaustive; rather, I name thirteen books that guided me in my own work, and continue to push me toward becoming the teacher I aspire to be. On the list, you will find a mix of hands-on pedagogical manuals (especially ones aimed at beginners); overviews of recent research on human learning; memoirs by exceptional educators; and books that consider how teaching participates in and disrupts systems of oppression. Some volumes do several of these things at once. As you browse, I hope you discover something of use for your own teaching practice, wherever you find yourself.

SELECT ANNOTATED BIBLIOGRAPHY OF PEDAGOGICAL RESOURCES

Ambrose, Susan A., Marsha C. Lovett, Michael W. Bridges, Marie K. Norman, and Michele DiPietro. *How Learning Works: Seven Research-Based Principles for Smart Teaching*. San Francisco: Jossey-Bass, 2010.

Written by experts in the science of teaching and learning, *How Learning Works* sums up current research in the field in seven accessible principles: (1) Students' prior knowledge can help or hinder learning; (2) How students organize knowledge influences how they learn and apply what they know; (3) Students' motivation determines, directs, and sustains what they do to learn; (4) To develop mastery, students must acquire component skills, practice integrating them, and know when to apply what they have learned; (5) Goal-directed practice coupled with targeted feedback enhances the quality of students' learning; (6) Students' current level of development interacts with the social, emotional, and intellectual climate of the course to impact learning; (7) To become self-directed learners, students must learn to monitor and adjust their approaches to learning. The authors illustrate these principles with real-life examples, and offer concrete classroom strategies for their implementation.

Bean, John C. *Engaging Ideas: The Professor's Guide to Integrating Writing, Critical Thinking, and Active Learning in the Classroom*. 2nd ed. San Francisco: Jossey-Bass, 2011.

When I first started reading Bean's book on the subway, I became so engrossed that I missed my stop. This professor-friendly volume is full of creative, high-impact strategies for promoting active learning through writing in any discipline. Bean discusses high- and low-stakes assignment design; coaching students to become active readers, thinkers, and writers; directing in-class activities; giving feedback; and assessing student work. The book's helpful layout makes it easy to return to it again and again for ideas and inspiration.

Deloria, Vine, Jr., and Daniel R. Wildcat. *Power and Place: Indian Education in America*. Golden, CO: Fulcrum Resources, 2001.

The sixteen essays in this volume show how the Native American experience at all levels of education in the United States has been affected by foundational differences between indigenous and Western metaphysics, and the ensuing divergences in ideas about education, technology, and the individual's relationship with the environment and community. Deloria and Wildcat advocate for a place-based curriculum that honors indigenous epistemologies, and offer suggestions for dismantling neocolonial educational structures. While the volume is especially useful for teachers working with Native students, any educator will benefit from this corrective to the mainstream erasure of indigenous perspectives.

Elbow, Peter. *Writing with Power: Techniques for Mastering the Writing Process*. 2nd ed. New York: Oxford University Press, 1998.

This is the book I wish I had read when working on my dissertation. It would have saved me months of agonizing over blank screens and pages. Elbow's advice is relevant to writing in any discipline, at any level, and can be easily applied to other kinds of creative work. His book contrasts the generative "yea-saying" and the critical "nay-saying" mindsets, providing imaginative exercises for getting started, overcoming anxiety and blocks, and harnessing the inner censor to produce powerful work. For writing-intensive courses, and for your own writing practice, I also recommend Elbow's *Writing without Teachers* (1973) and *Everyone Can Write* (2000).

Finkel, Donald L. *Teaching with Your Mouth Shut*. Portsmouth, NH: Heinemann Boynton/ Cook, 2000.

As a professor who has a hard time keeping her mouth shut, I find this book's challenge especially valuable. Drawing on the work of John Dewey, Finkel advocates moving away from teaching as talking, and toward teaching as creating a space in which students are able to learn. Both philosophical and pragmatic, *Teaching with Your Mouth Shut* offers an abundance of case studies, practical examples, and inquiry-based classroom strategies for promoting student learning, renegotiating academic power structures, and creating a more democratic educational environment.

Freire, Paulo. *Pedagogy of the Oppressed*. Translated by Myra Bergman Ramos, 50th anniversary ed. New York: Bloomsbury Academic, 2018.

In this foundational classic, Freire famously rejects the "banking" model of education: the unilateral transfer of information in which the student is positioned as a passive receptacle of static knowledge. Instead, Freire proposes a dialogic pedagogy of problem-posing that recognizes reality as a dynamic process to be named and shaped together by the teacher-turned-student and students-turned-teachers. This model of education helps students overcome their dehumanization to become subjects capable of transformative reflection and action. While adaptations of Freire's work often blunt its revolutionary edge, *Pedagogy of the Oppressed* remains a touchstone for any practitioner of critical pedagogy.

hooks, bell. *Teaching to Transgress: Education as the Practice of Freedom*. New York: Routledge, 1994.

This searing collection of essays should be required reading for any teacher stepping into an American classroom. Combining personal testimony, theory, and philosophical dialogue, hooks denounces the perpetuation of white supremacist, patriarchal, capitalist paradigms in modern academia. While confronting the painful realities of oppression and alienation, hooks articulates a vision of an embodied and holistic—even ecstatic—education that demands the labor of self-actualization from both students and professor.

Lang, James M. *On Course: A Week-by-Week Guide to Your First Semester of College Teaching*. Cambridge, MA: Harvard University Press, 2008.

In this practical guide, Lang mentors novices through preparing and teaching their first college course. The volume offers advice on getting ready for the semester and teaching the first class; using lectures, discussion, and small groups; designing assignments; grading; reenergizing the class; and closing the semester. Lang also addresses common classroom problems, and reminds the reader of their students' (and their own) humanity.

Lang, James M. *Small Teaching: Everyday Lessons from the Science of Learning*. San Francisco: Jossey-Bass, 2016.

Small Teaching is like a helpful and understanding friend. It offers the busy professor a wealth of evidence-based classroom activities (most of which can be implemented in five- to ten-minute segments, with minimal preparation) designed to promote active learning, long-term retention, transfer, and student engagement. Each user-friendly chapter contains a real-life anecdote illustrating its central concept, empirical studies supporting the practice in question, hands-on models for classroom application, a list of underlying principles, and an easily searchable bullet-point synopsis.

McKeachie, Wilbert, and Marilla Svinicki. *McKeachie's Teaching Tips: Strategies, Research, and Theory for College and University Teachers*. 14th ed. Belmont, CA: Wadsworth, Cengage Learning, 2014.

A pioneer of academic pedagogy, *McKeachie's Teaching Tips* offers a comprehensive overview of all matters related to college and university teaching, with guest chapters by leading voices in the field. This encyclopedic volume is useful for looking up specific questions and troubleshooting, both made easy by its detailed table of contents. Each section is followed by a supplementary reading list.

Nilson, Linda B. *Specifications Grading: Restoring Rigor, Motivating Students, and Saving Faculty Time*. Sterling, VA: Stylus, 2014.

Like many professors, I wish my institution didn't require grades at all, but Nilson's book has gone a long way in helping me make grading more meaningful and less onerous. Nilson proposes an efficient system of assessment in which students demonstrate mastery of outcomes by completing assignments for a pass/fail (with "pass" signifying a satisfactory attainment of the desired outcome, typically at "B" level). Students earn their overall course grade by submitting a certain number of assignments, or submitting assignments at a certain level of mastery. This system forces the professor to clearly articulate expectations ("specifications") for each assignment, and to prioritize process feedback, while eliminating time spent on calibrating individual grades. On the students' end, specifications grading promotes transparency, motivation, and agency, as each student gets to decide which final grade they wish to pursue.

Nilson, Linda B. *Teaching at Its Best: A Research-Based Resource for College Instructors*. San Francisco: Jossey-Bass, 2010.

This all-in-one volume offers a toolbox of pedagogical practices for academic teachers: preparing for the semester; experimenting with teaching formats and methods (with special emphasis on real-world, inquiry-based learning and problem-solving); promoting effective learning and knowledge retention; and assessing outcomes. Nilson addresses questions of cognitive development and motivation, as well as equity and access, grounding her advice in current research about human learning in general, and learning in higher education in particular.

Shor, Ira. *When Students Have Power: Negotiating Authority in a Critical Pedagogy*. Chicago: University of Chicago Press, 1996.

Shor's mixed-genre classic combines scholarly research, ethnography, and personal narrative to describe his experiments with power sharing in a course on literary utopias at the College of Staten Island. Shor offers multiple strategies for including students in decision-making, and illustrates the challenges and rewards of implementing critical pedagogy in a resistant classroom. I owe my obsession with classroom furniture to this transformational volume.

NOTES

1. Lenora Fulani and Fred Newman, *Let's Pretend* (New York: All Stars Project, 2011), https://allstars.org/wp-content/uploads/2016/05/Lets-Pretend-by-Newman-Fulani -January-2011.pdf.

2. James M. Lang, *On Course: A Week-by-Week Guide to Your First Semester of College Teaching* (Cambridge, MA: Harvard University Press, 2008).

17. Teaching the Large Lecture

GENEVIEVE CARPIO AND NEIL K. GARG

There are few tasks as daunting as facing a classroom with four hundred students staring at you as you stand at a lectern. Besides the potential for stage fright, which can hit even the most seasoned professors, we are often told throughout our academic training that the true measure of success is our number of publications. Yet the reality is that we are in a profession that regularly calls us to teach and perform for a large group of people. The large lecture class can be an incredible opportunity to find joy in a place in which we are frequently told to spend little time, and not frequently trained enough to spend our time. This kind of teaching, however, is increasingly being used as a metric to assess and reward professors, even those at traditional research universities. Shifting one's outlook to embrace teaching is particularly important for successfully running a large course. Drawing on our experiences teaching core courses across disciplinary divides (humanities and social sciences vs. math and sciences) at UCLA, we offer here advice for other academics working in a large lecture setting.

Setting the Tone

Students' experience of your classroom begins the moment they walk in the door. This is an ideal opportunity to set the tone for the class session ahead, and to help bridge the gap between the lectern and the auditorium. For instance, in addition to planning extra time to set up technology or check in with your teaching assistants (TAS), you can allocate an extra five minutes before class begins to interact with students. These exchanges can range from holding the door open and greeting individual students as they enter the classroom to sitting among students and asking how their day is going. In our largest lecture courses, in which over four hundred students enroll, it may be impossible to learn everybody's name, but these steps can let students know you are approachable and that you see them as more than a name or ID number on a roster.[1]

We have also found it effective to ease into formal lecture with a warm-up exercise. We recommend starting with a low-stakes activity that helps students transition from the outside world to inside the classroom. Instructing students to answer a few simple questions through polling, discussion, or writing in a class journal provides them an opportunity to reflect on primary learning objectives from the previous lecture, to preview themes related to the oncoming lecture, or to have fun with a topic that may seem tangentially related to the course. Rather than an accountability measure, these warm-up exercises help prepare students for the focus they will need to engage in lectures successfully. Such exercises help alleviate any noticeable disturbance as students trickle in and, more importantly, ensure that each class begins on time with a valuable activity.

Fostering Collaboration

Educational research shows that collaborative learning is a highly effective classroom practice that promotes student learning, fosters positive interaction with classmates, and teaches students to make connections through application. More so, collaborative learning is particularly beneficial to nontraditional students, who express greater interest, receive higher grades, and are retained at higher rates in these settings.[2]

The thought of integrating collaborative learning into your large lecture may seem overwhelming, but it needn't be. On one end of the spectrum, think-pair-share exercises—in which students journal independently about a question, pair with a classmate in an effort to solve the problem, and then share with the larger class—are a relatively painless way to encourage working together. On the other end of the spectrum, well-defined absolute grading schemes, with the opportunity to adjust in the favor of students if grades are unusually low, award collaboration and can help to counter the competition fostered by traditional curves that "weed" students out. Taking time to reiterate the advantages of study groups, the social benefits of getting to know one's classmates, and the value of learning to work together in both the classroom and the workplace can further help foster a collaborative spirit.

Promoting Creativity and Innovation through Assignments

The value of the large lecture exists well beyond its lessons for departmental majors, who will go on to take specialized courses in your field. Thus, it is important to help students understand the value of your course beyond its specific topic. Encouraging them to take a thematic approach to the class can help increase engagement and the value of their experience. That is, whether a student is enrolled in Introduction to Chicana/o Studies or Organic Chemistry, they can all gain something from the ways your particular field teaches them strategies for solving problems and offers tools for creative thinking. Assignment design (in-class and take-home) is a key place to foster these connections.

Two examples are illustrative here. In Introduction to Chicana/o Studies, rather than a traditional midterm, students are assigned a 'zine project in which they prepare a do-it-yourself booklet inspired by the print culture of the Chicana/o Movement. Many students use this opportunity to apply course themes to topics of personal import, such as family histories of activism, immigration, and identity formation. They express these lessons through pairing the written word with the creative arts, such as drawing, poetry, and collage. The 'zines recently became the basis for a public exhibit held at UCLA and many are now part of the library's permanent circulating collection.[3] In another example, in the class Organic Reactions and Pharmaceuticals, students have the option of creating music videos. This assignment encourages students to work in teams in order to share the lessons of organic chemistry through music and filmmaking for a public audience. Collectively, UCLA students have produced over five hundred YouTube videos, each encouraging new ways of approaching life science.[4]

Integrating creativity in assignment design offers students the opportunity to address pressing questions in innovative ways, and can lead to lasting products with value well beyond the classroom.

Integrating New Technologies: Clickers and Polling

When teaching a large lecture, you should consider all of the resources and tools available to you. New technologies offer exciting avenues for engaging students in real time. Clickers, in particular, have become commonplace in many university settings. Students frequently have clicker applications downloaded on their smart phones and many are already accustomed to their use. Although some professors are understandably hesitant to invest precious time in learning how to use tools like clickers, educational companies have done much to make them convenient, straightforward, and flexible. Chances are a clicker is much easier to use than you might expect and the investment is well spent, given the ways students benefit from seeing the data they generate in real time. Some particularly productive uses of polling technology include taking attendance, asking a warm-up question, and self-checks on how materials are being received and understood.

One of the potential pitfalls of clicker technology is that displaying and discussing the results of live polling can take up too much course time if used frequently (allow about five to ten minutes for each of these exercises). There's also the question of affordability, depending on your student population. For professors concerned with potential cost barriers, check with your university's library or technology office; many offer students free rentals. Or, if you are like one of us, there's always polling via raised hands.

Strive for Affordability

Students often struggle with course costs, and large lecture courses are no different. But attention to the prices of books and supplies here can have a positive effect on a much larger number of students. There are simple measures you can take to cut down costs with relative ease. Strategies include placing course books on reserve at the college library, allowing students to use old editions of new textbooks, and choosing texts available as e-books. Digital copies are often more affordable than print copies, and may even be available for free through your college network. Some faculty are shifting away from textbooks altogether, opting instead for online resources.

Disciplinary librarians are fantastic resources to consult with when seeking to cut course costs. They can often help you identify affordable resources or purchase new resources that can be made available to students online at no cost.

Tricky Subjects: Grading Conflicts

In any large class, the potential for grading conflicts grows with enrollment. But there are measures you can take to keep yourself sane when these problems arise. We recommend having a clear regrading policy that is stated explicitly on your syllabus. By offering your students a pathway to reach out to you when they feel they have received a grade in error, whether the professor or a teaching assistant completes the grading, you help ease stress and expedite correcting any misunderstanding that may have occurred. It is useful to provide a specific timeframe in which students can ask for a regrade (i.e., a week after the assignment has been returned), and a format for their request (i.e., written paragraph with a justification for the request). It can also be useful to share your rubric with students in advance, and to retain copies of exceptional responses for your records. These can be shared with students seeking to understand the difference between a high grade and a passing grade. Additional strategies you can engage to help reduce grading conflicts include careful attention to question design to reduce ambiguity; using grading software such as Gradescope; and eliminating grades on some assignments, for example, allowing students to self-check their progress through weekly problem sets or reading comprehension questions with answers posted online.

Likewise, it is important to have a clear policy on cheating and plagiarism in your syllabus. In the case of these violations, universities often require you to submit your policy before action is taken. We also recommend talking with students about the difference between collaboration and cheating early on; walking them through resources on proper citation; and discussing your class policy prior to handing out your first assignment. Being clear about your expectations can help cut down on student violations that occur unintentionally. In cases where academic dishonesty does occur, our advice is to be consistent and to follow university protocol. To do otherwise is time-consuming, confusing for all parties, and potentially damaging.

Fostering Healthy Dissent and a Safe Environment

In a large lecture, there is always the possibility of disagreement, dissent, or disruption. But in our experience, it has not happened often. It is more common that you will receive a question you do not know the answer to—and that's okay! In these cases, you can let the student know that you will follow up by discussing the question in the next lecture, by posting an answer online, or by writing to the student directly over email. Another useful strategy is not to answer the question at all, but rather reaffirm the value of the question, admit you do not know the answer, and talk through the steps someone would go through to find the answer, thereby highlighting students' own ability to find and think through the solution. For instance, "That's a great question that I do not know the answer to offhand. To answer that question, I would X, Y, and Z."

When heated dissent does occur, you have the option of walking students through the logic of your assertions using the tools that they have already been taught. If the discussion is not productive, you can invite the student or students to follow up with you after class. Doing so can prevent a handful of students from dominating valuable class time and give the agitated students an opportunity to cool down.

For many large lecture instructors, physical safety is a growing concern. In the wake of tragic campus shootings, some universities have taken new measures to address their ability to respond to emergency situations. At UCLA, for instance, administrators recently installed an extensive system that allows a central authority to lock classrooms remotely in case of a mass shooter. They also increased opportunities for active-shooter training among faculty and staff. Ultimately, ensuring a truly safe environment will involve taking a larger look at the root causes of gun violence. But instructors can and should take the time to know their classrooms and the resources available to them.

Working with TAs

Large lectures are a team effort. For those teaching a large lecture with the aid of TAs, graduate students comprise a large part of undergraduates' course experience. More so, graduates' involvement in your classroom will be a key part of their training. It's here that they will test and hone their pedagogy as future professors.[5] Thus, we treat our TAs like the colleagues they are, from engaging them in conversations during class to offering them the option to present small class modules. We've found that these efforts both engage undergraduate students, who have the opportunity to learn from talented graduates with their own exciting research agendas, and provide graduate students valuable experiences with the larger lecture format by answering student questions in real time and navigating the flows of a prepared in-class presentation.

In the large lecture setting, a weekly TA meeting is an effective means of discussing course subject matter, checking in on discussion sections, and soliciting feedback from graduate-student teachers. Likewise, flexible grading rubrics can help ensure uniformity across sections, while allowing graduate-student insights to be integrated into the assessment schema as grading takes place. For instance, in joint grading sessions or via Google Docs, rubrics can be expanded as TAs encounter unexpected but merit-filled answers. Grading together offers the added option of organizing an assembly line, in which the same person grades the same question, helping to save time through specialization, and ensuring consistency across exams.

Managing Your Workload and Self-Care

Teaching a large lecture course can feel like a one-person show. There is the stage, the microphone, and a demanding performance that requires preparation and enthusiasm when the curtain rises. Having a ritual as you make your way to class can help curb some of the jitters, such as watching a favorite You-Tube video, listening to an upbeat song, or rehearsing your presentation in advance. Given the daunting setting of the lecture course, you may feel the pressure to perform the role of "professor." This is particularly the case for those of us who do not fit the mold of instructor that students might expect. But this makes your presence and humanity all the more important.[6] Consider, for instance, the popular social media hashtag #ThisIsWhatAProfessorLooksLike, which sought to disrupt the assumption that professors are stoic, straight, white, middle-aged, able-bodied men through "selfies" of professors who challenge these stereotypes. Where the added weight of reaffirming one's expertise can create the pressure to denote infallibility—or to amass a large collection of tweed blazers—sharing personal stories of adversity and admitting when you don't know the answer to a question foregrounds your humanity and serves as a healthy model for students, many of whom are also confronting a highly competitive environment in which they are not always correct. The line between professional and personality can be tricky to navigate, but have faith in your expertise and look for comfort in being yourself (albeit a polished version of yourself). To be anyone else would be exhausting, time-consuming, and not nearly as interesting.

Practicing self-care means setting reasonable boundaries. Office hours can now be managed through online tools, which allow students to reserve meeting times and store information about those meetings, including students' names and topics of interest. Q&A boards are available on most course web portals and can be used to field commonly asked questions. A clear email policy can help students understand when and who it is appropriate to email and what type of responses they can expect. Likewise, multimedia sources and guest lectures can keep students engaged by diversifying the mode and tone of teaching, while also offering you a valuable pause from the high-energy practice of lecturing. Even with all of these tools, it's best to plan for your workload to shift toward teaching in the quarter or semester that you take on the large lecture. And it's not a bad idea to plan a nice break for the end of the quarter or semester as a reward for your hard work.

Keeping It Fresh

As noted earlier, teaching a large lecture can be exhausting and all-encompassing. Even if you have your lectures down cold, your media is fine-tuned, and your TAs are well seasoned, the demands of the large lecture can lead to burnout. If you have the option, we recommend rotating out of the course every few years. This helps ensure an opportunity for valuable recharging and a chance to rethink and refresh your approach to the course. Updating your reading list or meeting with your colleagues to discuss what new technologies and approaches they use in their classes can help put a new spin on your materials when they begin to feel "old hat." Academic conferences are another valuable setting to elicit new ideas and readings. Most offer pedagogical roundtables or panels that highlight new approaches to the classroom. More so, editors at the book exhibit are eager to help you brainstorm new additions to your syllabus. With a proper break, you can return to the classroom recharged and with some exciting new tools.

We write here as academics from two very different departmental backgrounds, one in the social sciences and the other in physical sciences, to highlight our collective experiences with large-format teaching that have been particularly effective for fostering a dynamic classroom experience.[7] More so, we write from our unique perspective as faculty in residence in the UCLA dormitories, where we physically live on campus and interact with thousands of students each year, through formal programming and informal interactions in the dorms. We've heard students' frustration when taking lecture courses in which professors avoid their students, offer no opportunities for feedback and self-checks outside of exams, and do not help students understand the value of course materials beyond their specific discipline. We've also heard students' excitement when they take a course with a professor who engages students beyond formal lecture, who allows them opportunities to see course tools at work through in-class demonstrations, and who assigns projects that allow for creativity beyond the traditional midterm. From this insider look at student life, we see the ways effective teaching in the large lecture setting can positively influence students in long-lasting ways by fostering collaboration, innovation, and problem-solving skills that span disciplines. And it's pretty cool.

NOTES

1. Richard E. Lyons, Marcella L. Kysilka, and George E. Pawlas, *The Adjunct Professor's Guide to Success: Surviving and Thriving in the College Classroom* (Boston: Allyn and Bacon, 1999).

2. Elizabeth F. Barkley, K. Patricia Cross, and Claire Howell Major, *Collaborative Learning Techniques: A Handbook for College Faculty* (San Francisco: Jossey-Bass, 2005); George Kuh, *High-Impact Educational Practices: What They Are, Who Has Access to Them, and Why They Matter* (Washington, DC: Association of American Colleges and Universities, 2008).

3. Reed Buck, "Q&A with Xaviera Flores and Doug Johnson, Co-Creators of the 'Las Causas' Zine Exhibit," *Powell Blog*, February 13, 2018, http://www.library.ucla.edu/blog

/powell/2018/02/13/qa-with-xaviera-flores-and-doug-johnson-cocreators-of-the-las-causas
-zine-exhibit.

4. Neil Garg, "Music Video Hall of Fame, Chem 14D (2010–2015)," http://tinyurl.com
/14dvideos.

5. Genevieve Carpio, Sharon Luk, and Adam Bush, "Building People's Histories:
Graduate Student Pedagogy, Undergraduate Education, and Collaboration with Community Partners," *Journal of American History* 99, no. 4 (2013): 1176–88.

6. Gabriella Gutiérrez y Muhs, Yolanda Flores Niemann, Carmen G. González, and
Angela P. Harris, *Presumed Incompetent: The Intersections of Race and Class for Women
in Academia* (Boulder: University of Colorado Press, 2012); Daryl G. Smith, *Diversity's
Promise for Higher Education: Making It Work* (Baltimore, MD: Johns Hopkins University
Press, 2006).

7. See also Sylvia Hurtado and Victoria L. Sork, *Enhancing Student Success and Building Inclusive Classrooms at UCLA*, Report to the Executive Vice Chancellor and Provost,
December 2015, http://wscuc.ucla.edu/wp-content/uploads/2019/01/C5_16_Report
_Enhancing_Student_Success-Building_Inclusive_Classrooms_at_UCLA_December
_2015.pdf.

18. Lessons from the #FergusonSyllabus

MARCIA CHATELAIN

August 2014 marked the passage of my seventh summer as a faculty member. August is a cruel month for academics; we mourn the end of our summer breaks from teaching in earnest when the calendar shifts from the freedom of July to the frenetic preparations of August. For many of us, our contracts resume, and we are inundated with emails from colleagues and students and reminders about ordering desk copies of our assigned books. We are forced to shift from our summer habits to the practices of the semester. We think about what we are going to teach, who we are going to teach, and, for history faculty like myself, we think about how we are going to make connections. As a specialist in twentieth-century African American history, it's not a stretch of the imagination or my teaching skills to help my students see the continuities of the rhetoric of the mid-century civil rights movement and the conversations they were privy to during the leadership of a black president. My courses on black women's leadership led them to ask questions about prominent women of color across sectors and in various communities. For me, the world outside of my classroom was always present, regardless of what we were reading, talking about, and grappling with on any given day. The first few days of August 2014 unfolded like the school years I had experienced before; I was preparing to teach my African American Women's Activism class and considering what I would tether the first lecture to—what news event would illustrate the themes of the course: continuity and change over time, interpretations of leadership, and gendered perspectives on the ways that movements are founded and grow.

Then, August 9 happened, and everything about my teaching life changed. Michael Brown's death in Ferguson, Missouri, his slaying at the hands of Officer Darren Wilson, on its surface, was not out of step with other tragedies of police brutality. A citizen of color is believed to have evoked fear. An agent of the law is allowed to use deadly force. A family and a community mourns. Yet, Brown's death in a St. Louis exurb—less than a hundred miles from where I spent my formative years as an undergraduate at the University of Missouri—refused to take the path of the tragedies that rise to the level of news one day and buried history the next. As an adopted Missourian—having spent my college years and several summers as a high school educator there—I felt indebted to the state, its taxpayers, and its citizens for affording me an opportunity to go to college. Having come to the university from a working-class background on a George C. Brooks Scholarship—which in 1997 was called a minority scholarship—my formal education and political education commenced the day I set foot on the campus in central Missouri. I was among a handful of black students in my incoming first-year class of thousands. I was among an even smaller number of students enrolled in the university's honors programs, and as a student of color, I was met with contempt by some and curiosity by others at a school that treated us "minorities" as critical nuisances to reform its image as a school that failed to open access, in a state that failed its black citizens, in a nation that protected these practices. At the time, as I was learning about the ins and outs of campus activism, I realized that a number of my fellow black, Latinx, Native, and Asian American friends were also out-of-staters; we seemed to be imported into the state to settle a debt that was paid on the backs of locals. Why were so few of my friends from St. Louis, Kansas City, Springfield, and Ferguson? It would take years for me to fully understand what it meant for black Missourians to still feel like the state's flagship public school was off-limits to them, and it wasn't until my alma mater made national news in 2015 that I would see all the pieces fit. But back in the summer of 2014, I was among the throngs of people tuned into cable news to keep up with the news from Ferguson. I thought the news cameras would leave eventually. I thought that this town in Missouri would fade from consciousness. Yet, as a few days of news coverage about Brown's death turned into nearly twenty-four-hour live coverage from Ferguson's main street, Florissant Avenue, and locals joined activists who traveled from around the state, nation, and world, Ferguson was not going to be forgotten. And Ferguson would have to join me in the classroom, on the first day of class and the last day of the semester; and, I soon discovered, Ferguson would radically transform the way I taught.

The stories from Ferguson continued to rise above the din of nightly news coverage to an educational opportunity for those interested in learning about the criminalization of the poor, the militarization of the police, and the legalization of racial discrimination through districting and voter disenfranchisement. The thoughtful accounts from Ferguson—some reported by journalists who braved tear gas and arrests, and others streamed from the social media accounts of activists who also braced themselves against bullets and billy clubs—were the building blocks of my small intervention in the moment: #FergusonSyllabus. The ask was simple: I reached out to my followers and friends on Twitter—mostly fellow academics—and asked them to commit the first day of class to Michael Brown, who was supposed to enter a vocational training program before his death, and the children of Ferguson, who would not have a normal first day of school because of the civil unrest. In acknowledging the empty desk in Brown's class and the empty classrooms in the schools that served Ferguson, I asked educators to band together to teach in solidarity with a community that had taught me and others so much, with their perseverance in the face of years of marginalization and their resilience in the face of state violence and grief. I didn't expect very much to come out of the ask. Teach something—anything—of substance about Ferguson on the first day of class. Have a conversation. Discuss a news article. Watch a documentary. Do something to remind our students that we learn in order to cultivate our approach, our methods, and our commitment to being in community. Twitter had long before been a medium for me to talk to other professors; to read their thoughts about everything from research and writing to humorous notes about the stresses of grading and the sadness about the end of summer. Twitter was the most efficient way that I had available to me to talk to my colleagues, to my like-minded friends who teach the "difficult" courses that require the courage and the strength to talk about racism, inequality, sexism, and violence. After engaging a few scholars about making a commitment to teach Ferguson on that first day, I received a few responses asking: Teach what? Teach how? These questions led to the birth of #FergusonSyllabus. The hashtag was a means of simply sharing ideas about how to use the disciplines we were trained in to amplify our contributions to better understanding Ferguson.

An invitation from the *Atlantic*'s technology editor, Alexis Madrigal, led to the first listing of #FergusonSyllabus material online. Although other educators had spun off #FergusonSyllabus-inspired projects, such as blog posts and even websites about material they were planning to present in class, the article for the *Atlantic* website was the first interaction between a community that was coalescing around teaching and a mainstream publication.[1] I had offered a few insights to National Public Radio and newspaper stories, but TheAtlantic .Com was able to show the texture of the #FergusonSyllabus and the material on Ferguson that reached back to the past, from the Supreme Court's ruling on the codification of segregation—*Plessy v. Ferguson* (1896)—and engaged the humanities and the sciences. In a short essay, "How to Teach Kids about What's Happening in Ferguson," I hurriedly gathered some of the ideas circulated on Twitter.[2] The #FergusonSyllabus incorporated the current reporting on the Ferguson crisis as well as accounts of St. Louis and its racial history, including a documentary on the city's failed public housing initiatives for newly arrived black migrants, *The Pruitt-Igoe Myth* (2011).[3] Educators also connected Ferguson to past moments of unrest, and recommended reflections on racial violence from earlier periods. The syllabus highlighted the continued relevance of James Baldwin's essay "A Talk to Teachers," in his 1985 essay collection *The Price of the Ticket* as well as Audre Lorde's meditation on activism, "Transformation of Silence into Language and Action," a speech first delivered in 1977, to the ways that activists had responded in Ferguson in 2014.[4] The *Atlantic* piece also included suggestions for educators of young children, like Eve Bunting's *Smoky Night* (illustrated by David Diaz, 1994), which features a child's perspective on the 1992 Los Angeles uprising.[5] The syllabus reminded educators that we have indeed been here before, meaning that we have a rich body of literature to draw from to inform how we teach in the midst of crisis; all we have to do is look and listen.

Developing #FergusonSyllabus was a challenge to my own investments in interdisciplinary thinking and method. Although I was trained in American Studies—a field deeply dependent on interdisciplinary research—I never considered how interdisciplinary collaboration operated in my teaching beyond directing my students to examine scholars outside of my dominant teaching and research frames, which usually relied on history and a bit of literature. Curating a syllabus project that extended beyond my dexterity with mostly urban history texts and assessments of civil rights movements invigorated my own thinking about how to model interdisciplinary analysis to my students. What did it mean to ask experts across disciplines to weigh in on a situation as chaotic and powerful as what was being broadcast every night in Ferguson? As I sent out tweets about what to teach and what questions could frame the classroom instruction and discussion about Ferguson, I realized that the peripheral goal of #FergusonSyllabus extended beyond breaking silences about race, imbalances in the justice system, and state violence. In many ways, #FergusonSyllabus was a challenge to the pleas of racial innocence of scholars who believe that their disciplinary orientation precludes the responsibility to consider the importance of race in what or how they teach. "I'm not an expert on race, how can I talk about Ferguson?" This question was posed to me in a number of ways: sometimes it was a confessional statement, and other times it was an act of evasion. Regardless of what motivated the concern, #FergusonSyllabus revealed that expertise on race was not a prerequisite to connecting the conditions that led to the unrest—the hypertargeting of the poor in Ferguson, racial segregation, inarticulate policies about policing and use of force—to the event itself. The recommendations that emerged from #FergusonSyllabus asked educators to teach an element, a factor, of what fueled the various responses to Ferguson—from residents to the activists who traveled to Missouri, to the White House and the attorney general, to the police unions—in order to engage our students on the complexity of understanding what was happening. I implored sociologists to illustrate theories about power by reading the reporting from Ferguson of long-experienced tensions between police and people in Ferguson. I asked my economist colleagues to consider the marked rise in poverty rates in Ferguson since 2000. I hoped that music scholars could talk about the use of chants and the adoption of freedom songs during protests. Chemists could introduce a lesson about tear gas and the health implications of its use in towns like Ferguson. Graphic design instructors could use the widely circulated data on the racially segregated and underresourced Ferguson-Florissant school district—from which Brown graduated high school—to create informational graphics to help people better visualize the data on economic disparity in the community.

Within a few days of introducing #FergusonSyllabus among the community of scholars I know through social media, the idea extended beyond my colleagues in academia. Elementary school and high school teachers reached out to me, sometimes privately through Twitter's direct message function, asking how they could talk about Ferguson to anxious students. They wanted to know how to engage the topics that emanated from Ferguson without violating directives to not talk about Ferguson. They wanted to be able to help students at homogenously white schools imagine the feelings of communities they had no context for understanding. The teachers wanted to play a part in making #FergusonSyllabus come alive without putting themselves in too much danger. As the tweets about #FergusonSyllabus circulated, journalists took heed and invited me to talk about the effort on radio, on television shows, and in newspaper articles. "Are kids too young to hear about this stuff?" I was asked if the classroom was the place for this level of discourse and, interview after interview, I was reminded of my gratitude to Missouri and my early undergraduate years: I loved teaching because it was the best part of political organizing.

Since initially making the case for teaching Ferguson, I have heard from scores of educators about their anxieties regarding talking about race in the classroom, and their fears about the political climates of their institutions that discourage them from publicly commenting on subjects deemed controversial. Teaching about what is sometimes euphemistically called "difficult topics" can be terrifying, but #FergusonSyllabus taught me that many educators can take pedagogical risks when they believe they are united in a common cause. Social media has the capacity to show us that we are not alone in our concerns, our approaches, and our commitments. I have discovered that #FergusonSyllabus's meaning to educators was as varied as the entries on the crowdsourced documents that were created from the suggestions tweeted and posted online. For educators who were at a loss about "what to do about Ferguson," teaching around the uprising was an act of solidarity, not only with the activists on the streets day in and day out, but also with the educators in and around Ferguson. While teachers and families awaited news of the reopening of Ferguson schools, local teachers volunteered to spend time with children at the Ferguson Public Library and joined the team at the St. Louis Arch, a National Park Service site, to ensure educational activities were available until the school year commenced.

For educators teaching against the grain of their institution, where silences about race and inequality permeated the culture, using #FergusonSyllabus disrupted their feelings of isolation when they searched Twitter. And as August turned into September, they could see examples of other educators "teaching Ferguson." Educators used the hashtag to share stories about successes, as well as misses, in introducing material; others shared links to digital projects created by students. On November 30, 2014, a St. Louis County grand jury refused to indict Officer Wilson in the killing of Michael Brown. The next day, the search for #FergusonSyllabus experienced an uptick on Twitter. Within a few months, #FergusonSyllabus was a known resource that educators could turn to in order to prepare for further discussions. As educators, we can talk to each other about our teaching, but social media allows us to show each other aspects of our teaching in real time. Whether it's encouraging our students to tweet our lectures, asking our colleagues to help us design our syllabi and assignments through crowdsourcing, or curating other syllabi projects, social media can help us create teaching communities outside of the confines of our departments and units. If the digital world can bring us more colleagues, teaching mentors, and supporters, we can find the encouragement we need during troubled times.

Teaching is always political in what knowledge is taught and what knowledge is concealed. Regardless of educators' motivations or framework, teaching is a powerful act because it prepares our students to engage as informed members of a society. Since the launch of #FergusonSyllabus, I have lectured about teaching, social media, and the conversations we need to be having in classrooms and communities about race and the quest for justice, at hundreds of schools. From third-grade teachers to faculty contemplating retirement, my conversations about teaching and technology have provided some insights about why

#FergusonSyllabus—and derivative initiatives, including the 2015 book *Charleston Syllabus* and other hashtags such as #TrumpSyllabus, and websites like Immigration Syllabus from the University of Minnesota—struck such a chord.[6] These lessons have stayed with me as students and educators searched for entry points after the rise of the Black Lives Matter movement, the uprising in Baltimore after the death of Freddie Gray in 2015, and the 2016 presidential election. The use of the word syllabus in this viral movement has moved beyond a description of a listing of readings and other educational material. It has become a shorthand for a response, driven by scholars, to remind a larger public about the importance of our disciplinary debates to solving pressing moral issues of our time. As George Lipsitz pointed to in his 2015 lecture, "Ferguson as a Failure of the Humanities," academics must see their work as originating the solutions to the problems of poverty, racism, privatization, and alienation.[7] #FergusonSyllabus was a small contribution to creating a global movement of scholars toward illustrating to our students why we teach and what they need to learn.

NOTES

1. Marcia Chatelain, "How to Teach Kids about What's Happening in Ferguson," *The Atlantic*, August 25, 2014, https://www.theatlantic.com/education/archive/2014/08/how-to-teach-kids-about-whats-happening-in-ferguson/379049/.

2. Chatelain, "How to Teach Kids about What's Happening in Ferguson."

3. Chad Freidrichs, dir., *The Pruitt-Igoe Myth* (First Run Features, 2011).

4. James Baldwin, "A Talk to Teachers," in *The Price of the Ticket* (New York: St. Martin's/Marek, 1985); Audre Lorde, "Transformation of Silence into Language and Action" (December 28, 1977), in *The Cancer Journals* (San Francisco: Spinsters Ink, 1980).

5. Eve Bunting, *Smoky Night* (San Diego, CA: Harcourt Brace, 1994).

6. Chad Williams, Kidada E. Williams, and Keisha N. Blain, eds., *Charleston Syllabus: Readings on Race, Racism, and Racial Violence* (Athens: University of Georgia Press, 2016); Immigration History Research Center at the University of Minnesota and the Immigration and Ethnic History Society, "Immigration Syllabus," January 26, 2017, https://editions.lib.umn.edu/immigrationsyllabus/.

7. George Lipsitz, "Ferguson as a Failure of the Humanities" (speech, Princeton, NJ, May 1, 2015), https://www.youtube.com/watch?v=mV3x0mk3kLQ.

19. Creative Approaches to Student Assessment

Structure of an Interdisciplinary Group Project

FREDERICO FREITAS

How can students learn interdisciplinary skills in the classroom? One approach is to introduce the thinking and practices of other disciplines into one's own course. It was the path I chose in my graduate seminar on the theory and methods of digital history. The course introduces three approaches of computational history—text analysis, network analysis, and GIS. Throughout the course, students not only discuss literature on different aspects of digital humanities, but also develop a research project based on hermeneutical interpretation of primary sources and data analysis through digital tools. Another approach is to pair up with faculty from other departments to offer joint courses that bridge the gap between disciplines. This was the path taken in the new visual narrative seminar at North Carolina State, where graduate and upper undergraduate students enrolled in courses in history (taught by me), computer science (taught by Arnav Jhala), and art and design (taught by Todd Berreth) work together on an interdisciplinary project that integrates the three fields.

In a typical semester, half of the meetings in the three courses are held jointly. Instructors form groups composed of students from all three disciplines, and their joint assignment is to develop the different components of a digital humanities project. The final project corresponds to 60 percent of the final grade of students in each class. Each semester, the three instructors choose a specific technology to be explored by all the groups. For example, in the first iteration of this co-taught visual narrative seminar, students are working with Unity, a game development platform, to create a virtual or augmented reality app that puts a user in the shoes of a person in the past. Besides developing the technical aspects of the project (i.e., coding, design), groups are also required to complete the humanistic task of picking a historical topic, finding primary sources, and framing a research question.

During a sixteen-week semester, groups complete a series of milestones designed to move students through the conceptualization, development, and finalization of the project. In the two first weeks of class, students take a survey on their skills and research interests, and are assigned to groups by the three instructors. The goal is to achieve a balance between students' complementary skills. In week three, groups turn in the first assignment—an exploratory report in which they present tentative topics and sources, choose a platform and describe the nature of the project, introduce visual culture related to the topics, and present references of prior art. The different components of this exploratory report expose students to the methods of the three disciplines—history, computer science, and design. This trident approach continues in the next assignments. In week five, students turn in a draft proposal that includes a well-defined topic, primary sources, and a research question, as well as a storyboard of the user experience and a conceptual demo as proof of technology. In week seven, each group presents their final research proposal, which serves as a roadmap for the rest of the semester. Students then have the opportunity to receive feedback from instructors and peers from other groups.

Although a significant portion of the development work happens out of the classroom, students also are allocated class time to work together on their project and receive feedback from instructors. There are two milestone checks before the final delivery, when groups give a short presentation on the progress of their projects. During finals week, students deliver their final product (e.g., a mobile app or a desktop online visualization) in a final critique session with the presence of members of the digital humanities, design, and computer science communities at North Carolina State. They also turn in a final report detailing the process of development, describing the performance of group members, and reflecting on the dialogue between the final product and the scholarship in each discipline. With this group project, we tried to create a hybrid assignment that speaks to specific questions in each field, while allowing students to work together across disciplinary boundaries.

Wiki Assignment

BRENDA ELSEY

Several years ago, I attended a THATCamp Feminisms East meeting at Barnard College, which included a wiki-edit-a-thon.[1] Session organizers presented compelling data about the paucity of women's and gender history on the website, as well as the disproportionate entries on the "Western" world. It inspired me to incorporate Wikipedia into my coursework, rather than shun it. As 10 percent of my students' course grade, they edit a Wikipedia page of their choosing, relevant to the course. The assignment requires that students use course materials to edit the entry, and that they properly cite them in the bibliographical or footnote section. We discuss the process of editing beforehand and ensure that students choose different entries in order to avoid editing over one another. There is a useful brochure to help students through the editing process.[2]

I've found that the Wikipedia assignment develops students' understanding of their first line of research. They also gain an appreciation for the skepticism of their teachers who have warned them about the use of the website. Nevertheless, students tend to feel empowered by the ability to change such an important public platform. From its inception in 2001, Wikipedia began to supersede the popularity of print encyclopedias, and now registers among the most-read webpages in the world. The most successful iterations of this assignment involved explicitly stating my intentions ahead of time.

An important objective of the assignment is for students to engage in a different way with course readings. My hope is that they better understand and articulate the contribution of the course texts as they survey the general information available to the public through Wikipedia. For example, in my colonial Latin America course, I assigned *Malintzin's Choices: An Indian Woman in the Conquest of Mexico*, by Camilla Townsend.[3] The student working on the entry of "La Malinche," or Malintzin, integrated information and arguments from the course text to discuss how the importance of Malintzin had been written out of accounts of the colonization of Mexico. She included evidence of Malintzin's importance to the Spanish, referring to sources from both Spanish and indigenous perspectives. The student went further and integrated other scholarly books and articles, voluntarily, to support her edits to the entry. During the discussions of the assignment, students expressed that they had a better understanding of what a monograph contributes to our general historical knowledge.

In terms of the assignment requirements, the students must add at least 250 words to one Wikipedia entry, and make additions to the bibliography. As part of the assignment, students write a summary of how they found the entry they chose to edit, the edits they made, the process of editing, and why they thought the change was significant. Their grade is based on the combination of the summary and the text of the edit itself. Typically, the assignment sparks a lively discussion on the day students hand it in. I try to leave an entire class session so that each person can speak for a couple of minutes about their experience.

Assignment: Writing Restaurant Reviews with Instagram
STEVEN ALVAREZ

At my first academic position at the University of Kentucky, I taught an undergraduate writing course exploring Mexican migration to the Bluegrass, focusing on themes of language and power, bilingualism, labor, family, and social justice. As a way to celebrate the end of the semester, I treated students to tacos in the barrio near campus, a barrio that many students had not known about. At Tortillería y Taquería Ramírez, the students expressed their amazement at a menu with food items they had never tasted. Naturally, students took out their cell phones and took photos of their tacos to post on Instagram. No doubt, this was the happiest I had seen the students all semester. Inspired by students' use of Instagram, I designed a photo-essay restaurant review assignment for what would become my new "Taco Literacy" course. This assignment requires students to explore the genre of the food review and create their own, while also teaching them the importance of social media as a tool to cultivate audiences and archive research. For the assignment, students compose a photo-essay reviewing a local Mexican restaurant, following a particular dish they have researched, and researching the history of the restaurant they review. Using the models of print and digital restaurant reviews they have read in class, students compose a piece that tells a story, using Instagram to illustrate their writing. I also ask students to include five translations of words from Spanish and describe the roots of the words, making note of indigenous loanwords. The text of the assignment includes six to eight photographs embedded within the body of the blog page, as well as captions. The length requirement is twelve hundred words, and must include the works cited and hyperlinked sources. The intersections of foodways, literacy, emotion, photography, social justice, and emergent bilingualism are rich material for writing projects at all levels.

Teaching Tactic: Dialogic Note-Taking
JEREMY V. CRUZ

I use this tactic to help students pay close attention to assigned texts, engage in active and structured note-taking, process learning verbally, build scholarly community, increase confidence, and feel greater group accountability within the learning process. Here are the steps:

1. Groups receive one or more questions from the professor, to guide engagement with course texts. Each group receives different questions.
2. Students read assigned texts and take personal notes.
3. Students collaborate with group members outside of class (in person or on Google Docs) to draft a response to the group's assigned question(s). Groups can vary in size and number, depending on class size and pedagogical needs. These groups are regular, preassigned discussion groups, allowing for reliable collaboration.
4. At the beginning of class, group members meet to ensure that their group has fully answered their assigned question(s), and that everyone is ready to explain the group's interpretations.
5. Each group sends one "ambassador" to a neighboring group. Each ambassador explains their group's answers to the question(s) posed by the professor. Group members who receive an ambassador take notes. Groups make note of any disagreements of interpretation. *The professor roams the room to correct misunderstandings regarding the process.*
6. Given time constraints, and the number and size of groups, the professor asks ambassadors to rotate through some or all of the groups.
7. Ambassadors return to their own groups. Group members share with ambassadors what they learned from other groups' ambassadors.
8. The professor responds to differences of interpretation that arose during the activity, and answers remaining questions about the assigned text.

Migrant Letters

ROMEO GUZMÁN

In my California Studies course, I use letter writing to replace the traditional five-page research essay. My students are required to pick an ethnic or migrant group that arrived in California in the nineteenth or twentieth century, and to write four letters from the perspective of a migrant. These letters, I instruct them, should demonstrate that they understand the genre of letter writing and the experience of the ethnic group they selected. Collectively, the four letters should document push and pull factors; legal, emotional, or political obstacles; transnational ties and connections; family and quotidian life; racism and discrimination; and work and joy, among other things. Students are required to use three to four peer-reviewed articles as secondary source material and are encouraged—when possible—to interview family members. My students enjoy using the "I" and the opportunity to use their historical imagination.

"Unofficial Archives"

ROMEO GUZMÁN

This is an assignment I use in my Introduction to Public History courses. I ask my students to think of their home as a source of historical knowledge and an archive of memories and material objects. I ask them to use a photograph or object (a belt buckle, a rolling pin, a piece of furniture) to construct a narrative about a person in their family, or their entire family or community. The word count on this assignment is flexible, but is often between 2,000 and 3,000 words. Students workshop their papers with each other in class, and are offered the opportunity to publish their stories on *Tropics of Meta*, an academic blog I help edit.

Bridging the Humanities and Hard Sciences: Transformational Learning through a Borderlands Classroom

SONIA HERNÁNDEZ AND TIFFANY JASMIN GONZÁLEZ

Two professors, two graduate assistants, and seventy-five undergraduate students from two academic disciplines (history and engineering) formed an interdisciplinary global classroom to expose undergraduate students to the Texas-Mexico borderlands. Funded by a Tier One Research Grant, the class took a three-day trip to the South Texas region to visit museums, historical landmarks, a wildlife refuge, a portion of the US-Mexico border wall, and several *colonias* (unincorporated neighborhoods). Law school professors with expertise in immigration, community development, and property law also met with the students.

An essential aspect of the trip was grouping students into teams of mixed majors. Students were expected to collaborate with each other and share research methods from their home disciplines. The final project required students to apply this interdisciplinary knowledge to communicating their personal and scholarly observations about the border region. Thus, along with promoting community engagement and service learning, this project required students to work outside of their disciplinary silos. Final projects included formal letters addressed to politicians regarding the devastating environmental consequences of a border wall, maps detailing environmental effects on wildlife, magazines on the history of the border, and scale models of historical landmarks, among other deliverables. In short, students approached the border region from various disciplinary perspectives via peer multidisciplinary learning.

Assignment: Describe and Defend

SHEILA MCMANUS

I use this trio of sequenced assignments in my freshman World History course, which covers ten thousand years of history across five continents in a single twelve-week semester. Each assignment's percentage of the final grade increases in steps (10 percent for the first one, 20 percent for the second one, and 30 percent for the final one).

The first D&D assignment requires students to choose the five events, periods, and/or individuals that they think are the most significant from the lectures and textbook reading they completed in roughly the first third of the course. They do a short 200- to 250-word write-up for each item, with 100 to 125 words on the description and 100 to 125 words explaining the criteria they used to make their choices, for a total length of 1,000 to 1,250 words for the whole assignment. After completing their individual assignments, students work in small teams in class to compare and contrast their lists before coming together as a whole class to discuss the top items that have emerged.

The second D&D covers approximately the middle third of the course. Students choose another five significant events, periods, or people, and write 200 to 250 words about each item, with roughly the same fifty-fifty split of description and defending their criteria. The students then go *back* to their first list of five items and choose their top three items from the ten they have chosen for the first two assignments. They write an additional 200 to 250 words on why they have chosen these three, and what patterns they notice about their own selection process. Have they chosen mostly military items, or political, or social, and why? Have they emphasized one time period or region over others, and why? The students are asked to be self-reflective and notice what these patterns reveal about what *they* think is important to study in history.

The third D&D follows the same format as the second one, beginning with choosing another five items from the final third of the course, and then revisiting the first two assignments to choose and analyze a final top three items out of their complete list of fifteen. The final word count for this assignment is between twelve hundred and fifteen hundred words, which is the same as the second one. After completing the individual written assignments, the students again work in small discussion teams in class to compare and contrast their lists. This leads to great discussion in their teams, and then as an entire class, about what they found significant in this expansive world history course.

Using Pinterest in the Classroom

LAURA PORTWOOD-STACER

I have used Pinterest in a media studies course—specifically focused on fashion and culture—with great success. I began by setting up a collective Pinterest account and giving all the students in the class access via a shared password. Each class period had a designated Pinterest board associated with it, and each student was tasked with pinning at least one image to the board that illustrated a concept from the assigned readings for that period. Along with the images, students provided captions that explained the connection they had drawn between the image and the course concepts. This assignment was successful for several reasons: (1) students had the opportunity to apply ideas from the course to real-life examples that felt relevant to them; (2) students could read, learn from, and build on each other's insights; (3) I was able to gauge students' understanding of the readings in advance of the in-class discussion; (4) the boards provided me with ready-to-hand examples I could use in my lectures while recognizing students during class for their contributions; (5) the class collectively produced a visually appealing archive of the course's content that they could return to during exam review; and (6) students gained facility with a social media platform that they could later use in their personal and professional lives.

Class Podcasts

MEGHAN ROBERTS

My students have always enjoyed thinking about the connections between early modern history and current events, but I had never designed a formal assignment channeling that interest. One day, when I was listening to one of my favorite historical podcasts, I realized: my students could produce podcasts of their own! For the final assignment of my Crime and Punishment seminar, small groups of students designed podcasts that linked the past to the present: prostitution in eighteenth-century London and present-day Las Vegas; the rise of "humane" prisons; the use of the insanity defense by would-be assassins of George III and Ronald Reagan; witch trials (both historical and as a rhetorical device to shut down the #MeToo movement); and so on. Using Apple's Garage Band software, they incorporated music, audio clips, interviews, and games. Their analysis was sharp and rooted in peer-reviewed scholarship and historical sources, which I could see because they submitted supplemental material with references.

NOTES

1. Barnard Center for Research on Women, "THATCamp Feminisms East," March 16, 2013, http://bcrw.barnard.edu/event/thatcamp-feminisms-east/.
2. "Editing Wikipedia: A Guide for Student Editors Supported by the Wiki Education Foundation," accessed April 2, 2020, https://upload.wikimedia.org/wikipedia/commons/e/e5/Editing_Wikipedia_brochure_%28Wiki_Education_Foundation%29_%282016%29.pdf.
3. Camilla Townsend, *Malintzin's Choices: An Indian Woman in the Conquest of Mexico* (Albuquerque: University of New Mexico Press, 2006).

20. Technology in Teaching

LAURA M. HARRISON

Two years ago, I banned electronic devices from my classes. This is a decision with which I struggled. I don't hate, fear, or otherwise oppose technology—a caveat that now seems required in any critique of it. And I'm not the kind of person who unilaterally bans things. Despite characterizations such as Matthew Numer's (2017) *Chronicle of Higher Education* piece, wherein he argues that faculty "brag" about banning technology, I'm highly uncomfortable with measures that smack of rigidity or authoritarianism. My experiences of devices sucking the energy, attention, and connection out of the classroom, however, eventually outweighed that discomfort.

In this essay, I will discuss how a device-free classroom can make teaching more effective and pleasurable. I will also share some strategies for teaching online, a skill set increasingly required in contemporary academia. My goal is to transcend the well-worn narratives about technology as either panacea or destroyer.

I will not land in the script of technology as simply a tool that works well or poorly depending on how it is used. I do not see technology as neutral; my views come close to Franklin Foer's as expressed in *World without Mind*, in which he describes technology itself as ideological:

> Algorithms fuel a sense of omnipotence, the condescending belief that our behavior can be altered, without our even being aware of the hand guiding a superior direction. There has always been a danger of the

engineering mindset, as it moves beyond its roots in building inanimate stuff and begins to design a more perfect social world. We are just screws and rivets in its grand design. (77)

My position is that technology is indeed ideological. If we let technology eclipse the relational aspects of the classroom in the name of providing education on the cheap, it becomes a means to the neoliberal end of the McDonaldization of higher education (Hayes, Wynyard, and Mandal 2017). This path also means pumping more public money into the hands of private educational technology corporations, a phenomenon Picciano and Spring (2013) exposed effectively in *The Great American Education-Industrial Complex: Ideology, Technology, and Profit*.

Exposing technology's nefarious aspects allows us to identify contexts where it can be reappropriated for more prosocial aims. As educators, we have agency over what ideology we support with our use of (or abstinence from) technology. If we employ technology in the service of a truly student-centered pedagogy, however, there are ways it can enhance that ethos.

Student-Centeredness in the Online Environment

Perhaps ironically, I began seeing the benefits of teaching online at about the same time I was starting to recognize the costs of devices while teaching in person. I was teaching a summer academic writing class that some students could not take on campus because of internships and other commitments that took them away for the summer. I reluctantly agreed to offer the course online and was surprised to see how much more progress many of the students made in this environment. What follows are some insights I gained based on both my observations and my students' advice.

LEVERAGE THE ONLINE ENVIRONMENT TO ADDRESS DIFFERENT LEVELS OF SKILL (AND ANXIETY)

Helping students improve their writing has to be one of the more frustrating and time-consuming aspects of academic life. We do not get much preparation for teaching generally, much less teaching writing specifically. Our jobs require us to write prolifically, so we tend to do it well and with at least some degree of pleasure. These qualities sometimes make it difficult for us to understand and teach those students with different experiences of writing.

There has been a trend toward faculty decreasing writing requirements in their courses (Berrett 2012). This is unfortunate, as employers lament the lack of writing skills in recent graduates (National Commission on Writing 2016).

Students need to write more, not less, yet the labor-intensiveness of the process often inhibits us from rising to this challenge.

The online environment helped me diagnose and treat some of the more labor-intensive aspects of teaching writing. For example, I knew that students varied in their college readiness in the area of writing, but I didn't fully appreciate how much my failure to address that variation made teaching writing more difficult than it needed to be. Once I created narrated presentations on topics like writing a sound thesis, using evidence to support an argument, and revising effectively, I made a dent in the problem of students being at such different skill levels. More advanced students could watch the videos once and move on to more challenging tasks. Less advanced students could watch the videos as many times as they needed and meet with me to address their specific questions.

I saved a lot of time by recording things I was tired of saying repeatedly. More advanced students benefited from not having to sit in class listening to things they already knew. Less advanced students were spared the difficult choice of struggling in silence or risking embarrassment by asking a question that might seem elementary to the other students. I value the community afforded by in-person classes, but I've also come to see how there are situations in which not constantly having to face other students is advantageous. When I teach scholarly writing online, struggling students are much more open with me about their challenges. They don't see the high achievers sailing through their assignments, and thus compete only with themselves. As a result, they ask better questions, which allows them to make more progress.

Similarly, high-performing students do not necessarily know they are at the top of the class, which I suspect causes less laurel-resting. They, too, don't have to worry about how they're coming across in a general classroom. I remember sitting in many a statistics class, wondering how the students who actually liked this subject felt in a room full of people with math anxiety. My online writing students are free of their fellow students' anxiety and thus able to lean into their enjoyment without being targets of scorn or envy.

LOOK FOR THE ADVANTAGES IN ONLINE EDUCATION

While I primarily teach writing online, I do occasionally teach other online courses as well. I argue that the live classroom is nearly always the most optimal experience for students, a point upon which I will expound in the next section. Hence, I believe contemporary academics must take up the banner of advocating for the preservation of the in-person educational experience. At the same time, we cannot deny the move toward more online offerings. Resistance is not futile, but it's also not always practical. It's tempting to approach online classes begrudgingly, but students are too often the casualties of that attitude. Therefore, it is better to mine the positives that can be exploited in the online environment.

The first advantage that jumped out at me when I began teaching online is the leveling potential of the virtual classroom. No longer could a few chatter-boxes dominate the conversation. Similarly, those students who need a couple of minutes to think before speaking benefited from the asynchronous discussions. In addition, the asynchronous environment can provide advantages for English-language learners. In my research on Chinese students, participants nearly universally expressed appreciation for professors who could slow things down enough for English-language learners to have time to translate (Su and Harrison 2016).

Slowing down also has some advantages in terms of civil discourse. As I write, I'm currently teaching Diversity in American Higher Education online. My students are primarily higher education administrators, so the purpose of this course is to provide an opportunity to delve deeply into the most pressing diversity challenges on college campuses. I revise the course frequently based on what is happening in the here and now, in order to keep it relevant. For example, the resurgence of student activism inspired me to focus more on civil discourse, since many of our students are called upon to navigate thorny issues such as free speech versus hateful language in their professional capacities as higher education leaders. We address some hot topics throughout the course; the ability to let my thoughts marinate before responding to students has helped me communicate more effectively than I might in the more palpable awkwardness or heat of the in-person classroom. My students have expressed similar feelings of gratitude for the time and space to collect their thoughts before "speaking" in the online environment.

Finally, having a transcript of online discussions can provide powerful modeling for students. An example of this pedagogical tool occurred in my online diversity class a couple of years ago. Two of the students engaged in respectful, but very candid, exchanges on several of the discussion threads in the class. Other students expressed concern that these students were embroiled in conflict, but it turned out that they were friends, perhaps of the Ruth Bader Ginsburg and Antonin Scalia variety. These students' comfort with conflict became a model for other students to stretch themselves to take intellectual risks and become braver about being challenged.

Despite these positive points, the students in this same class felt the constraints of the online environment. They wanted to engage more deeply as a learning community, and that required being live and in person. We eventually started meeting in person, which I think is a powerful statement, since these were students who chose an online program over an in-person one. Universities sell online programs as convenient, but it turns out that there are other, more important considerations in what constitutes an education.

Preserving the Classroom

Technology can enhance student learning when its use is motivated by that purpose. It cannot and should not, however, replace the classroom. My wife, an academic in Communication Studies, helped me develop an analogy for explaining this assertion. She talks of the importance of understanding positive, neutral, and destructive change in the context of technology's impact on journalism. For example, she has a great deal of nostalgia for newsprint, but concedes that it's not really a big deal whether people read news on paper or devices. The gutting of newsrooms, however, represents a truly problematic result of social-media-driven news. I see similarities with technology and education. When students first started taking notes on laptops, they experienced the benefit of storable, searchable notes without too many costs. Once a critical mass of students lost the ability to focus and started playing on GroupMe instead of contributing to the class, I felt it was my professional obligation to insist on device-free classrooms.

This was not a decision I made lightly, for two reasons. First, I do not gravitate toward rigid rules as solutions; I favor discussing concerns and trusting students to use their best judgment whenever possible. Unfortunately, this strategy consistently proved ineffective in my experience of technology in the classroom. If my evaluations are accurate, I'm a good teacher and my students are mostly very smart, motivated people. Yet the pull of technology seems to lure even the best students if their minds wander for even a minute. It became exhausting to keep repeating things students would have heard if they had not been trying to "multitask," an activity that has been proven futile (Ophir, Nass, and Wagner 2009). I tried all the softer tactics of being more entertaining, offering more breaks, and using my good classroom-rapport-building skills to address the issue directly. Despite these strategies and my repeated pleas to limit technology use to educational purposes, only an outright ban solved the problem.

The other reason I hesitated to enact a ban on devices is the very important point many have made about their role in assisting students with disabilities. I state both verbally and on the syllabus that I will, of course, honor technology accommodations for students with disabilities. This is my only legal obligation, but I understand the frequently made argument that students with disabilities may feel stigmatized, or more visible to their peers than they would like, by having to ask for an exception (Lang 2016). I take pride in my ability to be approachable and relatable to students, so I count on these qualities to make myself the kind of person with whom a student would feel comfortable engaging in a conversation about this issue. I have not yet been called upon to make such an accommodation, but am prepared to reevaluate the policy in light of this issue.

For now, the technology ban performs the job I was hoping it would in terms of facilitating a more productive and pleasant classroom environment. People often express surprise when I tell them how little revolt this policy has produced. I have used past students' complaints to anticipate and address current students' concerns upfront. For example, some students react defensively to the tech ban by indicating that they're tired of hearing "older" people complain about the things they think are fun. Therefore, I'm careful to frame the no-device policy in the positive language of our classroom community, rather than a negative attitude toward technology. Some students worry that they will not be able to handwrite as quickly as they can type, so I post my lectures online in order to assuage their fears about adequate note-taking (and speak to them a bit about strategic note-taking). I also post the greatest hits of the compelling research on the educational benefits of device-free classes to articulate the intentionality behind the policy. And if I see students get antsy, restless, or glazed-over during a lecture, I try to address this by including the student in the discussion I am leading, or giving the entire class a quick break.

Aside from these moments, I have received many unsolicited positive comments, particularly from older students weary of being texted constantly by needy children and employers. They like having a few hours a week during which they can be fully present, and being able to blame their lack of availability on their mean professor. Younger students, too, generally talk about our device-free classes as a novelty. It's not news to them that they are addicted to their phones; they actually seem to have more insight and honesty about this particular feature of modern life than their parents do. Young people have been fighting phones for their parents' attention for many years, so some of them seem to enjoy the adult attention afforded by the device-free policy.

More importantly, I tell students the truth about the real reason behind my device-free policy, which is that I don't want to miss out on them. I don't want to lose them to their screens. I admit that it's pure selfishness, that the pleasure of their company is what's in it for me. In addition, students need what Scharmer (2009) calls the "social field," that experience of community presence that generates more expansiveness and creative thinking than possible on one's own. So far, these reasons have convinced my students to go along with me on the merits of the device-free class.

Whether we teach online, in person, or both, we must insist on a practice that is student-centered in order to protect the integrity of what we claim to do in higher education. In *Alone Together*, Turkle (2011) writes of technology's impact on a variety of fields. We can harness the positive effects and ignore the neutral impacts; we need to take a stand against the negative impacts. Turkle provides a powerful example of a group of architects who reclaimed hand drawing as an aptitude too central to their identity to allow to be lost. Many of these architects supported computer-assisted design, but began to advocate for the preservation of hand drawing in academic programs when they noticed young professionals losing this sacred part of their professional identity.

Many will argue that any attempt to regain control over technology is simply aversion to change. Yet the substance of the change matters; there are things that need to change and things that are worthy of preservation. In just the past year, paper book sales outpaced e-books as people rediscovered the joy of reading without being plugged in. There has been a resurgence of interest in vinyl music as well. The point is, people can and do have paper books and e-books, streaming music services and record players. This logic can be extended to education. There can be both online and in-person classes (as well as hybrids). We can incorporate new possibilities without destroying all the value afforded by centuries of classroom learning.

I will close with the words of Palmer and Zajonc (2010), who articulate eloquently what I believe to be the best approach to hotly debated issues in higher education:

> If higher education is to keep evolving toward its full potential, it needs people who are so devoted to the educational enterprise that they have a lover's quarrel with the institution whenever they see it fall short of that potential—and are willing to translate that quarrel into positive action. (21)

We are in a moment when it is tempting to either dig in our heels against technological encroachment or accept it uncritically. Neither of these paths will lead to a desirable place for the future of higher education. The "lover's quarrel" option embodies the best of what could be a creative tension that allows us to cull the very best of both online and in-person learning. It is my hope that we can learn to live thoughtfully in that tension for the benefit of our current and future students.

WORKS CITED

Berrett, D. 2012. "An Old-School Notion: Writing Required." *Chronicle of Higher Education*, October 15. https://www.chronicle.com/article/An-Old-School-Notion-Writing/135106.

Foer, F. 2017. *World without Mind: The Existential Threat of Big Tech*. New York: Penguin.

Hayes, D., R. Wynyard, and L. Mandal. 2017. *The McDonaldization of Higher Education*. New York: Routledge.

Lang, J. 2016. "No, Banning Laptops Is Not the Answer." *Chronicle of Higher Education*, September 11. https://www.chronicle.com/article/No-Banning-Laptops-Is-Not-the /237752.

National Commission on Writing. 2016. *Design for Learning*. New York: College Board.

Numer, M. 2017. "Don't Insult Your Class by Banning Laptops." *Chronicle of Higher Education*, December 4. https://www.chronicle.com/article/Don-t-Insult-Your-Class-by /241972.

Ophir, E., Nass, C., and A. D. Wagner. 2009. "Cognitive Control in Media Multitaskers." *Proceedings of the National Academy of Sciences* 106.37: 15583–15587.

Palmer, P., and A. Zajonc. 2010. *The Heart of Higher Education: A Call to Renewal*. San Francisco: Jossey-Bass.

Picciano, A. G., and J. Spring. 2013. *The Great American Education-Industrial Complex: Ideology, Technology, and Profit*. New York: Routledge.

Scharmer, O. 2009. *Theory U: Leading from the Future as It Emerges*. San Francisco: Berrett-Koehler.

Su, M., and L. M. Harrison. 2016. "Being Wholesaled: An Investigation of Chinese International Students' Higher Education Experiences." *Journal of International Students* 26.4: 905–919.

Turkle, S. 2011. *Alone Together: Why We Expect More from Technology and Less from Each Other*. New York: Basic Books.

21. Neurodiversity in the Classroom

JOHN ELDER ROBISON AND KARIN WULF

A concerted effort to consider neurodiversity in the college classroom is essential for supporting neurodivergent students, and also offers important pedagogical opportunities. Not too long ago, most disability service requests were for physical disability. Today, the majority of such requests involve cognitive disability, and many fall under the neurodiversity umbrella. Neurodiversity is also reshaping disability activism and disability studies. It is creating opportunities for new areas of study, as the idea of neurodiversity touches every corner of today's university. Just as we recognize how constraining other kinds of expectations of what a "typical" student is might be (in terms of race, class, gender, age, and intergenerational experience of college), letting go of expectations for a standard neurology can enhance our ability to reach all students and create more dynamic, effective teaching.

Neurodiversity is the idea that neurological diversity is part of overall human diversity. The neurodiversity movement has emerged in response to the medical profession's identification of cognitive disorders—primarily autism, attention deficit disorder, dyslexia, and Tourette syndrome. These diagnostic labels focused entirely on disability, ignoring the reality that many diagnosed individuals have exceptional skills, too; they may be among the most impressive students in your college classroom. The people's adoption of neurodiversity as an identity is a response to perceived marginalization by medical professionals. The term is not a medical label; it was coined by an autistic social scientist who saw herself as "more than just disabled."

Over the past twenty years, changes to diagnostic standards have driven a surge in diagnoses of neurodevelopmental differences, producing a growing population of college students diagnosed with autism or ADHD. Some will arrive with neurodiversity awareness, others will learn about neurodiversity in school or in the community. Brain differences occur in more than 13 percent of the general population, according to Centers for Disease Control estimates. More than half that number have formal diagnoses by the time they reach college age.

A growing number of colleges and universities are starting to find ways to support neurodiversity. We have been teaching and working together since 2012, as part of William & Mary's Neurodiversity Initiative. This initiative works across campus to support students, faculty, and staff, though most of our efforts have focused on students. We address areas including admissions, study abroad, residential life, and especially classroom experience. Units all across campus have become engaged with this work, finding that supporting neurodiversity is not only part of their mission, but enhances experiences for all students. The Neurodiversity Student Group has become central to this work, advocating for student interests and joining us in making presentations and holding workshops.

Most students who were diagnosed as young children have some experience with the special education process. Some identify as neurodivergent without a formal diagnosis, since neurodiversity and neurodivergence are identity concepts that may describe a wide range of functions from disability to exceptionality. At William & Mary, we have seen students identify in this way during college, having made it through high school without any formal diagnosis, and others who pursue a diagnosis once they get to college.

Support for neurodiversity needs to operate at multiple levels, including the institution, the campus community, and the classroom. Neurodivergent students are at high risk for dropping out, and may find the social stress of college debilitating. So much of the college experience, from orientation to seminar-style coursework, includes high sensory demands and depends on discerning and managing implicit social information. "Why is college built for extroverts?" a student asked us early on. While extroversion and studying are not mutually exclusive, it is true that without accommodation for sensory and social sensitivity, college can be overwhelming.

The most straightforward classroom accommodations are about consultation and making the implicit explicit. Consulting with students from the first day of class, making the expectations and structure of the course clear for everyone, and surfacing some of the unwritten rules of the classroom environment are crucial for a neurodivergent student's success. This approach also lays a foundation for *all* students' success, and supports collaboration in learning.

Consulting with students about the classroom environment can take several forms. One is to make clear that accommodations can be discussed with the faculty member as well as any relevant university office. Another is to acknowledge the environment, whether because it lacks natural light, and artificial lighting can be distracting or painful for some; or because it is crowded; or because the acoustics are not suited to all learners. Reflecting openly on environmental problems allows students to know the instructor is aware of their challenges, and being heard is the first step in being helped. Another consultation might be on the nature of distractions in the classroom. Many faculty express concern about student distraction, and in fact some have advocated banning phones and laptops as a way to reduce distraction. For many students, however, the distractions of the physical plant (the low hum of fluorescent lights, for example) may be more disruptive. And for those with dysgraphia or other situations, laptops and phones are essential educational tools. Looking at why and how technology bans are implemented, in the context of the course and its format, is crucial for ensuring that students with accommodations are not singled out unfairly. Acknowledging that distraction presents itself differently can again simultaneously address the needs of specific students, and bring all students into a conversation about creating a productive learning environment.

Clarifying the structure and expectations of a course will help all students, but it is especially important for neurodivergent students for whom implicit requirements and abrupt transitions may make the course dramatically more difficult. An open-ended set of requirements that will rely on the students to absorb implicit rather than explicit sets of instructions and evaluation criteria will be detrimental for all, but again, much more difficult for neurodivergent students. When we meet with faculty groups to discuss this, we emphasize that we are not suggesting that any particular types of assignments or activities are wrong, only that all of them need to be explained clearly and fully.

The Neurodiversity Initiative at William & Mary has developed resources for faculty and students that offer guidance on some of these points. We have a presentation, for example, on the "hidden rules of seminars," which covers issues such as how to assess personal space in a seminar setting, how to gauge the appropriate number of contributions to the discussion, and how to enter into the discussion. We have another presentation on office hours, and others explicitly for faculty to create an inclusive classroom. In surveys, we have found that almost all students appreciate this sort of effort to make the implicit explicit, and that some are also particularly helpful, for example, for first-generation college students. All of these resources can be accessed on our website at www.wm.edu /sites/neurodiversity/resources. We are always looking to revise and improve these, and thus appreciate feedback.

Finding neurodivergent faculty leaders may be the first major challenge for any campus neurodiversity initiative. In the disability advocacy community, there is a famous mantra: *Nothing about us, without us.* One of us (John Robison) is openly neurodivergent. Given the size of the neurodivergent population, every college likely has a number of neurodivergent faculty. It is important that some of those faculty disclose their differences in order to have credibility and stand as role models for neurodivergent students.

Locating or developing other resources on your campus to support neurodiversity will become increasingly important to our increasingly diverse student body. Though it often presents with disability and requires thoughtful accommodations from the campus level (sensory-sensitive spaces) to the classroom and for the individual student, the work we do mutually—as neurotypical and neurodivergent faculty, staff, and students, as well as alumni and community members—is important to the entire campus community. But because neurodiversity, like other types of diversity, enriches community, it's also just a good thing to do. Attention to it can improve your teaching in the classroom and beyond. We have found that thinking about neurodiversity encourages reflection among faculty and staff. As one colleague remarked to us early on, "That word, neurodiversity, it really lowers the temperature on all sorts of differences."

22. "Typical Dreamer": Some Reflections on Teaching, Advising, and Advocating for Undocumented, Veteran, and Nontraditional Students

ELADIO BOBADILLA

In 2017, the *New York Times* profiled the "typical 'Dreamer.'" An average "Dreamer" came to the United States from Mexico at age six, lives in California, and is likely to hold a white-collar job.[1] A similar profile, published by the Department of Veterans Affairs a few years earlier, showed that the typical student veteran was male, older than the average college student, and likely to be married and have children. Such profiles are useful in some ways, but a careful look at (and beyond) the "averages" reveals an important contradiction: there is no such thing as a typical Dreamer or a typical veteran.[2] These student populations are made up of diverse individuals, with unique gifts, challenges, and needs. And yet, they do share something in common: their desire to get a higher education despite serious barriers.

Student populations like Dreamers and veterans pose a paradox and a challenge for educators, who have to be able to identify and recognize the collective groups and their needs in order to support them, while at the same time accepting that their expectations and preconceived notions about individuals within those groups may be incomplete or incorrect.

So, what can instructors and advisers do to help veteran, undocumented, and other nontraditional students succeed? First, academics should learn about the needs of the students they are teaching and serving: What challenges do they face? What kinds of issues stand in their way? Second, they can familiarize themselves with the resources that are available to those groups, such as campus- or community-based Veterans Affairs offices, counseling services, and legal clinics. And finally, they can work to make their classrooms (and any space in which student and teacher may interact) safe and welcoming places where all students will be supported, respected, and valued.

It is a positive sign that we are having this discussion in the pages of this volume and in our professional circles more generally. That wasn't always the case. "Back then all we had was the shadows," says S. Coronel, a formerly undocumented California man who, in the mid-1990s, dreamed of going to college but could not do so because of his immigration status. Despite an excellent academic record and a promising athletic profile, Coronel's undocumented status kept him from college. "At the time," he remembers, "students did not qualify for scholarships, financial aid, or in-state tuition." Worse, Proposition 187, California's now-infamous anti-immigrant ballot initiative, threatened to "make life impossible for all undocumented people."[3] Now a United States citizen, Coronel hopes to write a book that will tell his story and encourage undocumented youth to seek higher education. He wants other immigrants to have the opportunity he never did.

I am one of those more fortunate immigrants, though my path to academia was not a traditional or linear one. I was a first-generation student; neither of my parents had any formal education, and not one of my five siblings graduated from high school. I was the son of migrant farmworkers. I was the product of an open-enrollment institution (and before that, of self-paced distance courses and college-equivalency tests). I was a military veteran. And I had been undocumented for most of my childhood and adolescence. All of that made for a path that was not always easy. Thankfully, along the way I found teachers, scholars, mentors, and advisers who, whether instinctually or by virtue of their training or experience, knew what to do to help me succeed.

Not everyone is so fortunate, however, and despite the best efforts of those who lit my path, even I faced obstacles along the way. In what follows, I offer some reflections on my own experiences and on challenges for nontraditional students in higher education and the academy. Along with some insights from other scholars, I share some thoughts on how instructors and advisers might help undocumented students (often called Dreamers) and those who come from undocumented or mixed-status families, as well as veterans—and by extension, nontraditional students more generally. It would be impossible to speak for all undocumented, veteran, or nontraditional students or to offer a complete or comprehensive guide to teaching, mentoring, or working with these populations. Rather, I hope this serves as a starting point for important conversations in and beyond the classroom about how to better serve nontraditional students, especially (but not only) veterans and Dreamers.

First, some background on my own trajectory. I grew up in a village in southern Zacatecas, Mexico, where I lived with my mother and my older sister. We were poor. We lived in a small adobe house with no indoor plumbing, and our usual meals consisted of little more than corn, beans, and tortillas. My father, who had been working seasonally in the United States since the mid-1960s (he was a bracero—a contracted farmworker—toward the end of the program and has just celebrated his eighty-second birthday), left us for several months, sometimes a year or longer, to work in the United States. In 1996, after he was granted permanent resident ("green card") status, he brought us north with him. We settled in Delano, CA, an agricultural town made famous by the César Chávez–led farmworker struggle of the 1960s and 1970s. I did not have documents at that time, but my father believed that we all had a better chance at a dignified life in the United States than we did back home, and I was able to attend middle school and high school there.

One woman I interviewed for my dissertation on the history of the modern immigrants' rights movement said, "Who needs papers when you're a kid?" And she was at least partly right. Initially, I hardly thought about my immigration status. I focused my energy on learning English and on doing well in school. Soon enough, however, the realities of undocumented life caught up with me. As I grew older, I became more aware—and anxious—about the ever-present danger of deportation. Border Patrol sightings were common in the California Central Valley, even though it lies hundreds of miles from the border. And as many of my peers began talking about and preparing for college, I realized that higher education was probably out of reach for me. My parents were poor, and my undocumented status severely limited my opportunities. I began skipping school, flirting with gang activity, and failing classes. When I reached the beginning of my senior year, I decided I owed it to my parents and their sacrifices to at least graduate from high school. I took remedial courses, attended weekend and after-school make-up sessions, and scraped together enough credits for graduation. In 2004, I became the first person in my family to graduate from high school, and I began working the night shift at a local big-box warehouse. About a year after that, I received a piece of mail that changed my life. My green card had finally been approved.

The day after I got my official papers, in November of 2005, I walked into a recruiting station and joined the United States Navy in hopes of earning some money for college. After boot camp, I attended apprenticeship school in Meridian, Mississippi, and I was stationed in San Diego. In 2008, I was deployed to the Middle East in support of Operations Enduring Freedom and Iraqi Freedom. My duties were mostly mundane, and to stave off the boredom of life in deployment, I read widely. Two books in particular deeply shaped my thinking and aspirations: Howard Zinn's *A People's History of the United States*, and Joseph Heller's *Catch-22*. After reading those two books, I knew I wanted to be a historian. While still deployed, I began taking as many College Level Examination Program tests as I could, along with a couple of online classes. I also began to investigate where I could possibly gain acceptance, a major concern for me at the time, given my atrocious high school record. Community college was an option, but the structure of the GI Bill was not particularly well suited to that type of institution.[4] My wife, whom I had met in the service, suggested attending college in her home state of Utah, where spouses of residents of the state are usually granted in-state tuition and where most four-year colleges and universities have an open-enrollment policy.[5] Until then, I had no idea open-enrollment four-year colleges and universities even existed.

I began my undergraduate work at Weber State University in Ogden, Utah, in January 2010, on the GI Bill, and finished college in three years, thanks to the availability of evening, summer, and weekend classes there. At WSU, I met dedicated teacher-scholars who were accustomed to working with nontraditional students, though I suspect few had worked with undocumented (or formerly undocumented) students. I graduated in 2012 with a bachelor's degree, and I applied to several graduate programs. I attended Duke University from 2013 to 2019, when I earned my PhD in history.

I offer these details to explain that perhaps the most important lesson anyone can take from my experience is that every path to higher education and to academia is unique. Not everyone follows a linear path from high school to four-year college to graduate or professional school. And yet, much of higher education remains structured in a way that presumes this is the norm, or worse, the "correct" path. Unfortunately, this often limits the ways that faculty understand, teach, and advise their students. Whatever success I had was because of advisers at both the undergraduate and graduate levels who understood my particular trajectory, my specific academic needs, and my individual professional goals.

Still, even with a cadre of supportive advisers, there were moments in certain times and contexts when I felt I was not valued or heard. Some professors in college warned me against "rushing" to graduate in three years, failing to understand how the GI Bill was disbursed and structured (housing stipends, for example, are only paid out to veterans who are attending college full time, and they stop during breaks, including summers in which one is not enrolled full time).[6] In graduate school, I once had a painful conversation with a faculty member who could not understand why I was struggling more than my peers, many of whom came from prestigious colleges and universities and had much more theoretical, historiographical, and archival training than I did. During a particularly difficult period in graduate school, this faculty member more than once pressured me to drop out of the program, on several occasions (and at times publicly) telling me that "graduate school isn't for everyone." Over the years, I proved I was capable of learning and succeeding in my graduate work, but at the time, I came close to giving up. For some time, I believed that perhaps this professor was right—that a poor son of nearly illiterate farmworkers did not belong in graduate school. Eventually, with the backing of more supportive faculty members and outstanding advisers, I climbed out of that rut.

Even so, I would not have been able to fight for myself without access to higher education in the first place. My ability to graduate from college was part hard work and determination, sure, but also part luck, especially in getting my green card just a year after graduating from high school. But for millions of young people in this country, limited access to higher education because of their immigration status remains a tremendous challenge. Even after President Barack Obama instituted the Deferred Action for Childhood Arrivals program in 2012 to provide some relief for young undocumented people in the wake of Congress's failure to pass the Development, Relief, and Education for Alien Minors (DREAM, from which the term Dreamer is derived) Act, inaccessibility to higher education has remained a serious obstacle. This is especially true for undocumented youth who live in states that are unfriendly—or outwardly hostile—toward them. For example, while there are dozens of resource centers for undocumented students across the three higher education systems in California—which is one of twenty states that allows undocumented students to receive in-state tuition and has passed its own DREAM Act—students in other states are charged out-of-state tuition and have no such resources to help them navigate college admissions and the financial aid process.[7]

Worse still, some states not only lack resources, but they have made the process difficult and restrictive by design. One such example is the state of Georgia, which in the last decade has instituted some of the most draconian laws against undocumented youth anywhere in the country, going as far as barring undocumented students from selective state universities.[8] The situation in Georgia led to the founding of Freedom University, described by its founders and students as "a modern-day freedom school" that provides "college preparation classes, college and scholarship application assistance, and movement leadership training for undocumented students banned from equal access to public higher education" in the state.[9] Bethany Moreton, one of the founding members of FU Georgia who now teaches at Dartmouth University, said she learned a great deal from the experiment. Moreton was surprised to learn, for example, that "the single biggest issue" for the undocumented students she served in Georgia was transportation, since the state also denied undocumented people driver's licenses. Moreton also notes that while there was no shortage of volunteers to teach classes and mentor students, few wanted "to do the grunt work" necessary to support undocumented students, tasks such as "sending emails, making copies . . . very unglamorous, very unfun" but necessary work.

High-profile examples of civil disobedience brought a great deal of attention to the political and social struggles of undocumented students in Georgia.[10] But often the everyday needs and struggles of undocumented students across the country still go unheard and unaddressed. For many undocumented students, their status (or that of their families) is at the very least distracting, and it is often traumatic in ways few realize. Many of them live in constant fear of deportation or family separation, which despite the reports that have dominated the news in recent years, has been a reality for undocumented or mixed-status families for decades.[11] David-James Gonzales, who has taught at the University of Southern California and the University of California–Los Angeles and who now teaches at Brigham Young University, says instructors "should be aware of the mental and emotional stress undocumented students experience" every day "as a result of uncertainties pertaining to the immigration status of themselves, family, and community members." Gonzales says he has noted a "sharp rise" in students' anxiety since the 2016 election in particular.[12]

Gonzales says instructors can and often do make assumptions about undocumented students that make an already difficult situation worse. Even a gesture as innocuous as admiring a student's English-language proficiency can exacerbate matters. Coronel, for one, remembers often being told, "your English is so good." While well-meaning, such comments delegitimize the complex realities of undocumented life. Even as they're marked as "foreign," undocumented students often know nothing beyond the United States; many don't even speak their "native" language.[13] It has been a curious irony that undocumented status has often served to Americanize non-US-born youths. Personally, I remember the many times my classmates and friends spent summers in Mexico, visiting their grandparents and extended family, while I sat at home watching English-language television and practicing the language, at times furiously working to rid myself of my accent—not out of shame or internalized hate as some assumed, but out of something simpler: fear. I wanted to avoid standing out in hopes of avoiding being stopped or identified by immigration or the police.

Complex identities and intertwined realities often collide in odd, sometimes painful and humiliating ways, even in institutions that purport to be meritocratic and far removed from discriminatory times. In the military, my foreignness produced a number of obstacles and indignities. For one thing, non-naturalized service members are limited in the jobs, duties, and opportunities available to them, resulting in an unspoken policy of ongoing segregation in the military, despite the Pentagon's insistence that racial segregation in its services' ranks is a thing of the distant past.[14] And before I was granted citizenship, I—like many of the other thirty-five thousand non–US citizens in the military—was often reminded that I did not quite "belong" in the service, sometimes in subtle ways, sometimes not so subtle. As one example, for a time the Navy labeled all non-citizens in official correspondence, including email, as "FORNATS"—foreign nationals—and even appended the country domain of sailors' countries of origin to their official email addresses (something like first. last.mx@navy.mil).

I suppose that kind of thing is what in academic circles we might call a "microaggression."[15] But in the academy, it was often my veteran status that posed hurdles in my educational path. Feedback to my writing, for example, often revealed surprise at my skepticism of militarism and at my ability to think critically about social, historical, and political questions. It was not difficult to see that professors expected me to be overly militaristic, rigid, and unwilling to learn, common complaints about veterans.[16] For me, this was relatively easy to overcome, but stereotypes and unfamiliarity with veterans can be more pernicious and more consequential to those who have endured wartime trauma. Between 11 and 20 percent of Iraq and Afghanistan veterans suffer from post-traumatic stress disorder; recent surveys reveal that a staggering 71 to 90 percent of female veterans have been sexually harassed and one-third have been sexually assaulted; and nearly five million people have some form of service-related disability.[17]

Just as with undocumented students, the image many college instructors have in their minds of what a veteran looks like may not be the one they actually encounter. When they picture a Bronze Star combat medic, for example, they may not think of someone like Kate Dahlstrand, a decorated Iraq war veteran who recently finished her PhD at the University of Georgia.[18] Dahlstrand, who is a military historian and who has worked on collecting veterans' oral histories in Georgia, also reminds us that student veterans hope for a degree of sensitivity that is not always afforded them. Upon returning from Iraq and enrolling in college, Dahlstrand remembers being asked deeply insensitive and inappropriate questions in the classroom, among them, "What was the worst day like over there?" and "How many dead people did you see?" She says that "twenty years of constant warfare has taught many Americans" that such questions are "an invitation to angry outbursts." But perhaps better class management, including instructors that explicitly set ground rules for student discussions, or who were willing to step in and gently steer the conversation in another direction, might have prevented such episodes in the first place. But while "that sort of insensitivity isn't as obvious anymore," well-meaning but ultimately harmful inquiries and comments continue to plague veterans. Dahlstrand says she has often received "encouragement" in the form of comments like "you've been to war; you can certainly do this" and "this [academic] work must be nothing compared to combat." While well intentioned, such statements invalidate the struggles of academic life and place unrealistic and unfair expectations on student veterans, who may well be dealing with severe residual and ongoing stress or injury from their service while also dealing with the demanding rigors of academic life.

None of this is to suggest that instructors and academics ought to naturally and inherently possess the knowledge to deal with issues facing veterans, undocumented students, or for that matter, other vulnerable and nontraditional populations. Neither is it to suggest that instructors should act as therapists, social workers, or legal representatives. Indeed, one of the most important things academics can do, as Moreton puts it, is "know what we can contribute and what we have no business trying to contribute." In fact, attempting to serve as a "savior" to vulnerable students is risky territory, likely to lead to dependency at best and, in more serious cases, to inappropriate or exploitative relationships. Instructors and advisers, then, ought to remember, first and foremost, their limits and the boundaries of their positions—and work backward from there. While they cannot be therapists or legal advocates, instructors can offer support and create safe and welcoming environments for their students to learn and grow in. This seldom requires much effort or grand gestures; small ones can go a long way. Juan Coronado, an assistant professor at Central Connecticut State University who has taught both undocumented and veteran students, says that faculty members often find that something as simple as "veteran-friendly" and "Dreamer-friendly" stickers in faculty offices have helped veterans and undocumented students feel welcome. In the classroom, instructors can make clear that self-identifying is optional, and set ground rules for discussions about sensitive topics. And they can explain that while they cannot be all things to all students, they can be the first line of support who can connect students to the right resources.

In other words, what faculty can always provide to undocumented and veteran students to help them succeed is empathy, sensitivity, openness, and kindness. To avoid letting "diversity" and "inclusion" become mere buzzwords, academics need to take seriously questions of access, to take stock of their own blind spots, to be aware of their own limitations, and to educate themselves about the issues facing their nontraditional students. As scholars and educators, we often think of ourselves as producers of knowledge and as promoters of democracy. As such, we owe it to our students, our communities, and our profession to be better informed, better prepared, and better equipped to serve students from diverse backgrounds and experiences, including those who come from immigrant backgrounds and families, who are veterans, and who may otherwise have followed nontraditional paths to our classrooms.

NOTES

1. Alicia Parlapiano and Karen Yourish, "A Typical 'Dreamer' Lives in Los Angeles, Is from Mexico and Came to the U.S. at 6," *New York Times*, September 7, 2017, A17.

2. Department of Veterans Affairs, "Characteristics of Student Veterans" (VA Campus Toolkit Handout), reviewed April 22, 2014, https://www.mentalhealth.va.gov /studentveteran/docs/ed_todaysStudentVets.html, accessed July 10, 2019; Catharine Bond Hill, Martin Kurzweil, Elizabeth Davidson Pisacreta, and Emily Schwartz, "Enrolling More Veterans at High-Graduation-Rate Colleges and Universities," Ithaka S+R, January 10, 2019, https://doi.org/10.18665/sr.310816.

3. Daniel B. Wood, "California's Prop. 187 Puts Illegal Immigrants on Edge," *Christian Science Monitor*, November 22, 1994, https://www.csmonitor.com/1994/1122/22021.html.

4. Jon Marcus, "Community Colleges Rarely Graduate the Veterans They Recruit," *The Atlantic*, April 21, 2017, https://www.theatlantic.com/education/archive/2017/04/why -is-the-student-veteran-graduation-rate-so-low/523779/.

5. Courtney Tanner, "The Number of College Students in Utah Is Almost as Large as Salt Lake City's Population," *Salt Lake Tribune*, October 4, 2018, https://www.sltrib.com /news/education/2018/10/04/utah-valley-university/. See also "Step Up to Higher Education: 2018–19 College Guide," accessed January 28, 2020, https://stepuputah.com/site /uploads/2018/09/2018-19_college-guide.pdf.

6. Citation Nr: 1437385, Decision Date: 08/21/14, Archive Date: 08/27/14, Docket No. 11-23-891, On Appeal from the Department of Veterans Affairs Regional Office in St. Louis, MO, https://www.va.gov/vetapp14/Files5/1437385.txt.

7. The Campaign for College Opportunity, "Campus Resources for Undocumented Students," accessed June 9, 2019, https://collegecampaign.org/undoc-student-resources /; Nanette Asimov and Wyatt Buchanan, "Jerry Brown Signs Dream Act for Illegal Immigrants," *San Francisco Chronicle*, October 8, 2011, https://www.sfgate.com/news /article/Jerry-Brown-signs-Dream-Act-for-illegal-immigrants-2327890.php; Yara Simón, "Undocumented Students Can Receive in-State Tuition in These 20 States," *Remezcla*, June 19, 2019, https://remezcla.com/lists/culture/undocumented-students-in-state -tuition-20-states/.

8. Georgia Board of Regents Policy Manual, "4.1.6, Admission of Persons Not Lawfully Present in the United States," policy instituted October 2010, https://www.usg.edu /policymanual/section4/C327/#p4.1.6_admission_of_persons_not_lawfully_present_in _the_united_states.

9. Freedom University, "Who We Are," accessed June 4, 2019, https://freedom -university.org/home.

10. Lee Shearer, "9 Arrested during Freedom University Sit-in at UGA," *Athens Banner-Herald*, January 10, 2015, https://www.onlineathens.com/uga/2015-01-10/9-arrested -during-freedom-university-sit-uga; Mark Lieberman, "TV Comedian, Protesters Arrested at Georgia Higher Ed Meeting," *Inside Higher Education*, February 15, 2019, https://www .insidehighered.com/quicktakes/2019/02/15/tv-comedian-protesters-arrested-georgia -higher-ed-meeting.

11. Natalie Escobar, "Family Separation Isn't New," *The Atlantic*, August 14, 2018, https://www.theatlantic.com/family/archive/2018/08/us-immigration-policy-has -traumatized-children-for-nearly-100-years/567479/.

12. Victor Agbafe, "Immigration and the 2016 Election," *Harvard Political Review*, January 18, 2016, https://harvardpolitics.com/united-states/immigration-2016-election/.

13. Lulu Garcia-Navarro, "Deported after Living in the U.S. for 26 Years, He Navigates a New Life in Mexico," *NPR*, May 19, 2019, https://www.npr.org/2019/05/19/723739490 /deported-after-living-in-the-u-s-for-26-years-he-navigates-a-new-life-in-mexico.

14. Thomas E. Ricks, "Racial Inclusion and Diversity in the Armed Forces: Some Thoughts on Today," *Foreign Policy*, October 6, 2016, https://foreignpolicy.com/2016/10 /06/racial-inclusion-and-diversity-in-the-armed-forces-some-thoughts-on-today/.

15. Bradley Campbell and Jason Manning, "Microaggression and Changing Moral Cultures," *Chronicle of Higher Education*, July 9, 2015, https://www.chronicle.com/article /MicroaggressionChanging/231395.

16. Eladio Bobadilla, "'What It Means to Be a Citizen': Student Veterans in History Classrooms," *Perspectives on History*, January 9, 2017, https://www.historians.org /publications-and-directories/perspectives-on-history/january-2017/what-it-means-to-be -a-citizen-student-veterans-in-history-classrooms.

17. US Department of Veterans Affairs, "How Common Is PTSD in Veterans?," accessed June 18, 2019, https://www.ptsd.va.gov/understand/common/common_veterans.asp; National Resource Center for Domestic Violence, "Challenges Specific to Female Veterans," accessed June 20, 2019, https://vawnet.org/sc/challenges-specific-female-veterans; US Department of Veterans Affairs, "Statistical Trends: Veterans with a Service-Connected Disability, 1990 to 2018," May 2019, https://www.va.gov/vetdata/docs/Quickfacts/SCD _trends_FINAL_2018.pdf.

18. Lee Shearer, "Brothers in Arms?: Civil War Reality Predates Transgender Debate," *Athens Banner-Herald*, April 14, 2018, https://www.onlineathens.com/news/20180414 /brothers-in-arms-civil-war-reality-predates-transgender-debate.

23. Understanding Microaggressions

ANTAR TICHAVAKUNDA

Beyond a concept used by scholars to research identity, stereotypes, and belonging, the term "microaggression" has reached buzzword status. From internet think pieces to YouTube videos to Webster's dictionary, the word has become a part of our popular culture. The goal of this essay is to provide a general understanding of what microaggressions are, by defining them and then providing some examples of them from my own experience and research. I hope to help readers better identify microaggressions when they happen to you or somebody else (a student, for example), and to think about potential responses to such incidents.

Microaggressions are defined as subtle visual, verbal, and nonverbal insults about identity that can contribute to feelings of marginalization (Solórzano, Ceja, and Yosso 2000). Much work demonstrates the potentially devastating impact of microaggressions (e.g., Smith, Hung, and Franklin 2011; Yosso et al. 2009). Chester Pierce, a Black psychiatrist, first introduced the term "microaggressions" in 1978 as "subtle, stunning, often automatic, and nonverbal exchanges which are 'put downs' of Blacks by offenders" (66). Since then, the concept has been broadly applied to other types and aspects of identity (e.g., gender, class, religion, and ability). Microaggressions are varied, lying along the spectrum of unintentional to intentional, and context-based. An example of a microaggression might be a non-Black student at a predominantly white institution (PWI) assuming that a Black male plays on a sports team—for no other reason than his race and the stereotype of Black men gaining entry into college by way of athletics. As an undergraduate at a PWI myself, I was asked by many non-Black students, "Do you play on the basketball team?" or "Do you play a sport here?" for no other reason I could observe other than that I am a Black man. Another microaggression might be asking a South Asian person, "Where were you born?" or commenting, "Your English is really good." The assumption behind the question and observation is that the person was not born in the United States, for no other reason than their appearance or surname. The messaging behind these microaggressions is that the person is not an American. Microaggressions can also be nonverbal. Consider a white woman speeding up her pace and clutching her purse upon seeing a Latino or Black man on the same street. Although the woman does not say anything, her actions and body language express that she assumes the man is a criminal and potentially dangerous (Sue et al. 2007).

Another example comes from one of my research interviewees, a Black woman majoring in computer science. She was ostracized by her peers and recounted her experiences with microaggressions and, at times, clear displays of racism. Microaggressions sometimes manifested in non-Black students avoiding the seats next to her in lecture. An obvious manifestation of racism, however, involved an Asian American student refusing to help her with a problem set, saying, "You are going to get a job and I'm not." The clear assumption was that the Black woman had a better chance of acquiring a job solely because of her racial identity and desired "diversity." Regardless of how subtle a microaggression is, however, as Pierce (1978) argued, microaggressions are "only micro in name, since their very number requires a total effort that is incalculable" (520). For the interviewee, the only Black woman in her major, such actions resulted in psychological strain.

Campuses are diverse, racialized places (see, e.g., Harper and Hurtado 2007; Tichavakunda 2017) where misunderstandings and unintentional offenses are bound to occur. For that reason, we must make sure to consider the context in which microaggressions happen. Asking people where they are from at an orientation or during an icebreaker might not be considered a microaggression, given the nature of the event. The words, by themselves, matter—but context shapes whether or not an interaction might be understood as a microaggression.

Microaggressions research is contested. Some take issue with the name and question the validity of microaggressions research, arguing that such research makes strong claims without sufficient scientific evidence (Lilienfeld 2017). Others suggest that microaggressions are a symptom of a culture of victimhood and infantilization (Lukianoff and Haidt 2015). The debate between Derald Wing Sue, one of the foremost scholars of microaggressions research, and Scott Lilienfeld, a psychologist and critic of microaggressions research, is useful to examine (see Sue 2017; Lilienfeld 2017). Lilienfeld argues that microaggressions research is hinged on premises that lack "scientific evidence" (140). Sue, however, suggests that Lilienfeld's worldview fails to acknowledge clear evidence of the reality and impact of microaggressions. In making his point, Sue quotes the African proverb, "Until the lions have their story tellers, stories of the hunt will always glorify the hunter."

Microaggressions are certainly not bound only to the student experience. More recently, as a first-year professor, I have had to respond to people's assumptions that I am a student. Some of this, I am sure, has to do with my younger age, relative to other faculty. As such, on most occasions, I do not consider the question a microaggression. However, some people's reactions to hearing that I am a professor—looks of incredulity, confusion, and even anger—suggest that I do not fit the mold of how a professor should look. I respond in a variety of ways, sometimes with just a smile, sometimes with silence and eye contact, but always with the knowledge of the root of microaggressions—legacies of structural domination and oppressive ideologies based on identities. Regardless of my response, I make a point never to provide any further explanation to their looks of confusion. This experience, however, is shared by many other professors who do not identify as white heterosexual men. Two professors even started the #ThisIsWhatAProfessorLooksLike campaign to highlight scholars who were younger, people of color, women, and/or queer to challenge traditional, narrow depictions of professors.

Before offering words of advice about how to respond to a microaggression, I would like to preface my remarks by affirming that people manage stereotypes differently (McGee and Martin 2011). For example, in a recent study I conducted on Black engineering majors at a PWI, I asked participants how they would respond to the sentence "When I look at you, I don't see color." This statement is sometimes considered a microaggression because it denies a person's racialized realities or ethnic culture. Students suggested they would have responded in a variety of ways, from not being affected at all, to brushing off the statement, to using it as a moment of instruction. Responses, however, would depend on the participant's relationship with the deliverer of the microaggression. "I know I probably do things that upset people, so I want to give people the benefit of the doubt. . . . Some people I cut off because I'm not close with [them] either way. . . . With friends, . . . I'll sit down and talk to them," one person said. This strategy seemed to protect their peace and feelings. Others, however, were more vocal in their experiences and found peace in calling out a microaggression.

Similar to responding to microaggressions, there is no one or best way to avoid delivering a microaggression. Certainly, taking the initiative to learn about identities and cultures other than your own is helpful. In daily interactions with other people, avoiding an identity-based offense might be as simple as being more reflective and thoughtful about what statements or assumptions one makes (see Sue et al. 2007). Some scholars (e.g., Powell, Demetriou, and Fisher 2013; Rowe 2008) have also suggested applying *microaffirmations* to create a more positive and inclusive culture. Microaffirmations are small acts in a work or educational environment that facilitate feelings of support and belonging for people who might otherwise feel alienated in that environment. For example, in a predominantly male and white classroom, a Chicana student might feel distinctive and unwelcome. Microaffirmations are the steps one takes to subtly communicate to the student that she is welcome, matters, and is fully capable of thriving in the class. Examples of microaffirmations might include taking the time to learn and pronounce students' names correctly, constructing a syllabus with authors of different backgrounds and identities, or providing feedback to students and colleagues that emphasize their strengths (Powell, Demetriou, and Fisher 2013).

One of the reasons microaggressions research has taken such hold, I believe, is because it names an experience that is difficult to describe, yet common. I would recommend to other academics that they join or create a space or group of people with whom they can discuss these feelings of alienation. Whether it is an affinity group, a friend group, a mentor, or family members, being able to share your experience without feeling judged is important. Chester Pierce (1995) explained that the most perplexing burden of identity-based oppression in dealing with microaggressions is responding to them: "Knowing how and when to defend requires time and energy that oppressors cannot appreciate," he wrote (282). Throughout my educational and life journey, I have found power in naming for myself the microaggressions I have experienced. After naming the offense, I try my best to avoid giving the interaction any more energy or thought. Sometimes, however, I do replay the event over and over again in my mind. Other times, I share the experience with someone else for affirmation. We have power over how we react to microaggressions and the energy we give them in thought. In dealing with microaggressions, do what you feel is necessary to protect your peace.

WORKS CITED

Agarwal, P. 2019. "How Microaggressions Can Affect Wellbeing in the Workplace." *Forbes*, March 29. https://www.forbes.com/sites/pragyaagarwaleurope/2019/03/29/how-microaggressions-can-affect-wellbeing-in-the-workplace/#249a677b73cb.
Gant, E. 2017. "27 Workplace Microaggressions That'll Make You Ask 'How'd They Even Get Hired?'" *BuzzFeed*, October 8. https://www.buzzfeed.com/essencegant/workplace-microaggression-horror-stories.

Harper, S. R., and S. Hurtado. 2007. "Nine Themes in Campus Racial Climates and Implications for Institutional Transformation." *New Directions for Student Services* 120:7–24.

Italie, L. 2017. "Ghosting, Shade, Microaggression Hit Merriam-Webster Website." *Denver Post*, February 8. https://www.denverpost.com/2017/02/08/merriam-webster-new -words/.

Lilienfeld, S. O. 2017. "Microaggressions: Strong Claims, Inadequate Evidence." *Perspectives on Psychological Science* 12.1: 138–169.

Lukianoff, G., and J. Haidt. 2015. "The Coddling of the American Mind." *The Atlantic*, September. http://www.theatlantic.com/magazine/archive/2015/09/the-coddling-of -the-american-mind/399356/.

McGee, E. O., and D. B. Martin. 2011. "'You Would Not Believe What I Have to Go Through to Prove My Intellectual Value!': Stereotype Management among Academically Successful Black Mathematics and Engineering Students." *American Educational Research Journal* 48.6: 1347–1389.

Pierce, C. 1995. "Stress Analogs of Racism and Sexism: Terrorism, Torture, and Disaster." In *Mental Health, Racism, and Sexism*, edited by C. Willie, P. Rieker, B. Kramer, and B. Brown, 277–293. Pittsburgh: University of Pittsburgh Press.

Pierce, C., J. Carew, D. Pierce-Gonzalez, and D. Willis. 1978. "An Experiment in Racism: TV Commercials." In *Television and Education*, ed. C. Pierce, 62–88. Beverly Hills: Sage.

Powell, C., C. Demetriou, and A. Fisher. 2013. "Micro-Affirmations in Academic Advising: Small Acts, Big Impact." *The Mentor: Innovative Scholarship on Academic Advising* 15. https://doi.org/10.26209/MJ1561286.

Rowe, M. 2008. "Micro-Affirmations and Micro-Inequities." *Journal of the International Ombudsman Association* 1.1: 45–48.

Smith, W. A., M. Hung, and J. D. Franklin. 2011. "Racial Battle Fatigue and the MisEducation of Black Men: Racial Microaggressions, Societal Problems, and Environmental Stress." *Journal of Negro Education* 80.1: 63–82.

Solórzano, D. G., M. Ceja, and T. Yosso. 2000. "Critical Race Theory, Racial Microaggressions, and Campus Racial Climate: The Experiences of African American College Students." *Journal of Negro Education* 69.1: 60–73.

Sue, D. W. 2017. "Microaggressions and 'Evidence': Empirical or Experiential Reality?" *Perspectives on Psychological Science* 12.1: 170–172.

Sue, D. W., C. M. Capodilupo, G. C. Torino, J. M. Bucceri, A. Holder, K. L. Nadal, and M. Esquilin. 2007. "Racial Microaggressions in Everyday Life: Implications for Clinical Practice." *American Psychologist* 62.4: 271–286.

Tichavakunda, A. A. 2017. "Perceptions of Financial Aid: Black Students at a Predominantly White Institution." *Educational Forum* 81.1: 3–17.

Yosso, T., W. Smith, M. Ceja, and D. Solórzano. 2009. "Critical Race Theory, Racial Microaggressions, and Campus Racial Climate for Latina/o Undergraduates." *Harvard Educational Review* 79.4: 659–691.

24. Shifting Borders: Collaborative Teaching and Researching with Students on Latinx Roots in Oregon

LYNN STEPHEN

One of the fundamental jobs of cultural anthropology, one of my disciplines, is to codify the representation and resignification of difference. In this process, the borders, which form the outlines of our personal histories, are the first ones we have to excavate, confront, and cross. Once we have done that, we can focus in turn on the constant redrawing and resignification of boundaries marking difference that occurs around us. The study of shifting borders is thus an internal process as much as an exterior analytical exercise.

Here I use the concept of shifting borders to examine a collaborative process of teaching, learning, research, and knowledge production. I have participated in this process with five generations of students at the University of Oregon and co-teacher Gabriela Martínez, through a two-course sequence titled Latino Roots (see Stone 2017). I use our shared journey over a six-month period as a lens to examine how we built awareness and analysis about the categories of difference and borders which had functioned in our own roots and lives; moved to look historically at how these categories and borders were imagined, created, and given legal and political force; and then took these analyses and experiences into the production of oral history documentaries that attempted to explore the contextualized depth and breadth of Latin American and Latinx settlement and incorporation into the state of Oregon.

Borders of the Self

Proponents of activist and collaborative anthropology often propose subverting the objective/subjective distinction (Hale 2008; Leyva, Burguete, and Speed 2008; Stephen 2013). If we integrate that idea with research methodology, then the first step of investigation is to ask oneself the same questions that will be asked of others. In working with the student researchers I discuss here, this came first through having students consider their own family histories and roots. We can begin with the question, "Where do I come from—what are my roots?"

Of course, this is a question I first have to answer myself before asking my students to engage with it. In this class as well as in another graduate class I teach on Ethics, Epistemologies, and Ethnographic Research, I first talk about the positions that we have as students and faculty, which give us resources and access that we are obligated to use to support those we conduct research with and about. In Latino Roots, my co-teacher and I share our own stories with our students. In my case, I discuss my life in Chicago and in the suburbs growing up; beginning work at age fifteen; having parents who encouraged me in school; and getting into a very good liberal arts college that was the gateway to a PhD in anthropology. I discuss being white and being an academic as well as my commitment to activist and collaborative research. Unlike students, of course, I have the security of tenure and a very good salary. I acknowledge that but also share how I remained committed to activist and collaborative research while I was a graduate student. In general, I find that my students of color, as well as colleagues, are less interested in public acknowledgments of white privilege and more interested in the outcomes of my teaching and research—which hopefully demonstrate my commitment to engaged research that works at least partly in the service of those it is about.

Latino Roots classes are often about 40–50 percent Latinx students, a few African American students, and about 40–50 percent White students. The class is a graduate/undergraduate class so it has five to six graduate students in addition to undergraduates. The graduate students are often students of color (Latinx, Indigenous, Asian) and are from anthropology, journalism, and communication. The undergraduates come from widely different backgrounds, hailing from small towns in rural Oregon to Los Angeles. The class includes a range of majors, including anthropology, ethnic studies, journalism, political science, and others. Ethnic studies majors come to class equipped to discuss race, racism, and difference, and are a real resource for the class, as are most of the graduate students. Early on, our discussions of race and racism as a part of interrogating the racial-ethnic history of the US west may result in potential conflicts among students; but once we have gone through the exercise of everyone sharing their families' histories, students become seriously invested in the class and classmates. We also do a lot of small group work and work in pairs, which allows students to really get to know one another. They work together over two quarters (twenty weeks), outside of class, and for long hours in a lab editing their films. These experiences of pairing and putting students together across difference, drawing on skills and experiences they can offer each other, often is a transformative experience. This is a relatively small class (twenty five students total). The scale, along with the extended time together, allows students to really get to know and learn from one another. Such circumstances are privileged; other classes I teach, with bigger enrollments (one or two hundred), require careful work in discussion sections of twenty to twenty-five to try to bridge differences and potential conflicts.

Researchers who go through a process of self-reflection about where they come from, their work and community trajectories, and where they want to go in the future, have a basis for beginning to analyze the categories of difference that have permeated their life stories at different times. If these categories are excavated and turned over in the light of shared analysis and reflection, then the borders that they set up become clarified. If there is collective reflection about the categories that emerge in different people's stories, then there is both an individual and a collective process of dialogue and exchange about such categories.

The excavation of these categories of difference from students' own histories, and their shared analysis, debate, and discussion of how they work, provided the class with a rich corpus of information. The discussions produced an embedded and personally significant understanding and set of questions relating to categories of difference and the borders they create, which students could then use to analyze historical readings and bring into their oral history and film projects. When student researchers become aware of how these concepts have functioned in their own lives, where they have come from historically, they can push themselves individually and collectively to consider other ways of knowing and framing knowledge.

Historicizing Shifting Borders

One of the questions guiding our research and production of oral histories in audio and video form was: How do we represent the diversity of what is often called "Latino" history in a way that highlights the shifting racial and ethnic categories and boundaries that have accompanied the emergence of "Latino" as a contemporary category? A recent study carried out by the Pew Hispanic Center found that only 24 percent of those surveyed use the pan-ethnic terms

"Hispanic" or "Latino" to describe their identity, and that more than half (51 percent) use their family's country of origin to describe their identity (Taylor et al. 2012). Twenty-one percent use the term "American" most often. These results also vary by generation, length of time in the United States, and other factors. Even this contemporary picture suggests the complexity of the relationships between ethnicity, race, nationality, and region. If we put these categories into a longer historical view, the result is even more variable and nuanced. If categories of difference are constantly shifting, how do we understand the ways that they operate in people's lives today and in their family histories?

Once students explored the ways that categories of racial, ethnic, linguistic, national, legal, and geographic difference were embedded in their own family histories and experiences growing up, we set out to understand how these categories of difference had been mapped historically in the geographic and metaphoric space and place known now as Oregon. We also explored what kinds of borders were created and re-created in this process. How did shifting borders work in the history of what is now Oregon? We first studied Indigenous histories in our continent and emerging US-Mexico relations through exploring colonial and contemporary mapping of space, place, race, and ethnicity. Specific topics introduced the invention of "America" in the European imagination versus Indigenous concepts of space and time in their own territories; the epic Mexica migration from their ancestral homeland, Aztlán, to the shores of Lake Texcoco; settler colonialism and processes of elimination and assimilation; US empire-building in the territory of New Spain; loss of territory by Mexico in an unjust war; and the US colonial model in the Northwest, removing Native peoples and inviting in Anglo ranchers, miners, and farmers. A second part of this historical exploration was to look metaphorically and rhetorically at US immigration policy in the nineteenth and twentieth centuries. Of particular importance is a discussion of the fuzziness and mobility of the US-Mexican border until its racial consolidation in the 1920s and 1930s in the United States, the racialization of braceros (contracted laborers from Mexico who worked in US agriculture and on railroads from 1942 to 1964), farmworkers, and immigrant workers as "illegal" into the present; and the contemporary militarization of the physical border and criminalization of immigrants.

Contextualizing Racial/Ethnic Hierarchies

While reviewing these "snapshots" that illustrate how racial, ethnic, national, legal, and linguistic differences were created, codified, and resignified through time in what is now the state of Oregon, we also explored the concept of racialization and racial and ethnic hierarchies. In the larger context of US colonialism via American Indian nations and independent Mexico, globalization, and the integration of the US and Mexican economies, we studied the concept of racial formations as formulated by Howard Winant and Michael Omi (Omi and Winant 1986; Winant 2000). We also explore the concept of settler colonialism in Latin America as an ongoing process (see Speed 2019).

If we unpack the shifting racial formations of Oregon as a state since the mid-1850s, we can understand Oregon as a territorial space within which particular categories of socially constructed race have emerged at particular points in time to produce racial hierarchies, which are linked to specific sociopolitical conflicts and interests. Race is a category of difference written onto the human body in order to create discrete groups of people with differential rights and privileges, which justifies some groups as superior and others inferior because of "natural" intellectual, moral, temperament, and ability differences. In the history of Oregon in the larger scheme of US settler colonialism, phenotypical differences typical of human variation perceived as "color" difference were the basis for the creation and re-creation of different ranked racial groups at different points in time—with whites always in the superior position. This history includes the production of white supremacy; long-term anti-Black racism; lack of recognition of Native peoples; anti-Asian narratives in the 1930s and 1940s that resulted in internment during World War II; and more recently, the racialization of Mexican immigrants and Latinos as "illegal aliens."

Documenting Shifting Borders through Oral Histories

After reviewing the ways in which racial and ethnic formations were produced historically, and thinking about the categories of ethnic, racial, legal, national, and linguistic difference produced in larger Oregon history, the class moved to exploring the theme of shifting borders through the production of documentary films. The process involved the audiovisual documentation of one person's oral history, working closely with that person to write the script and choose images, music, and shots for a ten-minute final product. Most of the films were bilingual, in Spanish and English. Many students in the class had family members or close friends as the subjects of their documentaries. In the case of those students who focused on family members, they were essentially documenting their own stories as well. The fact that students collaborated with people they were already close to usually facilitated a participatory process that built on a prior established trust and connection. The self-reflection and collective exploration of socially constructed boundaries of difference in the students' lives and in Oregon's history resonated in each film produced.

DEPORTATION NATION: TRATANDO DE SOÑAR EN ENGLISH.
BY BYRON SUN. HTTPS://LATINOROOTS.UOREGON.EDU
/ARCHIVES/BYRON-SUN-2/
Byron began this project as a written narrative that he shared on an open class discussion board. His narrative focuses on his experience as a child, coming undocumented to the United States with his mother to join his father; being discovered and deported back to Guatemala where he was born; and then, after living there for a significant part of his adolescence, coming back to the United States legally for high school and college. The primary category of difference that constructs shifting borders in his life is legality. In class discussions he suggested that legal status also becomes a racial status in the US. He also references language and Indigenous ethnicity. I first quote his narrative and then discuss two key scenes from his film.

> I was born in Guatemala into the poverty that my father inherited by marrying my mother. By the age of three my mother and I had crossed all of Mexico. It took us one month because the coyote wanted to sexually abuse a younger woman in the group. The train helped us escape, taking us closer to the border and to the hands of another coyote. "¡Aaaa-puuu-ren-se!" Darkness . . . the smell . . . the rats . . . the American Dream . . . the sewage tunnel dumped us in San Ysidro; La Migra arrested us; I vomited in the back of the patrol-truck; they stripped us of our clothes checking for drugs; a few days went by and we got bailed out but never returned for our hearing.
>
> By the age of nine, I had lived in Van Nuys, California, for seven years. I was educated in English and spoke Español at home. My little brother was born in 1989. For Halloween I dressed up as Superman, Spiderman, Batman, and the Ninja Turtles. My father worked two jobs and my mother sometimes worked, and when she didn't she would pick vegetables from the back of the supermarket. In 1995, Immigration and Naturalization Service (INS) agents told my parents that my mother and I had ten days to leave the country with the possibility to return "legally" one day; otherwise we would be deported right there. Those ten days vanished quickly—disposable and hopeless—like the dreams of my parents that were destroyed with them.
>
> By the age of twelve in Guatemala City, I became accustomed to the violence, to the Indigenous people begging, to the drunken men fighting

over a dime, to the gun shots, to the dead bodies the next morning, to husbands beating their wives, to all the children with a plastic bag huffing the fifty cents worth of glue to forget their hunger, to the clapping of hands covered in corn dough making tortillas, to the blessings that I got from elderly women, to the hundreds of people walking in the streets talking, to having a small room with five pieces of furniture, to having to sleep in the same queen bed with my mother and brother, and to being separated from my father, who stayed in the US.

Byron begins his film with a slightly expanded version of the narrative above. He switches between Spanish and English, and the voice-over accompanies a visual collage of family photos that go with the story. The photographs are visually interwoven with a Google Earth map graphic which begins in Guatemala City with photographs of houses on the street where Byron was born, pulls back to an image of the whole country of Guatemala embedded in Central America, and then moves north to the United States–Mexico border. There, the map graphic moves further north to San Ysidro, California, and up to Van Nuys, California. The title appears, and the first image is a photo of Byron's dad as a young father. The film then cuts to the present, and his mother appears.

She begins to talk about how happy they were when they received a letter from the INS, telling them that they had an appointment to arrange legal residency for her and Byron. They went to the appointment and then something went wrong. "The officers told us we had a problem. Your wife and your son were arrested by Immigration. Your wife and son will have to leave the country voluntarily and ask for a pardon in Guatemala. . . . After the appointment there wasn't anything left and all our dreams started to vanish." The film follows the family selling their belongings, packing up, and saying goodbye. It also highlights the emotional pain that Byron's father and mother went through as they decided that they had to separate, because they were returning to nothing in Guatemala and had no money to take with them.

The second section of the film focuses on the sense of alienation Byron felt returning to Guatemala City at age twelve and being shocked by life there, again, following roughly his narrative above. But there were important experiences there as well.

My family's deportation wasn't only about sad experiences. It was also about happiness and a lot of important lessons. I was able to physically escape some of the difficult social conditions in Guatemala, but everything I saw there is still with me. The customs and life stories of the people. Finally, we got the pardon letter that we needed with my father's help. But instead of returning to Los Angeles, we came to Oregon.

The film ends with a shot of his family in Oregon.

Byron's autobiographical film centers on the emotional trauma and pain felt by all of his family members as a result of his and his mother's deportation. Byron uses geographical border crossing as a lens to look at the construction of other categories of difference that had a major impact in his life: legality, language, ethnicity, and class, in two different countries. His film shows his personal and intellectual journey as he first shared his story with classmates in discussions of difference, learned about historical processes of difference mapped onto the state of Oregon, and then produced his own film about the borders in his life and those of his family members. Byron is now a language arts teacher in Oregon. You can find out more about his personal journey at https://www.byronjosesun.com/.

Conclusions

Understanding of the shifting borders created by categories of difference comes through (1) self-reflexivity and exploration; (2) historical analysis of social narratives and key events which establish categories and boundaries of difference which change through time; and (3) collaborative research methods that permit the exploration of difference in the stories of project participants. Here I have highlighted these three processes in relation to a teaching and research project. While it is a very labor-intensive approach to teaching and research, I believe that the results illustrate how this three-pronged approach to exploring shifting borders encourages students to be self-aware and able to rethink borders with the participants in their research, in ways that conventional researchers may not. In addition, the presentation of research results in an audiovisual format allowed a much broader public to have access to what we learned. Our website, which features 62 of the videos produced by students and other related materials, is now a public resource that is being used in middle schools, high schools, and colleges, as well as by community organizations.[1]

This represents another shifting border as well. Knowledge produced within the university is made accessible and a part of the larger community from which it comes, rather than remaining bounded by the publishing conventions of the academy. As cultural anthropology continues to develop in this century, one of our greatest challenges is to continue to cross the borders of difference, which isolate us and what we produce from the communities we live in. We must train our students to conduct research that interrogates their own stories and makes accessible to those around them the histories and stories of those they work with.

NOTE

1. The website for the course and the student videos is located at https://latinoroots .uoregon.edu/archives/.

WORKS CITED

Hale, Charles, ed. 2008. *Engaging Contradictions: Theory, Politics, and Methods of Activist Scholarship.* Berkeley: University of California Press.

Leyva, Xochitl, Araceli Burguete, and Shannon Speed, eds. 2008. *Gobernar (en) la diversidad: Experiencias indígenas desde América Latina. Hacia la investigación de co-labor.* Mexico City: CIESAS, FLACSO Ecuador, and FLACSO Guatemala.

Omi, Michael, and Howard Winant. 1986. *Racial Formation in the United States: From the 1960s to the 1980s.* New York: Routledge and Kegan Paul.

Speed, Shannon. 2019. *Incarcerated Stories: Indigenous Women Migrants and Violence in the Settler-Capitalist State.* Chapel Hill: University of North Carolina Press.

Stephen, Lynn. 2013. *We Are the Face of Oaxaca: Testimony and Social Movements.* Durham, NC: Duke University Press.

Stone, Jason. 2017. "Latino Roots, Oregon Branches." *Around the O* (University of Oregon). https://around.uoregon.edu/latino-roots.

Taylor, Paul, Mark Hugo Lopez, Jessica Martínez, and Gabriel Velasco. 2012. *When Labels Don't Fit: Hispanics and Their Views of Identity.* Washington, DC: Pew Research Center.

25. The Florida Prison Education Project

KERI WATSON

In October 2017, I attended a session on prison education at the South Atlantic Modern Language Association's annual conference. The panel featured faculty and students from several higher education in prison programs in the Southeast. During the discussion, one of the presenters showed a pencil self-portrait of an incarcerated student. I immediately recognized the image as one made by a student in an art course I had taught for the Alabama Prison Arts and Education Project in the fall of 2012. Each Thursday afternoon for sixteen weeks, I packed drawing paper, pencils, charcoal, and a portable LCD projector, and drove an hour northeast of Montgomery to Elmore Correctional Facility. When I arrived at the prison, I checked in through the double gates, was searched, and was led to a multipurpose room where I taught the class. Class time consisted of discussing famous works of art and an art-making activity inspired by that day's lecture. One of the lessons I planned involved having the students draw self-portraits. I took a photograph of each man and then printed it on 8.5 × 11–inch paper. I gave each student the photocopied image, which he then used to create his graphite and charcoal self-portrait. As the panelist showed the picture to the audience, I was taken back to the day when I entered the prison with my camera, which had not been preauthorized. As a new faculty member just out of graduate school, who had never been in a prison before, I didn't recognize the magnitude of what I had done. I realize now that my actions must have caused the program director quite a bit of trouble, but sitting at the conference five years later, I saw the impact of my naïveté. I learned that this was the first time a camera had been used to teach a class as part of the Alabama Prison Arts and Education Project. Today, cameras are regularly brought into Alabama prisons as part of classes, giving students—many of whom have not seen their reflection or had their picture taken in years—the opportunity to see themselves and be seen by others.

Inspired by this panel and my experience teaching for the Alabama Prison Arts and Education Project, I returned home from the conference and met with a group of faculty at the University of Central Florida, where I am now an associate professor of art history, and decided to start a higher education in prison program in Orlando. Strategic planning, along with a few happy coincidences, helped the Florida Prison Education Project get off the ground:

- In the spring of 2017, Angel Sanchez, who had spent the majority of his young adult life in prison, was awarded the Order of Pegasus—the highest honor a UCF student can receive. His story captivated the community and galvanized campus support for our project. Sanchez, a former gang member, earned his GED while in prison, enrolled at Valencia College after his release, and then transferred to UCF. He graduated at the top of his class and is now a law student at the University of Miami.
- In the fall of 2017, UCF hosted a competition to select an interdisciplinary project that addressed a significant community challenge. After a vote by UCF faculty, staff, and community stakeholders, and with support from the Vice Provost of Regional Campuses and Outreach and the Vice Provost for Digital Learning, the Florida Prison Education Project was selected. This designation gave us institutional support and ten thousand dollars in seed funding from the university.
- Our team has worked strategically to align our goals with those of our university. Specifically, the Florida Prison Education Project supports UCF's Mission and Strategic Plan by expanding educational access and serving at-risk populations. The Florida Prison Education Project also partners with UCF's Office of Digital Learning to leverage technology to enhance learning and with UCF DirectConnect to support the educational success and degree attainment of prison-transfer students. In addition, the Florida Prison Education Project provides research, service, and mentoring opportunities to current UCF faculty and students.
- We started small. We initiated our relationship with the Florida Department of Corrections by offering two National Endowment

for the Arts Big Read–sponsored book clubs at the Central Florida Reception Center, a mixed security men's prison located fourteen miles from the UCF campus. We provided faculty discussion leaders and complimentary copies of the selected novel to thirty-two men who participated in the pilot program. This initial offering helped us establish trust with the incarcerated students, as well as with the warden of the Central Florida Reception Center and the education coordinator for the Florida Department of Corrections. We continue to operate in good faith with the Florida Department of Corrections to try and match their needs to our goals.

Prison education is at the forefront of the national conversation about criminal justice reform, and the University of Central Florida, as one of the largest universities in the United States, is leveraging its scale to impact Florida's criminal justice system. Since receiving designation as a UCF Community Challenge Initiative, the Florida Prison Education Project has collected more than five thousand books for Florida prison libraries and offered fifteen classes to two hundred incarcerated students. Currently, the Florida Prison Education Project offers continuing education courses to men incarcerated at the Central Florida Reception Center in Orlando, but we plan to expand our services to Polk Correctional Institute, Zephyrhills Correctional Institute, and Lowell Correctional Institute (the largest women's facility in the United States). Twenty-four UCF faculty from art, art history, education, English, history, humanities, mass communication, mathematics, physics, political science, religious studies, social work, and theater have volunteered to teach with our project, but by partnering with other colleges and universities and developing online courses, we hope to bring college-level courses to men and women incarcerated throughout the state. The primary impediment to the expansion of our course offerings is funding, but we are raising money through UCF's foundation, as well as applying for grants to support our programming.

Research has shown the relationship between a state's criminal justice system and its wider political and economic landscape, and this is particularly relevant in the South, where history, politics, and religion have combined to encourage a penal system based on retribution rather than rehabilitation. In Florida, the rate of incarceration has increased 1,000 percent since 1978, and Florida now has the third-largest prison system in the United States, with nearly 100,000 people behind bars. Nearly three million Floridians have a criminal record, and Orlando has one of the highest incarceration rates in the nation.

Despite a swelling prison population and overwhelming evidence to support the effectiveness of correctional education, Florida provides limited educational opportunities to those who are incarcerated, even though many of its prisoners do not have a high school diploma or college education. In an effort to help the Department of Corrections meet the needs of incarcerated people, the Florida Prison Education Project now provides college-level courses to those in prison in Central Florida. With this move, UCF joins Florida Gateway College, which provides college courses to men at Columbia Correctional Institution in Lake City as part of the Second Chance Pell Grant Initiative; Stetson University, which provides college courses to men at Tomoka Correctional Institution in Daytona Beach as part of their Community Education Project; ESUBA, an educational program that brings together Miami-Dade students and those incarcerated in South Florida; and Exchange for Change, which facilitates anonymous writing exchanges between people who are incarcerated and students in South Florida. Together, these programs are working to make a difference in the lives of people in Florida.

26. So, You Want to Start a College-in-Prison Program?

KATHRYN J. FOX

If you are reading this, I assume you have been thinking about launching a higher education program in a prison. There are many considerations and steps in this process. The order could probably differ from this one, but here are the main concerns to address.

1. **Feasibility considerations**
   a. Think about where you are in your career, and if you have the bandwidth, and more importantly, the institutional support to carry this out. (You will need a cheerleader or comrade to help!)
   b. How will you fund this program? Will your institution "waive" tuition for incarcerated students? Or will you fundraise? Can you apply for funding without a track record of success?
   c. Is there a prison within a reasonable distance? If the nearest facility is a county jail, the population will be too transient. Consider how far is reasonable for instructors to commute.
   d. Will the Department of Corrections be on board? You may encounter some resistance on the part of staff who feel prisoners should not be entitled to this benefit.
   e. How will students progress? What will you offer? If you plan to offer a degree, you will need to create a cohort to move through the program.

Will you be able to create a cohort? Does the facility have sufficient numbers of college-ready students who have long sentences?

2. Negotiations
    a. At the institutional level—Who will manually process applications, transcript requests, financial aid resolution?
    b. At the Department of Corrections level—How will you recruit and screen applicants? What correctional staff time is expected to move people for education, or to assist with the program? How will your schedule of courses work around facility schedules?
    c. At the programmatic level—How will you solicit and screen faculty instructors? How will you decide which courses to offer? Who will create an application process? Will students need remediation?
    d. At the facility level—How will problems be addressed? What if students are removed for disciplinary reasons? Or moved to another facility? How will you manage bringing in books and other materials? What can you manage, assuming students have no internet access?

3. Legal considerations
    a. General Counsel—You will need to work with General Counsel about any concerns they may have, especially around risks and responsibilities, and particularly if you are bringing on-campus students into facilities.
    b. Risk Management—You will need to work with risk management and create a Memorandum of Understanding between your institution and the Department of Corrections about the assumption of risk and liability and transportation.
    c. Family Educational Rights and Privacy Act (FERPA)—You will need to think about how to honor this federal requirement, given that students cannot request a transcript online, and anything mailed to a student in a facility will be read by correctional staff.
    d. Disability Accommodations—You will need to determine how best to provide accommodation services to students identified as having a learning or other disability.

4. Time and effort considerations
    a. Is all this blood, sweat, and tears worth it? Totally.

27. Service Learning: Doing Development in West Africa

CHARLES PIOT

The number of US university students traveling abroad to engage in small-scale development efforts in Africa, Asia, and Latin America has increased dramatically over the past decade. The students volunteer in rural health clinics; set up microlending initiatives; build schools and dig wells; organize the export of local textiles—and the list goes on. This essay draws inspiration from a set of projects undertaken by Duke University students since 2008 in two villages in northern Togo, West Africa.[1] The projects are inexpensive, aim small, and are tethered to a common theme: youth culture/youth flight. Among other efforts, these students have built a cybercafe, organized a microfinance initiative for teens, set up a writers' collective, and installed a village health insurance system. They engage their projects with commitment and creativity—and with the courage it takes to live locally and subsist on food that is foreign to the palate, while also being exposed to tropical fevers and dysentery. They come from a variety of backgrounds and a range of academic majors, and there are invariably more women than men. They often do not know one another before setting out, but typically develop deep friendships and work hard together to achieve their projects' aims.

I never intended to be a development anthropologist; my graduate education trained me to look down on anything "applied," which not only seemed anti-theory but also smacked of complicity. When I was first in the field in the mid-1980s, I ran the other way when I saw a development worker or a missionary. My generation of anthropologists aimed to defend and give voice to other ways of being in the world rather than to change or colonize them. Now, many years later, I am intrigued by missionaries and development workers—not merely as objects of study but also as fellow travelers, for I have become something of a development agent myself. I have set up a fund in my fieldwork village, contributing royalties from book sales to a village development account, and I now take students there each summer to engage in small development efforts.

So, what changed? Today, anthropologists no longer imagine that we might be able to access pure social forms outside entangled global histories, and have abandoned the naïve view that the anthropologist studying everyday life in a village might be a detached observer, having little effect on what he or she is studying. Student culture and university practices have also changed. Whether deriving from the cachet that the phrase "global university" has on college campuses today or from a desire to do good in the world, or both, today's college students are signing up for semester and summer abroad programs in record numbers. While there are specificities to each program, and to the locales where students end up, the programs are largely driven by a common impulse: students' desire to travel and learn and make a difference in the world.

It is easy to be cynical about this new student culture, this quiet social movement that aims to bring change through personal initiative. Is this enthusiasm not more about résumé building or adventure—"academic tourism" or "voluntourism," some have called it—than making a difference? Is it not driven by naïve assumptions about development and what it means to "make an impact"? Is this sort of do-it-yourself development not the distillation of a neoliberal political economy and zeitgeist that has conquered the world and reduced development to individual initiative? How can a US college student, typically from the suburbs, parachute into a village in Africa or Latin America for a few months, with minimal local knowledge, and really hope to make a difference?

This is all true, of course, and I spend much of my undergraduate Development and Africa class criticizing the view that development can accomplish anything at all without a deep understanding of local culture, politics, and history. Yet, I have also found students' youthful idealism irresistible and many of their projects inspiring. More importantly, whatever their motivations, their efforts are hailed by those in the villages where I conduct research, and their work has had a positive impact on local lives.

My involvement in student-led development started by chance—because an administrator asked if I would mentor three students who were planning summer internships in Ghana. I told her I was not keen on going to Ghana but that if she had students who spoke French and wanted to work in Togo, I would consider it. Two weeks later, she sent over six interested students, all with French-language skills. After vetting them, I agreed to take three.

When they arrived that summer, I set them up with internships and home-stay families. I then left to do my own research, telling them I would return three weeks later and wanted each to come up with a project to work on during their last month that might make a difference in local lives. To my surprise, two of the students came up with quirky-brilliant ideas that, in twenty-five years in the area, had never crossed my mind. One of these, a health insurance plan, was implemented the following year and is still in place today. Moreover, at the end of the summer, villagers pleaded with me to bring more students the follow-ing year. They were thankful not only for the projects, but also for the money the students injected into the local economy, and for their good humor in the face of everyday challenges. Most important, they felt acknowledged by the fact that students from far away had chosen their village in which to live and work. "You've given us many small things over the years," a friend said as I was leaving for the start of classes that fall, "but bringing these students is the best thing you've ever done."

Inspired by the students' projects and knowing they would need follow-up—but also sobered by my interlocutor's frank appraisal of my own long-standing attempts to reciprocate local generosity—I decided to bring another cohort the following summer. They turned out to be as good as the first group. And so it went: each year a new cohort brought new ideas and energy, and the projects kept morphing in interesting ways. Moreover, these students have opened new vistas for me—not only applied, but also theoretical.

By any standard, the Kabre villages in northern Togo, where the students carry out their projects, are materially poor. There is no electricity or running water; houses are covered with thatch or tin; fields are cultivated by hand; poor soil and a harsh climate impede crop cultivation. While weekly markets en-able the circulation of local foodstuffs, they provide little opportunity for extra income. Moreover, the health challenges in this area of West Africa are legion, with tropical fevers and intestinal parasites a constant in the lives of all. Up to 50 percent of family income is spent on health care each year.

What can be done in an area like this, especially when virtually all attempts at "development" have failed? As an initial step, I insist that the students' educa-tional process must begin before arriving in the field—that they take courses on African culture and politics, and sign up for an independent study in which they read broadly in anthropological and historical literatures on West Africa and begin to brainstorm their projects. Many projects have begun with a research proposal—"I want to study traditional medicines, to determine their effectiveness and to think about ways they might be integrated into clinic practice"—that further gets them into the literature and into a researcher's mindset. The fact that eight cohorts have been to the same place means that they can also learn from those who have gone before.

Some of the student projects have succeeded brilliantly, others were unsuccessful; some have been abandoned, while some have focused on research more than intervention. The first thing I tell students is to lower their expectations, even to assume failure—that failure can be instructive. The second is to remain open-minded and flexible, always on the lookout for surprises. Some have switched projects altogether in midstream, and most have had to innovate along the way; these improvisational moments have made all the difference. Third, and perhaps most important, I urge students to adopt an attitude of humility toward the local and assume that local knowledge (about crops, soils, markets, health) will trump outsider knowledge most of the time—that one's first instinct should be to find out from villagers how and why they do what they do. I thus insisted that a student who wanted to set up a microfinance initiative spend her first weeks sitting with women in the market, learning the ins and outs of local payment and debt systems. When another student became frustrated with inconsistent attendance at the writers' club she had started, I suggested she make the rounds of teachers and students to learn more about attitudes toward literacy. One of the most gratifying aspects of this experiment has been its organic nature. From the beginning, it has been a work in progress, one idea and project leading to another, one stray comment or insight opening a new set of possibilities. At every step, students' orientation to local culture, history, and society has been critical.

The majority of projects have addressed health—both because of real needs in the villages and because global health is a popular area of study today. The health insurance scheme the students designed—which offered family coverage for only four dollars a year—entailed a surprising set of challenges. It has been a financial win-win—families save more on the medicine they purchase than they spend enrolling, and the clinic makes money from the exchange. But at its peak, only twenty-three out of two hundred families had signed up, with enrollment dipping to sixteen families in 2013. Some prefer herbal medicine, which healers dispense free of charge, or they do not trust clinic workers. Others mentioned that having to pay the annual premium on a fixed day was burdensome. Yet others said that paying to treat an illness you do not yet have could put you at spiritual risk, potentially bringing on the illness. Moreover, the idea of insurance is culturally alien to local sensibilities. The Kabre do not otherwise gamble their money on unknown futures; nor do they pay into a general fund that covers those in need while failing to reimburse those without (but who have already paid in). The logic that underlies insurance—hedging against the future, deploying "population" as a category, measuring individuals against population-level norms—assumes that people are already inside a distinctively Euro-American cultural order that normalizes insuring one's fate against unknown futures. A partial solution was found when one student studied the clinic's books and compared the expenditures of those who were insured against those who were not (but who still visited the clinic). She then made the rounds of both groups, pointing out the savings of those who had enrolled. Five new families enrolled within a week; in 2015, forty-seven families were enrolled.

More recent projects have grown out of students' research on male teens migrating from the villages in Togo to farms in Benin and Nigeria. Local authority figures have opposed this exodus, but teens leave anyway, often sneaking off in the middle of the night. "We work hard here and have nothing to show for it at the end of the year," they assert. "We work hard in Nigeria, too, but in the end we come back with a motorcycle or a 'video' [TV and DVD player]." This social drama (between teens and parents) inspired projects that aimed not to stem the migratory tide—an impossible task—but to make life more palatable for those who remain behind.

The centerpiece of our efforts was the installation of a solar-powered internet café in the village of Farendé. Two students designed a website to announce the project and raise funds to purchase laptops and four large solar panels, and sent them to Togo by express mail. They assembled everything themselves, connecting to the internet through a local cellphone tower. Now this small village—well off the beaten path, without electricity or the usual amenities—is connected because of a couple of enterprising students. Many projects have been organized around this cybercafe. One student offered typing and internet classes; another created a writers' club that met twice a week to share work (about everyday life in the village), offering students computer access so they could type their essays, and publishing those essays online at the end of the summer.

Despite all the good intentions, hard work, and positive responses, it is worth considering the complications of installing a cybercafe in a village like this. Who will oversee its operation? How can it be both affordable and self-sustaining? How can the equipment be safeguarded? How does one ensure that monies end up in the right pockets? How can one spread computer literacy in a village where most have never seen a computer before? Even at the seemingly low price of sixty cents an hour, most locals could not afford to use the cybercafe. In one month in 2013, it had only three visitors—all adults—and made only fifty cents. Most of the cybercafe's income came from charging cell phones (with electricity generated by the solar panels), not from computer use, making this state-of-the-art cybercafe into little more than the village's charging station. There were also whispers that funds were being misappropriated by the young woman who tended the register and by the director. Someone broke in at night and made off with three of the laptops. For all of this, the project still has legs. The thief did not touch the pricier solar panels—which are riveted to the roof—and laptops are easily replaced. A night guard has been hired, and checks against disappearing funds have been put into place. The cybercafe now offers free computer access to youth one morning a week, which has begun to create a clientele.

This is how it goes with development: the best-laid plans usually go awry. But it is through setback that such designs become better adapted; that utopian dreams are brought down to earth and retrofitted to the local. Over time, new projects have come and gone, and while the center has held steady—the health insurance scheme, the cybercafe, microfinance, and the writers' workshop remain staples—other projects are being added: latrine sanitation, a universal nut sheller, a second internet café, an archival and oral history project, Zumba classes. It is the improvisatory, roll-with-the-punches nature of this work that not only makes it fresh and interesting—opening up new challenges and possibilities each year—but also lends it a flexibility that larger development initiatives lack.

Some of the more successful projects require no money at all. The insurance scheme is exemplary, as is the writers' project. In its second year, the writers' workshop enrolled eighteen students who embraced an idea to write a one-hundred-page novel in a month. By writing four pages a day, and never looking back, ten of the eighteen achieved their goal. Several of the novellas, especially those with a focus on everyday life in the villages, were surprisingly good and were bundled together for publication—at a printing press in the capital that charged five hundred dollars for 250 copies. These young authors are thrilled to see their work published, and a synergy has developed: in focusing on everyday life in the villages, many wrote poignant narratives about youth leaving for Nigeria—accounts of conversations between parents and children about the pros and cons of leaving, descriptions of travails on the farms of Nigeria and in the bars of Benin. Since this migratory phenomenon is the larger context that subtends all of our projects, having local teens write about it deepens and adds nuance to our ethnographic archive. Moreover, this project has fostered other initiatives we are now digitizing: the novellas along with transcriptions from the interviews we do each year with youth who have migrated; writings of Farendé researchers trained by an early French missionary; and student-collected oral histories from village elders about Kabre origins (which reveal fascinating, often contested histories with contemporary political implications).

These are all low-intensity and mostly inexpensive, sometimes free, interventions that focus largely on human potential and things immaterial. They tap into youthful energy on both sides: opening doors of desire for Farendé youth while hitting US students in their soft spot. American students are digital creatures sutured to their devices and, at least in this context, enjoy teaching others how to use them. Student engineers enjoy building things; English majors relish the opportunity to teach writing; global health students dive into almost anything health-related. This is the upbeat, utopian side of student culture today, an impulse I find hard to resist.

Can such endeavors be scaled up and made available to students elsewhere and in other settings? Duke students are fortunate that their university is able to bankroll up to forty student projects around the world each summer—in part because it has been trying to flee its reputation as a basketball and party school[2]—but other universities are today following suit, seeing abroad engagement as integral to education in the twenty-first century.[3] The cost to each student, while significant, is not prohibitive: between four thousand and five thousand dollars for a plane ticket and room and board for two months. A key to such a program's success is getting faculty buy-in, either by granting courses off or by convincing faculty that the experience can be research-enhancing. For my part, the latter has produced surprises at every step. Student questions and research agendas during the summer have opened new research directions for me, and lead to new publications. Moreover, when I am in the field with students, I have time on my hands—time for daily writing and research—while students work on their projects with community partners. For me, it has all been a win-win.

As should be obvious by now, when designing projects, accessing local knowledge is key to success. Introducing a mechanical nut sheller, for instance, requires familiarity not only with techniques of processing but also with local regimes of rights and access. How should gender and age orient access? While the Kabre do most of their work in groups, they do not own property in common. Who will "own" and repair the nut sheller? The student who initiated the Writers' Society learned that students who enjoy reading outside class are made fun of and have to conceal their books. And how does one deal with local views that computer use may lead to witch attacks—with users afraid to open messages or attachments from those they do not recognize? The outsider is usually at pains to find resolutions and invariably will commit errors of judgment. It is much better to let villagers sort things out according to local protocols and organizational principles.

Knowledge about local politics is also indispensable to project implementation. Countless development projects in this area have foundered because protocols were not followed, authorities were not consulted, or jealousy interfered. Initiatives are vulnerable to local authorities who want to be in charge of all that happens in their realm and to profit from it financially. Thus far, we have been fortunate to keep Farendé's and Kuwdé's chiefs at bay—another advantage of not only remaining small in scale and flying below the radar, but also of years of building relationships with chiefs (including the occasional greasing of palms). There are also influential civil servants in the capital who have an abiding interest in the villages, and are prepared to run interference if things go awry. Still, the delicacy of the relationship to power is real and gets factored into all that we do.

In addition to preparatory training during the semester before they leave, we meet for lunch twice a week throughout their time in the villages to brainstorm and troubleshoot their projects. During these sessions, we hold language lessons and discuss cultural puzzles, oddities, and misunderstandings that have arisen during the week. Two months is not enough time to acquire deep local understanding, of course, but it is enough to instill an attitude of respect and humility toward the local and to learn when to ask others for help. It also makes a difference that there is continuity from one year to the next—of student projects and assistants and community partners who have worked with the group. They carry knowledge about projects forward. And the students write up summaries and best practices—dos and don'ts—of their projects, with suggestions for the next generation of students. Finally, failure ought to be seen as constitutive. Each of these projects has experienced false starts, missteps, detours, profound setbacks, and flat-out failure. But for each setback or failure, lessons have been learned, and there have been some modest successes—and the projects have more traction today than they did before. Once you accept that failure is guaranteed, it opens the way to exploring why and how things did not work and how they might work better in the future.

NOTES

1. A longer version of this essay and contributions by students are collected in Charles Piot, ed., *Doing Development in West Africa: A Reader by and for Undergraduates* (Durham, NC: Duke University Press, 2016).

2. The Duke lacrosse scandal in 2007 spawned DukeEngage as a way, administrators hoped, to rebrand the school's identity—and it worked. Today, entering Duke students

list DukeEngage as their top reason for attending the university, unlike ten years ago, when basketball topped the list.

3. Among others, Tufts, Harvard, Stanford, Notre Dame, and Berkeley have launched similar programs, with Harvard's president announcing that "Harvard should be ready to provide summer internship opportunities in service for students—any student who wants one." Shera S. Avi-Yonah and Delano R. Franklin, "Harvard Unveils Summer Service Program for the Class of 2023," *Harvard Crimson*, April 29, 2019, https://www.thecrimson.com/article/2019/4/29/public-service-program-2023/.

28. Mentoring for Success across the Academic Spectrum

JOY GASTON GAYLES AND BRIDGET TURNER KELLY

There is wide agreement that mentoring is important and necessary to help students and faculty achieve their professional goals in higher education settings. Although mentoring is important, it is not well understood in the academy. People have different ideas about what mentoring means, what it looks like, and how it should be structured. The lack of shared understanding about mentoring leads to unevenness in terms of the extent to which people's needs are met, particularly those new to the academy. Rockquemore and Laszloffy (2008) define mentoring as a way to socialize students and faculty new to the institution through sharing information that is pertinent to success. Mentor relationships can be short- or long-term, but the goal is the same: to center the mentee's experience, and offer guidance and support that serves their best interests.

In this chapter, we share stories about mentoring to introduce some of the challenges and opportunities at various levels within the academy. The reality is that at every step of the academic ladder from undergraduate, graduate, and postdoctoral to the tenure track, there is a need for mentoring. At each step, there are unwritten rules, new expectations and requirements for success, and skills needed for navigating a new phase of one's career. Here, we offer recommendations and strategies that are grounded in the needs of undergraduates, graduates, and early career faculty.

Mentoring Undergraduate Students: A Story of Multiple Mentors

BRIDGET TURNER KELLY

Meeting Lauren was inspirational, and one of the best mentoring experiences I have ever had with an undergraduate student. When I learned about the type of work Lauren wanted to do as a Ronald E. McNair student, I was excited to be her official program mentor, because we had a shared interest in underrepresented students at historically White universities (HWUS). Lauren's status as a McNair student meant she received funding and resources to complete an undergraduate research project with a faculty mentor, and funding and preparation to attend graduate school. I took Lauren out to lunch and asked her about her experience at the HWU she attended, and where I worked as an associate professor. She discussed how she did not have any faculty of color or many students of color in her classes. In order to expose Lauren to successful Black women who had already completed college, we decided to create a study focused on Black women who graduated from HWUS to find out what factors helped or hindered their progress and, in some cases, their decision to pursue graduate school. Lauren completed the entire study with me, from the IRB proposal, to sixteen interviews with Black alumnae, to presenting the study at a national research conference, to publishing a peer-reviewed manuscript with me and my research team. In the end, Lauren benefited from a network of mentors that included me, my graduate student research team, and the Black women in the study. She successfully completed her undergraduate and master's degrees and is now working in her chosen field.

Challenges and Opportunities for Mentoring Undergraduate Students

Fortunately, the empirical research has caught up with practice in many universities, and policies and programs are more accessible to students to engage in formal mentoring, particularly at research universities. For instance, Provosts' and Undergraduate Research Offices are offering funding to undergraduate students and faculty who conduct research together. The funding from the McNair program was coupled with undergraduate research funding that Lauren had applied for, enabling us to travel to interviews and pay for professional transcription. In addition, this funding assisted Lauren in traveling to an out-of-state conference to present our research. There are also opportunities to mentor students as teaching assistants, or as advisers to study-abroad trips or student organizations.

On the other hand, there are many challenges to mentoring undergraduate students. Often, students like Lauren seek mentors who share some of their salient identities; but at many institutions, the number of faculty of color is disproportionately low in comparison to the number of students of color. Faculty at research universities also are discouraged from mentoring undergraduate students, as it can take time away from research and scholarship. Even when universities incentivize faculty-undergraduate collaboration or research, faculty often believe that undergraduate students do not have the necessary skills and experience for the work. In liberal arts colleges where teaching is a much larger component of tenure, mentoring students can be viewed as an investment of time that could be better spent on pedagogical or curricular development. Faculty also may feel unprepared for mentoring, particularly when students bring issues to mentors that involve mental health, abuse, or trauma. What I found from my longitudinal study of twenty-two women faculty at research universities was that mentoring students was the main reason most faculty chose their career, as opposed to working in industry or professional associations. Yet the investment it takes to mentor students well, including becoming knowledgeable about resources, or when and how to refer students to counseling or Title IX officers, is often not factored into tenure and promotion requirements at many universities.

Strategies for Mentoring Undergraduates

Since mentoring is not highly rewarded, faculty need to have incentives such as time release or additional salary for working with undergraduates, as it can be time-consuming. Another approach is the utilization of graduate students to mentor and advise undergraduate students alongside faculty. This tiered approach is effective with teaching and can be effective with mentoring as well. Understanding the demographics on the college campus is important, so that you can fill a need for mentoring when new hire opportunities come around. Faculty who have demonstrated evidence of working with and mentoring individuals with salient identities and other aspects of importance for diversity should be sought after. Last, mentoring should not be a solo endeavor. Faculty Affairs offices have numerous trainings and resources to equip faculty with assisting students and getting students in contact with appropriate counselors, health advocates, and academic support programs.

Mentoring Graduate Students

When I first met Kristin, I was impressed with not only her academic background but also the way she carried herself. What stood out the most was her passion for justice, inclusion, and equity. She began her PhD with me serving as her academic adviser and assistantship supervisor, and I was somewhat perplexed as to how to get into a deeper relationship with Kristin because during the first year, it felt as though her work and school life were all I was privy to in our weekly check-ins. I am an intrusive adviser and believe in asking students about their whole lives, because I think it impacts their work and well-being. When I asked Kristin about her life outside of school, I got very curt answers. It was not until the second and third years of working together that she let me into more of her life. Kristin and I are the same in a lot of ways, going straight through to the PhD from our master's and bachelor's degrees, and doing our dissertations on the impact of a social justice curriculum and pedagogy on students' development. Yet, we do not share ethnicity, race, nationality, or personality type. In order to gain Kristin's trust and build a mutually beneficial relationship, I let her into my home, introduced her to my partner, kids, colleagues, and friends. She served as my teaching assistant and I discussed my fears, vulnerabilities, frustrations, and joys with her in the class. She eventually led my research team and organized national conference presentations on research we gathered. Kristin introduced me to her family, and shared her grief and joy at major incidents in her life. We published several articles together while she was a student and well past her graduation. What gives me the most pride about our mentoring relationship is the friendship we have now, and how Kristin found her way to a career that is in our field, but not as a faculty member. It is an ideal fit for her, and it helped me learn how to mentor someone to be on a path that is right for them, and not just a carbon copy of the path I have chosen for myself.

CHALLENGES AND OPPORTUNITIES FOR MENTORING GRADUATE STUDENTS

Often, we form mentoring relationships with students after serving as their adviser or professor, or working with them on a research project. One of the difficulties in forming reciprocal relationships with students is the power difference. It is the responsibility of the faculty member to limit that as much as possible, through sharing vulnerabilities and stories of when they were in the same position; showing a genuine interest in students' lives outside of school work; and seeking the students' insights on teaching, research, and service.

Another difficulty can be the sometimes ambiguous expectations each has for the relationship. Recently, my institution mandated that Graduate Research Expectations be written and signed by both the graduate research assistant and their faculty supervisor. The form requires a conversation between the student and the faculty to make explicit each person's responsibilities; what schedule the two agree to; what procedures and best practices will be followed; and the professional development plan for the student, agreed to by both. These are for graduate students with faculty supervisors, but the same need exists for mentor and mentees to be explicit about unwritten rules of communication and culture that are often assumed or expected by faculty without being communicated to students. Graduate students and faculty who work together should be clear on when and how email should be returned, how feedback is given, how authorship will be handled on manuscripts, and whether or not working on other faculty's research is encouraged.

When a strong mentoring relationship exists, there are numerous benefits for the faculty member and the student. Students who know that someone is investing in their success have an easier time succeeding, and faculty benefit from mentoring someone new to the field. Students can also be great advocates for faculty when they nominate mentors for awards or speak highly of mentorship with prospective students. And they can relay the importance of mentoring to administrators and decision-makers on policies and practices that impact faculty time, resources, and workload. In addition, mentees can learn the hidden curriculum of graduate school that can help fuel their success. Mentors learn more about current research, new pedagogies, and ways of navigating the university from a reciprocal relationship with a mentee.

STRATEGIES FOR MENTORING GRADUATE STUDENTS

What is clear in Lauren's and Kristin's stories is I am not their only mentor. Kristin has other mentors in supervisors, colleagues, and former doctoral students. I learned a valuable lesson about multiple mentors from Christine Wiseman, President Emerita of Saint Xavier University, who said that three different type of mentors are helpful throughout one's journey: (1) a situational mentor who can be called upon when you have to make an important decision (e.g., whether to take a position, stay in a position, or switch academic advisers); (2) a seasonal mentor that you check in with four times a year who can offer perspective over a longer time period of connecting with you; and (3) an inspirational mentor that writes or speaks in such a way that uplifts and guides. The inspirational mentor may be someone you never meet, but someone who is prolific and whose work you can read to assist you in your journey. Often, we can provide inspirational mentors to students by having them read a myriad of works by diverse scholars that connect with them in ways we cannot. Letting students know which one, if any, of these multiple mentor roles we can fulfill helps them to know where they can go to get other needs met (Consortium on Race, Gender and Ethnicity 2012).

Mentoring Early Career Faculty

NEW KIDS ON THE BLOCK STORY (JOY GASTON GAYLES)

When Sasha joined the program faculty at my institution, I was excited to have a new colleague, particularly one who looked like me. At my institution, there are very few faculty of color. In my program area, I was the only one for several years before Sasha was hired. Although I was excited that Sasha joined the faculty, I quickly realized that I was not sure how to help her be successful. As a mid-career faculty member, I was dealing with a lot of challenges with privilege and power. For example, when I experienced microaggressions or differential treatment in the classroom due to my race and gender, I did not have a safe space to problem-solve these issues. Within my program and department, being one of few faculty of color was connected to my feelings of lack of belonging and fit. Because I was overwhelmed with writing deadlines, doctoral advisees, service requests, and a poor racial/ethnic climate, I was at a loss for how best to support my new colleague as she navigated her new role and expectations. Over time, Sasha and I became friends, and she spent quality time with me and my kids on the weekends. She even became a part of my social circle outside of academia. While I was able to help Sasha acclimate socially, I knew she needed more than that—she also needed support for her professional development. I invited her to be a part of a writing accountability group that I started within my college. This accountability group consisted of faculty within different program areas across the college as well as mid-career and early career faculty. I also thought about ways to collaborate with Sasha on writing projects that aligned with her research interests. As a result, we coauthored on writing projects as a way to build her portfolio as well as hold each other accountable for an important evaluation endeavor.

CHALLENGES AND OPPORTUNITIES FOR EARLY
CAREER FACULTY

Many early career faculty report that they started their positions feeling that graduate school left them unprepared for *how* to be a faculty member (Eddy and Gayles 2008; Whitt 1991). The reality is that new faculty begin their careers with a lot of questions, ranging from how to navigate the campus cultural climate and environment to how to "say no" to a colleague who holds a higher rank than they do. In addition, some new faculty do not feel comfortable asking questions or sharing aspects of their personal lives that may be impacting their productivity. They can feel an extreme sense of isolation and loneliness due to navigating their new careers on their own without communities of support (Rockquemore and Laszloffy 2008).

STRATEGIES FOR SUPPORTING EARLY CAREER FACULTY:
A COMMUNITY APPROACH

The challenges that early career faculty experience can be viewed as opportunities to better support and provide strategies to help new professionals achieve success. Much of the research and writing conducted by faculty members happens in silos, as they are expected to establish themselves as independent scholars. However, working independently does not always lead to the kind of consistent productivity that is necessary to earn tenure and promotion. It is much more effective for faculty to work in community with other scholars and colleagues to hold themselves accountable, obtain answers to their "how to" questions, and receive advice on how to navigate the tenure track.

Many times, new faculty are paired with a senior faculty member when they arrive on campus. This traditional model of mentoring assumes that every mentor match works the same, and that one faculty member can address all of the needs of their new colleague. A better approach to mentoring is to identify multiple faculty members and campus resources to make sure new faculty's needs are met. Faculty development offices around the country have started writing and accountability groups to provide structure for research and writing in the context of a supportive community. Joining such groups is a great way for new faculty to meet and engage with other faculty at the university and expand their support network. Institutions are also partnering with the largest faculty development center in the country, The National Center for Faculty Development and Diversity (NCFDD). NCFDD is an independent center that offers webinars, coaching, accountability, writing challenges, and multiweek courses on topics related to faculty success. Further, NCFDD is most well known for its twelve-week Faculty Bootcamp, which teaches faculty concrete skills and strategies that lead to explosive productivity, work-life balance, and healthy relationships.

Conclusion

In this chapter, we shared our experiences with mentoring at various levels within the academy, and discussed challenges and opportunities for effective mentoring at each level. Mentoring is important at all stages of the career ladder, from undergraduate through senior level faculty. Every time individuals advance in their careers, they must learn and navigate new expectations and rules to achieve success. A common approach is for individuals to do more of the same as they advance in the academy, which is not an effective strategy for success. For example, many undergraduates quickly realize that they need to learn new study-habit skills and advocate for themselves in order to make progress toward degree attainment. In the same way, graduate students must advance their writing, research, and time-management skills to achieve success in graduate school. It is important to recognize that having needs and questions (e.g., professional and personal) when starting a new role is normal. Further, many individuals will need assistance with learning what they may not know about their new role and expectations, identifying resources to enhance their skills, and cultivating communities of support. Effective mentoring can help socialize undergraduates, graduates, and faculty into their new roles and expectations with greater ease. It will require rethinking traditional approaches to mentoring, and instead centering the needs of the mentee to create a network of mentors and support.

WORKS CITED

Austin, A. E. 2002. "Preparing the Next Generation of Faculty: Graduate School as Socialization to the Academic Career." *Journal of Higher Education* 73.1: 94–122.

Consortium on Race, Gender and Ethnicity. 2012. "Mentoring Conversations: Doctoral Students Reflect on Relationships with Advisors: The 10 Things We Wish Our Advisors Knew." *Research Connections.* http://crge.umd.edu/wp-content/uploads/2017/07/RC 2012.pdf.

Eddy, P. L., and J. L. Gaston Gayles. 2008. "New Faculty on the Block: Issues of Stress and Support." *Journal of Human Behavior in the Social Environment* 17.1–2: 89–106.

Rockquemore, K., and T. A. Laszloffy. 2008. *The Black Academic's Guide to Winning Tenure—Without Losing Your Soul.* Boulder, CO: Rienner.

Whitt, E. J. 1991. "'Hit the Ground Running': Experiences of New Faculty in a School of Education." *Review of Higher Education* 14.2: 177–197.

29. Anonymous: Making the Best of a Peer Review

SHARON P. HOLLAND

Writing for Readers

One of the most important yet thankless tasks you will undertake as a member of the professoriate with a tenure line in an academic department is the review of scholarly work for the purposes of departmental promotion and for university presses. It is a task that graduate school does not prepare us for, and it is extremely important. For that reason, it can be daunting—a predicament only exacerbated by its totally unscripted nature. Since these letters and reviews are confidential (for the most part—and I will get to the question of confidentiality in the second part of this piece), it is impossible to land on a template or example of the genre, and the closest we come to it will be the evaluations we write for our graduate students as they approach the market. Moreover, there is no box to check in your own papers for promotion that will indicate how many of these letters you write in any given year—it is an expectation that we all do them to some degree, and that we do them quite often. It is common knowledge that women perform this task more often than our male colleagues, but that should be no surprise to any of us, given the culture of the institutions we serve.

Your relationship with this genre of writing in your career will be mixed with love and hate. Finding the time to consider a colleague's work in any capacity is a process of juggling an already too-full work week, and—make no mistake about it—it is a deeply personal and political process. I hope the strategies below will help you both navigate and, dare I say, enjoy this aspect of what will surely be a serious demand on your time.

I think the first order of business is to understand that within the genre of reviews, personnel decisions and manuscript reviews are *not* the same animal. In the former, you attempt—with both precision and some manner of skill—to cover the arc of a colleague's career, citing their principle arguments and their impact on the field. In the latter, your task is more open-ended, and you can feel free to propose friendly amendments to the author's work, often challenging the ideas collected therein, or wrestling with some thorny issue that is not quite articulated but needs to be. Understanding the nature of the beast will allow you to write the most effective letter you can.

In the first instance, the personnel decision can be an opportunity to consider the work of a scholar whose work you *should* know, but do not. It is a wonderful way to be introduced to someone. Whether this someone is friend or stranger, your own work will be enriched if you take the task seriously enough to engage with their ideas. I see these letters not as an opportunity to bring my own interests to bear, but to illuminate the interests of the colleague I am writing for to a body of individuals—appointment and promotion committees at the dean and provost levels—who will, for the most part, be wholly unused to the work before them. *That* should be your only goal, and none other. How do you approach the work before you with generosity and an eye toward making it legible to scholars outside the field? This work becomes even more crucial and valuable when you labor in often stigmatized fields that are believed to be wholly outside the normal work of the university. The task of your letter becomes twofold: to place the field squarely within the university committee's line of vision and explain its relationship to the broader work of the overarching discipline; and to state the importance of your colleague's work to both the traditional discipline and the burgeoning field. This is why your work is always already political, and understanding those stakes can bring clarity and pleasure to the task at hand. In this regard, you become a fierce advocate for the kind of work this scholar wants to do, and the place they hold or would like to hold in the profession. Your job is to write to that space, explaining the author's work with generosity and clarity. Perhaps this is the ultimate nerd's pleasure, but I can think of nothing more satisfying than coming to the end of a three-page letter having deeply considered the mind of a colleague, having basked in the ray of light that they shine upon the world around us.

In the second instance, the manuscript review is the chance to engage with often cutting-edge work in the field—to truly consider the impact of a colleague's work, how it will be read and received by generations to come. The question of impact on the field is no small one, and it is covered in both subgenres of writing. However, in manuscript reviews this question is more difficult. You must come at it with a critical eye, and you must also lay your own ego aside—even when scholars fail to cite you (so annoying!)—and invest in new directions and problems in the field. To this end, you must constantly be willing to understand the difference between a readerly resistance to being led in a new direction and those moments when scholars (particularly young scholars with first books) simply need a bit of clarity to connect the dots in a manuscript that will no doubt be impactful for the field. In essence, be willing to learn something new, and in turn help authors to take that something new to a wider audience. Understand that the means or the conveyance by which an author gets from point A to point B might not be your cup of tea, but ask yourself: does it have to be? I often find that so many of the books around us interrogate the same territory, as if the conversation was somehow narrowly truncated by some magical force, and now everyone is speaking a similar language. If we look around and all we see are the same set of epistemological communities staring us in the face at the book exhibit, we have only our unimaginative manuscript reviews to blame. If we want a set of fresh and innovative ideas in the marketplace of knowledge, we have to be generous enough in our critique and our praise to let those new ideas onto the playing field. In this way, manuscript reviews, I would argue, help foster the next generation of scholarly work.

Why All of This Matters

I want to travel from my general comments about manuscript reviews and promotion letters to a few examples from my own career trajectory, to better illuminate what's at stake. My reader's reports for my first monograph were relatively positive. One reader seemed to "get" my project and the second reader, while lauding its accomplishments, still wanted me to write a "big book." Scholars in my field were used to writing books that took the survey approach—they found a topic, researched any and everything related to it, and then wrote across sometimes hundreds of works to prove their point. My generation of scholars were pulling away from that kind of book, and the press I went with was rather maverick in publishing some of our earlier work. In fact, this latter point brings me to one of the most important understandings a writer should have about their work and its relationship to a press. Much like the fashion industry, presses are like houses—house of Versace, Chanel, etc.—and editors cultivate their reading lists very carefully to build recognition for their authors, and for the innovative work that the press puts forward. Knowing what press you are writing your review for is just as important as the manuscript itself. Many of us producing intellectual work in the field of LGBTQ studies are indebted to Ken

Wissoker, who took a chance on our quirky books and minds and encouraged us to choose his house and consider it a home. University press editors, if they are any good, are strong-minded and they know the field. And if they are wise, they do no gatekeeping but cull carefully and with intention. Do not be discouraged over a negative manuscript review. I have seen more than one book rejected by a press find a home in another, and go on to be an award-winning contribution to the intellectual work of the field.

There are several takeaways from my first experience with this process of manuscript review. It has always intrigued me that the reader who tends to disagree with you becomes "the second reader," as if their comments were somehow subordinate to the first reader, who looks like a hero next to the grumpy second, the naysayer. If you find yourself in this position as a reader, remember that this book *will* come back to you for review. If you have strong disagreement with an argument or paradigm, make sure to let the review sit for a few days—even a week if you can afford it—and come back to it. This is a bit of insurance against the "having a bad day and I hate having to do this when I have other work (my work) to do" response. Been there, done that. In hindsight, I realize that my response to those readers of my first book project was probably more cheeky than it should have been—I tried to be measured, but I did argue passionately for the kind of book I wanted to write. When the revised manuscript came back to the second reader, they took more than half a year to read it; when the review finally came in, their commitment to its publication was damning—they said, in essence, that the press could publish the book if they wanted to. Meh. Meanwhile, back at the plantation where I worked, I had informed my review committee in the run-up to tenure that my reports were in, and that I had made the necessary corrections and responded to readers. That was September. When February rolled around and I still had no word from the press, the situation on the ground at my institution became rather dire. Since no one had heard of such a long time between first- and second-round reports, my senior colleagues jumped to the conclusion that I was clearly not being entirely honest about the process. I was in conversation with my editor, but I wasn't sure how to advocate for myself, and I don't think I communicated how dire my situation actually was. In short, I was a young faculty member trying to build a career in a hostile working environment—a fact of living institutionally that has haunted my working life and will continue to do so into my retirement.

Moreover—and here's where all that intersectionality work that we do comes in—I was between a rock and a hard place. I was the only out, queer black woman in the college. Any place that I've been I've had to desegregate. While some might assume the benefit of the doubt when it comes to the above, what to do when that "benefit" doesn't transfer to your body, your gender? During a recent Modern Language Association meeting, a colleague disclosed the name of my absentee reader; I think they were trying to encourage me and let me know that this person had my back, so all would be okay. When my editor received the review, he phoned. I disclosed that I knew who the reader was. He seemed relieved and wanted to know, because the report was basically useless, if I had had some kind of professional falling out with this person. I responded that I had not, that the issue stemmed from a family conflict that had nothing to do with me but implicated me nonetheless. There were several lessons for all of us here: if your editor is an advocate—and mine certainly is and was—then talk to them about what's going on for you on the ground. It will help them to help you. Second, I learned how kinship networks can work in academic circles and how we all know one another; we are locked in a pseudointimacy that is at times beneficial and at other times demoralizing. Authors producing cutting-edge work need to know and hold that sharp edges cut both ways, so be kind and patient with yourself and your community, and most of all, reach out for help when you need it from those who can actually make a difference.

Being flippant in a review serves no one. We have to remember that at the end of the day, the editor of a press has to answer to the board, and so the argument for publication of a book has to be made across the two reviews. Period. To make matters worse, I knew who this person was, and when I got the call from my editor, I was to pick them up at the airport the next afternoon and host them for three days on my campus, as I had put their name forward for a senior position in my department. I was torn between my loyalty to self and my fierce loyalty to what it means to be a person of African descent in predominantly white spaces. When the chair asked me (again) that next morning what was up with my book, I responded to protect the candidacy of that individual and told the chair that I thought a second review was late or something like that. I am sure my response didn't inspire confidence. They didn't believe me because they knew something was funky, but what was I to say? The reasons why I wanted to protect this senior person wouldn't have registered with them *culturally*—it would have seemed absurd to them to put someone else's career over my own. On the other hand, had I told the truth, they would have believed it somewhat unprofessional to call out a senior person in my field who was in flight to our campus as we spoke. They would have been absolutely unable to put their white liberal self on the shelf and imagine that there could be any such conflict between folks of color. In this thorny equation, white persons tend to fear being called racist if they mess with black folks' business, so when it comes to institutional intersectional microaggression, you are basically on your own.

I learned this lesson the hard way, but it was my second time around, as my postdoc had prepared me for what was to come. To put it simply, it was a very long week in my young professional life. The only person who knew the whole story of that awful week was the late Lora Romero, who held me while I cried and plied me with whiskey and cigarettes. The story of her slow unraveling before all of us is another chapter in my professional life. Suffice it to say, I miss her warmth and her smile, and we kept each other's secrets well. Too well, as it turned out.

So why does this story matter? I want to help scholars approach a genre of writing that is unfamiliar to them. I also want to note how important that work is to the young scholar on the ground who might be struggling to survive at a predominantly white institution (PWI). This is all the more reason to take the review process seriously, to be clear about what *you* want to see in a book and what kinds of moves the author is making that might be paradigm-shifting or risky for the discipline. If this is the case, your review should state up front what you feel the stakes are for the larger discipline, and then you should create a roadmap of those important stakes, viewing the project on its own merits rather than in relationship to the field *as you know it*. This is no small task, and in many ways a contradictory one. But I promise that when you do this work, some parts of your own closed mind will be opened too, and your own work will be enriched. There is no greater pleasure than being at a conference and meeting an author for whom I've written an anonymous review. It is a small queer pleasure indeed to take pride in their being published, and to see how such intellectual acknowledgment can be transporting for someone trying to make their way through what can be a brutal and brutalizing profession.

Fast-forward almost twenty years to my promotion to the rank of full professor. Duke University 2010. In the spring of 2009, the associate dean had a meeting with me to tell me that it was time for me to come up. Up to that point, my time at Duke had been nothing short of a nightmare, everything that could go wrong did go wrong. It made my time at Stanford—where I endured Lora Romero's suicide and encountered such harassment from the chair of the department that staff would apologize to me after individual meetings with her and senior faculty would joke about how much the chair hated me—look . . . well, not so bad. I came up for full professorship not so much because I believed in an equitable process at Duke but because it was time to leave or stay (again) and if the dean was just setting me up for failure, so be it. In the aftermath of the denial, of course, the letters people wrote for me were redacted in part by supporters angry at what had happened to me. And here is perhaps the second lesson in letter-writing—while your letter is designed to be confidential, if the case goes south or gets gnarly in any way, the confidentiality of those letters can be undermined. What was told to me is that a few reviewers chose to take issue with my second monograph—some arguing with my work for a number of pages. I think we all know that this kind of work might be great for a conference paper—I'm a big girl and can take whatever criticism comes my way—but it is wholly inappropriate for a letter of promotion to any rank, as those Appointments, Promotion, and Tenure (AP&T) committee members who read it will undoubtedly read it with bias. We should always remember that first task: advocacy in the face of college committees who might know nothing at all about the field.

The moral of this story: When we write letters of support for promotion or manuscript review, we have to hold onto our fierce belief in the importance of intellectual work, with a good sense of what's at stake in the process. On the conference circuit, after being denied promotion to the rank of full professor, I watched as colleague after colleague registered shock and awe when I informed them about my promotion debacle. Shock and awe from a professoriate who write *every*day and *every*where about the injustices of the institution? Our collective inability to understand the stakes when we write and the situation on the ground where we work is profound, and only illuminates for me the sense that the problem is both inside and outside. We must remember the full community of scholars, and that some of us who are truly on the margins and at the intersection of the discipline have daily lives that look more like a hellscape than an academic career. This is why writing for colleagues is such a daunting and important task, but also a special pleasure because I can do the work unfettered; I can make the case for the full person who lives and works in what might be thoroughly deplorable circumstances; and, most importantly, I can pay it forward.

30. Questions to Ask Yourself about Requests for Service

LORI FLORES AND JOCELYN OLCOTT

Invitations to perform departmental, institutional, and professional service are just that—they are invitations, not contractual obligations. That said, as with any invitation, there are questions to consider before you accept or decline.

1. WHO'S THE "HOST"?

Service duties can offer you different opportunities for exposure to colleagues and administrators and for affiliations with groups. Whether the invitation comes from a horizontal direction (a peer in another department or institution) or a vertical one (from a dean or president at your own school or a student asking you to sponsor a campus organization), take time to consider the short- and long-term benefits of serving. If you are asked to serve on a committee convened by the provost, for example, you might feel that you have little choice in the matter or that demurring will be more difficult. While this may be true, ask yourself if it would be a good opportunity to foster relationships with colleagues outside your department or to establish greater name recognition and visibility for yourself at your institution. There is nothing wrong with thinking strategically about your *yeses* and *nos*. In terms of service to the profession, keep in mind the different demands of serving on a prize committee (a lot of reading and work in a concentrated amount of time) versus a conference program and logistics committee (more meetings and email discussions but spread out over a longer period of time). Before you give your host a definite answer, ask about their expectations. How many meetings will the committee have? When will be its busiest season or time? How many terms or years are you expected to serve? All of these are reasonable and smart questions to ask.

2. WHO ELSE IS INVITED?

Service commitments often expose you—for better and for worse—to people outside your immediate circle. On the upside, you'll have a chance to build alliances with people who might share your convictions. You could come away from the experience with more friends and mentors to add to your support network. On the downside, you might find yourself in conflict with colleagues who have different priorities, a competitive outlook, or higher rank or more power than you. Sometimes, a little reconnaissance can yield more information about who else will be serving on a committee with you, and that information can then factor into your decision to accept or politely decline. If the guest list will be a surprise, remind yourself that it will be a good opportunity to practice your diplomacy. However, be wary of any service that doesn't have strong or appropriate leadership from the get-go.

3. WHAT AM I BRINGING TO THE PARTY? WHAT'S MY ROLE?

The first thing that anyone will do to convince you to take on a service commitment will be to flatter you by telling you why you are *the perfect person* for the job. Before you agree, separate the flattery from your own objectives. Try to get concrete information about what your role will be. If you will be the most junior colleague on a university-wide committee, for example, ask yourself (and trusted others) why that might be. Does the head of the committee truly want the input of a newer colleague, or might this be a setup to put a more vulnerable person on a collision course with the dean? If you notice you're the only woman or person of color on a committee, is this a valuable opportunity to shape the agenda, or do you get the sense that you'll only be fulfilling some demographic tokenism without having any real influence? You might want to ask around about who has served on this committee in the past (if it has existed before) and chat with someone who will give you an honest answer about their experience. If their assessment (or your own intuition) leads you to think you will be ill-suited for the role—whether because of your other commitments or because of your temperament or vulnerability—there are ways to give a gracious *no*. You can give a particular reason (overcommitment, the need to focus on a particular task) or no reason at all; if you feel it would soften the blow, you can suggest someone else you think would be better suited or excited for the opportunity.

4. HOW MUCH TIME AND MONEY WILL IT TAKE?

As with any invitation, you'll want to think about how much time it will entail—not just meetings or tasks themselves but also travel time, disruption of other activity, preparation for meetings, and the emotional time and energy taken up by combative situations. Some service commitments are fairly straightforward and simply involve showing up and offering your perspective; most, however, will involve other demands on your time. Make sure you get a sense of the time involved and make a clear-eyed assessment of how much time you will dedicate and whether it will lead to situations that might create additional distractions. As for money, some professional service requires traveling to particular conferences or meeting sites. If you do not foresee yourself funding that travel with institutional money or by paying your own way, take that under serious consideration. Some askers might be more privileged in terms of funding or might not be mindful of others' financial situations. Be honest about your limitations, and if you still really want to serve, ask if it might be possible to do so remotely.

5. DO I HAVE A CONFLICT?

You should check to make sure not only that you don't have another invitation for the same time but also that you are not overcommitted in general. Remember: no one but you keeps track of everything that you're doing; make sure you don't exceed whatever quotas you've established for yourself about different forms of service. It might be helpful to make a list or grid of everything you are doing (committees, manuscript reviews, undergraduate organization advising, getting graduate students through qualifying exams and dissertations, and so forth) to give you a striking visual way of determining whether you're able to give a real and enthusiastic *yes* to something. And, of course, you should not accept an invitation if it would create a conflict of interest—for example, serving on a promotion committee for someone with whom you are romantically involved or serving on a grant committee where you have a financial interest.

6. HAVE I GIVEN MYSELF ENOUGH TIME TO DECIDE?

Never accept an invitation right away. This isn't a matter of being coy and playing hard-to-get: you want to have enough time to figure out what the commitment will mean in practical terms. You might want to consult with mentors and other colleagues as well as friends and family members, particularly if your plans might affect them. If you don't want to keep the asker hanging while you deliberate, send them a quick reply that you need appropriate time to check your various calendars. While they might make you feel pressed to give a quick answer, refrain from doing so. On their end, asking you is very likely something on their "to-do" list that they want to check off quickly and get off their desk. The consequences for you, however, are longer-reaching.

7. CAN I LEAVE EARLY?

There's always the chance that you'll arrive at the party and realize that you cannot stay for as long as you thought. Perhaps one of the other guests is someone you'd rather avoid, or the conversation puts you in an awkward or marginal position. Obviously, you would prefer not to have to back out of something before you have fulfilled your commitment, but it's worth finding out what the professional and reputational consequences might be if you find that you must.

8. DO I WANT TO GET INVITED BACK?

Some service commitments can give you insights into the ways your institution functions and might help you explore career options within academia. If, for example, you're interested in pursuing administrative opportunities, it makes sense to accept service that allows you to learn how decisions are made and budgets determined. If you're interested in curricular reform, it makes sense to serve on your department's undergraduate studies committee or even take on the duties as director of undergraduate studies. Be strategic if you want to see one invitation turn into more—say *yes* to the things that will develop the particular skills needed for a role you hope to have in the future.

To sum up: A *yes* to something means a *no* to something else. Think seriously about whether you will be fine with a particular opportunity taking your time and energy away from other invitations that may come your way. If so, that's great! But keep that running log of all your *yeses* so that you don't find yourself buried and resentful under a pile of them.

On the flip side, a *no* to something can mean a *yes* to something else. Remind yourself that in a reply to a host, you can always say, "I have to decline this time, but please keep me in mind for something else." Do not let a *no* plague your conscience; you might very well be opening yourself up to accept something later that feels more exciting and in line with your priorities and passions.

PART III

Issues in Today's Academy

The contributions in this part of the handbook speak to some of the most dramatic national developments that have taken place in recent years, including new economic pressures; transformative (and increasingly demanding) technologies; family formations; louder conversations about sexual misconduct and various forms of racial violence; and an uptick in anxiety, isolation, and depression in people of all ages. All of these things, plus other societal shifts, reverberate in academia and academics' lives. Indeed, it can sometimes feel like things are moving so quickly that the ground is shifting beneath our feet.

For many of the questions taken up here, it will be useful to consult the student and faculty handbooks at your institution to get a sense of the relevant policies. For issues related to sexual harassment and emotional health, for example, some schools have specific required-reporting policies that mandate faculty to convey to the appropriate offices any student reports related to these matters. Most institutions have policies about how to accommodate undergraduate and graduate students with physical or learning disabilities. Many colleges and universities now have programs that encourage faculty to reach out to their surrounding communities through civic engagement and service-learning programs, and have offices dedicated to supporting those efforts.

Perhaps one of the most dramatic changes that has occurred in the past decade is that many scholars have turned to social media to have a presence as public intellectuals. These technologies offer opportunities and pitfalls for academics, allowing us to bring our expertise to bear on public questions in a timely fashion, but also exposing us to public scrutiny when comments might be taken out of context. Social media have also provoked new questions about academic freedom, as faculty may weigh in on issues that lie outside their areas of expertise in spaces that are simultaneously public and private. Meanwhile, many faculty members may feel pressure from their employers to have a social media presence either for themselves or for their departments, adding another time-consuming task to their weekly to-do lists. Natalia Mehlman Petrzela explains the opportunities and challenges of developing a prominent social media presence as an academic, and N. D. B. Connolly describes his experiences producing a podcast as a form of what he calls "public teaching."

The contributions here are far from exhaustive treatments of these matters, and new questions arise every day. But these essays point to many of the issues that colleagues might consider when navigating issues and expectations that may seem apart from the conventional expectations of research, teaching, and service. Michelle Falkoff offers reflections on the role that student evaluations have come to play in the academy, and how academics should use them. Lauren Hall-Lew and Heidi Harley, both adoptive parents (a demographic that gets short shrift in discussions of academic work-family balance), offer advice about "setting a healthy boundary between caregiving and work" in a career in which both will consume as much time and energy as we allow them. Stephen Kuusisto speaks to the persistent marginalization of differently abled people.

Issues that dominate headlines spark intense debates in colleges and universities. Matthew Finkin discusses the differences between the protections of the First Amendment and academic freedom, as well as instances wherein there are tensions between different forms of academic freedom. Cary Nelson draws on expertise gained as president of the American Association of University Professors (AAUP) to examine the precarity resulting from academia's overwhelming reliance on non-tenure-track faculty. David Schultz explores the changes in administration and governance in what has emerged as the "corporate university," and the resulting pressures on academics to be productive, efficient, and marketable at all times. Elizabeth Hutchison discusses obligations, expectations, and best practices for addressing sexual harassment and sexual violence, whether it involves students, staff, or colleagues. To bring this handbook to an end, anthropologist Kelly Fayard recounts how she has cultivated allies in her efforts to decolonize the academy and recognize Native communities.

Taken together, the essays in this section offer reflections about how to navigate institutions that are designed to reflect upon the world around them, but remain inextricable from that world. The changing social, economic, and technological landscape places new expectations on faculty but also creates chances for us to have a greater impact on the communities—whether on a household scale or a global scale—in which we live and work.

31. Navigating Social Media as an Academic

NATALIA MEHLMAN PETRZELA

I am a digital immigrant. In stark contrast to the "natives" just a few years my junior, I organized my high school papers on index cards and, in college, emailed once daily at the library. But by the time I became a professor in 2009, I was navigating new terrain, created by social media and the digital technologies that enabled them. My strongest recollection of this era was a sense that while social media was fun, it could only distract from scholarship. I let friend requests from colleagues languish (baby pictures and workout updates would only reveal me as unserious, right?) and even deleted the "sent from my Blackberry" signature that would reveal I was ever untethered from my desk. I was dimly aware of a field called "digital humanities," but even online archives felt far from the heart of an endeavor I defined by the mostly solitary, tactile spaces of libraries that smelled of old books, and my solid wood desk.

That I'm writing this essay—and for a university press—is evidence that the landscape has changed. When I first began using social media to share ideas with colleagues, I emphasized that new media created opportunities for traditionally recognized modes of intellectual expression. It was, and still is, true: social media has led directly to my participation in conference panels, contributions to edited volumes, and publication in venerable—print!—outlets such as the *New York Times* and the *Chronicle of Higher Education*.

But social media is now exciting to me for the opportunities it creates that are unique to our age. Syllabi coalesce—publicly! freely!—as the news breaks. Rich threads filled with primary sources and sharp insights make the rounds.

Thoughtful, peer-edited blogs are accessible in terms of prose and cost. Podcasts privilege the smart commentary often reduced to a sound byte in popular media. Writing accountability groups collectively inspire grad students and tenured professors alike. Networks amplify often-silenced marginalized voices, and create a virtual cheering section for the accomplishments of academic life that can be illegible to those outside of it—securing a job that requires moving to a remote location for a low salary, or the acceptance of an article for no pay that will not be published for two years.

I use social media for all the above, but also find it professionally valuable in ways that don't correspond to cv lines. I often share about parenting, exercise, and travel, and I am especially gratified when younger scholars thank me for modeling how professors can unabashedly exist outside the academy. Conferences can now feel different thanks to the digital versions of each other we come to know, as it is common to enjoy a degree of intimacy afforded by social media's albeit imperfect window onto who we are beyond our acknowledgments.

That said, social media is no utopia for academics or anyone, especially women and minorities. Old structures of authority apply, and social media offers a 24/7 opportunity to run afoul of them, with professional consequences far beyond one's follower count. I see this when graduate students get blowback for tweeting too intrepidly; even senior scholars are targeted for florid Facebook rants, and women of color get death threats for daring to speak out at all. I'm hardly immune: when I tweeted about the dubiousness of touting press secretary Sarah Huckabee Sanders's appointment as a feminist accomplishment, conservative blogs—and eventually Fox News—seized on it and, for a couple of days, my mentions were filled with profanity and threats. Less aggressively, but arguably more impactful on my career, sidelong remarks from some colleagues about the superficiality of social media make clear that others perceive the time I spend on these platforms as a waste.

I try to amplify the online voices of graduate students, contingent faculty, and marginalized communities to do a small part to challenge these forces. Yet, I also remind myself, and anyone who will listen, to be deliberate about social media use: think before posting, as I do, about whether the potential repercussions are worth it. Do you want to spend the next several hours or more being called terrible names, or worse? Would you say what you tweeted to a colleague's face? Would you be embarrassed if it were a *New York Times* headline? What does your point of view add to the conversation? It is important for all of us to remember that the apparent anonymity of sharing from our screens is misleading, and when the urge to be mean-spirited or intellectually careless, or to weigh in on every news item becomes irresistible, it's time to take a break! I have removed Twitter and Facebook from my phone several times for this reason.

Understanding the promises and pitfalls of this new realm is especially salient as scholars like me push to recognize public engagement as a legitimate form of expression for academics, while others understandably worry that maintaining an online presence will become yet another requirement of an already demanding job. Scholars who invest time and energy engaging in and elevating the popular discourse through these media should be acknowledged for it. I have been pleased that my institution supports my work in this realm as complementary to, rather than a distraction from, my research, teaching, and service. Still, when people compliment my "bravery" for "getting out there," I want to reply that if anything deserves praise, it's my stamina. Precisely because I know public engagement is not uniformly valued among colleagues—and because I truly do value peer-reviewed, traditional publishing and teaching as the core of a scholarly career—I have always made sure that I meet and even exceed these professional standards, in part because I do this work. I completely understand the anxiety of some junior colleagues who worry that they don't have enough of a public profile but also that cultivating one could work against them. They are right, and there is no easy, singular answer to this quandary.

It is exciting, and even thrilling, to chart this new territory with other scholars, and to interact with publics far beyond what was possible less than a decade ago. It's up to us to consider the impact of this shift and to create new norms that will consider the many possible forms of public engagement for scholars, including how to value them more legibly and meaningfully as part of an academic career. For all this enthusiasm, however, I am reminded of an ambivalent realization I had when a scholar at a conference in Europe referred to a tweet I had written two years earlier: words I had dashed off in haste—and assumed, on some level, had disappeared into the ether—really can last forever. Most importantly, perhaps, I must admit I found it nearly impossible to write this short piece without checking my feeds multiple times. I am certainly more distractible than I was in a notification-free era that could be lonely, but was also characterized by a quiet I now find difficult to recapture. I guess I'm lucky to remember those days at all.

32. My Social Media Philosophy in (Roughly) One Thousand Words

N. D. B. CONNOLLY

I consider social media and podcasting useful for researching, organizing, and what I like to call "public teaching."

You can get content almost anywhere these days. But as history professors, we've been uniquely prepared to consider and amend the stories that the general public tells itself about the past. We've been placed, too, in a position to provide and present strong evidence—*archival* evidence—in a compelling way, usually through narrative.

My work as a host on the podcast *BackStory* (which began airing in 2008 and which I joined from 2017 to 2020) has proven critical for teaching in public. We enjoyed over 100,000 listeners every week. That's a lot of teaching! Moreover, as historians, we cohosts constantly learned from each other about historical facts, interpretations, and how to present ideas. That has made my public teaching, via podcasting, a boon to my skill set and knowledge base as a classroom teacher.

With my own experience of growth in mind, I believe it incumbent on historians to understand and wield ever-evolving genres of storytelling. That used to mean books, articles, films, radio, and literature. Now, it includes web-based content such as blogs, digital mapping, Facebook posts, Twitter threads, and podcasting. As long as we embrace these new platforms *as genres* of historical narration, we can innovate and deepen what these platforms can do. If we treat them as cognate to "real history"—and if we don't continue pressing for our universities to consider and reward this labor *as* labor—we're contributing to academic historians' potential obsolescence. In these times, that strikes me as especially dangerous.

Considering, in fact, the politics of knowledge-making, I've found social media remarkably effective at organizing scholars to help humanize and improve our professional institutions. I've personally been party to efforts begun via social media to improve editorial practice at major journals, to petition against political appointments from a place of scholarly expertise, and to redress topical oversights in trade publications. Each time, these have been collective efforts. And they've become so common in our wider profession as to go largely unremarked and unframed as part of our general job description. (Even if that's becoming more and more the case.)

Organizing via social media has clear scholarly benefits. Facebook, especially, can allow you to whip up an immediate academic conference on whatever topic you need. Often in mere minutes (and without leaving the couch), I've been able to marshal help tracking down arcane sources, reading barely intelligible archival records, and laying out the contours of a pressing scholarly debate. I gave up social media for a time to focus on writing. It was the research aspect of social media, though, that brought me back.

That said, I've also learned a few lessons to help me navigate the newness of these platforms and digital modes of knowledge-sharing and -making.

First, the importance of taking breaks from digital platforms can't be ignored. The draw of immediate gratification, distraction, and sometimes bald voyeurism, can make social media a poor and toxic substitute for working through a tough patch of writing or an archival dead end. There's no magic formula for balancing one's "digital diet." Mostly, I think, it requires being honest with oneself about how social media makes one feel, especially when compared to how one feels cracking a research riddle or completing a powerful piece of writing. No lyrical Facebook post or foe-vanquishing on Twitter can really compete with that.

Second, recognize that not everyone will appreciate your online contribution as much as you do. It's increasingly true that scholars with large Twitter followings can command higher speaking fees or heftier book advances, based on their perceived marketability. For those scholars merely holding or interested in pursuing an academic job, however, university administrations do not yet hire, tenure, or promote based on one's social media impact. (Again, not *yet*.) They can and have, however, terminated professors for exercising their free speech online. This is not to dissuade anyone from using direct or even sharp language on one's platform of choice. It is, rather, to make a direct economic point. You can't take social capital built online into the Ivory Tower, any more than you can spend pesos or rupees at a Walmart in Indianapolis. The currencies are not equivalent. Knowing this can go a long way toward mitigating one's expectations of and investment in particular platforms.

Third, one should remain mindful of the consequences—really, the dangers—of subjecting one's work or ideas to social media, *and protect oneself accordingly.* Those out in the world who believe your perspective to be dangerous or costly—for them personally or for their imagined group—will often find an unsavory way to let you know it. Over my years of public teaching via op-eds and social media, I've received some pretty bracing messages, replete with death threats, n-bombs, and JPEGs of the Confederate flag. As a general rule of thumb, it's advisable to consider how much your distaste for hate mail outweighs your desire for media exposure. More specifically, take concrete steps to keep your home address offline, protect your data from hackers, and, if ever threatened, take such threats seriously by activating the necessary security or law-enforcement measures.

33. Moving beyond Student Teaching Evaluations

MICHELLE FALKOFF

Few who have ever worked in higher education would be surprised to learn that more evidence has come out showing that student evaluations of teaching are often biased. In a recent study on gender bias in student evaluations in *PS: Political Science & Politics*, Kristina M. W. Mitchell and Jonathan Martin argue that academic institutions must stop giving an inordinate amount of weight to student evaluations when making employment decisions until the institutions can account for, address, and eliminate bias.[1] Unfortunately, there is no consensus on how best to do that, and gender is not the only kind of bias at issue. Still, it is time for academic institutions to do better.

Evidence of gender bias has been available for a long time. Even the most cursory search reveals multiple studies going back to the 1980s that examine the role of gender bias in academic evaluations, published in journals such as the *Journal of Educational Psychology* and *Research in Higher Education*.[2] More recently, researchers for publications such as the *Journal of Diversity in Higher Education* have investigated the effect of other kinds of bias, such as racial and ethnic bias, and have found equally problematic outcomes.[3] Even biases that fall outside traditional categories of discrimination, such as student negativity toward classes they perceive as overly challenging or taxing, harm educational institutions' ability to use student evaluations to gauge teacher effectiveness. Professors who are perceived to be difficult, or who teach difficult material, may receive lower evaluations, despite students often having greater success in later courses based on what they learned from those professors, as one study found.[4]

Student evaluations have also become less reliable over the years because most schools have switched to online systems. The American Association of University Professors (AAUP) ran a comprehensive survey of faculty members about teaching evaluations. This survey noted that the rate of return for student evaluations has gone down precipitously in the electronic age, and that the tone of student comments has started to resemble that of internet message boards, with more abuse and bullying.[5] Students who were aware of some or all of their grades in advance of completing the evaluations tended to be harder on faculty, in both written comments and numerical assessment. This decrease in reliability and consistency also contributes to the ineffectiveness of student evaluations as a primary metric for faculty assessment.

While it may be possible to improve evaluations by trying to account for or eliminate bias (such as changing the questions, discounting numbers to account for bias, or coming up with alternative strategies for obtaining student feedback), the better approach is to look at alternative means of assessing faculty performance. In particular, it is time to stop relying primarily on one approach and move to a more holistic strategy, in which multiple factors contribute to a more accurate, consistent, and well-rounded assessment.

My experience as director of the Communication and Legal Reasoning program at Northwestern University's Pritzker School of Law has convinced me that a holistic approach to faculty evaluation is more appropriate than reliance on student evaluations alone. Our course is part of the required curriculum, and my faculty includes a majority of women. Students do not get to choose their professors, are graded on a curve, and receive extensive critical feedback during the semester before they complete their evaluations. This means that students often use their evaluations to express their frustration with the difficulty of the course overall, and often lash out at faculty members. As a result, student evaluations are far less helpful than I would like in assessing what faculty members do well, or where faculty members need improvement. This makes it necessary to parse the distinction between students' frustrations that are natural byproducts of the difficulty of the course, and actual teaching issues that impede student learning.

To that end, the University of Michigan Center on Learning and Teaching emphasizes the importance of using more than one evaluative methodology, regardless of what the methodologies are.[6] The Center suggests including assessment of how faculty members deliver their instruction; how they plan their courses; how they assess the students themselves; and other factors, including feedback from students, colleagues, and supervisors. The AAUP survey authors also suggested a holistic approach to evaluation. Based on faculty feedback, they recommended clearer institutional assessment policies, assessment by multiple constituencies that included but were not limited to students, and an increased emphasis on mentoring.

At my own institution, I have found alternative methods of assessing faculty extremely effective. These methods include watching faculty classes (whether via video or in person), reviewing course materials, reading faculty self-evaluations, and meeting with faculty members one-on-one to discuss performance. With a clear sense of how faculty members perceive their own course, student feedback is easier to contextualize, and it becomes possible to determine whether student concerns are legitimate or are typical for classes as demanding as first-year law school classes tend to be. The Searle Center for Advanced Teaching and Learning at Northwestern is also helpful in providing guidance to faculty who wish to improve their teaching. The Center holds workshops and programs for groups of faculty on various topics related to teaching, and Center employees also work with individual faculty members, including visiting classes and providing personalized feedback.

Of course, student feedback remains important, and at the law school we have taken steps to make the evaluations more useful for both students and faculty. Faculty members can personalize their evaluations to ask questions they feel are likely to be valuable. My program's evaluations include, for example, some questions permitting the students to evaluate their own performance. These provide context for their other responses, both for themselves and for faculty members. The university is also in the process of reviewing its overall approach to student feedback, as are many other institutions.

Holding teaching faculty members to high standards is important and student feedback is relevant; but if academic institutions do not take steps to assess faculty members more holistically, they run the risk of losing talented faculty for reasons that are not only inappropriate but may well be illegal. Moving beyond reliance on student evaluations may involve taking more time and effort to evaluate faculty members, but it will also help us ensure that we are helping teachers succeed while eliminating the possibility that bias will play a role in making or breaking their careers.

NOTES

1. Kristina M. W. Mitchell and Jonathan Martin, "Gender Bias in Student Evaluations," PS: Political Science & Politics 51.3 (2018): 648–52.

2. Susan A. Basow and Nancy T. Silberg, "Student Evaluations of College Professors: Are Female and Male Professors Rated Differently?" Journal of Educational Psychology

79.3 (1987): 308–14; Henry Wigington, Nona Tollefson, and Edme Rodriguez, "Students' Ratings of Instructors Revisited: Interactions among Class and Instructor Variables," *Research in Higher Education* 30.3 (1989): 331–44.

3. Landon D. Reid, "The Role of Perceived Race and Gender in the Evaluation of College Teaching on RateMyProfessors.com," *Journal of Diversity in Higher Education* 3.3 (2010): 137–52.

4. Anya Kamenetz, "Student Course Evaluations Get an 'F,'" NPR Ed, 26 September 2014, https://www.npr.org/sections/ed/2014/09/26/345515451/student-course-evaluations-get-an-f.

5. Craig Vasey and Linda Carroll, "How Do We Evaluate Teaching? Findings from a Survey of Faculty Members," AAUP online, May–June 2016, https://www.aaup.org/article/how-do-we-evaluate-teaching#.WrFBzOgbNPY.

6. University of Michigan Center for Research on Learning and Teaching, "Methods of Evaluating Teaching," http://www.crlt.umich.edu/resources/evaluation-teaching/methods, accessed January 28, 2020.

34. Work-Family Balance in Academia

LAUREN HALL-LEW AND HEIDI HARLEY

Every day, our work is affected by our home life. A good night's sleep can foster productivity, while an argument over breakfast can ruin your day. Long term, our family lives can deeply impact the resources we have to carry out tasks at work. In this chapter, we draw on our experiences as adoptive parents—a type of parent who is not often explicitly included in discussions of life in academia—to discuss caring for and growing a family while working in the academy. We use our experiences to illustrate the sometimes unexpected ways that family stress and complexity can impact an academic career, and we discuss strategies for achieving balance.

First, we'll introduce ourselves.

Lauren's Story

My husband and I have a daughter, born in 2012, and a son, born in 2016. Both lived with foster families from birth and joined our family as toddlers. We are Americans, living in the United Kingdom since 2009. A common path to adoption in the UK is through the foster care system. After a child is placed with prospective adoptive parents, there is a "settling in" period of several months before the legal adoption begins. This is a stressful time. Prospective parents are parenting a child they've only just met and who will be struggling emotionally with the transition. The children may have emotional or cognitive delays because of the circumstances that led to their being in foster care. And since children in foster care are not often relinquished voluntarily by their birth parents, there are sometimes long and fraught court proceedings. Isla was placed with us in March 2014 and we expected to legally adopt her that September, but it took four court dates, finishing in December. I was working full time that semester, and it was sometimes difficult to be fully present at work.

My first few years as a parent were spent learning to radically change the expectations I had for my work productivity. Despite the fact that my husband took full-time adoption leave for a year and then returned to his job (in academic administration) part time for caregiving reasons, Isla still seemed to require every ounce of my energy and attention when I wasn't at work, and even sometimes when I was. I was always tired, and often sick. Even when she was in day care, the intensity of her needs in the mornings, evenings, and on weekends was often overwhelming. When my son came home a few years later, the feeling more than doubled, and I reached a new level of burnout. My self-care strategy is to cultivate support. I've amassed a pile of books about parenting, adoption, and childhood trauma. I go to therapy and am active in online support groups. Together, these efforts help me manage, and even enjoy, both parenting and academic life.

Heidi's Story

We have two boys, one born in 2012 and one in 2017, both placed with us at birth through domestic open adoption in the United States. We adopted as older parents; I was forty-two in 2012, and my husband was fifty. Our first adoption was through a large national agency, and it went about as easily as possible. We were chosen by Jasper's birth mom after only a month of waiting. Her vision for the adoption was clear, and we had a lot of time to get to know each other, to the point that she invited us into the delivery room. My husband cut the cord; I was the first to hold Jasper; we have been together since his first breath. Since then, we have stayed in regular contact with his birth family and settled into our respective familial roles well. Despite this, it was an emotionally fraught process, full of fears and tears and interpersonal challenges. Our second adoption was a much bumpier process, although I experienced the bumps with much more equanimity. We renewed our home study, paid our second set of agency fees, sent in our materials, and waited. A year went by, then two, then three—and then our national agency went bankrupt, taking our fees and our hopes of a second adoption with it. (Adopting through an agency in the United States, either domestically or internationally, is an expensive proposition. Agency fees are in the tens of thousands of dollars, a significant percentage of an annual academic salary, especially at an early career stage. Agency fees also don't include legal costs or birth parent support costs, which add another few thousand to the total expense. In contrast, there are very minimal costs when adopting from foster care.) But a few months later, the local agency that did our home study on behalf of the national agency called with a potential match! We were fortunate to be able to afford the third fee, and so we matched with a couple in our state who were making their decision late in the pregnancy. Jaxson was born two weeks later; we met him about five hours after birth. His birth mom's postpartum emotional journey was volatile, and responding supportively to her feelings was a big new emotional challenge for me.

As for Lauren, adoption for me has meant a lot of reading, counseling support, and seeking out experienced mentors, as well as changes to my work life. Open adoption, besides the sometimes challenging interpersonal dynamics, has also brought new logistical challenges, such as taking time for visits with our new extended families. Parenting through open adoption has sharply curtailed my academic travel even more than biological parenting would have, despite the fact that like Lauren, I have a very supportive partner who does a large share of the caregiving, having reduced his work schedule to part time for that purpose. Because of our partners' support, both Lauren and I have more flexibility for work-related travel than we might if we were single. As for my day-to-day life, there is no more attending to the millions of chores of academia at home. My new boundaries have their upside, however. Parenthood has made both going to work (I get to get some work done!) and coming home (I get to see my darlings!) more rewarding.

Caregiving while an Academic

The challenges of adoptive parenting overlap quite a bit with any kind of caregiving: loss of leisure time, loss of sleep, and increases in stress. This can often result in increases in physical and mental illness, and difficulties completing work-related tasks of various sorts. We discuss our experiences with these challenges, and our advice for addressing them, by focusing on two general issues: time and energy.

YOUR TIME

Challenges to work-family "balance" are felt most acutely at the day-to-day level. When you are someone's primary caregiver, your personal time is not, strictly speaking, ever your own. There are times when this state is immediate (e.g., when feeding or bathing that other person), but even at work, your time might need to be spent on caregiving duties (e.g., scheduling a doctor's appointment).

When caregiving for a high-needs individual, it can be impossible to accomplish that kind of task while simultaneously attending to their immediate needs.

Different family situations require different amounts of this organizational work. A central feature of adopting, for example, is the massive amount of time and paperwork involved. In Lauren's case, the most time-consuming part of the process was the home visitation, which follows six weeks of preparatory training. When UK-based parents adopt from foster care, they are represented by a seventy- to eighty-page document that the social worker assembles after about nine months of fortnightly home visits, which always take place during the workday. The document includes personal information about the prospective adopters; medical checks; criminal background checks; safety checks of the home; and three letters of recommendation, the writers of whom are also interviewed. The prospective adopters are interviewed by a panel before starting to look at profiles of available children, which itself can take months or years. Heidi went through a similar home-study process in the United States, with two social worker visits, criminal checks, medical affidavits, and three letters of support from nonrelatives. Open adoption in the United States also requires a kind of familial promotional brochure with pictures and text, for birth mothers to look at as they choose which families to consider for their baby. Heidi found assembling that document to be about as stressful and time-consuming as assembling her tenure dossier.

The day-to-day demands of caregiving require resetting your expectations for a "productive" day, and being understanding about the fact that your workday may necessarily be structured differently than it used to be, or differently from that of your peers. You might put in more hours in the evenings or weekends just to work the same number of hours as your colleagues; or you might rule out working at home entirely, putting more pressure on your time in the office. On the one hand, the flexibility built into the academic work schedule in US and UK cultures is an advantage. On the other hand, becoming a caregiver necessitates building healthy boundaries: recognizing that there are times when work takes priority over caregiving, and vice versa, and being deliberate about when those times are. As children get older, their school-dictated schedules sharply constrain their caregivers' availability. If you had been a binge-writing night owl, as we both were, you either need to transition to a nine-to-five, planned-increment schedule for writing, or schedule your writing binges in collaboration with your caregiving support network. Being a primary caregiver is a major change and, like all change, it's not always easy. For some, it may be tempting to transfer a quality of perfectionism from an academic context to a caregiving one (e.g., being the "perfect parent"), and this temptation must be avoided at all costs, lest you burn out at both ends.

Setting healthy boundaries between caregiving and work is also the bottom line for how to navigate the challenges of the longer-term demands on your time. For example, some academics are advised to see their sabbatical as an ideal time to have children. This is *bad* advice. The effect is to deprive you of a research-focused sabbatical that your childless peers are taking, with commensurate effects on your research output. If you have access to parental leave, claim it separately from research leave. If you have a child during sabbatical, pause the research leave from the moment you begin parental leave, and resume it at the completion of parental leave. Don't expect to do *any* academic work while on parental leave. If you can manage some here and there, great; but you are on personal leave for good reason, and the demands of that reason mean that even the smallest academic task can feel overwhelming. It may feel uncomfortable, after having dedicated your life to obtaining a PhD, to suddenly abandon your academic work for months, but we both found that it was necessary.

There may also be pressure to limit the length of leave. Tenure-track academics, especially, worry that any break in progression toward tenure will be evaluated negatively. While penalizing tenure applicants for caregiver leave is, in our opinion, unethical, we can't promise it won't happen. But all things being equal, we recommend taking as much leave as possible. Check with your human resources department about how much leave you're entitled to, as this varies from place to place. For those adopting, we hope that you find yourselves at institutions that allow for the same leave as birth parents. While adoptive parents don't need to recover from childbirth, they need time to heal other wounds and bond with their child. (Colleagues and students may need to be educated about this, though we hope less and less so in the future.) And, of course, caring for any newborn is a 24/7 prospect for months.

Another challenge is medium-term planning: teaching, examining graduate students, attending conferences, and so on. Your caregiving can be required very suddenly and unexpectedly, and that state of anticipation can be very stressful. With pregnancy, a premature birth or miscarriage can have a devastating impact on an academic's ability to work at all, not to mention throwing all of their medium-term (and long-term) planning out the window. With adoption, the timeline is extremely hard to predict. Practically, it makes it hard to plan for the various scheduled aspects of academic life. It can be frustrating to be unable to make definite plans, to have to say "no" more, and to have to cancel plans you were looking forward to, sometimes at the last minute. We recommend intentionally resetting your own expectations, recognizing that these things go hand in hand with caregiving. Seeing the silver lining can help: being forced to choose your work travel much more carefully is not necessarily a bad thing, as it can help you clarify priorities and streamline research goals. Your support network is key. It's also important to maintain open lines of communication with your colleagues, especially those most likely to cover your teaching and administrative duties while you're away.

The challenge of long-term planning is a defining difference between, for example, caring for an elder, which may be more likely later in your career, and caring for a child, which may be more likely earlier. Adopting and giving birth also affect long-term planning differently. Although there are fewer biological constraints on the age you can be when adopting, there are more constraints in terms of academic life stage. While it's possible to get pregnant while on the job market, and move with a new baby, this is not possible with adoption. Bringing an adoptive child into your home requires absolute stability, for legal and administrative reasons but also for emotional and psychological ones. Children need a highly predictable environment in order to thrive in the initial years after placement. Both of us essentially had tenure when we started our adoption processes. For some, the intensity and uncertainty of being on the tenure track may make it a challenging time to begin an adoption journey.

YOUR ENERGY

Caregiving differs widely in terms of its physical demands, but there is no doubt that any caregiving depletes your energy level. The loss of sleep, for example, can be so profound that it can be difficult to even get to work, or to function at work at even a basic level. Sleep deprivation can affect people of different ages differently as well, as physical resilience varies significantly across the lifespan. Anyone experiencing a truly deep level of exhaustion might consider a medical leave of absence, finding alternative caregiving support, or both. This is one key reason why personal leave should never be combined with research leave.

Caregiving can be exhausting even when you're well rested. You are responsible for another person's schedule in addition to your own, and maintaining multiple schedules can be mentally taxing. Beyond the day-to-day, there is a huge cost to mental energy in terms of big-picture decision-making, whether it be deciding to adopt a child (and the difficult circumstances that might lead to that decision), deciding to move a parent to a nursing facility, deciding to go back on the job market for the sake of your family's needs, and so on.

These aspects of caregiving can be emotionally draining, as can emotional demands felt on a day-to-day basis. People in care don't have full capacity to care for themselves. That restricted capacity is something they likely have an emotional response to, whether it's a toddler learning to share or a partner with a sudden illness. Caregivers are engaged in empathy work, taking on the emotional experiences of those they care for, and this can be as depleting as the loss of sleep or the juggling of schedules. It encroaches on the same reserves that we draw upon as academics in our supervisory or mentorship capacities—what they call "pastoral care" in the UK. New caregivers might find that reservoirs of patience and empathy may run a bit dry in the most intense years of caregiving, whenever they come.

Managing your emotional energy is a challenging aspect of work-family balance for adoptive parents. Adoption differs from pregnancy in having more variables and unfamiliar corners, each an additional tax on your emotional reserves. The first few months of an adoption placement are spent building attachment between individuals who are basically strangers when the placement begins. It can mean allowing for, yet simultaneously soothing, the child's fear, anxiety, and anger at having their world turned upside down. It can mean welcoming the child's birth family into your life, and recognizing and supporting their process as well as your own. It requires the conscious cultivation of more patience and empathy than we had ever imagined: for your child, birth family, foster family, your partner, and you, on top of the usual challenges of parenting any child. It takes time for everyone to settle into their new life together, to trust one another, and to bond. It can feel very long and very hard, and the effect on academic life is tremendous.

Work can also be emotionally challenging, and so we cannot stress enough how important it is to anticipate the emotional strain of caregiving, and put support structures in place to keep up morale. For example, schedule more breaks in your workday, connect with others in your situation, and consider psychotherapy to help you talk and work through your struggles and questions. If you are involved in the aspects of academia that entail emotional labor, such as student supervision, expect to cut back. Much of the energy we give our students is like the energy we give our children. It's important for colleagues to understand your situation, and to set up both practical support (e.g., who can cover your teaching at the last minute) and emotional support.

Conclusion

While every academic's experience with caregiving will be different, we hope that the experiences and advice we've shared here are general enough to apply to a range of situations. There are, of course, endless positives to being a caregiver, just as there are many positives to being an academic! But both present particular challenges and stressors, and the best way to mitigate those is to go in with eyes open: inform yourself, revisit your own expectations, and cultivate reliable and varied networks of practical and emotional support. Nurture your own resilience to maximize the rewards for everyone.

35. Ableism in the Academy: It's What's for Breakfast

STEPHEN KUUSISTO

Ableism is akin to racism or homophobia, but with one difference: the assumption that physically challenged bodies are "someone else's issue" remains largely unexamined outside academic or activist circles within disability communities.

—Stephen Kuusisto, before his first cup of coffee

You can't include the disabled in whatever is meant by "diversity" until the problem above is addressed.

—Kuusisto, after his second cup of coffee

That the disabled belong in special offices, sequestered environments, is a hangover from the nineteenth century. Just as people of color or women still experience cruel nineteenth-century headaches, the disabled do also. The academy taught racial separation, "the White Man's Burden," and eugenics, and promoted the medical and psychological inferiority of women and people of color throughout the 1800s and long into the twentieth century. The hierarchies of post-secondary education in the United States remain in an amnesiac state—you see, I've even chosen an ableist metaphor to make the point. Where disability is concerned, college administrators see no reason to address the structural dynamics of outworn and damaging ideas—after all, disability is about accommodations, and doesn't a special office take care of that?

—Kuusisto, after a bowl of oatmeal

The last sentence above is always spoken by the able-bodied. The disabled don't say this. They say, "We're part of the village now."

The able-bodied say, "You're part of the village only insofar as it's convenient. Go to your special office."

—Kuusisto, after walking his dog

Loose Notes

— The special office is always in an out-of-the-way location.

— The special office is always understaffed.

— The special office gives faculty and administration permission to think "the disabled" (who are really cash-paying students—your sister, your friend, your neighbor) are a complicated problem, requiring sequestered and specialized "treatment."

— This is an outworn model for disability engagement.

— Faculty and staff need to be brought into the twenty-first century where disability is concerned.

— This cannot be accomplished if able-bodied faculty, staff, and administration cannot confront the legacies of ableist thinking.

— No one likes to be called ableist. Just as some white people hate to be called out for white privilege and say, "but I have a black friend," thereby proving their privilege, ableists are fond of saying "I CARE about disability," which often means, "I want to change the subject."

— This is what I like to call the ableist shrug. If the able-bodied believe themselves progressive but fail to assist the disabled when they experience obstacles, then they're extending ableism.

—Kuusisto, after a shower

NOTE

Originally published on Kuusisto's blog, *Planet of the Blind*, May 2, 2018, https://stephenkuusisto.com/?s=ableism+in+the+academy.

36. Free Speech and Academic Freedom

MATTHEW W. FINKIN

As long as centers of power are displeased—angered or outraged—with what professors write, teach, or say, and seek to sanction the speaker, irrespective of adherence to the standard of care for disciplinary utterance or respect for the robustness of speech in a political forum, academic freedom will be threatened. Threats have most often come from outside the university: from "benefactors," as founders of the American Association of University Professors (AAUP) put it in 1915 (297), and from "public opinion" which they saw as the "chief menace" at the time. The record was ample on that account, and of long standing. In 1854, Edward G. Loring, a US commissioner and lecturer at the Harvard law school, was denied reappointment by vote of Harvard's Board of Overseers, a body elected by the state legislature, rejecting the recommendation of both the law faculty and the Harvard Corporation. As commissioner, Loring had recently enforced the Fugitive Slave Act, as he was legally bound to do even as he detested it. Such was the state of public opinion that the fugitive had to be placed under a military guard lest a crowd rescue him during his return.

Over the course of the twentieth century and into the twenty-first, the professoriate encountered the legislative prohibition on instruction in evolution and the requirement that equal time be given to creationism; the imposition of loyalty oaths; a drumbeat of investigations into subversive teachings; attempts to ban speakers at public universities; and efforts to legislate "balance" in instruction. In these controversies, the words free speech and academic freedom have sometimes been deployed interchangeably. But academic freedom is not free speech.

The two have different sources, perform different functions, and are subject to different standards. They may overlap at some points but diverge at others.

Freedom of Speech

The First Amendment enjoins Congress to "make no law . . . abridging the freedom of speech." At its core, it protects political speech, speech intricately tied to the vitality of democratic government. The Supreme Court has emphasized that political speech must be allowed to be "robust," "unfettered," "uninhibited," without connection to the speaker's status or education, or whether what the speaker has to say is well or poorly informed, or even if it is utter nonsense. However, the prohibition applies only to state actors. Public colleges and universities are governed by the First Amendment; private institutions are not.

For much of American history, however, public employment was outside the zone of speech protection. As a justice of the Massachusetts Supreme Court, Oliver Wendell Holmes Jr., opined in 1892 in the case of a police officer fired for disparaging the management of his department, "The petitioner may have a constitutional right to talk politics, but he has no constitutional right to be a policeman" (*McAuliffe* 1892, 220). In 1927, the Supreme Court of Tennessee saw no infirmity in a law criminalizing speech uttered by a teacher in one of the state's schoolrooms or university classrooms: the teaching of evolution. The teacher was named Scopes. The US Supreme Court reversed course in 1968, when a school board in Illinois dismissed high school teacher Marvin Pickering for "disloyalty" in writing a letter in the local newspaper criticizing the board's financial management.

The *Pickering* Court started out with what would seem to be a categorical imperative: public employees, including schoolteachers, do not "relinquish the First Amendment rights they otherwise enjoy as citizens to comment on matters of public interest," including comments "in connection with the operation of the public schools in which they work" (568). However, what would seem at first blush to extend the right of robust, unfettered, uninhibited political speech to public employees was immediately circumscribed in three consequential regards that were to take on a thick texture in the Court's unfolding jurisprudence.

First, the Court's reference to "matters of public interest" was not simply descriptive. The Court subsequently clarified that constitutionally protected speech must address an issue of concern to the community at large. Speech of merely personal, parochial, or intramural concern is not protected. Second, the *Pickering* Court stressed that government "has interests as an employer in regulating the speech of its employees that differ significantly" from those it has in regulating the speech of the citizenry at large; that is, "in promoting the efficiency of the public service," to maintain "discipline by immediate supervisors or harmony among co-workers"(568–70). Thus, speech otherwise protected as concordant with that robust and uninhibited political or social debate the Court extolled might be so robust, so uninhibited as to so disturb one's coworkers, supervisors, or clients that it should lose protection. Third, the Court revisited its reference in *Pickering* to employee speech *"as a citizen* on matters of public concern" (*Connick* 1983, 138) when an assistant district attorney was disciplined for protesting that the office was railroading a criminal defendant. The Court held that the lawyer spoke not "as a citizen" at all but rather pursuant to his "official duties" (*Pickering* 1968, 578); when speaking in that capacity, the First Amendment simply did not apply. Justice Souter dissented, noting that the holding imperiled the constitutional protection for university professors who teach—speak—"pursuant to [their] official duties" (578). The majority recognized Justice Souter's concern for academic freedom "at least as a constitutional *value*" (emphasis added) and that speech of that nature might not be fully accounted for in its decision. "We need not," said the Court, "and for that reason do not, decide whether the analysis we conduct today would apply in the same manner to a case involving speech *related to* scholarship or teaching" (*Garcetti* 2006, 13; emphasis added.) What that means remains unsettled.

What is settled is that when addressing the public on an issue of public concern, there is no duty to investigate, to actually know what one is talking about. The speaker can be sued in defamation for the utterance of an injurious lie. But even then, the speaker must know the facts to have been false or have reason to have known them to be so. Matters of opinion are not actionable at all. Anyone is free to mount the proverbial soapbox—or, today, a virtual one—to declare that Poland started the Second World War by attacking Germany; global warming is a hoax perpetuated by a secret cabal; 90 percent of murders and rapes in America are committed by unlawful aliens. Such is the Constitution's commitment to the robustness of political speech.

Academic Freedom: The 1915 *Declaration*

Even as Justice Holmes uttered his aphorism about the hapless policeman, the American professoriate, turning to the model of the German research university, sought recognition of their right to speak contrary to the dictates of the trustees who appoint them. The effort coalesced in the 1915 founding of the AAUP and its issuance of a manifesto, the *Declaration of Principles on Academic Freedom and Academic Tenure* (AAUP 2006a). The *Declaration* lays out the several bases for academic freedom, the phrase borrowed from the German usage. Two of these bear emphasis here.

First was the nature of the institution. A university is a public trust devoted to the promotion of inquiry, the advancement of the sum of human knowledge, the instilling in students of the capacity for and exercise of critical thought. The modern university is not founded to propagate a faith nor to transmit the preferred doctrine of its donors. Institutions of that nature did exist and they have every right to, but, the *Declaration* maintained, they are essentially proprietary in nature and should not be allowed to fly under false colors.

Toward these ends, the professoriate was asserted to play a distinct and critical role, grounded in what Robert Post has called "disciplinarity" that imposes standards of care in utterance. As the *Declaration* put it, "The claim to freedom of teaching is made in the interest of the integrity and of the progress of scientific inquiry; it is, therefore, only those who carry on their work in the temper of the scientific inquirer who may justly assert this claim" (AAUP 2006a, 298). A professor of modern European history who pronounces that Poland attacked Germany in 1939, a professor of climatology who claims that global warming is a conspiratorial fabrication, a sociologist of crime who asserts that aliens are responsible for the lion's share of violent crime can be called to account on how they have arrived at these conclusions, to show that their methods are disciplinarily acceptable. If they cannot, unlike our soapbox orator, they could well face institutional sanction. Political speech does not preclude fabulism or charlatanism. Disciplinary speech does.

The 1915 *Declaration*'s emphasis on disciplinarity has drawn criticism on the grounds that as academic freedom is meant to encourage new departures and ways of thinking and seeing that challenge prevailing pieties, the discipline's power to reject the new and restore the old violates academic freedom. But even critics of this stripe agree that there must be *some* standard of measure that only those knowledgeable are equipped to make. Academic judgments have to be made distinguishing the valuable from the meretricious, the insightful from the superficial, the scholarly from the political. The task is inherent in the academic enterprise. Judgments of that sort, made on academic grounds, do not violate academic freedom; making them is a responsibility that cannot be shirked.

Note that at its core, academic freedom is at once narrower and deeper than freedom of political speech. Narrower because it is grounded in disciplinary discourse. Deeper because, unlike the speech of a government worker sanctionable on fear of disruption or disharmony, the exercise of academic freedom cannot be subject to any such constraint: to hold the utterance of new ideas and theories, when the fruit of competent inquiry, hostage to sacrosanct authority or the vicissitudes of public hostility would be fatal to the advancement of knowledge. The lesson is as old as Galileo.

Even as the 1915 *Declaration* appealed to reason, it lacked purchase in administrative circles at the time; nor did it have or was it intended to have legal effect. However, its ideas germinated, and the need for some common understanding became apparent. The result was a document jointly negotiated by the AAUP and the Association of American Colleges, the *1940 Statement of Principles on Academic Freedom and Tenure* (AAUP 2015a) which is now endorsed by well over two hundred learned societies and disciplinary organizations, and referenced or echoed in hundreds of institutional regulations and faculty handbooks. In this way, the *1940 Statement* has been given institutional and at times legal effect.

Three aspects of the *1940 Statement* bear emphasis. First, it does not undertake separately to explicate the theory of academic freedom; it rests on the contemporary understanding. Second, it is a compact made by the profession's representative with a representative of the administrations principally of liberal arts colleges, and reflects the concerns of that bargaining partner. Third, its administration was tacitly conceded to be the function of the AAUP, undertaken by its Committee A on Academic Freedom and Tenure, which would place a gloss of meaning on academic freedom.

The *1940 Statement* provides that those governed by it should be assured freedom of teaching, research, and publication, but it expands on two other categories. It says that college and university teachers are "officers of an educational institution" as well as citizens, and their freedom to speak in those capacities is separately assured. The former aspect came to be called "intramural utterance," speech about institutional policies and actions uttered as a member of the faculty at large or in service to some university body. The latter came to be called "extramural utterance"; not that it need be expressed outside the institution's walls, but rather that it addressed issues in the larger community. A word on each.

As members of a faculty, professors are engaged by institutional practice and policies in a variety of service functions, developing, proposing, critiquing, and administering institutional policies—within their academic units, in school and campus committees, and in elected faculty senates and councils. The *1940 Statement* extends academic freedom to a faculty member's speech in these capacities; indeed, to speech simply as a faculty member critical of institutional policy or administrative action. The need for and logic of this extension should be obvious; but, as it is advanced under the head of academic freedom, it differs from free speech under the First Amendment.

If speakers seek to ground protection for intramural speech in the First Amendment, they would immediately confront a double bind. If they speak as critics outside the structure of faculty governance, they run the risk of their speech being found either to address a topic too parochial to be of interest to the larger community, or too pregnant with disruption or disharmony and so, by either route, to be constitutionally unprotected. If they speak as members of an institutional body, a committee or faculty senate, they would run the risk of that speech being found to have been uttered in an "official capacity" and so to be unprotected on that ground, *unless* the Court's cautioning dictum in response to Justice Souter is given judicial weight *and* a court sees the speech as sufficiently "related to scholarships or teaching" to warrant protection. As an AAUP report explained, the bind arises only when the First Amendment is looked to as the source of constraint. But academic freedom was not rooted in the First Amendment, and its assurance by institutional policy need not be driven by constitutional law. Express assurance of freedom to address institutional policies or action can be accomplished by institutional policy; and fast upon the AAUP's report, a number of major institutions took just that action.

Extramural utterance applies to nondisciplinary discourse directed to the larger community, treating political, economic, social, or other issues (i.e., to "speech as a citizen"). Of all the aspects of academic freedom, this has been the most difficult. At the threshold, it is by no means obvious that nondisciplinary speech should be treated as a matter of academic freedom at all—why academics, when speaking as citizens, should be treated differently from any other citizen. Perhaps because academics in public institutions in 1940 had no constitutional protection for their political speech at all, and because the drafting organizations thought it important that faculty be free to address issues of public policy, they included speech "as a citizen" in the 1940 *Statement*. In doing so, however, they hedged it with constraints of their own. When college and university teachers

> speak or write as citizens, they should be free from institutional censorship or discipline, but their special position in the community imposes special obligations. As scholars and educational officers, they should remember that the public may judge their profession and their institution by their utterances. Hence they should at all times be accurate, should exercise appropriate restraint, should show respect for the opinions of others, and should make every effort to indicate that they are not speaking for the institution. (AAUP 2015a, 14)

For the most part, the last clause has fallen into disuse: few today believe that speakers who identify themselves by institutional affiliation are speaking on the institution's behalf. But the rest of it, and the profession's effort to extricate itself from a concession inconsistent with the theory of academic freedom, has had a tortuous history.

The underlying concern seems to be one of public relations: that the institution could suffer the wrath of donors and political leaders outraged by what a faculty member might say. The record then, as now, is replete with just such episodes; whence the prudential call for "appropriate restraint." The question is whether the anticipatory capitulation to public outrage was either workable or wise. One obvious problem is that it may be difficult to segregate disciplinary address—to which a professional standard of care, but only a professional standard of care, attaches—from political address to which these "special obligations" attach. Is a professor of environmental studies, a professor of American-Russian relations, a philosopher of medical ethics who speaks publicly to the environmental, international relations, or medical funding policies of the federal government held to a disciplinary standard of care or to a standard of "appropriate restraint"? Apart from this conundrum, there are inevitably cases in which no element of disciplinary connectedness is involved. Nearly a half century ago, William Shockley, a Nobel Prize–winning physicist at Stanford, declared the intellectual inferiority of blacks. His classes were disrupted and his appearances on other campuses either canceled or boisterously protested. Was he subject to sanction because what he said wanted in "appropriate restraint"? In the event, his arguments were subject to exacting scrutiny and criticism. His professorship was unaffected.

The "special obligations" clause presents two other problems. First, because it hinges on the vicissitudes of public reaction, it supplies no principled or ascertainable standard to guide the speaker beforehand. The second problem lies in the institutional consequences of assuming the role of censor. "If a university or college censors what its professors may say," Abbott Lawrence Lowell said in 1917, "if it restrains them from uttering something it does not approve, it thereby assumes responsibility for that which it permits them to say. This is logical and inevitable, but it is a responsibility which an institution of learning would be very unwise in assuming" (AAUP 1918, 14).

The AAUP struggled with the status of this clause in the 1960s: was it regulatory, such that one could be discharged for lack of "appropriate restraint"? Or was it an avuncular admonition without institutional consequences? In 1964, Committee A attempted to put these questions to rest in a *Statement on Extramural Utterances*. "The controlling principle," it said, "is that a faculty member's expression of opinion as a citizen cannot constitute grounds for dismissal unless it clearly demonstrates the faculty member's unfitness for his or her position. Extramural utterances rarely bear upon the faculty member's fitness for this position" (AAUP 1965, 29).

This seems to close the door to institutional sanction, mostly. What it leaves ajar is the unexplored zone of "unfitness." For the most part institutions have steered clear of trying to draw it. When Ward Churchill (2001), a professor of American Indian Studies at the University of Colorado, called the victims of the terrorist attack on the World Trade Center "little Eichmanns," discipline was not imposed for having said it—though it instigated inquiry into professional derelictions that led to his dismissal. But in 2018, the Supreme Court of Wisconsin entered the fray in the wake of the suspension of a professor at Marquette University on the basis of the findings and recommendation of a faculty hearing committee. He had publicly criticized a young instructor's classroom behavior, calling it an egregious case of "political correctness." The university grounded its decision in the 1940 *Statement*'s recognition of special obligations. The court, stressing the AAUP's "rarely bear" admonition found that the professor's utterance did not render him "unfit." Insofar as the court disregarded a collegial judgment of the responsibility that the faculty member owed a person who, though given teaching duties, was in graduate study and to whom the ethical obligations professors owe to students obtained, the decision is more than questionable. Even so, the court's refusal to extend the "special obligations" clause to what it understood, incorrectly, as public political utterance is notable.

As this controversy and others have shown, academic freedom can be threatened from within. Two issues feature prominently in illuminating the extent to which academic freedom is understood and respected on campus: (1) the imposition of restrictions on what can be uttered in the name of fostering an "inclusive" or "welcoming" or "respectful" educational environment; and (2) efforts to have the university accede to the demands of the BDS movement, to boycott, divest, and sanction the state of Israel and those connected to it. A word on each.

Welcomeness

The AAUP's 1966 *Statement on Professional Ethics* (2015b) provides that "as teachers, professors encourage the free pursuit of learning in their students. They hold before them the best scholarly and ethical standards of their discipline. . . . They avoid any exploitation, harassment, or discriminatory treatment of students." Plainly, a teacher would be acting unethically in holding a student up to scorn, to demean or belittle. But that is not what speech codes are about. They reach speech in the classroom that is in exercise of academic freedom but to which some students take offense, as well as to public utterance having the same effect, *vide* William Shockley (Wicker 1973). Apart from the incapacity of the standard to provide any ascertainable guide to what may be said—"hostile," "uncivil," "unwelcome," "offensive"—the conflict with academic freedom is palpable. A dispassionate unpacking of ideas—political, economic, religious, social, scientific—that challenge a student's most cherished beliefs, that might go to the core of their very sense of self, is protected by academic freedom however much offense a student might take by it. These policies hold faculty speech hostage to just such adventitious subjective reactions. The effect is to cast a pall over the classroom and over the campus, to stultify learning.

Administrations that have embraced speech restrictions in the name of civility are fully aware of the conflict. The administration of Marquette University candidly argued to the Wisconsin Supreme Court, echoing a line of reasoning taken by others, that "academic freedom is just one value that must be balanced against 'other values core to their mission'" (*McAdams* 2018, 732). The court rejected the argument. So has the AAUP. Its 1994 *Statement on Freedom of Expression and Campus Speech Codes* closes on this note: "Free speech is not simply an aspect of the educational enterprise to be weighed against other desirable ends. It is the very precondition of the academic enterprise itself" (AAUP 2015c, 362). Thus far, the courts have saved the academy from its folly: all reported decisions have held such speech codes to be unconstitutional.

BDS

The focus is not on the BDS movement's larger ends, it is on the tactic it deploys. That involves what in labor law parlance is called a "secondary boycott": it seeks to impose a cost on parties with whom it has no direct conflict—Israeli universities, businesses that invest or do business with or in Israel—to get those secondary parties to pressure their primary target, the state of Israel. It would do so by having US universities "boycott" Israeli ones and divest their endowments and pension funds of securities in companies that do business in Israel. In terms of academic freedom, however, the two—boycott and divestment—are quite different. Let us take the boycott first.

The BDS movement explains that its "boycott" of Israeli universities refers to "Israeli academic institutions only and not to individual scholars." The distinction is nonsensical: when one collaborates with an Israeli or French or Japanese colleague or group on some shared research or other common academic endeavor, one is necessarily engaged with one's collaborators' institutions. It is quite impossible to boycott—which means a total refusal to deal, a disengagement—an Israeli university without boycotting the Israeli scholars it houses. The AAUP has condemned the academic boycott as a violation of academic freedom, as it "strikes directly at the free exchange of ideas" (AAUP 2006b, 41).

Divestiture is more interesting. In reaction to the movement, several states have applied the secondary boycott to an opposite effect, divesting themselves or their pension funds of the securities of companies that honor the boycott of Israel. There is more to this than the obvious irony, that once the secondary boycott is taken to be a legitimate weapon, it simply becomes a matter of whose ox is to be gored. What is involved is how divesture relates to intellectual freedom.

Criticism of these anti-boycott divestiture laws rests on the claim that divestiture necessarily affects the climate of intellectual freedom on the campus: by signaling support of Israel, the institution delegitimizes and so suppresses criticism of it. Regental pronouncement on a current controversy might well have such an effect. Were the governing board of a university to declare it to be university policy that a war be supported, and supported unflinchingly, dissenting faculty might well be more than reticent to speak their minds, as was much the case in the First World War. But there is no evidence that the divestiture of securities has had any such effect. Since 2015, for example, Illinois law has prohibited the state's university retirement systems from having holdings in Iran-restricted companies, Sudan-restricted companies, and companies that boycott Israel. Yet, BDS activity at public institutions in that state has not abated.

With respect to the climate of the campus, it could well be the case that the most significant threat to academic freedom comes from internal structural change—the erosion of tenure. The dismissal of a tenured professor because of what they have said requires a hearing and proof of professional unfitness. Faculty lacking that protection might well be reticent to speak or even to come to the aid of a colleague, to speak out in their defense. The economist Fritz Machlup (1964, 122) found that in 1955, somewhere between 53 percent and 65 percent of university faculty had tenure. He termed this figure distressingly low. In 2015, about a third of the full-time faculty in four-year public institutions and a quarter in private ones had tenure, even as there has been a rise in the use of part-time, non-tenure-eligible faculty. Without a significant cohort of tenured faculty willing and free to exercise their academic freedom and to come to the aid of it when threatened, the health of academic freedom going forward remains to be seen.

WORKS CITED

American Association of University Professors. 1918. "Recent Academic Freedom Discussion." *Bulletin of the American Association of University Professors* 4, no. 3 (February): 11–15.
American Association of University Professors. 1965. "Committee A *Statement on Extramural Utterances*." *AAUP Bulletin* 51, no. 1: 1-95. https://www.jstor.org/stable/40223224?seq=1#metadata_info_tab_contents.

American Association of University Professors. 2006a. "1915 *Declaration of Principles on Academic Freedom and Academic Tenure*." In AAUP *Policy Documents and Reports*, 10th edition, 291–301. Washington, DC: AAUP.

American Association of University Professors. 2006b. "On Academic Boycotts." *Academe: Bulletin of the AAUP* 92 (September–October): 39–43.

American Association of University Professors. 2015a. "1940 *Statement of Principles on Academic Freedom and Tenure with 1970 Interpretive Comments*." In AAUP *Policy Documents and Reports*, 11th ed., 13–19. Baltimore, MD: Johns Hopkins University Press.

American Association of University Professors. 2015b. "1966 *Statement on Professional Ethics*." In AAUP *Policy Documents and Reports*, 11th ed., 145–46. Baltimore, MD: Johns Hopkins University Press.

American Association of University Professors. 2015c. "1994 *Statement on Freedom of Expression and Campus Speech Codes*." In AAUP *Policy Documents and Reports*, 11th ed., 361–62. Baltimore, MD: Johns Hopkins University Press.

Churchill, Ward. 2001. "Some People Push Back: On the Justice of Roosting Chickens." *Pockets of Resistance* 11 (September). https://cryptome.org/ward-churchill.htm.

Connick v. Myers. 1983. 461 U.S. 138. Accessed April 2, 2020. https://supreme.justia.com/cases/federal/us/461/138/.

DelFattore, Joan. 2010. *Knowledge in the Making: Academic Freedom and Free Speech in America's Schools and Universities*. New Haven, CT: Yale University Press.

Doumani, Beshara, ed. 2006. *Academic Freedom after September 11*. Cambridge, MA: Zone Books.

Finkin, Matthew, ed. 1996. *The Case for Tenure*. Ithaca, NY: ILR.

Finkin, Matthew, and Robert Post. 2009. *For the Common Good: Principles of American Academic Freedom*. New Haven, CT: Yale University Press.

Garcetti et al. v. Ceballos. 2006. 547 U.S. 425. Accessed April 2, 2020. https://www.supremecourt.gov/opinions/05pdf/04-473.pdf.

Machlup, Fritz. 1964. "In Defense of Academic Tenure." *AAUP Bulletin* 50, no. 2 (1964): 112–24.

McAdams v. Marquette University. 2018. 914 N.W.2d 708. Accessed April 2, 2020. https://law.justia.com/cases/wisconsin/supreme-court/2018/2017ap001240.html.

McAuliffe v. Mayor of New Bedford. 1892. 155 Mass. 216; 29 N.E. 517. Accessed April 2, 2020. http://masscases.com/cases/sjc/155/155mass216.html.

O'Neil, Robert M. 1997. *Free Speech in the College Community*. Bloomington: Indiana University Press.

Pickering v. Board of Education. 1968. 391 U.S. 563. Accessed April 2, 2020. https://supreme.justia.com/cases/federal/us/391/563/.

Post, Robert. 2012. *Democracy, Expertise, and Academic Freedom: A First Amendment Jurisprudence for the Modern State*. New Haven, CT: Yale University Press.

Turk, James L., ed. 2014. *Academic Freedom in Conflict: The Struggle over Free Speech Rights in the University*. Toronto: Lorimer.

Van Alstyne, William W., ed. 1993. *Freedom and Tenure in the Academy*. Durham, NC: Duke University Press.

Wicker, Tom. 1973. "The Shockley Case: In the Nation." *New York Times*, November 16, 41.

37. Contingency

CARY NELSON

In 1969, 78 percent of US faculty nationally were tenured or tenure-eligible and treated as permanent hires. By 1975, this figure had slipped to 75 percent or less.[1] That slow point-by-point decline has accelerated and continued ever since. As we approach 2020, it is barely 25 percent, with the majority of faculty being "temporary," though many such temporary faculty teach in that category for their whole working lives. Moreover, except for minor passing upticks, the academic job market for full-time jobs has been in a state of collapse since 1970. Since a terminal MA or PhD is no longer a ticket to a full-time job and a traditional career, graduate student employees are also part of the gig economy's temporary employees. Contrary to the view that most precarious teachers prefer part-time employment, a 2015 study published in the *Journal of Higher Education*, based on survey data from four thousand part-time faculty, demonstrated that 73 percent want full-time jobs but cannot find them.[2]

Other countries show high reliance on long-term "temporary" faculty as well. Of those not eligible for tenure, some are categorized as part-time or contingent, while others may teach on renewable contracts at various fractions of a full-time appointment. The terms "contingent" and "precarious" are largely interchangeable, though in a given country one term may predominate. The two terms also have somewhat different connotations. "Contingent" emphasizes the contractual character of a temporary appointment; it is contingent on contract renewal and on campus instructional needs, sometimes on how many students are enrolled in a given course. "Precarious" emphasizes how faculty members with no job security experience such an appointment and lifestyle. Mexico uses "precarious" as the operative category, whereas Canada prefers "sessional," referring to the fact that those faculty teach session by session, or semester by semester.[3] Although compensation rates vary, most such faculty are compensated on a per-course basis, not by way of a full-time salary with benefits.

Some contingent appointments represent hidden full-time appointments; in such cases, a person may teach the same number of courses as a full-time faculty member but still be defined as a part-timer. Indeed, at colleges and universities that have two- or three-course limits for faculty members, contingent faculty may also teach a higher load. My own campus, the University of Illinois at Urbana-Champaign, limits tenure or tenure-eligible faculty in the humanities to two courses per semester, whereas contingent faculty typically teach three. Some science faculty at research universities teach but two or three courses over an entire year, in which case the difference between tenured and precarious teaching loads is greater still, though science faculty also often supervise a lab funded by grant applications they have to submit.

People who cannot live on the resulting income may supplement their university income by taking on additional courses at community colleges, which often have no tenure system at all. In larger metropolitan areas, where there are a large number of colleges and universities available—Atlanta, Boston, Chicago, Houston, Los Angeles, and New York are obvious examples—contingent faculty members may travel some distances to assemble a semester teaching load of eight to ten courses per semester at multiple campuses and institutions, in an effort to cobble together what generally still remains less than a middle-class income. That has led to contingent faculty being informally referred to as "freeway flyers."

Faculty teaching at multiple campuses obviously do not have one office they can call their own; indeed, they may literally have no private office or any office at all on a given campus. Their teaching materials may reside in the trunk of their car. Office hours, if they can be called that, may be held in a campus cafeteria, library, or student union. Arranging face-to-face, one-on-one meetings with precarious faculty on hectic schedules can be difficult for students. Contacting a truly temporary faculty member for a letter of recommendation can be impossible. To highlight the consequences for students, people began using the motto "Faculty working conditions are student learning conditions."

The problem is experienced most directly in local terms, how it affects a given campus and its employees, but the national statistic clearly points to an industry-wide phenomenon—indeed, a deep-seated, industry-wide crisis. The crisis plays out not just in terms of how faculty are compensated, but also in terms of how higher education is funded, what percentage of its resources are spent directly on instruction, faculty status and role in decision-making, and on the social status of college teaching. Higher education is now conducted on a foundation of cheap instructional labor; reversing that national and international trend is likely to prove impossible. Even collective bargaining has not had any impact on the reliance on precarious labor. For many years, the problem was blamed on the overproduction of PhDs, making it easy to hire those devoted to a teaching career who were willing to accept substandard salaries if they had no other option. But there has never been a dearth of classes to teach; the problem has been the underproduction of good jobs.

Even under the best current working conditions for contingent faculty, conditions few enjoy—for example, a three-course load per fifteen-week semester at seven thousand dollars per course—actually supporting a family on a contingent salary is virtually impossible. Indeed, that higher end of the compensation range is unlikely in nonunionized campuses or areas without a large pool of underemployed PhDs. Per-course compensation of three thousand dollars or less is far more common. The consequent family income puts many precarious faculty below the poverty line, with many eligible for food supplements and other social benefits that are themselves precarious.[4] In Mexico, the availability of government food supplements is considered part of the total compensation package. In reality, the most livable contingent faculty working conditions obtain when a family member or partner has a full-time job with a substantially better income.

Strategies for Addressing Contingency

Precarity, or contingency—in national terms the mass employment of faculty in underpaid teaching jobs without job security—is increasingly a problem without a solution. If there was a moment when faculty themselves might have rallied to resist that growing employment trend, that moment was the 1970s and 1980s, before the shift away from tenure-eligible positions became decisive. It would be easy to say that faculty did not see it coming, but the programs that made the shift to contingency more rapidly saw no meaningful faculty resistance. The problem, it may be argued, was careerism, the domination of faculty thinking by narrow self-interest. Organizing to resist the wave of contingent appointments, moreover, would have required collective action, a sense of solidarity, and a willingness to prioritize the health of the academic profession as a whole. Nothing in faculty training or psychology, let alone the higher education reward system, pointed in that direction. The moment passed, and we are now in the brave new world of disposable teachers.

The fatal delay in addressing the precarity problem was, it must be said, prolonged by the failure of the major relevant faculty professional organizations to acknowledge the problem, let alone make any effort to solve it. The two faculty groups with the core responsibility to confront contingency were the Modern Language Association (MLA) and the American Association of University Professors (AAUP). The MLA represents English and foreign language professors, and thus has considerable power to address how composition, introductory literature, and foreign-language courses are taught. Those are the subject areas with the largest concentration of precarious faculty. The AAUP has had the unique responsibility to define appropriate faculty working conditions and responsibilities since the organization was founded in 1915. Both groups remained in denial for over a generation, first pretending that the problem did not exist, and then denying its seriousness. Until the new millennium, the AAUP held to the increasingly irrelevant principle that all faculty teaching more than six years were eligible for tenure.

Unfortunately, improving the conditions of precarity now requires somewhat the same collective commitments that the profession failed to manifest decades ago. What cannot in any realistic assessment be achieved is a return to tenure, job security, and stable careers for the majority of faculty. That does not mean that issue-specific faculty consensus and solidarity are not possible; but it does mean that broad-based collaboration behind—and advocacy for—the whole range of interrelated principles and working conditions that affect precarity may be out of reach. On the other hand, all faculty would likely support the notion that anyone teaching half time or more should receive paid health care coverage, something most union contracts provide. Even in the absence of overall reform, such improvements in working conditions are a huge benefit.

Efforts to address contingency have in many cases made the problem worse for the faculty members most affected:

1. Following AAUP guidelines, some campuses decided that contingent faculty should be limited to six years of employment, since they would have to be given tenure in their seventh year. Those campuses would then typically refuse to renew precarious faculty for a seventh year, instead simply hiring a different contingent teacher. Needless to say, the faculty members who had their employment terminated did not experience this either as a benefit or a principled decision.

2. Many campuses restricted the number of courses a contingent faculty member was permitted to teach so as to differentiate between tenured and part-time faculty, and thereby escape the accusation they were violating

AAUP guidelines and exploiting faculty who were really full time. The major effect of such policies was to increase the freeway flyer phenomenon, as faculty struggled to assemble a viable income.

Some campuses have introduced compensation for contingent faculty whose courses are canceled because of low enrollment, given that, unlike tenured faculty, they are usually not assigned a different course and instead are out of a job. But the sums paid may seem more symbolic than substantive. Georgetown University paid $300 for a canceled course as of the late 2010s, whereas Notre Dame de Namur University near San Francisco paid $250.[5] One partial solution has given some relief to contingent faculty and reduced the precarity of their employment: multiyear renewable contracts, generally with two- or three-year terms, but sometimes with five-year terms. This approach has made a real difference, though it obviously still provides for set renewal dates that establish points of job uncertainty and precariousness. That uncertainty can lead faculty to avoid controversial speech or classroom assignments throughout their contract period.

Equally problematic is the suggestion that research universities establish a two-tier tenured faculty, one devoted entirely to teaching and one in which research is expected.[6] While that could have the clear benefit of enlarging the tenure-eligible faculty pool, it is difficult to imagine that the non-research faculty would have the same status, prestige, influence, or salary.

On many campuses, moreover, there is at least one further impediment to any effort to repair contingent faculty working conditions: the active distrust and hostility that often obtains between tenured and precarious faculty. It has long been obvious that, as a two-track employment system hardened in place, a divided faculty culture with competing interests would evolve as well. The starkest evidence of that divided culture is revealed when contingent faculty resist the limited conversion of contingent to tenured faculty lines, recognizing that reduction of their numbers will come with a reduction in contingent faculty power and influence, as well as fewer courses for contingent faculty to teach.

The practices that can be instituted to reduce this divided faculty culture of antagonism include: (1) ensuring that contingent faculty not only have the right to participate in all governance processes, from department meetings to the faculty senate, but are also compensated for doing so; (2) providing contingent faculty with office space where they can meet students and store teaching materials (otherwise, contingent faculty tend to become invisible, a status that not only alienates them but also makes them easier to exploit); and (3) achieving genuine per-course compensation parity for contingent and tenured faculty.

The second of these steps has proven relatively easy to institute, while the first and the third have so far proven impossible for most campuses.

The context in which diverging interests can become most obvious is in collective bargaining, which, paradoxically, is also about the only way to improve precarious working conditions. Contract negotiations involve tension and conflict over priorities for both reform and resources. And the administration's representatives are always concerned with the financial cost for any benefit won, and thus may resist improvements for either faculty group. The administration's representatives may not be able to resist pitting contingent and tenure-eligible faculty against one another. Perhaps worse still, there can be a trade-off between financial benefits and academic freedom guarantees. To manage and avoid or at least reduce these effects, contingent and tenured faculty on the same campus must either try to be in one bargaining unit, or collaborate to coordinate bargaining demands. But some faculty from both camps will resist being in one bargaining unit—either from fear and distrust, or from elitism and mutual contempt. The University of Oregon won a single union for all, which resulted in a high degree of coordination and solidarity for both groups. The trustees at the University of Illinois at Chicago refused to bargain with a combined unit, so full-time and part-time faculty had to accept the more difficult option of bargaining separately and coordinating priorities outside negotiating sessions.[7]

Yet trust between the two groups can be established through dialogue and a record of mutually agreeable organizing and bargaining plans. A commitment from tenured faculty to make contingent faculty compensation the highest priority in a first negotiation can go a long way toward building that trust. Salary parity, however, will never be achieved if the two groups receive the same percentage raises. There needs to be frank recognition that assigning tenured and contingent faculty the same annual percentage raises will actually increase salary disparities in absolute dollars over time. Multiyear contracts are not a perfect substitute for tenure, but they are far better than the brutal alternative of semester-by-semester or annual contracts. Renewals, however, should take place by the end of the current teaching semester, not in late summer, as is too often the case. Contingent faculty members also need strong, clear grievance procedures, preferably with a union formally representing the grievant. Effective grievance procedures do, however, require faculty solidarity, along with formal protection against reprisals for filing grievances. Grievance procedures outside union contracts are often ineffective.

Some collective-bargaining agreements have given contingent faculty substantial raises over the life of the contract. These include Washington University in St. Louis (26 percent), Boston University (29 to 68 percent), and Point Park University in Pennsylvania (23 percent).[8]

As I write, however, the potential for collective bargaining in higher education faces existential challenges on two fronts. These challenges not only put new recognition drives in danger, but also threaten the viability of existing locals. The Trump-era National Labor Relations Board (NLRB) that oversees private-sector unions is set to curtail bargaining rights on several fronts. Given the opportunity to revisit graduate student employee bargaining rights, it is sure to reverse the Obama-era NLRB and withdraw them. Meanwhile, although it is absurd to declare part-time faculty "managerial" employees under the terms of the US Supreme Court's 1980 ruling in NLRB v. *Yeshiva University* and deny them bargaining rights as a consequence, some private institutions have been willing to make that argument nonetheless. Long-term efforts to get the court to reverse itself are clearly dead. Equally serious is the US Supreme Court's June 2018 ruling in *Janus v. AFSCME Council 31*, which withdrew the right of public-sector unions to charge an agency fee to all employees who benefit from union-negotiated contracts. That decision will be seriously damaging to all public-sector unions, but it will hit contingent faculty bargaining particularly severely, as even modest union dues can be a burden for low-wage employees.

These developments are even more painful when one understands the progress made both in contingent faculty benefits and in contingent faculty / tenured faculty relationships by unions that represent both groups and have focused on them over the last generation. The statewide California Faculty Association (CFA) representing the state university system is a prime example. Recognizing that there was serious hostility between the two constituencies, the CFA made confronting them a priority. They established special planning mechanisms so that contingent faculty could collectively set their own priorities, and then emphasized improving their salaries and benefits in salary negotiations. At the same time, they worked successfully to build union-wide solidarity.[9]

The CFA was also among the unions that recognized that, over the last generation and more, the qualifications of most entry-level contingent and tenure-eligible faculty have become essentially the same. They have the same advanced degrees, the same teaching experience, and often the same research accomplishments. Of course, over time the record of accomplishments may diverge, but denying contingent faculty recognition and rewards for serious achievements—and defining job responsibilities to preclude them—is not only inhumane, but also a betrayal of the collegial values that should define higher education.

Precarity and Academic Freedom

The dramatic rise in the percentage of precarious faculty in the academy has broken the fundamental bond between job security and academic freedom. Put simply, if you can be fired at will or nonrenewed for controversial teaching assignments or public statements, you do not really have academic freedom. The practical consequences of dissolving the link between academic freedom and tenure thus include potential degradation of the quality of classroom instruction. When contingent faculty are vulnerable to dismissal or nonrenewal for assigning controversial readings in the humanities, or promoting unpopular consensus positions in the sciences, instruction will suffer. The result is already apparent—widespread faculty self-censorship. It is pointless to expect courage to rule when faculty livelihoods and family security hang by the thread of at-will employment.

These two elements of faculty status, tenure and academic freedom, are interdependent, and they are reinforced by a third: shared governance. Shared governance provides the principles and the practical arrangements by which faculty members and administrators negotiate all those areas of campus life in which faculty have a vested interest, from hiring policies to professional standards to the curriculum. But contingent faculty paid on a per-course basis often view shared governance as unpaid labor. People with high teaching loads, moreover, typically have no time for committee service or participation in the faculty senate. At campuses without tenure, meaningful shared governance often disappears, including faculty authority over the curriculum. That means disciplinary expertise can be largely cut out of curriculum planning. Protections for academic freedom disappear at the same time. The expectation that faculty will have a major influence over both the curriculum and hiring decisions combines academic freedom and shared-governance principles. Academic freedom for faculty who have no voice in governance is an illusion.

Unfortunately, the broad consensual support that prioritized academic freedom, which once prevailed in the academy, may be declining. Indeed, at least in the humanities, academic freedom itself is no longer a sacred value. Over the last few years, some humanities students and faculty find academic freedom worse than an inconvenience. It gets in the way of an effort to suppress campus speech that they find morally or politically abhorrent. They hold values they believe superior to academic freedom, and argue that campus communities need to be protected from speech they consider dangerous. Beginning about 2010, we saw increased incidents of organized student/faculty efforts to shut down invited far-right or conservative speakers whose views they reject. One may pose a critical question in response: would the same constituency rally behind an effort to protect the job of an outspoken contingent faculty member holding views they found objectionable? The prevailing assumption for many decades was that the pressure to punish unpopular political speech came exclusively from outside the academy, the restrictions on speech during World War I and the McCarthy period being key examples. The internal arguments that academic freedom must give way before preferred political convictions suggest that the academy itself can put academic freedom at risk. No group will prove more vulnerable to such pressures than our most precarious colleagues.

Conclusion

Administrators addicted to the cheap instruction that contingent employment makes possible often fail to see that the quality of their institutions will suffer, not because contingent faculty are less dedicated or less qualified, but—as pointed out above—because faculty working conditions are student learning conditions. Student retention and achievement are both curtailed by overreliance on precarious labor. What administrators do realize, however, is not only that exploiting precarious labor makes it easier to fund other priorities, but also that increased reliance on precarity alters the power differential on campus: faculty are weaker and administrators are stronger. On campuses where all faculty are contingent, including some community colleges, shared governance can be essentially nonexistent. That may seem tempting to administrators in the short run, but the loss of the checks and balances developed over a century will not serve the academy's interest in the long run.

Overall, it is far better for colleges and universities to have one faculty, not two faculties fundamentally divided by status and compensation. But with multiple external political and ideological forces—and internal economic ones—working against that goal, navigating a progressive road forward has become increasingly daunting. The compensation and governing gaps between administrators, tenured faculty, and precarious faculty, moreover, in many ways mirror employment inequities in the US workforce writ large. In that regard, universities reflect the hourglass economy that disenfranchises and impoverishes workers in many industries.

To be optimistic under these conditions is unwarranted. At the local level, faculty will need to build working relationships throughout their communities so that these trends can be collaboratively resisted. Nationally, change across these fronts will require activism on a scale not seen for decades. That is not impossible; indeed, a first step is being realistic about what it will require to repair the damage that contingency has done to higher education.

1. Exactly when the ratio of tenure-eligible to part-time faculty was reversed or flipped depends on what starting point you choose. The statistics address the number of faculty in each category, since a nationwide count of the number of courses taught in each category does not exist. On many campuses, that data is maintained only by individual departments, not centrally, if it is maintained at all.

2. See M. Kevin Eagan Jr., Audrey J. Jaeger, and Ashley Grantham, "Supporting the Academic Majority: Policies and Practices Related to Part-Time Faculty's Job Satisfaction," *Journal of Higher Education* 86 (May–June 2015): 448–83.

3. See Cary Nelson, "The Problem of Contingent Labor," in *The Business of Higher Education*, edited by David Siegel and John Knapp (New York: Praeger, 2009), 175–98; and "Legacies of Misrule: Our Contingent Future" in Cary Nelson, *No University Is an Island: Saving Academic Freedom* (New York: New York University Press, 2010), 79–106.

4. For evidence that 25 percent of US part-time faculty are eligible for public assistance like food stamps, see Ken Jacobs, Ian Perry, and Jenifer MacGillvary, "The High Public Cost of Low Wages: Low Wages Cost U.S. Taxpayers $152.8 Billion Each Year in Public Support for Working Families," UC Berkeley Labor Center, April 13, 2015, http://laborcenter.berkeley.edu/the-high-public-cost-of-low-wages/.

5. These figures are cited from Kim Tolley and Kristen Edwards, "Reflections on the Possibilities and Limitations of Collective Bargaining," in *Professors in the Gig Economy: Unionizing Adjunct Faculty in America*, edited by Kim Tolley (Baltimore, MD: Johns Hopkins University Press, 2018), 186–202.

6. Michael Bérubé and Jennifer Ruth champion that solution in *The Humanities, Higher Education, and Academic Freedom: Three Necessary Arguments* (New York: Palgrave Macmillan, 2015).

7. In conjunction with my AAUP presidency, I participated in the Illinois and Oregon campaigns and followed developments closely.

8. These figures are cited from Kim Tolley and Kristen Edwards, "Reflections on the Possibilities and Limitations of Collective Bargaining," in *Professors in the Gig Economy*, edited by Tolley, 186–202.

9. As part of my union organizing work and research, I made several visits to California Faculty Association meetings and interviewed members and leaders extensively. For a case study of one local, see Kim Geron and Gretchen M. Reevy, "California State University, East Bay: Alignment of Contingent and Tenure-Track Faculty Interests and Goals," in *Professors in the Gig Economy*, edited by Tolley, 172–86.

38. The Corporate University in the Age of Trump

DAVID SCHULTZ

American colleges and universities are mired in a crisis largely of their own making—the problem of how to bridge the gap between the promise of a quality affordable education and generating a business plan that provides the resources to deliver that goal. The prevailing solution over the last four decades has been to create a neoliberal or corporate university model, adopting a plan heavy on business metrics, light on a meaningful faculty voice, and questionable in terms of the educational quality it offers, except perhaps at the most elite institutions. This model has transplanted, or competes with, an older rival, one that many still ascribe to but which increasingly appears untenable or disfavored by higher-education administrators and the Trump presidency.

The Corporate University Business Plan

Since the end of World War II, two business models have defined American higher education. The first was the Dewey model that dominated until the 1970s, and which still lingers on in our hopes. The second, a corporate model, flourished until the economic crash in 2008 and still limps on, but is perhaps facing unprecedented assaults on its existence during the 2020 coronavirus pandemic.

The first post–World War II business model began with the return of military veterans after 1945, and it lasted through the matriculation of the baby boomers from college in the 1970s. This was a model that produced an ever-expanding number of colleges for a growing population seeking to secure a college degree.

It coincided with the height of the Cold War, during which public funding for state schools was regarded as part of an important effort to achieve techno-logical and political supremacy over communism. It witnessed the expansion of more middle- and working-class students entering college. This was the democ-ratization of college, made possible by the expansion of inexpensive public univer-sities, generous grants and scholarships, and low-interest loans. Higher educa-tion was seen not simply as a private good, wherein students bore the costs, but a public good worthy of taxpayer investment.

Public institutions were key to this model. They were public in that they received most, if not all, of their money either from tax dollars to subsidize tuition and costs, or federal money in the form of research grants for faculty. Private schools, too, benefited from the grants that were available to their stu-dents. The business model then was simple: public tax dollars, federal aid, and an expanding population of often first-generation students attending college at low tuition in state institutions and subsidized private schools. Let us call this the Dewey business model, named after John Dewey, whose theories on educa-tion emphasized the democratic functions of education, seeking to inculcate citizenship values though schools. This is the model upon which shared gover-nance, tenure, and the American Association of University Professors princi-ples are based.

The Dewey model, however, began to collapse in the mid-1970s. Inflationary pressures caused by Vietnam, the energy embargoes of the 1970s, and recession-ary forces from relative declines in American economic productivity produced significant economic shocks—including to the public sector, where many state and local governments edged toward bankruptcy.

Efforts to relieve declining corporate profits and productivity led to efforts to restructure the economy, including cutting back on government services. The response under Ronald Reagan was an attempt to retrench the state through decreases in government expenditures for social welfare programs, cutbacks on business regulations, resistance to labor rights, and tax cuts. These proposals are collectively referred to as neoliberalism, and they sought to restore profit-ability and autonomy to free markets with the belief that, unfettered by the government, they would restore productivity.

Neoliberalism had a major impact on higher education. Beginning under President Carter and increasing under Ronald Reagan, the federal and state gov-ernments cut taxes and public expenditures. The combination of the two meant a retrenchment to the Dewey business model, as support for public institutions decreased and federal money dried up. For example, in the 1970s, Governor Hugh Carey imposed dramatic cuts to the State University of New York system. There were also financial pressures placed on the City University of New York and the City College of New York at that time.

Higher education needed a new business model, and found it in the corporate university. In this model, administrators increasingly use corporate structures and management styles to run colleges and universities. This includes abandoning the shared governance model of the American Association of University Professors, under which faculty had a real voice in the running of the school, including over curriculum; selection of department chairs, deans, and presidents; and determination of many of the other policies affecting the academy. The corporate university replaced the shared governance model with one more typical of a business corporation.

For the corporate university, many decisions, including increasingly those affecting curriculum, are determined by a top-down pyramid style of authority. University administration—often composed not of typical academics, but those with business or corporate backgrounds—preempted many of the decisions faculty used to make. Under a corporate model, the trustees, composed of more business leaders than before, select the president, often with minimal input from the faculty. The president, in turn, selects the deans, department heads, and other administrative personnel—again with minimal or no faculty voice. The most extreme version of this corporate model was the rise of private, for-profit colleges such as Walden, Capella, and even Trump University.

The corporate university took control of the curriculum in several ways in order to generate revenue. The new business model found its most powerful income stream in profession education. The number of these programs rapidly expanded, with high-priced tuition. They were sold to applicants with the claim that the price would be more than made up by graduates' future incomes. This model accelerated with the emergence of the internet and online classes, and was especially perfected with the for-profit schools. In the case of online programs, a specialist designs the curriculum for courses and sells it to the school, and then the university hires adjunct faculty to deliver the canned class. The costs of offering a class are reduced, the potential size of the classes is maximized, and it is simple to change the curriculum to reflect new market needs or preferences. Traditional schools, seeing this model flourish, began emulating it by expanding online programs and minimally investing in traditional full-time faculty, opting instead to hire contingent and part-time faculty. If liberal arts used to be defined as offering a breadth of classes premised on what schools thought students needed to know, now it is based on what is profitable to offer.

Third, the new corporate curriculum required a standardized curriculum, teaching methods, and performance metrics, both within and across schools. Bringing Fordism and scientific management principles to higher education meant standardization of classes and easier processes of replacing one professor with another, or having one person develop the curriculum and others become inexpensive "content providers." This standardization of teaching is exactly what accrediting agencies are doing with the push to define and measure learning outcomes. It enhances commodification of curriculum, and it also provides an easily quantifiable measure of teaching to determine productivity—how many students are enrolled and the course's profit margins. This commodified curriculum is also behind pressures to teach larger and more classes, merge programs, or drop majors that do not sustain university bottom lines. Link all this to pay-for-performance and elimination of tenure, and one has the perfect market model for schools that allow administrators and students to rank and judge programs and professors. This is what the *U.S. News & World Report* does.

This corporate business model worked until 2008, when it died along with the economic policies that had nourished it since the late 1970s. The global economic collapse produced even more pressures on the government to reduce educational expenditures. After an initial decline in recession enrollment, this model came back—but with students required to assume even more debt to finance their education. Unlike previous post–World War II recessions, the 2008–9 one dramatically wiped out $13 trillion of wealth, and consumer debt skyrocketed. Student loan debt ballooned and is now greater than personal consumer debt, exceeding $1.5 trillion. The average student loan debt for a graduate of the class of 2008 was $23,400; for the class of 2016, that number had reached $37,100, according to *Forbes*.[1] Students are tapping out—they have no money to finance further education, and it is unclear if they can continue to borrow at the rates they did in the past. While the Obama administration tried to regulate some of the worst student lending processes and reign in the worst practices of the proprietary schools, the Trump administration is undoing these efforts.

The result? Except for the elite, well-financed Harvards of the world, most schools are forced to find new revenue streams. In some cases, it is real raises in tuition; in others, it is lower admission standards and expanded enrollment, thus the pressure for larger classes and higher teaching loads. Culturally, many say that perhaps college is not for all, but the reality is that higher education is trapped. Lacking more public resources, they will be forced to act even more corporate to stay afloat, by implementing even more business practices that replicate what they have been doing for the last four decades. It is a failed model that may soon lead to lot of colleges going bankrupt, especially after the 2020 coronavirus pandemic, but there is no alternative to it.

The corporate business model has crashed. Even such mainstream publications as the *Economist*, in its August 4, 2012, issue, noted the collapse of this old model.[2] It was a bubble that burst, much like the real estate bubble in 2008. But in actuality, it was a model waiting to burst. The corporate business model functioned as an education Ponzi scheme. Higher education paid for programs by raking in dollars from rapidly expanding professional programs, and selling degrees on the promise that the high tuition costs would be worth it to students. But all Ponzi schemes eventually collapse.

Faculty as Workers: The End of Shared Governance

The Supreme Court's 1980 NLRB v. *Yeshiva University* decision declared that faculty at private universities were not employees under the National Labor Relations Act, and therefore were ineligible to form a union.[3] Because faculty engaged in shared governance at a university—participating in crucial decision-making in the creation of curriculum, in defining academic standards, and even in having a say over finances—they were more like managers than they were employees.

Yeshiva University gave powerful impetus to the corporate university. In entertaining the fiction that faculty have a voice in a university, the decision empowered administrators to restructure schools in a top-down corporate manner, without the worry that a union or a threat of unionization would serve as a countervailing power. But as universities took advantage of *Yeshiva University*, they created a workplace where faculty had a diminished voice. No longer was there shared governance; instead, it was a corporate setting, with faculty occupying roles similar to workers in traditional corporations. The time was coming to revisit the fiction of *Yeshiva University*. This is precisely what the NLRB did in its December 2014 decision *Pacific Lutheran University v. SEIU*.[4]

Pacific Lutheran University recognized that the nature of universities has changed significantly in the last forty years, with many schools taking on more characteristics of a traditional top-down corporate model of governance. According to the decision, for faculty to be considered managerial, they must have a real and meaningful role over more than just academic affairs such as the creation and selection of curriculum. Instead, other factors considered are the roles faculty have in issues such as enrollment management, finances, and creation of new programs or schools.

Quoting the NLRB decision: "In order for decisions in a particular policy area to be attributed to the faculty, the party asserting managerial status must demonstrate that faculty actually exercise control or make effective recommendations." The decision further states that "faculty recommendations are 'effective' if they routinely become operative without independent review by the administration."[5] This is significant. It means that simply pointing to handbooks or official policies is not enough. A school must prove that faculty have a real say over a range of these matters for them to be considered managerial and therefore ineligible to create a union.

In supporting its decision, the NLRB noted the significant changes that had taken place in higher education since *Yeshiva University* was issued. Again, quoting *Pacific Lutheran University*:

> Time appears to have confirmed the wisdom of the Court's decision to address only the case then before it. Over the 30-plus years since *Yeshiva* was decided, the university model of delivering higher education has evolved considerably. . . .
>
> Indeed, our experience applying *Yeshiva* has generally shown that colleges and universities are increasingly run by administrators, which has the effect of concentrating and centering authority away from the faculty in a way that was contemplated in *Yeshiva*, but found not to exist at Yeshiva University itself.[6]

Among the ways in which universities have corporatized has been the increasing use of contingent and part-time faculty. Such faculty, *Pacific Lutheran University* notes, hardly has the same shared governance voice presupposed in *Yeshiva*.

Pacific Lutheran University charts two possibilities for the corporate university. Option one dictates that colleges and universities restructure, and give faculty a meaningful and effective voice along the lines and criteria delineated in the decision. Such a restructuring poses a major threat to the current corporate model. Option two accepts the realities of the new corporate model, allowing for faculty at private schools to unionize. Unionization, too, challenges the current top-down model, forcing administrators and trustees to acknowledge publicly what their institutions have become, while opening them up for the potential to have collective bargaining change the way decisions are made on campus. Neither of these choices sit well with the current corporate model. *Pacific Lutheran* held out the promise of faculty being able to unionize, but it is unclear if the decision survives a Trump NLRB. Additionally, the 2018 Supreme Court decision in *Janus v. AFSCME*, declaring that public-sector unions cannot collect mandatory dues, potentially undercuts the possibility that faculty, at least at public schools, can take advantage of them.[7]

Conclusion

The corporate university has created the conditions for its own demise. Its top-down restructuring and relentless pursuit of Ponzi-like revenue schemes that include pricey and expansive enrollments have come to a bust. The 2008 recession demonstrated the limits of the financial business model, and the *Pacific Lutheran University* decision revealed the problems with its governance fiction. What awaits the corporate university is not clear in terms of what, if anything, will replace it, or how it will respond to these shocks to its business model. Trump administration policies aim to deregulate the corporate university as an effort to save it; yet what is certain is that the current model has reached its limits, and something new must emerge for higher education to remain viable in the future.

NOTES

1. Zack Friedman, "Student Loan Debt Statistics in 2019: A $1.5 Trillion Crisis." *Forbes*, February 25, 2019, https://www.forbes.com/sites/zackfriedman/2019/02/25/student-loan-debt-statistics-2019/#7381ba2d133f.

2. "The College-Cost Calamity," *The Economist*, August 4, 2012, https://www.economist.com/business/2012/08/04/the-college-cost-calamity.

3. NLRB v. Yeshiva University, 444 U.S. 672 (1980).

4. *Pacific Lutheran University v. SEIU*, 361 N.L.R.B. 1404 (2014).

5. *Pacific Lutheran University v. SEIU*, 1422.

6. *Pacific Lutheran University v. SEIU*, 1422

7. *Janus v. AFSCME*, 585 U.S. ___ (138 S. Ct. 2448; 201 L. Ed. 2d 924 [2018]).

39. Making Campus Safer: Academics Fighting Sexual Violence and Sexual Harassment

ELIZABETH QUAY HUTCHISON

A student sits in your office, asking for an extension on the final paper, saying that they have not been coming to class because of "personal issues." After skirting the issue, maybe seeing something like doubt cross your face, they blurt out the rape. They may cry, they may not. You see their pain—maybe as a survivor yourself, you begin to feel it—and you struggle: what are you supposed to do? Maybe you immediately offer the extension, something you normally do when there's a death in the family or a medical crisis. But in this situation, faced with the trauma and confusion so evident in the student's speech, body language, or tears, you might ask yourself whether there's more you can do for them. And then they tell you: it was another student, at a party. Or it was your senior colleague, someone who has harassed you as well. What *now*?

Given the frequency with which college students experience sexual assault, these kinds of faculty-student encounters happen a lot, and with increasing frequency in the wake of greater public discussion about sexual assault over the last ten years.[1] Some of us in the academy certainly handle such disclosures more than others, just because of the subjects we teach or the politics we embody. And perhaps we have ourselves been harassed or assaulted—within the university or beyond—or we have witnessed the sexual harassment of others, whether faculty, graduate students, or staff.[2] Sometimes we know a colleague accused of sexual misconduct, or we have faced a complaint ourselves.[3] But following the Obama-era reforms to federal oversight of Title IX, academics have also been inundated with messages about Title IX compliance, either through trainings at our home institutions or through news accounts about the latest campus rape or faculty harassment scandals. If disclosures like the one described above become formal complaints to university authorities, they also often result in what trauma researchers Smith and Freyd have termed "institutional betrayal"—the failure of colleges and universities to respond effectively to the needs of survivors, thereby increasing significantly the risk of causing them even greater trauma.[4] As in the many aspects of academic life addressed in this volume, faculty often find themselves unprepared to respond to sexual misconduct, whether they hear about it, witness it, or experience it themselves. Yes, we may have learned the university's rules for reporting sexual misconduct, joined a faculty task force, or studied the yearly campus climate reports. But how do we respond to sexual misconduct, not only when we hear about it from students, but also when we find ourselves the target of sexual violence and sexual harassment (svsh), retaliation, or a complaint? What is our responsibility—as professionals, as university employees, and as human beings—to those affected by sexual misconduct in the academy?[5]

If you work at a college or university in the United States, your administration's response to increased federal oversight has very likely included revising its svsh policies, defining what constitutes sexual misconduct, how investigations should proceed, and what sanctions may apply. Many institutions also require all employees to report any disclosure of svsh to a designated university official, immediately and without the consent of the person who experienced the sexual misconduct.[6] Although such policies have spurred a significant expansion of student services and support, they have largely neglected faculty and staff employees, considered only in their roles as potential perpetrators and reporters, but not as victims, bystanders, or advocates.[7] While some faculty prefer this exclusion, it has nevertheless left many of us without the knowledge and the tools we need—as teachers, research supervisors, and administrators who maintain the modern university—to respond appropriately and effectively to sexual misconduct on campus.

This chapter confronts the invisibility of faculty in the most common responses to campus sexual violence, drawing on current research on prevalence, discussing the negative effects of federally mandated intervention, and suggesting how academics can help to reduce svsh in the university. Understood within the framework of "institutional betrayal"—a term that describes the risk posed to victims by the inadequate response to their complaints within military, religious, and educational institutions—sexual violence and harassment can only be effectively addressed if faculty, staff, and students take an active role in Title IX compliance. Compliance mechanisms derived from legal definitions of workplace harassment, which typically do not address the power inequities that inhere in higher education, have been inadequate to the challenges of making our campuses safe. Further, compliance-based approaches increase the likelihood of academics' unwitting participation in institutional betrayal and inhibit our ability—as teachers and colleagues—to advance institutional courage.[8] Every disclosure about sexual misconduct we hear, every incident of verbal harassment we witness, provides academics with an opportunity to demonstrate awareness, knowledge, and sensitivity to the person victimized by it.[9] Moreover, unless higher education's most permanent workforce—the embattled tenure-stream faculty—become change agents in the quest to provide educational access and workplace safety for all members of the university community, SVSH will remain an intractable problem on our campuses.

Whereas the previous edition of *The Academic's Handbook* addressed how faculty might better "anticipate and avoid misperceptions of harassment," the current version—drafted on the one-year anniversary of the #MeToo movement and finalized on the cusp of new laws that roll back Obama-era Title IX guidelines—asks instead how academics might move beyond compliance, not only by responding better to individual students and colleagues targeted by this violence, but also by working to improve the university's capacity to respond effectively and unequivocally to campus sexual violence. Even as public attention has increased the visibility of sexual coercion and unwanted sexual attention in academia, growing awareness of the more widespread (and underreported) prevalence of gender harassment—verbal and nonverbal behaviors that convey hostility, objectification, exclusion, or second-class status about members of one gender—poses new challenges for academics, particularly in STEM fields.[10] As long-term and privileged leaders in the university community, tenure-stream faculty are uniquely positioned to build alliances with staff and students to decrease the prevalence of SVSH in higher education. The final section of this chapter suggests how academics, by learning about their institution's policies, offering support to survivors, documenting complaints of sexual misconduct, and working to improve the university's response, can make our campuses safer places to work, teach, and learn.

Title IX: From Sports Equality to Freedom from Assault

From "Take Back the Night" marches of the 1970s to the creation of women's studies programs, and through the longer struggle to diversify college admissions and hiring, feminist scholars and their allies have long struggled to advance the fundamental premise of Title IX legislation, signed into law in 1972:

"No person in the United States shall, on the basis of sex, be excluded from participation in, be denied the benefits of, or be subjected to discrimination under any education program or activity receiving Federal financial assistance."[11] The passage of Title IX corresponded to the expansion of women's, feminist, gender, and sexuality studies in higher education, as well as increasing numbers of tenure-track women faculty willing to formally complain about sexual misconduct, often at significant personal and professional cost. Recognizing that sexual violence and harassment have constituted persistent barriers to the advancement of women in academic departments, scholarly research, and administrative hiring, women (particularly those who also experience discrimination as sexual, gender, and racial minorities) have struggled both individually and collectively against discrimination and harassment in the university environment. Although Title IX compliance initially focused on securing female students' equal access to athletics teams, the problem of rape and harassment on college campuses meanwhile festered, spurring complaints, student disciplinary hearings, and civil and criminal litigation that was often resolved (or dismissed) quietly behind office doors.[12] The result has been a persistent pattern of toleration for SVSH on college campuses—by university attorneys, upper-level administrators, coaches, deans, and faculty—a pattern that both enabled perpetrators of sexual misconduct and consistently undermined their accusers. Not until the uproar generated by high-profile campus rape scandals in the 1990s—frequently linked to student behavior in athletics and campus fraternities—did the prevalence of sexual violence on college campuses, and the failure of universities to address it, become a topic of national concern.[13]

Growing awareness of campus sexual violence, along with the success of other laws addressing violence against women passed in the 1990s (both national and international), laid a strong foundation for Title IX's transformation in the last twenty years into a mechanism for expanded federal oversight of women's and girls' access to education. After 2008, the US Department of Education (DOE) pursued an aggressive agenda to assess university compliance with Title IX, Clery, and other campus safety measures, issuing letters of guidance for campus officials and threats of punitive action to those found wanting. Since April 2011, the DOE has opened 502 Title IX investigations on college campuses, resolving just 197 of them by June 2020. And after 2013, the Department of Justice also became involved, creating agreements to secure Title IX compliance with the University of Montana, Wheaton College, and the University of New Mexico.[14] The expansion of university compliance mechanisms also created a veritable industry in Title IX services—a network of Title IX coordinators, attorneys, and advocates who in turn provide training seminars, campus climate survey tools, sexual harassment policy templates, and marketing advice to beleaguered university administrators.[15] In US higher education of the early twenty-first century, the enhanced scope and compliance framework of Title IX indeed brought national attention to the problem of campus sexual violence, but was often limited by its focus on peer sexual violence, leaving universities to regulate faculty and staff sexual misconduct through employment and civil rights law. Significantly, while administrators regularly use SVSH and student conduct policies to sanction student misconduct, they have been less successful in addressing sexual misconduct—both *by* and *against*—faculty and staff.[16]

The expansion of Title IX enforcement on university campuses in the past decade has generated responses from across the political spectrum, from critics who argue that federal intervention in SVSH goes too far, does not go far enough, and/or is fundamentally misguided. Conservatives have long criticized the DOE-led increase of the university's role in sanctioning sexual misconduct, challenging the definition, investigation, and sanctions of Title IX by universities.[17] On the other hand, feminist/queer critiques of Title IX point out that university SVSH policies have failed to support the most vulnerable populations, such as minority, LGBTQ, and disabled students.[18] For its part, the American Association of University Professors has weighed in on the "History, Uses, and Abuses of Title IX," documenting how many university administrations have implemented Title IX in ways that undermine academic freedom and/or employment rights of faculty.[19] In August 2020, the Trump administration will implement new regulations defining Title IX compliance in K–12 and higher education, including measures that narrow the definition of sexual harassment, limit the geographical scope of university response, and require live hearings with cross-examination for all postsecondary institutions, measures that will have a chilling effect on reports of sexual assault and harassment.[20]

Moreover, after a decade of Title IX–inspired changes to how universities handle sexual misconduct, research findings have begun to show the limits, and even the damage, caused by those efforts.[21] Recent studies have shown, for example, how the most frequent manifestations of institutional compliance—such as universal mandatory reporting, required sexual assault awareness training, and Title IX investigation and hearings processes—themselves have unintended negative consequences, such as discouraging reports of sexual violence, negative gender norming, and retraumatization of assault victims.[22] Ongoing studies of prevalence/climate, student cultures and behavior, trauma and crisis intervention, institutional behavior, and the Title IX legal framework have repeatedly challenged the efficacy of a compliance approach to campus SVSH.[23] A growing body of research on peer sexual violence has also revealed the complexity of student behaviors in relation to alcohol, partying, and hooking up, with important implications for how we think about institutional response.[24] Research on campus sexual violence has repeatedly exposed the limitations inherent in both federal and university interventions that fail to consider the vulnerabilities, violence, and misconduct of university employees, both staff and faculty. How can universities learn to prevent and respond safely to sexual violence without first understanding, educating, and enlisting the support of staff and faculty who are both subject to and responsible for implementing university policies? Given all of the uncertainties of the Title IX landscape, and the requirements imposed by our home institutions—be they required trainings, mandatory reporting, or respectful campus policies—what are the faculty, considered here both individually and collectively, to do?

Academics and SVSH

So how are academics implicated and involved in responding to campus sexual violence? The answer goes far deeper than policies warning instructors not to "fraternize" with students might suggest, to the most troubling realms of the training, mentorship, scholarship, and professional standards of our academic disciplines. What a cursory glance at blogs and publications on higher education reveals is an enduring pattern of sexual harassment among scholars, and between faculty and students, about which we often lack more than anecdotal information. Subject to both the gendered expectations common in any workplace and the particular pressures of unwritten codes of scholarly collegiality, faculty and graduate students targeted by sexual misconduct struggle mightily, often at great cost to themselves, to identify and take action against sexual harassment.

To take just one well-documented example, the story of Terry Karl, a political scientist hired on the tenure track in 1980 by Harvard University, contains all of the above elements. Subjected to repeated sexual overtures, unwanted physical contact, and threats of reprisal by her senior colleague Jorge Domínguez, in January 1983, Karl began to formally raise her concerns with university administrators, documenting the incidents of harassment and her concerns about their impact on her professional standing. Administrative intervention was so minimal and without sanction to Domínguez that Karl chose to leave for a position at Stanford rather than remain at Harvard.[25] At a distance of 30 years, one can easily see how a different institutional context—such as the existence of clear SVSH policies and a Title IX office—might have ameliorated the negative professional and personal effects on Karl. But her case still perfectly illustrates the ways that the university setting, usually in combination with broader academic culture, continues to enable harassment, discourage reporting, and punish complainants. A 2016 study showed that even as sexual harassment has become more readily identifiable, only 11 percent of female faculty who experience sexual harassment have reported it.[26] In the end, then as now, it is just easier and safer for a faculty member (or student or staff, for that matter) to leave for another department or institution than to file an official complaint and risk retaliation, which perpetrators regularly apply with impunity in the academic context.[27] Male privilege, research dollars, and the diminishing of sexual harassment as a "real" problem—even in the current context of heightened Title IX action in most universities—all mitigate against the safety and professional well-being of those who complain.[28] On the other hand, because sexual harassment undermines the integrity of research itself, federal grant agencies[29] and academic associations[30] have recently issued new guidelines on sexual harassment and other forms of bias. But in an institutional context, particularly as federal oversight through Title IX morphs and declines, academics continue to have little incentive to report sexual misconduct, turning instead to the age-old strategies of avoiding perpetrators, surviving through tenure, or leaving the university or the profession.

The problems named above really begin with how academics have been socialized to gendered rules of professional behavior. Certain academic fields have infamously tended to be more prone to endemic sexual misconduct, because of factors such as persistent gender imbalance in graduate programs and at all faculty ranks, extreme dependency in mentor relations, and the physical isolation of labs or distant field sites.[31] Recent research on higher education has revealed the persistence of high levels of faculty sexual harassment toward graduate students and its negative impact on students' mental health, progress to degree, and standing.[32] Graduate students and medical residents—the research and teaching faculty of tomorrow—have historically been subjected to high levels of sexual misconduct and racial/gender/sexual/sexuality/disability discrimination, behaviors prohibited by both federal civil rights law and university policy. But the price of even informal complaint can be untenably high for those who report misconduct. In many academic fields in which women remain underrepresented at senior ranks, the relationship between overt gender harassment and regular sexual misconduct remains a painful reality. Combined with the invisibility of faculty and staff in university Title IX compliance systems, and the vulnerability of most university employees within them, sexual misconduct remains largely unseen and unaddressed. We, the university's faculty employees, are often required to report sexual misconduct in a context rife with insecurity, both personal and professional.[33]

Even for the most privileged actors in higher education—the shrinking numbers of tenure-stream faculty—recourse to complaint is rife with professional risk, even beyond the real or implied threat to achieving tenure. While it remains difficult to fire tenured faculty without cause, colleagues openly accused of misconduct have ready access to professional retaliation, from denial of grant funding and program support to the filing of countercomplaints, all of which can be as devastating as they are difficult to prove. Those who submit formal complaints, moreover, often experience immediate repercussions of accusing a colleague (or supervisor) of sexual misconduct. The discomfort of continuing to operate in work environments subject to investigation, as well as the long waiting time for investigations to be completed, increases stress and trauma for the complainant. As in the Karl case, the failure to create or enforce (or otherwise incentivize) professional behavior at the level of departments and professional associations has encouraged enabling and risk-averse responses from university administrators and senior academics. Finally, because faculty enjoy the additional protections of academic freedom, university administrators (including legal counsel) often assume that faculty also enjoy additional protection from verified complaints of sexual violence and sexual harassment. This is incorrect, but this widespread perception serves as a brake on meaningful sanctions for faculty misconduct.[34]

How Academics Can Respond—Some Suggestions

Institutional responses that fail to consider and involve faculty in their efforts to diagnose, design, and execute Title IX mandates will have limited or contradictory effects on campus sexual assault. This contradiction arises from the fact that even the basic remedies designed to protect our students must be implemented and supported through institutional and professional relationships that are shot through with power imbalances. In addition, work environments currently expose survivors, reporters, and advocates to virtually unchecked retaliation from peers and supervisors. We have to first recognize the vulnerabilities inherent in professional relationships—including the likelihood of faculty members' experience of harassment and well-founded fear of professional retaliation—before we can empower faculty participation, both individual and collective, in meaningful responses to campus sexual violence and harassment.

Given the ongoing uncertainties of Title IX law and guidance, as well as the great variety of policies in place at universities, how can we as academics respond effectively to the prevalence of sexual violence and harassment on college campuses? Faculty at every rank can try some of the following steps to protect themselves, support others, and improve their institution's response to sexual misconduct:

1. **Learn the System:** Study your institution's policies for defining, reporting, investigating, and sanctioning sexual misconduct, asking whether these policies effectively promote equal access to education and a safe workplace for students, faculty, and staff. Universities must not only prohibit sexual misconduct, but are also required by Title VII to sanction any retaliation that occurs as a result of reporting SVSH, usually through whistleblower protection policies. Find out whether your institution's policies, including the manner in which they are implemented, encourage the identification of sexual misconduct and protect those targeted for SVSH and retaliation. If existing policies have negative impact on survivors and reporters, raise these failures with your administration, compliance office, and/or faculty governance leaders, and demand changes that will better support survivors and reporters of SVSH.[35]

2. **Support Survivors:** When you witness or hear about an incident (or repeated occurrence) of sexual violence or harassment, start by listening to those aggrieved and offering to connect them to *confidential* support services. Victims of sexual misconduct benefit tremendously from being heard without judgment and offered supportive measures that affirm their sense of control—over their stories as well as their physical safety.[36] Unless you have the authority to intervene and correct the abuse—usually assigned to those at the level of Chair and above—your first obligation is to the victim, whose well-being may suffer further damage if you report to university officials without first securing their consent. Unless someone is in immediate danger, consider the risks the survivor may face if you share their story without their consent. If your university requires mandatory reporting of Title IX violations, you can comply with the spirit of such policies—while also respecting a victim's request for privacy—by referring them to your institution's confidential service advocates.

3. **Document Everything:** If you file a complaint under your university's sexual harassment policies or support a student, staff member, or faculty colleague in doing so, document every step of this process and avail yourself of any reliable support and reporting services in the community. As is often the case, university officials may be unable or unwilling to fully investigate a complaint or sanction the perpetrator, or they may even seek to cover up the complaint to avoid risk of negative publicity or lawsuit. In these circumstances, it is imperative that you accompany survivors (or seek accompaniment) in administrative interviews and hearings, save relevant correspondence and reports, and construct timelines to monitor the administration's response. Such materials are critical for mounting

administrative appeals as well as seeking legal remedies to situations that the university may fail to resolve.

4. **Support Institutional Courage:** As members of the university community and academic disciplines, we participate—often unwittingly—in the acts of betrayal and courage carried out by our universities and the academy as a whole. As teachers, academics bear primary responsibility for creating a supportive classroom environment, and can offer clear instructions to our students about the confidentiality and accommodations we can offer them if they report sexual misconduct to us.[37] Bring your knowledge and concerns about sexual harassment to the appropriate venues for faculty governance, shared governance, union organization, and administrative leadership, pressing for policies that are both research-based and survivor-centered. If your university resists these efforts, get your tenured colleagues together, work with student and staff associations, and cultivate alliances with campus advocates and investigators to press for change. Finally, push the upper administration to provide real leadership on campus sexual violence; these leaders should provide appropriate messaging and resources to address the persistence of svsh.

5. **Participate in #AcademicMeToo Movements:** For many faculty, the struggle against sexual harassment is not contained within the university, but extends to their work with professional associations in their disciplines. A slew of academic associations and the National Science Foundation have already established new procedures for considering complaints (or findings) of sexual harassment that should influence decision-making about publication, research grants, committee membership, and professional honors. Join a working group or a review panel and make your opinions known.

Although this chapter has focused on how we can respond to svsh in an institutional context—namely, the teaching and professional relationships that shape academics' experience at colleges and universities—even this approach risks over-determining just how we fight sexual misconduct. When someone we know or we ourselves are the target of sexual violence or harassment, we do well to recognize, like Cortina and Fitzgerald, that "like rape, sexual harassment is both a legal concept and an experience, and it is important to recognize that these are not the same."[38] Before we rush to make an official report, or otherwise try to "fix" the problem, we should stop to identify the needs and secure the safety of those experiencing svsh. Further, when we fight our institution's practices of institutional betrayal, we must beware the temptation to focus primarily (as have so many university leaders) on those efforts that serve chiefly to show compliance with federal law. Rather, we must also, in Nicola Gavey's words, work against the beliefs and practices about sex that "scaffold" sexual violence.[39] As the authors of the National Academies of Science, Engineering, and Medicine's 2018 report argued, without increased transparency and accountability, advances in diversity and inclusion, and effective leadership at all levels of academic life, policies that prohibit sexual violence and harassment alone hold little promise for reducing sexual violence. By listening to and supporting those targeted by svsh and bringing faculty experience to bear on efforts to promote institutional courage, we academics can indeed make our classrooms, programs, and universities safer places to work, teach, and study.

NOTES

The author thanks the students, staff, and faculty who have shared their experiences of sexual harassment and sexual violence, which inspired this chapter and have transformed the way the University of New Mexico responds to sexual misconduct. The author also recognizes her colleagues of Faculty SAFE UNM and the staff of the Women's and LGBTQ Resource Centers, the LoboRESPECT Advocacy Center, and the Office of Equal Opportunity at UNM for their tireless work on behalf of our community.

1. Recent studies show the prevalence of sexual assault in the general population to be one in three women, and 20–25 percent among college students. K. C. Basile, S. G. Smith, M. J. Breiding, M. C. Black, and R. Mahendra, "Sexual Violence Surveillance: Uniform Definitions and Recommended Data Elements," version 2.0, (Atlanta: National Center for Injury Prevention and Control, Centers for Disease Control and Prevention, 2014); C. A. Mellins, K. Walsh, A. L. Sarvet, M. Wall, L. Gilbert, J. S. Santelli, et al., "Sexual Assault Incidents among College Undergraduates: Prevalence and Factors Associated with Risk," *PLoS ONE* 12:11 (2017): e0186471.

2. National Academies of Sciences, Engineering, and Medicine, *Sexual Harassment of Women: Climate, Culture, and Consequences in Academic Sciences, Engineering, and Medicine* (Washington, DC: National Academies Press, 2018), chapter 3, "Sexual Harassment in Academic Sciences, Engineering, and Medicine"; for critical analysis of prevalence research methodologies, see especially 30–41. The National Academies' 2018 study has spurred cooperation among over sixty institutions of higher education across the country in the "Action Collaborative on Preventing Sexual Harassment in Higher Education," November 19, 2019, http://sites.nationalacademies.org/sites/sexualharassmentcollaborative/index.htm.

3. This chapter uses "sexual misconduct" and "sexual violence and sexual harassment" (svsh) to refer to a range of activities prohibited by law and/or university policy, including sexual assault and sexual harassment. Sexual harassment is defined by the Equal Employment Opportunity Commission as "Unwelcome sexual advances, requests for sexual favors, and other verbal or physical conduct of a sexual nature constitute sexual harass-

ment when this conduct explicitly or implicitly affects an individual's employment, unreasonably interferes with an individual's work performance, or creates an intimidating, hostile, or offensive work environment." USEEOC, "Facts about Sexual Harassment," https://www.eeoc.gov/eeoc/publications/fs-sex.cfm (accessed February 20, 2020).

4. Carly Parnitzke Smith and Jennifer J. Freyd, "Institutional Betrayal," *American Psychologist* 69:6 (September 2014): 575–587.

5. Although this chapter focuses on response to unwanted sexual attention or sexual coercion ("come-ons"), an important body of research centers the more pervasive incidence of gender harassment ("put-downs") in the academy. The National Academies' recent report, *Sexual Harassment of Women*, relied on decades of research to show a strong correlation between gender harassment—behaviors that insult, humiliate, or ostracize women—and the incidence of sexual harassment and coercion. Noting that gender harassment is often conducted by multiple actors and tolerated by supervisors, the report found higher levels of sexual harassment in institutions where leadership was uninformed or unresponsive to reports of harassment: "This means that institutions can take concrete steps to reduce sexual harassment by making systemwide changes that demonstrate how seriously they take this issue and that reflect that they are listening to those who courageously speak up to report their sexual harassment experiences." NASEM, *Sexual Harassment of Women*, x.

6. Universal mandatory reporting policies—not required by Title IX but embedded in university sexual harassment policies in all but a handful of universities—have spurred opposition from professional and legal associations as well as faculty organized on several campuses. See K. J. Holland, L. M. Cortina, and J. J. Freyd, "Compelled Disclosure of College Sexual Assault," *American Psychologist* 73:3 (February 2018): 256–268; Merle H. Weiner, "A Principled and Legal Approach to Title IX Reporting," *Tennessee Law Review* 85:71 (2017): 71–188; Leora D. Freedman, "Faculty as Responsible Employees: To Be or Not to Be," paper presented at the 55th Annual Conference of the National Association of College and University Attorneys, Washington, DC, 2015; Sine Anahita, "Trouble with Title IX: Mandatory Reporting, Title IX Profiteers and Administrators, and Academic Governance," *Academe*, May–June 2017, https://www.aaup.org/article/trouble-title-ix#.Xk8fO2hKi7o.

7. Consider, for example, the sexual harassment that many faculty and staff have already experienced—up to and including assault—in the course of their undergraduate or graduate training, which can have long-lasting and deleterious effects on education, career, and private life: Claire Raymond and Sarah Corse, "A Distorting Mirror: Educational Trajectory after College Sexual Assault," *Feminist Studies* 44:2 (2018): 464–490.

8. "Institutional courage," a term coined by psychologist Jennifer Freyd in 2014, refers to institutions' systematic attempts to enhance accountability and transparency in their response to sexual assault. See Jennifer J. Freyd and Alec M. Smidt, "So You Want to Address Sexual Harassment and Assault in Your Organization? *Training* Is Not Enough; *Education* Is Necessary," *Journal of Trauma and Dissociation* 20:5 (2019): 489–494. Freyd now directs the Project on Institutional Courage, https://www.jjfreyd.com/project-on -institutional-courage (accessed February 20, 2020).

9. Survivor advocates, as well as recent findings in psychology, emphasize the importance of how individuals, including academics, respond to incidents and disclosures of sexual violence: Emily R. Dworkin, Charlotte D. Brill, and Sarah E. Ullman, "Social

Reactions to Disclosure of Interpersonal Violence and Psychopathology: A Systematic Review and Meta-Analysis," *Clinical Psychology Review* 72 (2019), https://doi.org/10.1016/j.cpr.2019.101750; Alejandra Mabel Rosales, "If You Experience Sexual Harassment You Must Report It . . . Right?," *Intersections: Critical Issues in Education* 2:1 (2018): 45–47; Katherine J. Holland and Lilia M. Cortina, "'It Happens to Girls All the Time': Examining Sexual Assault Survivors' Reasons for Not Using Campus Supports," *American Journal of Community Psychology* 59 (2017): 50–64; NASEM, *Sexual Harassment of Women*, 79–82.

10. On the high correlation between workplace gender harassment and the prevalence of physical assault, see Louise F. Fitzgerald and Lilia M. Cortina, "Sexual Harassment in Work Organizations: A View from the 21st Century," in APA *Handbook of the Psychology of Women: Perspectives on Women's Private and Public Lives*, edited by Cheryl B. Travis, Jacquelyn W. White, Alexandra Rutherford, Wendi S. Williams, Sarah L. Cook, and Karen Fraser Wyche (Washington, D.C.: American Psychological Association, 2018), 215–234.

11. 20 USCA, Sec. 168, Title IX (1972).

12. The landmark 1977 case of *Olivarius v. Yale University*, though unsuccessful, was the first attempt to argue that sexual harassment constitutes a violation of Title IX, inspiring a series of further lawsuits and Catharine MacKinnon's important volume, *Sexual Harassment of Working Women: A Case of Sex Discrimination* (New Haven, CT: Yale University Press, 1979).

13. For an excellent reference work on the origins and transformation of Title IX, see Susan Ware, *Title IX: A Brief History with Documents* (Long Grove, IL: Waveland, 2007). On sexual violence in college athletics, see Jessica Luther, *Unsportsmanlike Conduct: College Football and the Politics of Rape* (Brooklyn, NY: Akashic, 2016).

14. See the *Chronicle of Higher Education* Title IX tracking page at https://projects.chronicle.com/titleix/ (accessed June 13, 2020).

15. Anahita, "Trouble with Title IX"; Lauren F. Lichty, Rebecca Campbell, and Jayne Schuiteman, "Developing a University-Wide Institutional Response to Sexual Assault and Relationship Violence," *Journal of Prevention and Intervention in the Community* 36:1–2 (2008): 5–22.

16. The focus on student sexual assault complaints has been so intense that university general counsels have sometimes been unwilling to recognize Title IX complaints by staff and faculty. See the discussions at NACUA's 55th annual conference, "Title IX and VAWA Issues Specific to Employees and the Employment Relationship," Washington, D.C., June 28–July 1, 2015.

17. The Foundation for Individual Rights in Education (FIRE) argues that Title IX violates the free speech of individuals sanctioned under university policies. See Conor Friedersdorf, "How Sexual-Harassment Policies Are Diminishing Academic Freedom," *Atlantic*, October 20, 2015. Another widely read critique of recent Title IX implementation is Laura Kipnis's *Unwanted Advances: Sexual Paranoia Comes to Campus* (New York: Harper, 2017).

18. Nancy Chi Cantalupo, "And Even More of Us Are Brave: Intersectionality and Sexual Harassment of Women Students of Color," *Harvard Journal of Law and Gender* 42:1 (2018): 3–81; Jennifer Doyle, *Campus Sex, Campus Security* (South Pasadena, CA: Semiotext(e), 2015); Rana Jaleel, "Title IX and Feminism on Campus," *Academe*, January–February 2018, https://www.aaup.org/article/title-ix-and-feminism-campus#.Xk8l82hKi7o.

19. American Association of University Professors, "The History, Uses, and Abuses of Title IX," Report of the Committee A on Academic Freedom and Tenure and of the Committee on Women in the Academic Profession, adopted by the AAUP in June 2016. https://www.aaup.org/file/TitleIXreport.pdf.

20. Department of Education, "Title IX: Summary of Major Provisions of the Department of Education's Title IX Final Rule," https://www2.ed.gov/about/offices/list/ocr/docs/titleix-summary.pdf (accessed June 13, 2020); Sarah Brown, "What Colleges Need to Know about the New Title IX Rules," *Chronicle of Higher Education*, May 6, 2020; Greta Anderson, "ACLU, Survivor Advocate Groups Sue Dept. of Education," *Inside Higher Ed*, May 15, 2020.

21. NASM, *Sexual Harassment of Women*, chapter 2, "Sexual Harassment Research."

22. Justine E. Tinkler, "How Do Sexual Harassment Policies Shape Gender Beliefs? An Exploration of the Moderating Effects of Norm Adherence and Gender," *Social Science Research* 42:5 (2013): 1269–1283; Mala Htun, Carlos Contreras, Melanie Dominguez, Francesca Jensenius, and Justine Tinkler, "Effects of Mandatory Sexual Misconduct Training on College Campuses," paper presented at Midwest Political Science Association Annual Meeting, Chicago, April 5–8, 2018, and American Political Science Association Annual Meeting, Boston, August 30–September 2, 2018.

23. Much of this research has emerged at the University of Oregon, where psychologist Jennifer Freyd's Dynamics Lab has generated research findings on trauma and institutional betrayal, work that has also advanced UO campus engagement with university policies on SVSH. See the Dynamics Lab publications at https://dynamic.uoregon.edu/ (accessed February 20, 2020); Weiner, "Principled and Legal Approach."

24. Research on student social behaviors related to sexual assault has been the focus of the Sexual Health Initiative to Foster Transformation (SHIFT) at Columbia University: https://www.mailman.columbia.edu/research/sexual-health-initiative-foster-transformation (accessed February 20, 2020). See Jennifer S. Hirsch and Shamus Khan, *Sexual Citizens: A Landmark Study of Sex, Power, and Assault on Campus* (New York: Norton, 2020)

25. Tom Bartlett and Nell Gluckman, "She Left Harvard: He Got to Stay," *Chronicle of Higher Education*, February 27, 2018. Domínguez has since been retired and seen his privileges revoked by the university. See Colleen Flaherty, "Harvard Revokes Emeritus Status and Retirement Privileges from Professor Who Was Found to Have Harassed Women for Decades," *Inside Higher Ed*, May 10, 2019.

26. USMSPB (US Merit Systems Protection Board), *Update on Sexual Harassment in the Federal Workplace* (2018), https://www.mspb.gov/MSPBSEARCH/viewdocs.aspx?docnumber=1500639&version=1506232&application=ACROBAT.

27. Lilia Cortina and V. J. Magley, "Raising Voice, Risking Retaliation: Events Following Interpersonal Mistreatment in the Workplace," *Journal of Occupational Health Psychology* (2003), https://doi.org/10.1037/1076-8998.8.4.247; NASM, *Sexual Harassment*, chapter 4, "Job and Health Outcomes of Sexual Harassment and How Women Respond to Sexual Harassment," 67–92.

28. Psychologist Jennifer Freyd refers to the likely responses that further discourage both informal and formal complaints to authorities as DARVO: Deny, Attack, and Reverse Victim and Offender. Institutions that fail to sanction offenders or prevent retaliation

engage in "Institutional DARVO." See S. Harsey, E. Zurbriggen, and J. Freyd, "Perpetrator Responses to Victim Confrontation: DARVO and Victim Self-Blame," *Journal of Aggression, Maltreatment and Trauma* 26 (2017): 644–663.

29. National Aeronautics and Space Association, "Compliance Requirements for NASA Grantees," https://missionstem.nasa.gov/compliance-requirements-nasa-grantees .html (accessed February 20, 2020); National Institutes of Health, "1311—Preventing and Addressing Harassment and Inappropriate Conduct," NIH *Policy Manual*, https:// policymanual.nih.gov/1311 (accessed February 20, 2020); National Science Foundation, "Reporting Requirements Regarding Findings of Sexual Harassment, Other Forms of Harassment, or Sexual Assault," *Federal Register* 83:43 (March 5, 2018): 9342–9343, https://www.federalregister.gov/d/2018-04374.

30. See, for example, the American Geophysical Union, "AGU Scientific Integrity and Professional Ethics," August 2017, https://www.agu.org/-/media/Files/AGU -Scientific-Integrity-and-Professional-Ethics-Policy.pdf; American Association for the Advancement of Science, "Revocation Process," https://www.aaas.org/programs/fellows /revocation-process (accessed February 20, 2020); American Historical Association, "Sexual Harassment Policy (2018)," https://www.historians.org/about-aha-and -membership/governance/policies-and-documents-of-the-association/sexual-harassment -policy (accessed February 20, 2020); Latin American Studies Association, "Anti-Harassment Policy," https://www.lasaweb.org/en/anti-harassment-policy/ (accessed February 20, 2020); American Philosophical Association, "Discrimination Complaint Procedure," https://www.apaonline.org/page/discrim_complaint (accessed February 20, 2020); American Anthropological Association, "Policy on Sexual Harassment and Sexual Assault," http://s3.amazonaws.com/rdcms-aaa/files/production/public/AAA_SH_Policy _2018.pdf (accessed February 20, 2020).

31. For research on SVSH in field research contexts, see K. B. H. Clancy, R. G. Nelson, J. N. Rutherford, and K. Hinde, "Survey of Academic Field Experiences (SAFE): Trainees Report Harassment and Assault," *PLoS ONE* 9:7 (2014): e102172, https://doi.org/10.1371 /journal.pone.0102172; Robin G. Nelson, Julienne N. Rutherford, Katie Hinde, and Kathryn B. H. Clancy, "Signaling Safety: Characterizing Fieldwork Experiences and Their Implications for Career Trajectories," *American Anthropologist* 119:4 (December 2017): 710–722; Rebecca Hanson and Patricia Richards, *Harassed: Gender, Bodies, and Ethnographic Research* (Oakland: University of California Press, 2019).

32. Nancy Chi Cantalupo and William C. Kidder, "A Systematic Look at a Serious Problem: Sexual Harassment of Students by University Faculty," *Utah Law Review* 3:4 (2018): 671–786.

33. While any university employee who is required to report incidents of sexual harassment may themselves be drawn into a subsequent investigation or become a target of retaliation, staff, graduate students, and contingent faculty—including those who belong to ethnic and sexual minorities—are even more vulnerable: Alexis Henshaw, "The Challenges for Adjuncts When Supporting and Counseling Sexual Assault Victims," *Inside Higher Ed*, June 23, 2017.

34. A fuller discussion of how Title IX regulations and OCR guidance have been insufficiently attentive to the protection of academic freedom can be found in AAUP, "The History, Uses and Abuses of Title IX."

35. Following the Department of Justice's findings on noncompliance with Title IX at the University of New Mexico in April 2016, faculty organized a movement for mutual support and collective action at the university, "Faculty for a Sexual Assault–Free Environment," or Faculty SAFE UNM. These and other efforts have successfully mobilized faculty authority and expertise to maintain pressure on university administrations and influence the direction of institutional change in recent years.

36. M. M. Foynes and J. J. Freyd. "The Impact of Skills Training on Responses to the Disclosure of Mistreatment," *Psychology of Violence* 1 (2017): 66–77. See also Freyd's tips for listening to disclosures of SVSH at https://dynamic.uoregon.edu/jjf/disclosure/good listener.html (accessed February 20, 2020).

37. Your institution's Title IX Coordinator may suggest language for course syllabi regarding relevant services and employee reporting requirements for SVSH, but instructors may choose to rely instead on the American Association of University Professors' "Statement on Professional Ethics," which requires that professors protect students' academic freedom and "respect[s] the confidential nature of the relationship between professor and student." https://www.aaup.org/report/statement-professional-ethics.

38. Fitzgerald and Cortina, "Sexual Harassment in Work Organizations," 5.

39. Nicola Gavey, *Just Sex? The Cultural Scaffolding of Rape* (London: Routledge, 2005). Thanks to M. Gabriela Torres for this important insight and for sharing M. Gabriela Torres and Dianna Shandy, "Taking Leadership and Remaking Academic Communities," *Anthropology News* 59:3 (2018): e119–122.

40. Decolonizing and Building Community

KELLY FAYARD

I was an undergraduate at Duke when I decided that I would get a PhD in anthropology, but it was not exactly my idea. To be honest, I had never considered a life in academia. However, when I decided my final project for a "Native North America" class would focus on my own tribe, the Poarch Band of Creek Indians located in southern Alabama, I came across books and articles that gave me pause. They circulated ideas that totally contradicted my experience growing up in and around Poarch. The lack of information was also upsetting: while there were a handful of books about southeastern Indians at the time, the majority of anthropological Native studies were reserved for the tribes out West.

I approached my professor to lament this lack of study. "Well," he replied, "you'll just have to get your PhD in anthropology!" And so I did.

Anthropology has been a discipline that Native people have long avoided due to the colonial nature of the discipline, as well as the historical mistreatment of many Native groups and individuals by anthropologists. Examples of anthropologists digging up burials, recording sacred ceremonies against the wishes of the Native nations involved, or stealing culturally significant objects are abundant in the field. In 1969, with the rise of the Red Power movement, Vine Deloria Jr. wrote a scathing review of this treatment in his book *Custer Died for Your Sins*, which began a more systematic critique of anthropology by Native American scholars.[1] While anthropology as a discipline has been self-reflexive and has begun to deal with its historical sins, there are many practitioners who continue to thrive within the asymmetrical power imbalances placed upon Native groups with whom they have relationships. However, because many Native scholars are interested in entering into these anthropological discussions, more Native anthropologists have emerged in the field since the 1990s. I entered the Department of Anthropology at the University of Michigan in the fall of 2004. Within a few weeks of my arrival on campus to begin my graduate work, I found a few Native students in the departments of History and American Culture. By the time I was writing my dissertation, there were over a dozen Native PhD students at Michigan. We worked together and supported, celebrated, and socialized with each other. We also had a strong Native studies faculty and allies who worked with us. We built community. In turn, the community supported and nourished our spirits and our intellect. It was an indigenous nerd's paradise!

While in graduate school, however, I did begin to understand that while I had built such a strong support system with other Native graduate students, the broader discipline of anthropology was not going to be as supportive or accepting. At my first American Anthropological Association annual meeting, for example, an older anthropologist familiar with my tribe approached me and said "I never thought I'd see the day that a Poarch Creek would be at the AAAS!" This was the beginning of my understanding that the discipline, as much as it had grown, had not necessarily created the space for me—and others like me—to become a part of it.

My anthropological "fieldwork" was really "home work." It was important to me to do community-based research that would ultimately help the tribe. Following the suggestions of Linda Tuhiwai Smith in *Decolonizing Methodologies*, I wanted to build meaningful connections between me (the researcher), the products of my research, and my community of origin.[2] I went on a listening tour in which I asked elders and tribal leaders what kind of work would be meaningful to them. Community-engaged research is where my passion lies.

My return to Ann Arbor to write my dissertation coincided with the height of a nasty battle between Michigan tribes and the Museum of Anthropology at the University of Michigan, to return the remains of thousands of Native people that were being held in a field house near the football stadium. To say that I was made to feel unwelcome in the anthropology department is an understatement. Fortunately, a graduate student group called Ethnography as Activism stepped in as allies. While none of these students were Native, they wanted their department to be on the right side of the debate and to understand and follow the spirit of the Native American Graves Protection and Repatriation Act (NAGPRA), rather than merely the letter of the law. This was the first time I experienced firsthand working with allies, and it was a beautiful thing. Because of Ethnography as Activism, the Native Graduate Caucus, and the Michigan tribes, the Vice Provost of Research created a NAGPRA council at the University of Michigan to handle NAGPRA claims. This was a victory, and it influenced how I came to envision building community at a university with different stakeholders, as well as within the local and state tribal communities.

As I was finishing my dissertation, a job at a small liberal arts college in Maine opened; the search was for an anthropologist of Native North America. I applied, received an offer for a tenure-track position, and moved to Maine immediately after defending my dissertation. The transition from a supportive Native community to a campus where I was the only Native faculty member was very difficult. To make matters more complicated, even though there were large and vibrant Native communities in Maine, I found no tangible connections between these tribes and the college.

After working as a faculty member of anthropology for four years and successfully being reappointed, I began to think about the trajectory of my career. In my reappointment letter, the department warned me about participating in too many campus events and spending too much time dedicated to students. This was my favorite part of the job. I could not shake the feeling that the first-generation or low-income students and students of color were not getting enough support at the college. I began to wonder how I could fill a different role that would allow me to help build a supportive and inclusive community for students who are too often left to figure it out for themselves—or who, like me as an undergraduate, felt woefully underprepared and lost in an elite university setting. And, I wanted to explore more opportunities to develop relationships between Native students on campus and Native communities where I was located.

It has become clear to me through working in multiple educational settings— public and private, small colleges and large universities—that a barrier to building successful relationships between community members and the institution is the baggage that each institution carries with it. Even as a Native faculty member or administrator, I have found that reaching out to Native communities is made more complicated by the historical wrongdoings of my institution which can, in many cases, outweigh the good intentions of campus leaders. I have always attempted to build connections with local Native communities so that I might bring students more awareness about the land they occupy while at school, beyond just hearing the names of tribes in formal land acknowledgments before events. Again, this has been made easier or harder, depending on the specific relationship between the institution and the local tribes. Acknowledging this historical context cannot be overemphasized as a factor in building these relationships.

To approach these relationships productively requires us to think outside of usual academic hierarchies, especially in older elite institutions where hierarchy is important. For example, I work to invite Indigenous people who come from all walks of life. When they arrive on campus, instead of using the usual hierarchical indicators of recognition to welcome them, such as graduate degrees or prestigious home institutions, I give a genuine warm and hearty greeting to a fellow Native. This is one way that I strive to decolonize the academy. Just because I have a PhD, this does not mean that I am more informed or more intelligent than any of my fellow Natives. Many elder Native intellectuals were denied the right to an education, and a lack of a degree should not preclude their being treated as important dignitaries when they visit campus. It takes a great amount of effort to convince the rest of campus of this. For example, in my experience, some institutions on a campus may have students or lower-level administrators reach out to local tribal government leaders. There is not an acknowledgment that tribal governments are sovereign and that in order to be respectful, the institution should treat a tribal chair as a head of a foreign state, should they visit campus. I spend a lot of time helping my colleagues understand the gravity of tribal sovereignty and all that it entails.

Beyond building community between institutions and local Native communities, I am also responsible for creating community among my institution's diverse Native students. At Yale, we have students from reservations in South Dakota, the Big Island of Hawai'i, and urban centers across the United States, and others claim indigenous roots traced to tribes in Mexico and Central and South America. Some students come fluent in their language and culture, others have no connection to their Native identity at all, and others fall on the spectrum in between. We try very hard to make sure that students are first and foremost supported in their own identity—be that Blackfeet, Lakota, Diné, Creek, Choctaw, Kanaka Maoli, Mohawk, or any of the other dozens of tribes our students represent. Part of the way that we facilitate this is through our language program (funded by our lone Native faculty member, Professor Ned Blackhawk). We offer (via Skype) up to eight Indigenous languages per semester for students to take in community classes. This way, our community is strengthened at the same time that students' tribal identity is strengthened. Beyond the language classes, the Native American Cultural Center works to bring in Native artists, scholars, and intellectuals in order to bolster and converge our students' personal identities and interests with their scholarly pursuits and interests.

I am fortunate to work at an institution where students have worked to create space for the Native community. Many other institutions, public and private alike, do not have space or resources dedicated to the Native community. Yale is a place where one can see how student activism has changed the campus for the better. The Native American Cultural Center is made possible by an incredibly generous alum who has endowed a budget for the center and for the assistant dean position. The space that we have has made a huge difference in how we are able to recruit Native students to campus. There is a definite privilege that comes with working at a private institution—we are able to take up physical space on campus and employ dedicated staff members for Native students and other students of color. It is important to acknowledge, however, the generations of students who spoke out and worked to make all of this a possibility. It is also important to understand that even with the tremendous resources Yale has, the Native and Indigenous population comprises less than two percent of the student body, so our funding is predicated upon that. The reality is that much of my time is spent fundraising!

Some of our biggest successes at the NACC are when we come together as a Native community to celebrate our students. At the end of each year, we travel to Mohegan Sun Casino and Resort (so we can be at a Native-owned business) for our annual graduation dinner. It is here, during the open mic, that one can hear the love and the trust that has been built between students, faculty, and staff through the NACC. It is at this ceremony that one can hear what an impact the NACC has had on students. It is here that one can learn how much a space like the Native American Cultural Center matters to these students. It is here that one recognizes how much our Native students have had to overcome in order to be successful in an educational system that was not created to educate nor welcome them. It is here that we celebrate together all that we have overcome.

NOTES

1. Vine Deloria Jr., *Custer Died for Your Sins: An Indian Manifesto* (Norman: University of Oklahoma Press, 1969).

2. Linda Tuhiwai Smith, *Decolonizing Methodologies: Research and Indigenous Peoples* (New York: Zed, 1999).

Contributors

LUIS ALVAREZ is Associate Professor at the University of California at San Diego, where he has served as the director of the Institute of Arts and Humanities and of the Chicanx Latinx Studies Program.

STEVEN ALVAREZ is Associate Professor of English at St. John's University. He is the author of *Brokering Tareas: Mexican Immigrant Families Translanguaging Homework Literacies* (State University of New York Press, 2017) and *Community Literacies en Confianza: Learning from Bilingual After-School Programs* (National Council of Teachers of English, 2017).

ELADIO BOBADILLA is Assistant Professor of History at the University of Kentucky. His research focuses on twentieth-century US history, particularly ethnic and immigration history and the history of social movements. He is a US Navy veteran and recipient of many awards and fellowships, including the 2020 Herbert Gutman Dissertation Prize. His first book will be published as part of the Working Class in American History series of the University of Illinois Press.

GENEVIEVE CARPIO is Assistant Professor in the César E. Chávez Department of Chicana/o Studies at the University of California at Los Angeles. She is author of *Collisions at the Crossroads: How Place and Mobility Make Race* (University of California Press, 2019).

MARCIA CHATELAIN is Professor of History at Georgetown University. She is the author of *South Side Girls: Growing up in the Great Migration* (Duke University Press, 2015) and *Franchise: The Golden Arches in Black America* (Liveright, 2020).

ERNESTO CHÁVEZ is Professor of History at the University of Texas at El Paso. He has published two books, *¡Mi Raza Primero! (My People First!): Nationalism, Identity, and Insurgency in the Chicano Movement in Los Angeles, 1966–1978* (University of California Press, 2002) and *The U.S. War with Mexico: A Brief History with Documents* (Bedford/St. Martin's, 2007). He is writing a critical biography of Mexican-born actor Ramón Novarro, tentatively titled *Body and Soul: The Closeted Performance of Ramón Novarro*. An article on this subject appeared in the September 2011 issue of the *Journal of the History of Sexuality*.

MIROSLAVA CHÁVEZ-GARCÍA is Professor of History at the University of California at Santa Barbara and holds affiliations in the Departments of Chicana/o Studies and Feminist Studies. Her most recent book, *Migrant Longing: Letter Writing across the U.S.-Mexico Borderlands* (University of North Carolina Press, 2018), is a history of migration, courtship, and identity as told through more than three hundred personal letters exchanged across the US-Mexico borderlands among family members and friends.

N. D. B. CONNOLLY is Herbert Baxter Adams Associate Professor of History at Johns Hopkins University and the author of *A World More Concrete: Real Estate and the Remaking of Jim Crow South Florida* (University of Chicago Press, 2014). Until 2020, he also served as a cohost of the weekly podcast *BackStory*.

JEREMY V. CRUZ is Assistant Professor of Theological Ethics at St. John's University. His research interests are at the intersections of Christian political theology, egalitarian moral theory, and labor studies.

CATHY N. DAVIDSON is founding director of the Futures Initiative and Distinguished Professor in the program in English, the MA in Digital Humanities, and the MS in Data Analysis and Visualization at the Graduate Center, City University of New York. She is also cofounder and codirector of HASTAC. Davidson was appointed by President Obama and confirmed by the Senate to serve on the National Council on the Humanities from 2011 to 2017 and served on the board of directors of Mozilla from 2012 to 2018. Davidson's *The New Education: How to Revolutionize the University to Prepare Students for a World in Flux* (Basic Books, 2017) won the 2019 Frederic W. Ness Book Award from the Association of American Colleges and Universities.

SARAH DEUTSCH is Professor of History at Duke University. She is the author of three books, most recently *Women and the City: Gender, Space, and Power in Boston, 1870–1940* (Oxford University Press, 2000), and numerous articles and book chapters, including "Labor, Land, and Protest since Statehood," in *Telling New Mexico: A New History*, edited by Marta Weigle (University of New Mexico Press, 2009). She has served as program cochair for annual conferences of the American Studies Association and the Organization of American Historians, as dean of the Faculty of Social Sciences at Duke, as chair of the Executive Committee of Delegates of the American Council of Learned Societies, and on the executive committee of the Organization of American Historians. Her current book project is *Making a Modern West, 1898–1942*.

BRENDA ELSEY is Associate Professor of History at Hofstra University. She is the coauthor (with Joshua Nadel) of *Futbolera: A History of Women and Sports in Latin America* (University of Texas Press, 2019) and author of *Citizens and Sportsmen: Fútbol and Politics in Twentieth-Century Chile* (University of Texas Press, 2012). She has also published numerous academic articles on gender and popular culture in Latin America. She is development lead for the Fare network in the Americas, an NGO that fights discrimination in soccer and develops grassroots projects using soccer for social justice. She is the cohost of the weekly sport and feminism podcast *Burn It All Down*.

SYLVANNA M. FALCÓN is Associate Professor in the Department of Latin American and Latino Studies and director of the Research Center for the Americas at the University of California at Santa Cruz. She is the award-winning author of *Power Interrupted: Antiracist and Feminist Activism inside the United Nations* (University of Washington Press, 2016).

MICHELLE FALKOFF is a graduate of the Columbia University Law School and the Iowa Writers' Workshop and currently serves as Director of Communication and Legal Reasoning at Northwestern University's Pritzker School of Law. She is also the author of several young adult novels, including *Playlist for the Dead* (HarperCollins, 2015), *Pushing Perfect* (HarperCollins, 2016), *Questions I Want to Ask You* (HarperCollins, 2018), and *How to Pack for the End of the World* (HarperCollins, 2020).

KELLY FAYARD is Assistant Professor of Anthropology at the University of Denver, where she teaches a variety of classes on contemporary Native Americans. She served as director of the Yale Native American Cultural Center from 2015 to 2019.

MATTHEW W. FINKIN is a Professor of Law at the University of Illinois. He has also served as general counsel to the American Association of University Professors.

LORI FLORES is Associate Professor of History at Stony Brook University and the author of *Grounds for Dreaming: Mexican Americans, Mexican Immigrants, and the California Farmworker Movement* (Yale University Press, 2016).

KATHRYN J. FOX is Professor of Sociology at the University of Vermont. She teaches in the area of criminal justice and conducts research on community reintegration after prison. She is director of the University of Vermont's Liberal Arts in Prison Program, which is part of the Bard Prison Initiative's Consortium for the Liberal Arts in Prison.

FREDERICO FREITAS is Assistant Professor of Latin American and Digital History at North Carolina State University and an investigator at the Visual Narrative Initiative. He has most recently published the edited volume *Big Water: The Making of the Borderlands between Brazil, Argentina, and Paraguay* (University of Arizona Press, 2018).

NEIL K. GARG is Professor and the Kenneth N. Trueblood Endowed Chair in Chemistry and Biochemistry at the University of California at Los Angeles.

NANIBAA' A. GARRISON is an Associate Professor at the University of California at Los Angeles in the Institute for Society and Genetics and the Department of Medicine's Institute for Precision Health and the Division of General Internal Medicine and Health Services Research. Her research focuses on bioethics, genetics, and community engagement with Indigenous peoples. She is an enrolled member of the Navajo Nation.

JOY GASTON GAYLES is Professor of Higher Education and University Faculty Scholar at North Carolina State University. Her research focuses on access and success in postsecondary education.

TIFFANY JASMIN GONZÁLEZ is an American Association of University Women Fellow and a PhD candidate in History at Texas A&M University at College Station. Her dissertation, "Representation for a Change: Women in Government and the Chicana/o Civil Rights Movement in Texas," details the political labor that Latinas conducted to shape American government for their inclusion since the 1970s.

CYNTHIA R. GREENLEE is a North Carolina–based intentionally independent scholar and journalist who writes about African American history, gender, the law, and reproduction in the post–Civil War US South. For the 2019–20 year, she was an Open Society Foundations Media Justice Fellow.

ROMEO GUZMÁN is Assistant Professor of US History at Claremont Graduate University. He is the coeditor of *East of East: The Making of Greater El Monte* (Rutgers University Press, 2020).

LAUREN HALL-LEW is Reader in Linguistics and English Language at the University of Edinburgh. She is a sociolinguist specializing in phonetic variation and change, particularly with respect to accents of English in the United States and Scotland.

DAVID HANSEN is the Associate University Librarian for Research, Collections, and Scholarly Communications at Duke University Libraries, where he is also the lead copyright and information policy officer. His background is in intellectual property law. Before joining Duke, he held academic positions at the University of North Carolina School of Law and the University of California at Berkeley School of Law.

HEIDI HARLEY is Professor of Linguistics at the University of Arizona, where she has worked since 1999. She has supervised over twenty doctoral dissertations and published over seventy articles on the abstract grammar underlying the structure of words and sentences cross-linguistically.

LAURA M. HARRISON is Professor in the Department of Counseling and Higher Education at Ohio University. She is the author of four books; her most recent work is *Teaching Struggling Students: Lessons Learned from Both Sides of the Classroom* (Palgrave Macmillan, 2019).

SONIA HERNÁNDEZ is a former Fulbright fellow and Associate Professor of History at Texas A&M University who specializes in the intersections of gender and labor in the US-Mexican borderlands, Chicana/o history, and modern Mexico. She is the author of *Working Women into the Borderlands* (Texas A&M University Press, 2014).

SHARON P. HOLLAND is the Townsend Ludington Distinguished Endowed Professor and chair of American Studies at the University of North Carolina at Chapel Hill. She is the author of *Raising the Dead: Readings of Death and (Black) Subjectivity* (Duke University Press, 2000) and *The Erotic Life of Racism* (Duke University Press, 2012) as well as the coauthor, with Tiya Miles, of *Crossing Waters/Crossing Worlds: The African Diaspora in Indian Country* (Duke University Press, 2006).

ELIZABETH QUAY HUTCHISON is Professor of History and director of the Feminist Research Institute at the University of New Mexico. In 2016, she cofounded Faculty for a Sexual Assault–Free Environment at the University of New Mexico (Faculty SAFE UNM), and she now participates in the National Academies of Science, Engineering, and Medicine's Action Collaborative on Preventing Sexual Harassment in Higher Education.

DEBORAH JAKUBS is Rita DiGiallonardo Holloway University Librarian and Vice Provost for Library Affairs as well as Adjunct Associate Professor of History at Duke University. She is a past president of the Association of Research Libraries and a member of the board of the Open Library Foundation.

BRIDGET TURNER KELLY is Associate Professor of Student Affairs at the University of Maryland at College Park. Her scholarship focuses on marginalized populations in higher education, such as women and faculty of color. She is the editor of the National Association of Student Personnel Administrators' *Journal of Student Affairs Research and Practice*.

KAREN KELSKY is Founder and CEO of The Professor Is In and the author of *The Professor Is In: The Essential Guide to Turning Your Ph.D. into a Job* (Random House, 2015). She speaks nationally and internationally on academic and postacademic career development for scholars, is a biweekly columnist for the *Chronicle of Higher Education* and cohosts the podcast *The Professor Is In*.

STEPHEN KUUSISTO is the author of *Have Dog, Will Travel: A Poet's Journey* (Simon and Schuster, 2018). He teaches at Syracuse University.

MAGDALENA MĄCZYŃSKA is Associate Professor of English and World Literatures at Marymount Manhattan College and the author of *The Gospel According to the Novelist: Religious Scripture and Contemporary Fiction* (Bloomsbury, 2015).

SHEILA MCMANUS is Professor of History at the University of Lethbridge. She is passionate about teaching and learning in higher education and has received multiple teaching awards, including the university's Distinguished Teaching Award, the ULSU Teaching Excellence Award, and the ULSU Award for Outstanding Dedication to Students.

CARY NELSON, Jubilee Professor of Liberal Arts and Sciences at the University of Illinois at Urbana-Champaign, is the author or editor of thirty-three books and the author of three hundred essays, many on higher education.

JOCELYN OLCOTT is the Margaret Taylor Smith Director of Gender, Sexuality, and Feminist Studies and Professor of History and of International Comparative Studies at Duke University. She is the author of *Revolutionary Women in Postrevolutionary Mexico* (Duke

University Press, 2006) and *International Women's Year: The Greatest Consciousness-Raising Event in History* (Oxford University Press, 2017) and the coeditor of *Sex in Revolution: Gender, Politics, and Power in Modern Mexico* (Duke University Press, 2007).

ROSANNA KATHLEEN OLSEN is a scientist at the Rotman Research Institute, Baycrest Health Sciences, and Assistant Professor in the Department of Psychology at the University of Toronto. Dr. Olsen's research is centered on understanding how the brain supports memory and how memory-related brain regions change as we age.

NATALIA MEHLMAN PETRZELA is Associate Professor of History at the New School and the author of *Classroom Wars: Language, Sex, and the Making of Modern Political Culture* (Oxford University Press, 2015). Her current book project is *Fit Nation: How America Embraced Exercise as the Government Abandoned It*, and she is a cohost of the *Past Present* podcast.

CHARLES PIOT is Professor of Cultural Anthropology at Duke University, where he has a joint appointment in African and African American Studies. His area of specialization is the political economy and cultural history of rural West Africa. His recent book, *Doing Development in West Africa: A Reader by and for Undergraduates* (Duke University Press, 2016), describes small-scale development projects that his students have carried out in the villages of northern Togo.

BRYAN PITTS is assistant director of the Latin American Institute at the University of California at Los Angeles. He is completing a book on the shifting relationship of the Brazilian political class to the military and to civil society during the country's 1964–85 military dictatorship. He also studies the intersection of sex, race, and nationality in Brazil, particularly in gay publications and among gay tourists. His work has appeared in journals such as the *Hispanic American Historical Review* and *Revista Brasileira de História*, and he writes regularly on contemporary Brazilian politics for media outlets in both the United States and Brazil.

SARAH PORTNOY is Associate Professor of Teaching in the Departments of Latin American and Iberian Cultures and American Studies and Ethnicity at the University of Southern California. Her area of specialization is Latinx food culture and food justice in US Latinx communities. Her book *Food, Health, and Culture in Latino Los Angeles* (Rowman and Littlefield, 2016) has received recognition for its contributions to the field of food justice and Latinx food culture. She has written about Latinx food culture for the *Los Angeles Times*, *Los Angeles Weekly*, and numerous academic publications.

LAURA PORTWOOD-STACER is a developmental editor and publishing consultant for academic authors at ManuscriptWorks.com. She is currently writing a handbook on scholarly book proposals, under contract with Princeton University Press. Portwood-Stacer previously taught media studies at New York University and the University of Southern California.

YURIDIA RAMÍREZ is a Ford Foundation Fellow and Assistant Professor of History at the University of Illinois at Urbana-Champaign. She is currently working on a book, tentatively titled *Indigeneity on the Move: Transborder Politics from Michoacán to North Carolina*, a historical and interdisciplinary analysis of a diasporic indigenous community and its transforming sense of indigeneity.

MEGHAN K. ROBERTS is a scholar of early modern Europe and Associate Professor of History at Bowdoin College. She is the author of *Sentimental Savants: Philosophical Families in Enlightenment France* (University of Chicago, 2016) and is currently working on a book about medical expertise and moral authority. For more on her teaching and research, see meghankroberts.com.

JOHN ELDER ROBISON is the Neurodiversity Scholar at the College of William and Mary. He is also the author of *Look Me in the Eye* (Crown, 2007), one of his five *New York Times* best-selling books about his life on the autism spectrum. He served two terms on the Interagency Autism Coordinating Committee for the US Department of Health and Human Services and serves as an autism and neurodiversity adviser to other federal agencies.

DAVID SCHULTZ is Professor of Political Science at Hamline University and Professor of Law at the University of Minnesota. He is the author of more than thirty-five books and two hundred articles on American politics and law.

LYNN STEPHEN is Phillip H. Knight Chair and Distinguished Professor of Anthropology at the University of Oregon as well as a past president of the Latin American Studies Association. Her current research focuses on gender violence and access to justice for indigenous women; migration, immigration, and asylum; transborder/transnational studies; gender, race, and ethnicity; and testimony and self-representation in Mexico, Guatemala, El Salvador, and the United States.

JAMES E. SUTTON received his PhD in Sociology with an emphasis on crime and community from Ohio State University. His published works have examined a range of topics, including sexual assault in prison, gangs, state corporate offending, and the use of life events calendars to improve the reliability and validity of self-reported interview data. He is currently chair of the Department of Sociology, chair of the Institutional Review Board, and Associate Professor of Sociology at Hobart and William Smith Colleges.

ANTAR A. TICHAVAKUNDA is Assistant Professor of Education at the University of Cincinnati. He uses sociological frameworks and critical race theory to examine college access, Black campus life, and the experiential core of the campus experience.

KERI WATSON received her PhD from Florida State University. She is Associate Professor of Art History at the University of Central Florida and the founding director of the Florida Prison Education Project. Her research on art, activism, and high-impact pedagogies as they relate to prison education has been supported by the National Endowment for the Arts, the Institute of Museum and Library Services, and the Association of American Colleges and Universities.

KEN WISSOKER is Senior Executive Editor at Duke University Press, acquiring books in the humanities, social sciences, media, and the arts. He joined the press as an acquisitions editor in 1991 and has published over 1,000 books that have won over 150 prizes. He also serves as Director of Intellectual Publics at the Graduate Center, City University of New York. He speaks regularly on publishing at universities in the United States and around the world.

KARIN WULF is executive director of the Omohundro Institute of Early American History and Culture, Professor of History at the College of William and Mary, and cochair of neurodiversity at William and Mary.

Index

boundaries, setting of: between faculty and students, 200, 235; labor-related, 3, 62, 64, 247–50; parenthood/caregiving and, 252, 267–69; time and energy–related, 42, 69, 162. *See also* work-life balance

Boycott, Divestment, Sanctions (BDS) movement, 282–83

Brigham Young University, 198

Brown, Michael, 166–67

California Faculty Association (CFA), 291

campus visit, 13–15

Capella, 297

caregiving, 266–71

Carey, Hugh, 296

Carter, Jimmy, 296

Centers for Disease Control (CDC), 190

Central Connecticut State University, 200

Charleston Syllabus, 171

Chávez, César, 195

cheating, 92, 160

Chronicle of Higher Education, 73, 181, 255

Churchill, Ward, 281

City College of New York, 297

City University of New York, 297

Clery Act, 305

collaboration, 98, 157, 209, 211–15; coauthorship, 115; interdisciplinary, 168, 182, 187

collegiality, 13, 23, 45

Common Rule, 96

community building, 5, 19–22, 54, 58, 319, 321–22. *See also* networks, support

community outreach, 50–51, 54, 208–16

community colleges, 67, 286, 293

conferences, 21–22, 42, 56, 61. *See also* presentations

contingent employment, 16, 286–92, 297. *See also* adjunct positions

contracts: employment, 16, 24–27, 38, 49, 290; publishing, 134–36

copyright, 138–39

Coronado, Juan, 200

Coronel, S., 194, 198

Cortina, Lilia M., 311

cover letters, 21, 128

crowdsourcing, 5, 68, 165–71

Creek Indians, 318–19

Custer Died for Your Sins (Deloria), 318

DACA (Deferred Action for Childhood Arrivals), 197

Dahlstrand, Kate, 199–200

Dartmouth University, 197

data, sharing of, 91, 115–16. *See also* research, ethics of

debt, student, 38, 298

Declaration of Principles on Academic Freedom and Academic Tenure (1915), 276–78

Decolonizing Methodologies (Smith), 319

Deferred Action for Childhood Arrivals (DACA), 197

Deloria, Vine, Jr., 318

depression, 251. See also mental health

Development, Relief, and Education for Alien Minors (DREAM) Act, 197

Dewey model, 295–96

Digital Science, 88

digital scholarship, 85, 91; #FergusonSyllabus, 165–71; libraries, 82–94; podcasts, 179, 256, 258; social media, 5, 35, 167, 251, 252, 255–60

disabilities, 189, 190, 191, 282–83; ableism, 272–73

discrimination: ableism, 272–73; gender harassment, 304, 313–14; in graduate school, 19, 21; microaggressions, 20, 199, 203–7, 237, 244; and salaries, 26; and student evaluations, 261; and Title IX, 305. *See also* marginalization; racism; sexism; underrepresentation

dissertations, 10, 36, 48, 90, 153, 249; revision into book, 129–32

diversity, 19, 35, 73, 184, 210, 272–73; neurodiversity, 189–92. *See also* underrepresentation

DREAM (Development, Relief, and Education for Alien Minors) Act, 197

Dreamers, 193–201

Duke University, 19, 29, 32, 196, 223, 229, 230–31n2, 245, 318

Elsevier, 87–89

employment contracts, 16, 24–27, 38, 49, 290

experiential learning, 50–51; service learning, 223–31

external review, 42, 57. *See also* peer review

Facebook. *See* social media

faculty of color, 20, 57–58, 67, 233, 234, 237

Second Chance Pell Grant Initiative, 220
self-care, 42–43; interview process and, 15; support networks and, 266; professional commitments and 58, 161–62, 269–71. *See also* boundaries, setting of; mental health; work-life balance
service, 4, 30, 67–69; departmental, 54, 56–58; strategic selection of, 39, 41, 58–59, 69, 247–50
service learning, 223–31
sexism, 4, 167, 256, 262, 272. *See also* discrimination; women
sexual violence and sexual harassment (SVSH), 302–17. *See also* women
Shockley, William, 280–81
Simons Foundation: Funding Opportunities in Math, Life Sciences, Physical Sciences, and Autism, 73
Smith, Carly Parnitzke, 303
Smith, Linda Tuhiwai, 319
social media, 5, 35, 185, 251, 252, 255–60; Facebook, 28, 125, 257–59; Instagram, 125, 175; Pinterest, 179; Twitter, 4, 118, 122, 125, 167–70, 257–59; YouTube, 147, 158, 162, 203
Sociologists for Women in Society, 39
Souter, David, 279
South Atlantic Modern Language Association, 217
Spring, Joel, 182
staff, 190, 192, 273, 322; department, 39, 40, 60, 64, 245; grant support for, 72; harassment of, 302–11; recognizing, 44, 46; supervision of, 31, 64
Stanford University, 81, 90, 92, 231, 245, 280, 307
start-up funds, 26, 138
State University of New York, 296
Statement on Freedom of Expression and Campus Speech Codes (1994), 282
Statement of Principles on Academic Freedom and Tenure (1940), 278–80
Statement on Professional Ethics (1966), 281–82
STEM (science, technology, engineering, and math): departments, 10; fields, 31, 304; grants, 72–73; job offers, 16; journals, 85–86, 92
Stetson University, 220
student evaluations, 261–63

students of color, 20, 32, 209, 234, 320. *See also* Asian Americans; Black people; Indigenous people; Latinxs; Native Americans; underrepresentation
Sue, Derald Wing, 204
support networks. *See* networks, support
SVSH (sexual violence and sexual harassment), 302–17. *See also* women

teaching assistants, 159, 161, 233, 235
teaching, 38, 46, 50, 56, 67, 199; assignment design, 147, 158, 173–79; course design, 51, 53, 61, 165–71, 191–92, 208–16; large format, 156–64; online, 182–87, 297; political topics, 169, 170; in prisons, 217–22; small format, 142–55; student evaluations and, 261–63; technology in, 51, 68, 158–59, 174, 179, 181–88, 191
technology: and research, 83, 86; in the classroom, 5, 51, 68, 156, 159, 170, 172–73, 181–87, 191, 218; in libraries, 90–92; in presentations, 46; in publishing, 89
tenure, 3–4, 56–59; disappearance of, 283, 285, 296, 298; letters for, 1, 42, 240–41, 245–46; pressures from, 269; untenured positions, 38–44, 58, 237
#ThisIsWhatAProfessorLooksLike, 4, 162, 205
Title IX, 234, 302–17
Title VII, 310
Togo, 223–30
Toward an Open Monograph Ecosystem (TOME), 137
Townsend, Camilla, 174
Tropics of Meta (blog), 177
Trump, Donald, 291, 295–301, 306
Trump University, 297
#TrumpSyllabus, 171
Turkle, Sherry, 187
Twitter. *See* social media

underrepresentation: among faculty, 4, 56, 57, 162, 243–45; among students, 18, 166; service commitments and, 248. *See also* discrimination; marginalization
undocumented students, 3, 193–200, 213–15
unionization, 25, 30, 287–88, 290–91, 299–300, 311. *See also* American Association of University Presses (AAUP); representation, faculty